Upgrading You[r]
to Multimedia

Steven A. Thompson

with
Keith Aleshire and Dave Gibbons

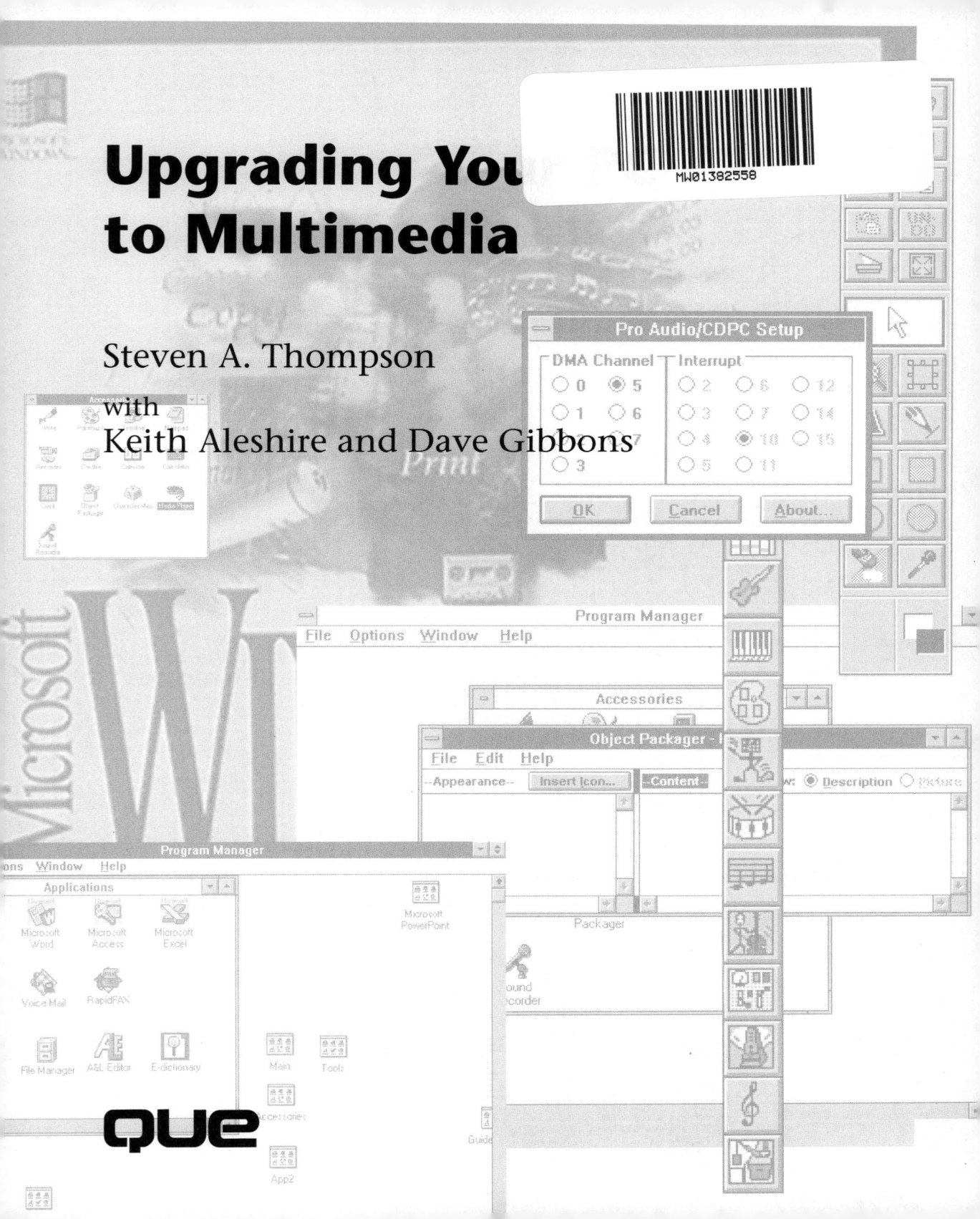

MW01382558

Pro Audio/CDPC Setup

DMA Channel
- ○ 0 ● 5
- ○ 1 ○ 6
- ○ 7
- ○ 3

Interrupt
- ○ 2 ○ 8 ○ 12
- ○ 3 ○ 7 ○ 14
- ○ 4 ● 10 ○ 15
- ○ 5 ○ 11

OK   Cancel   About...

que

Upgrading Your PC to Multimedia

Publisher: David P. Ewing

Associate Publisher: Don Roche, Jr.

Managing Editor: Michael Cunningham

Marketing Manager: Greg Wiegand

Associate Product Marketing Manager: Stacy Collins

Dedication

I dedicate this book to you, the reader. It was written specifically with you in mind.

Now that the book is complete I can dedicate my time, energy, and love to the people I love the most. At the top of the list is my beautiful wife, Lisa. She really is beautiful, inside and out. My family is very special to me: Mom (words can't express how much your children love you), Keith, Kellie, Cindy, and Dad (whose memory is an everlasting thought). My best friend, technical advisor, and sounding board in life, John Bradbury. Cathy Roberts, whose confidence in me is both reassuring and inspiring. Those who are very special friends, appearing in chronological order: Sheree Roberts, Marco Pacelli, Mike Pooler, Jodene Goldenring, Barry Giordano, Brian, Dennis, and Jay Lacny. If you want to know how you rank in order of importance, you'll have to look at my speed dial numbers.

—Steve Thompson

Credits

Publishing Manager
Nancy Stevenson

Acquisitions Editor
Jenny L. Watson

Product Director
Kathie-Jo Arnoff

Product Development Specialist
Lisa A. Bucki

Production Editor
Thomas F. Hayes

Copy Editors
Charles K. Bowles
Geneil Breeze
Noelle Gasco
Lisa M. Gebken
Patrick Kanouse
Julie A. McNamee
Nicole L. Rodandello

Technical Editors
Michael Watson
Anthony Schafer

Acquisitions Coordinator
Jill L. Pursell

Book Designer
Paula Carroll

Cover Designer
Dan Armstrong

Production Team
Stephen Adams
Stephen Carlin
Kim Cofer
Maxine Dillingham
Karen Dodson
Chad Dressler
DiMonique Ford
Karen L. Gregor
Aren Howell
Daryl R. Kessler
Malinda Lowder
Brian-Kent Proffitt
Kaylene Riemen
Michael Thomas
Suzanne Tully

Indexer
Johnna VanHoose

Composed in *Stone Serif* and *MCPdigital* by Que Corporation

About the Authors

Keith R. Aleshire is a Phi Beta Kappa graduate from the University of Minnesota School of Journalism. He has worked for various high-tech firms, including Northgate Computer Systems, Digi International and LaserMaster Corp. He has been a senior producer and columnist for the PRODIGY service and writes for several computer magazines. He has written three national books and is president and CEO of Strike Twice Corp.

Dave Gibbons is a former technical trainer and writer for DATASTORM TECHNOLOGIES in Columbia, MO, and LaserMaster Technologies in Eden Prairie, MN. He began his professional writing career in chilly Cando, ND, at age 16. Now a free-lance writer and consultant, Dave spends much of his free time rock climbing on the Internet (dgibbons@bigcat.missouri.edu).

Over the past 12 years **Steve Thompson** has gained experience working in various capacities within the computer industry: Programmer, Senior Systems Analyst, Regional Manager of Information Systems, Technical Support Manager, Data Base Administrator, and Local Area Network Manager. However, it was not always his intent to become a systems professional.

In 1981, while still in high school, Steve's life forever changed. His parents coerced him to pursue a computer career rather than becoming a musician. He stopped playing the saxophone and took the computer class. The course was the first of its kind in the small desert community of Yucca Valley, CA. It was love at first sight.

While still in high school, Steve took an evening course in computer programming at the College of the Desert. He then secured his first paying job as a computer operator at the Harley-Davidson shop in town. Eventually, Steve graduated from high school and went on to earn his Bachelor of Science in Computer Information Systems from DeVry Institute of Technology.

Currently Steve authors books, lectures, and operates a small consulting firm in San Diego, CA. You can reach Steve on CompuServe at 76304,2445 or take the following off-ramp when traveling the information superhighway (76304,2445@compuserv.com).

Acknowledgements

I would like to thank Mike Morrison for sharing his knowledge, experience, and most important, putting me in contact with the right people. A special thanks to Jenny Watson, who guided me through the tough times and made this all possible. I also appreciate the efforts of all the editors, especially Tom Hayes, who worked diligently to make this book a valuable resource to all the readers.

—*Steve Thompson*

Trademark Acknowledgments

All terms mentioned in this book that are known to be trademarks or service marks have been appropriately capitalized. Que cannot attest to the accuracy of this information. Use of a term in this book should not be regarded as affecting the validity of any trademark or service mark.

Contents at a Glance

Table of Contents

II Multimedia Components   71

3 Adding a CD-ROM Drive   73

Introduction

Multimedia is a technological revolution unlike anything else. With multimedia, yesterday's dream has become today's reality.

Science fiction writers used to dazzle their readers' imaginations with stories of computers that had personalities: Computers that would talk to you, listen to your commands and act upon them; computers that interacted with you, that would teach you art, science, history, nature, sports, and trivia; computers with personalities you enjoyed because you created them; computers that could even have your voice.

Today, these systems are reality. You can get one at the local computer store. Your neighbor may already have one. Millions of people have purchased CD-ROM drives, sound cards, speakers and other multimedia add-ons. One company, Creative Labs, has sold more than five million computer boards that produce multimedia-based sound.

In a nutshell, multimedia systems let you combine text, still images, full-motion video and animation, sound, and interactivity. Multimedia application programs you play on a multimedia-equipped system are like a movie (including the music), but are even better because you can interact with them! For example, if *Gone with the Wind* were converted to a multimedia application, you might be able to choose a new ending and have Rhett say, "Frankly, Scarlett, I'd rather live in Toledo" or something equally entertaining.

The Exploding Multimedia Market

It's not just the computer enthusiast who is buying into multimedia. Businesses, too, are flocking to multimedia in droves. From major corporations to individuals working at home, business users see unprecedented opportunities in the immediate and long-term future. Some of the businesses using multimedia are already realizing tangible benefits.

The multimedia industry is growing at a phenomenal rate. According to Multimedia Development Group statistics, the multimedia industry is expected to grow from today's $3 billion base to $25 billion by 1998.

The multimedia industry will eventually become twice the size of the home video market and five times the size of the motion picture industry. Digital networks are being installed by local telephone and cable companies. These networks will deliver multimedia directly to your home. Even now you can go to a photo store and have your pictures developed and then stored on a compact disc (CD).

Multimedia is quickly becoming *status quo*. Everywhere you look you see multimedia products—sound boards, advanced video cards, CD-ROM drives, speakers, MIDI keyboards, and CDs. Millions have already purchased CD-ROM drives, and millions more are expected to follow. Experts anticipate that over 10 million people will own a CD-ROM drive for their computer by the end of this year.

Selling with Multimedia

Not only is multimedia a technology people are buying, it also is a technology many businesses are using for marketing and selling. You may have noticed billboards with an illustration of a drape covering a large object. Printed in large letters is the statement, *The Kiosks Are Coming!* After a few weeks the billboards were updated, the drape was removed and the object underneath was revealed—they were kiosks for electronically finding apartments.

Many businesses are using kiosks to interactively market their products and services. What is a kiosk? Simply put, it's multimedia in a box; an electronic newsstand. On the outside, you have a fancy, attention-getting display box. On the inside, there is a multimedia computer. You simply go up to the kiosk and either type in your request or select options from a touch-sensitive screen. In the case of the apartment kiosk just mentioned, you go and enter in your preferences—one bedroom, green carpet, purple appliances, and $1,002 per month. You are then presented with the apartments that match your criteria.

Kiosks are a great way for clients to be informed of the products and services offered by a company. At the same time, it is an ideal tool for companies to use for collecting marketing data about the client—personal preferences, background, annual income, name, and so on.

Most people hate giving personal information to salespeople, yet they'll tell a computer everything about themselves because people are less defensive when interacting with a computer. When it asks a question, you give it an answer. It also can be fun. For example, would you play a game that tested your IQ? Sure you would. Especially if the names of all the geniuses, including yours, were in bold letters for all to see. Your esteem is built up, and so is the business' marketing database.

Will You Upgrade?

"The first step binds one to the second."

— French proverb

In fact, it really isn't a question of *if* you are going to upgrade to multimedia; it's a question of *when*. Multimedia is fun and effective. The more you begin to understand multimedia, the more you love it. It is addictive. It's the opium of the computer people.

There are many skeptics who say multimedia is just a fad. It won't last, they say. Are they correct?

- Is multimedia just a fad?
- Are there viable applications of multimedia?
- Do people want multimedia?

You need to analyze these questions for yourself. Why, for example, did you pick up this book from the shelf and begin to look at it? There are probably hundreds of others to choose from. Have you been interested in multimedia all your life? Why is it that suddenly this topic interests you? No doubt it's because everyone is talking about multimedia and many are doing it.

Sure, there are naysayers and skeptics, but that's nothing new. There are those like the Luddites in the early 1800s who feared losing their jobs to technology so much that they organized themselves and destroyed manufacturing machinery. Conversely, there are those who recognize advancements in technology as opportunities and seize them.

Technological Society

"The world is moving so fast these days that the man who says it can't be done is generally interrupted by someone doing it."

- Elbert Hubbard

If you have been associated with the computer industry for even a short period of time, then you've seen many changes. The changes in the past 12 years have been phenomenal. Even if you have had no association with the computer industry, it's hard to ignore the technological improvements the computer is responsible for. Advancements in computer technology have, without question, had a significant impact on society. For instance,

- How many times do you go to the bank now and actually go up to a teller?
- How many supermarkets have you gone to that don't use lasers for reading UPC codes?

- Have you used a rotary dial phone lately?

- Do you have to physically change channels on your TV, or do you use a remote?

- Have you recently called someone who doesn't have an answering machine?

- Have you recently received a letter typed on a typewriter?

Many of these changes have been subtle. Some drastic. What's ironic about multimedia, though, is that multimedia is changing our methods of dealing with information. Multimedia is technology changing technology. It's changing how we interact with computers, how we learn, how we teach, and how we are entertained. From hobbies to critical business functions, multimedia is having a profound impact on how we, as a society, relate to ourselves and the world about us.

Technology Defining Society

Multimedia is a *defining technology*. Essentially, it is a technology that society will use to explain our culture—science, philosophy, or art. It is a technology used as a metaphor in explaining ourselves.

Now wait a minute! Why are we talking about metaphors and theories? This is a book on upgrading your PC, not a Computer Science Appreciation Course. The reason is clear.

Multimedia is an important technology. It is changing traditional ways of doing things: the ways businesses market their products and services; the way we teach and learn; the way we are entertained. Multimedia is changing the way we view ourselves, and is helping bring new ideas into focus.

Multimedia is a technology that is significant enough to change our society. In his book *Turings Man,* J. David Bolter wrote:

> *"Technology does not call forth major cultural changes by itself, but it does bring ideas into a new focus by explaining or exemplifying them in new ways to larger audiences."*

Multimedia is bringing ideas into a new focus and delivering them to an extremely large audience. Throughout history, civilization used metaphors defining technologies of their time to explain their culture. Bolter identified some of the metaphors used:

- Plato compared the created universe to a spindle. In the *Republic*, Plato described the heavens revolving about a "spindle of Necessity."

- Aristotle used metaphors of clay formed on the potter's wheel to explain reality from form and matter.

- Descartes likened animals as mechanisms similar to clocks. This metaphor applied to the clockwork mechanisms during his era.

- Scientists in the 19th century and early 20th century have regularly compared the universe to a combustion engine that is slowly squandering its fuel. Humans also were likened as machines with gears and parts that operated upon fuel (food). This is a metaphor derived from the industrial revolution.

Today the computer is constantly serving as a metaphor for the human mind. Ever heard the saying, "We're like computers?" You might have even said it yourself. Multimedia takes this one step further by making your computer more human.

It's Alive!

Multimedia is to computers what the breath of life is to humans. It makes your computer come alive. It gives your computer a personality. It makes learning enjoyable. It entertains. It is one of the most effective forms of communication available today. Multimedia takes text, sound, graphics, video, and animation and encapsulates it into an effective, informative, and entertaining presentation.

This Book's For You

This book makes you aware of multimedia and shows you how to upgrade your PC so you can become a part of this inevitable technology. This book teaches you exactly what multimedia is, where it came from, and where it is going. The individual components of multimedia are identified and explained. You need knowledge to make intelligent buying decisions; therefore, the less you know, the more susceptible you are to making a costly, wrong decision. Reading this book gives you the knowledge you need to survive this technology revolution.

You don't have to be a computer scientist to read this book; although if you are one, you will find it to be a good reference and an effective tool for helping others. Even if you have never touched a computer before, you will find this book to be an informative guide. It provides you with an understanding of what everyone is talking about: multimedia!

The next three sections explain the contents of this book and provides an overall view of the many topics discussed.

Part I: Building a Multimedia Foundation

In this part, the term *multimedia* is defined and explained. The different uses of multimedia also are identified. Basic computer requirements also are provided. These requirements allow you to assess the current status of your computer system. Answers are provided to the following questions:

- Can my computer handle multimedia?

- Should I upgrade or buy new?

- If I can't buy a complete system now, what should I buy to prepare for the future?

- What is memory and how much do I need, if any?

- Should I get ISA, EISA, MCA, VL-Bus, or PCI?

- Do I need IDE or SCSI?

The first part focuses on the question, "Can your computer handle multimedia?" In addition to identifying and defining technical terms, a brief history of technology is provided. It is generally easier to comprehend technology when you have a clear understanding of when it was started, why it was started, and by whom.

Part II: Multimedia Components

In this part, the individual components of multimedia are clearly identified. Each component is explained in detail. It is important to know what each item is and how it will, or will not, benefit you. Each topic starts off very general and then proceeds to a more technical understanding. Upon completing this section, you will have a thorough understanding of multimedia and will have learned how you can add the following capabilities to your computer:

- CD-ROM technology

- Sound processing

- Image processing

- Full-motion video and animation

- Musical Instrument Digital Interface (MIDI)

Once you know what your computer has (Part I) and what it needs to be *truly* multimedia (Part II), you are then ready to begin investing in multimedia.

Part III: Investing in Multimedia

This part will save you tens, hundreds, and possibly thousands of dollars. It is common to see people make bad decisions. You have probably heard the old cliché, "The best offense is a good defense." This couldn't be more true than with purchasing computer hardware and software. Your defense is knowledge of technology and knowing your needs. Your offense is in knowing where to go to buy the products you need. With the defense of knowledge that you acquired in Parts I and II, this section will direct you to offensively pursue legitimate, economical sources of multimedia products and services.

The only thing you need to do now is get started.

Helpful Hints

As you read this book you will notice a few helpful conventions used throughout. These include tips, notes, cautions, and even special sections that provide overviews of subsequent topics. Each of these offer different benefits to you and are explained as follows:

Tip

A *Tip* is provided as an action you should take. Tips are based upon the current topic being discussed. They are usually brief hints about multimedia.

Caution

A *Caution* is more serious than a Tip. Ignoring cautions can adversely affect you or your PC. Cautions are provided to help you avoid problems. If it is not serious, and does not necessarily require an action by you, then a Note will be used.

Note

Notes are provided as mental reminders. They don't necessarily require any action on your part, nor do they present any adverse circumstances. A Note is simply a general comment—something to file away, mentally, as a reminder. Notes can be more lengthy than Tips. Sometimes Notes provide ancillary information based upon the topic being discussed.

From Here...

Another convention you will notice is the *From Here* section at the end of each chapter. This section provides a glimpse into the next chapter. It prepares you for the next subject.

From here you will proceed to "Part I: Building a Multimedia Foundation." This helps you understand your multimedia needs. The components of multimedia are defined so you can understand the scope of upgrading your PC to multimedia. The business and personal needs of multimedia also are discussed.

Part I

Building a Multimedia Foundation

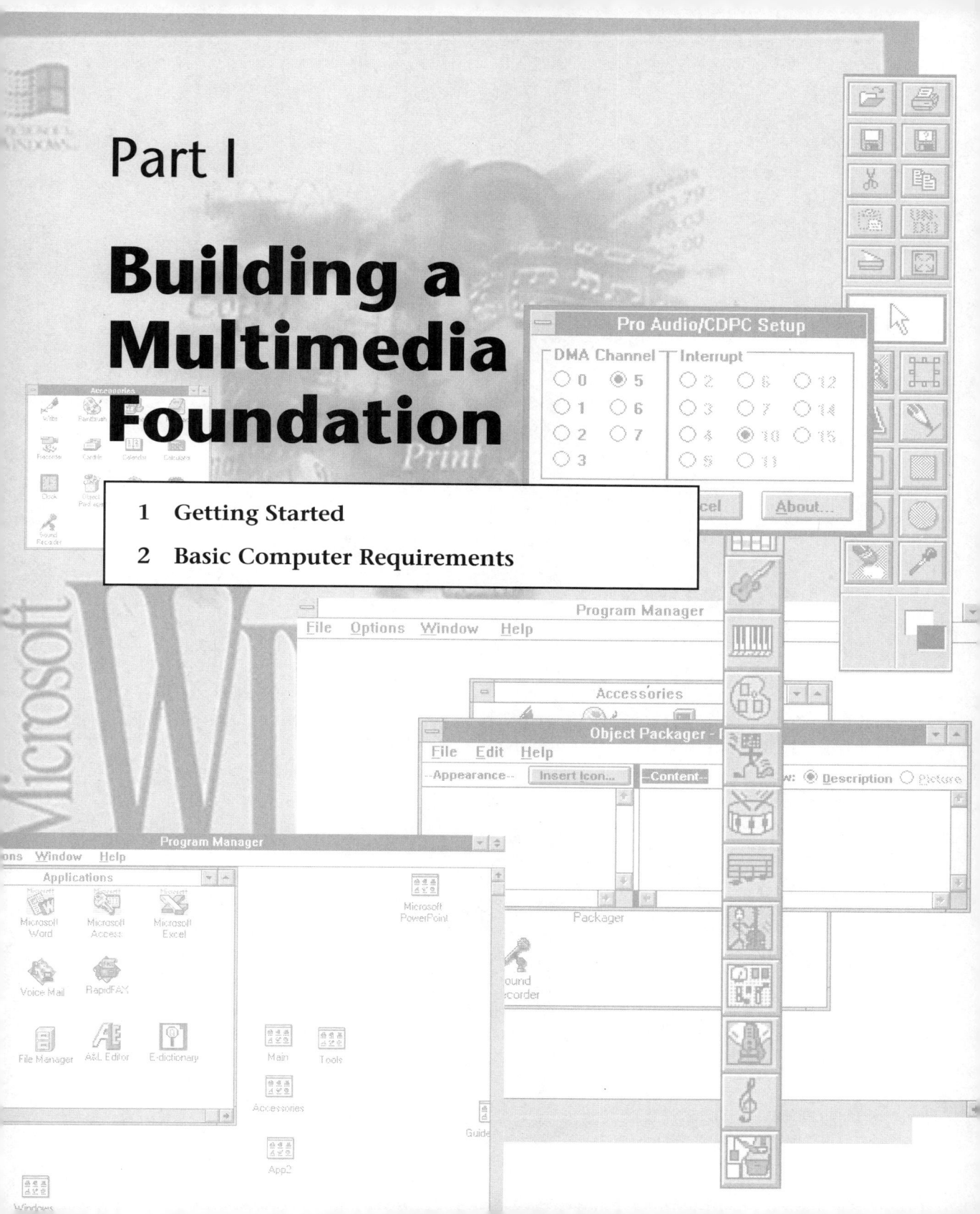

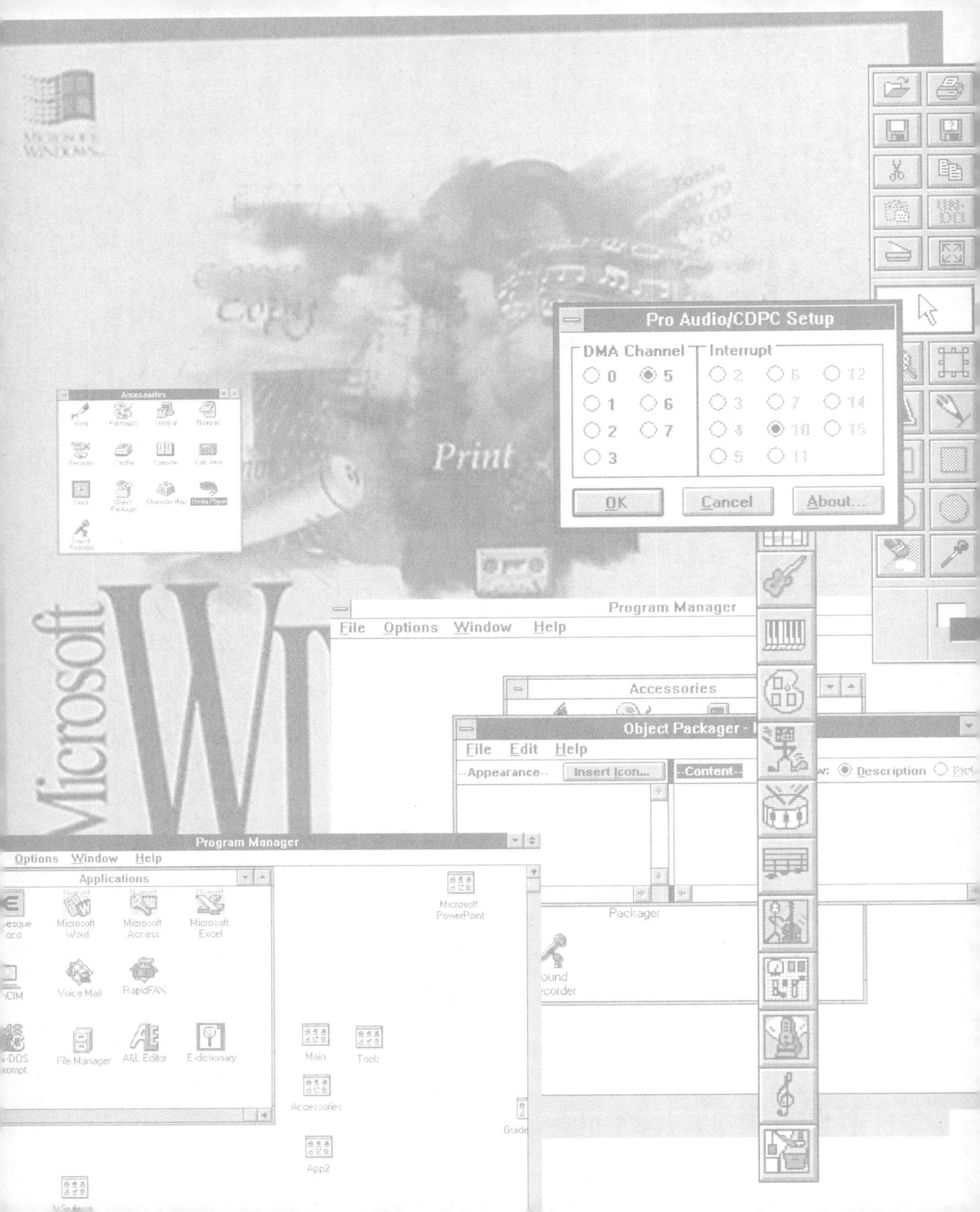

Chapter 1

Getting Started

When upgrading your PC to multimedia, you need to know *what* to buy and *when* to buy it. This chapter discusses *when* you should buy; then it proceeds to offer you advice on how you can determine *what* to buy. The first issue, *when to buy*, is illustrated via a hypothetical scenario. The second issue, *what to buy*, is determined by helping you assess your needs.

Buying computer hardware and software is not an easy task. It gets easier, however, as you gain experience. Although when new technologies surface, you find yourself back at square one. This can become frustrating, especially if you're a technical person who has suddenly realized that technology has passed you by. When this occurs, you may find it tempting to just dive in and sort out all of the details later.

Red-Hot Money

Once you make the decision to buy multimedia, the money in your pocket starts heating up. Now it's red-hot. "It's burning a hole in your pocket," as your father often said.

It took you three weeks to make the decision to buy—now you've decided you're not going to waste any more time. Off you go, to the first computer dealer you find. You have to act quick because it's late in the afternoon, and daylight is running out. You have to buy everything and get back home to install it before midnight.

When you get to the store, you run in and buy the most colorful box containing the product you are seeking. Since you didn't identify your *needs*, you rely upon alluring advertisement. After all, the company has to be good in order to spend that much money on such a colorful box. You run up to the cash register, flop down the money, and out the door you go. Not bad. It only took you five minutes to purchase the most complex part. Buying everything else should be a snap.

Now you drive to the next store. You heard that this one component is real important so you select the most expensive one you can find. It has to be good if it costs a lot, right? You pay for it and then go on to the next store. You are running low on money; from now on you've got to be more thrifty. When you get to the third store you buy a fast, but inexpensive, CD-ROM drive. Just the basic one. You don't need all that extra photo stuff, right? You're done. Well, at least all the major items are out of the way. Now you can be real cheap and get the remaining pieces. You dash up and down the aisles selecting the stuff with the lowest number on the price tag. Even though you were thrifty you don't have any money. Not to worry, you have plastic. With everything purchased, the only thing you need to do now is to install it.

You finally make it back home. You burst through the door and tear open all the boxes. The ancillary junk gets tossed into the corner: registration cards, boring documents, loose screws, and odd wires that you probably don't need. Using your natural gift of problem solving, you analyze each component and connect them. Some of them don't fit together so you have to use brute force. You flip on the power switch and nothing works. You're up all night long. Actually, you spend the next six weeks trying to make everything work.

Those liars! They said the product was easy to install. They said it was fast. They said the quality was great. But it took you six weeks to install the product, and the performance is equivalent to a moped. You've seen better quality in a Yugo. You spend hours queued in the technical support black hole. When you finally get someone, you spend 10 minutes yelling at them: "Multimedia, ha! It's just hype."

Sound familiar?

Using Gray Matter before Green Matter

If you are fortunate, you've only heard of situations like this and never actually experienced them. You use your head first and your money second. You don't make rash decisions. You learned a long time ago that planning up front saves your behind. You make educated decisions in a logical manner. You need to take the following steps:

1. Familiarize yourself with the terms and technology.

2. Understand your needs.

3. Identify products that meet your needs.

4. Shop for the best prices.

5. Purchase the products.

6. Properly install the products.

7. Complete and send all warranties and registrations.

8. Set aside time to learn and enjoy the new technology.

Because you have taken these steps, you have a good understanding of all the components you purchased. You have avoided many problems. Also, you have achieved balance. You purchased enough to satisfy current and future needs, but you didn't over buy. You're the type of buyer who lays a solid foundation to build upon. You are nothing like the buyer in the first scenario that makes purchases haphazardly. You don't smart when you buy; you buy smart.

The Buyer You Should Be

It is better to plan before you buy. You must lay a good technology foundation before you begin to build. Imagine what would happen if a skyscraper were built on a poorly designed, or non-existent foundation. The skyscraper would collapse. So will your multi-media system if you don't educate yourself first, plan next, and then finally buy. The very fact that you're reading this book is a good indication of diligent research.

Understanding What Multimedia Is

Do you need multimedia? Really, is it something that will benefit you? Will you find it enjoyable? Do you actually know what multimedia is? Are you aware of how people are using multimedia?

These are all questions that you should think about, especially if you're getting started in multimedia. The next several paragraphs answer these questions for you. First, let's take a mental snapshot of multimedia. The true definition of *multimedia* (according to the 5th Edition of Que's *Computer User's Dictionary*) is a "computer-based method of presenting information by using more than one medium of communication, such as text, graphics, and sound, emphasizing interactivity."

Whether you realize it or not, you've been using a form of multimedia for years. Television and movies are multimedia. They use two media: picture and sound. If you've ever rented a foreign film, you may have experienced another medium along with the picture and sound—text. Movie producers use all of these media, or vehicles of communication, to tell a story. The images paint the picture in your mind, the voices and text tell the story, and the music creates the emotion.

Television and movies aren't as effective if they only use one medium. A good example of this is the old silent footage of family movies that are stored in your attic. Silent family movies may be entertaining to watch; however, if this were the only medium available, we would quickly lose enthusiasm and would no longer find them entertaining.

Computers used to be like old silent movies and presented data only on one medium, the CRT (cathode ray tube) or monitor. Eventually sound was integrated, through a puny speaker that only beeped or buzzed. As technology progressed, more media became available to computer users: color screens were made available, graphics quality improved, and sound technology advanced. Today we have sophisticated computers that can produce photographic images, realistic animation, and digital sounds. The result is just as realistic as a movie: sights, sounds, and action.

Realizing that you have been entertained and possibly educated by multimedia, you can begin to understand what it is. The reason it is called multimedia is because it uses multiple vehicles of communication: pictures, sound, text, music, and animation. Now, are you ready to run out and start buying? Well, it may be wise to first explore why you are interested in multimedia. Specifically, you should be asking yourself if you really need multimedia. The next section covers this topic in detail.

Do You Need Multimedia?

Multimedia is expensive. If it only cost $10, you could treat it as a disposable item. If you didn't like it, you could throw it away. However, it's not $10. Actually, you're going to have to add a couple of zeros to that number to fully upgrade your computer to multimedia.

Is it worth it? Well, that depends on your needs. If you can identify your needs, you can easily justify the cost. This section helps you explore why or even if you need multimedia. Of course, the age, model, memory capacity, and name brand of your computer are all factors that could affect the cost of upgrading to multimedia.

I See It, I Hear It, I Want It

The movie *The Gods Must Be Crazy* is about a tribe of bushmen. Completely removed from civilization, the tribe had never been in contact with modern society. One of the tribesman was suddenly struck by an object that fell from the sky. The tribesman thought this was a gift from the gods. Actually, what really hit him was an empty soda bottle thrown by a pilot flying overhead in an airplane.

Once the other tribespeople heard what had happened and actually saw this "gift" from the gods, they became interested. They had never seen anything like it before. They began to covet the god's gift. In an effort to get their hands on it they created all sorts of needs. Soon they couldn't do anything without it. This simple object became integral to every aspect of their lives.

When thinking of multimedia, this movie comes to mind. Although multimedia didn't fall out of the sky, it is something that many computer users want, once they see and hear it. Since we want it, we create all kinds of needs to justify the purchase. To restate this point, personal needs of multimedia are usually derived out of a sincere desire. You may have seen a multimedia PC in the store. Maybe you read about multimedia and it interested you. Or possibly a friend or family member has shown you what they can do on their computer, and what you can't do on yours. Whatever the case, you saw it, you liked it, and now you want it.

Personal Uses for Multimedia

There are several personal needs to identify. Maybe you want multimedia because you are interested in learning how to play a musical instrument—such as a piano, guitar, or saxophone—or you may want to learn how to paint. Or maybe reading is your favorite pastime and you want multimedia so you can read the electronic books you've noticed at the bookstore. What about education? Multimedia can provide you with more reference material on one CD than some people can find in their community library. Personal needs fit into the following categories:

- *Education.* From toddlers to adults, multimedia is used as an effective training tool. Multimedia titles range from learning how to count and identify colors to advanced programs that teach you another language or some advanced math.

- *Reference.* One CD-ROM can contain volumes of encyclopedias. Coupled with this storage capacity, multimedia also delivers sound, animation, hyper-text, and full-motion video. All of this at a fraction of the cost of traditional reference books and encyclopedias. Also, you don't need bookshelves for multimedia; just a small CD holder will suffice.

- *Entertainment.* Some justify the need for multimedia entirely upon entertainment. Multimedia games are more enjoyable and realistic, simply because more mediums are made available, such as sound effects, music, animation, and real voices. Also, some forms of multimedia entertainment are educational and make learning fun.

- *Self-improvement.* Some multimedia programs are strictly directed towards self-improvement. For example, one program simulates the job interview process to prepare you for the *live interview*.

There are gray areas. Some entertainment programs also can be educational. Self-improvement can be considered educational, or visa-versa. Also, reference programs may be entertaining. It is not important to scrutinize categories. What is important is to recognize these categories exist and from them you can identify your personal multimedia needs.

Business Uses for Multimedia

Multimedia is not just fun and games. It can be a viable profession, too. If you have access to any on-line service (CompuServe, America Online, Internet, Prodigy, and so on.) you may have perused areas that deal with multimedia. Possibly, you've seen all the postings for job opportunities:

- MIDI Composer Wanted.

- Wanted! Animator.

- Help Wanted!

- DTP Professional Needed.

- Multimedia Consultant Wanted.

- Please help! Need Multimedia Expert.

If you think this is too good to be true, test it out. Look at the messages posted in the on-line forums, or read the classified ads in the newspapers. The jobs and opportunities are there. If you are considering multimedia as a career, or if you're currently a multimedia professional, you will enjoy this section.

In today's business environment, information and communication are essential. You need information on yourself and your competition. You also need to provide information to your employees, business partners, and clients (see fig. 1.1). Multimedia is an effective way of processing and presenting information. Multimedia also is an ideal communication tool. For these reasons, many businesses are realizing the need for multimedia and are beginning to employ it. Some of these uses are:

- *Employee Training.* Multimedia is interactive and makes education more enjoyable. Also, all the mediums available to multimedia provide a variety of communication tools. Some multimedia training programs also offer scoring and trainee histories to show improvements.

- *Marketing.* The sights and sounds of multimedia attract attention. Businesses capitalize on these features to market their products and services and make themselves known. Kiosks are one example of multimedia marketing. Besides presenting information, multimedia marketing is very effective at gathering data on prospects.

- *Sales.* An effective multimedia presentation is capable of establishing an image. Multimedia sounds can arouse certain emotions and communicate with live voices. The visuals of multimedia can communicate key points. Businesses use these mediums to convince prospects to become clients.

- *Product Support.* Many businesses are using animation and full-motion video to *show* how to perform a certain task rather than try and *explain* how something is done. This is an example of how multimedia benefits product support. Watching a video of someone performing a task is quicker and easier to understand than reading a technical guide. This is prompting some businesses to develop multimedia-based product support.

Fig. 1.1
The Toshiba T6600C is equipped for sight, sound, and quality video and can help enhance business presentations.

There are many examples of businesses currently using multimedia. The legal profession uses multimedia to present their cases to juries. Imagine having all of your exhibits available at the push of a button. While your opponent is fumbling around with bulky displays, you can instantly replay an animated sequence that clearly shows your client is innocent, or guilty if you're the prosecutor.

Another application of multimedia in business is client presentations. Your competition thinks they've already won the contract because they're using color slides. Then you skip in with a laptop computer and give a full color presentation that includes live video with stereo sound. Obviously, you're more capable than the competition and, therefore, able to charge twice as much.

Technical support and *help desk* functions also are greatly improved with multimedia. Instead of having to wade through a large manual or spend hours on the phone, you can provide your customers multimedia-based training (MBT). With MBT you can show actual pictures and present full-motion video, or even animation to liven it up. All this can fit onto a single compact disc (CD) that you can provide to each client. If your business has a computer network, you can implement CD servers so that everyone can have access to your training, support, and presentations.

Justifying the Need for Multimedia

Justifying the need for multimedia can be easy or difficult depending on your situation. If you're purchasing multimedia for yourself, then the only person you have to convince is yourself. If it's more than just *you*, then you have to convince the others, too; this may include your spouse, in-laws, children, attorneys, family physicians, and spiritual advisors. If you're going to use multimedia for business, you may have a real challenge because you'll need to convince your boss. Proving the absolute necessity of multimedia to your boss will probably require that you go through the gauntlet of management authorization.

The nice thing about multimedia, and what distinguishes it from all the other technologies, is that you can see it and hear it. This is not always the case with other forms of technology. Consider, for example, trying to convince your boss that you need a $10,000 network analyzer just to sit and listen in on traffic on your company's Local Area Network. Now there is a real challenge.

With multimedia, however, people can see the benefits. The only obstacle to overcome is how to get your boss in front of a multimedia demo. If they have already seen multimedia in action, your job may be easier. Typically, when you see multimedia, you immediately want it.

If your superiors don't perceive the same need as you do, you'll have to sharpen your sales skills. Here are a few pointers:

■ *Create a client need.* This can be done by educating a client on the benefits of multimedia. Typically, when a client speaks, the company listens, especially if it's a major client.

- ■ *Calculate cost savings.* Effective training can save a company thousands of dollars. Multimedia is one of the most effective training methods available. Also, think of all of the storage space you can save when you throw away all of those reference books. How much does your company spend on 411 directory assistance? Now you can get every telephone number in the United States on CD-ROM.

- ■ *Improve your boss's image.* Invest personal time to prepare a quick presentation that your boss can use at the next manager's meeting. Your boss typically likes it when you improve his or her image.

- ■ *Gain/maintain competitive advantage.* If the competition has a professional multimedia presentation that they are going to take to your client, beware. They may snatch business away from you. Thwarting these efforts is a sure-fire way to not only get authorization for purchasing multimedia, but you may get a bonus and promotion as well.

The preceding list also applies to personal use, especially the first two items. First, you have to create a need. Your parents or spouse must be educated on the benefits of multimedia. The cost savings for personal use are not as apparent as is the case with business use. But it can be assessed. For less than $90 (provided you already have a multimedia PC), you can purchase a complete set of encyclopedias on CD-ROM. This is a significant savings compared to buying a large set of bulky bound books or spending time to trek back and forth to the library.

As you can see, there are many ways you can justify the need for multimedia. Let's assume that you've justified the need. All you need to do now is just buy it, right? Well, what are you going to buy? Just a CD-ROM? It is important to note that multimedia is much more than CD-ROM. It's more than quality sound or animation. Multimedia is made up of several components. You need to understand these components to make sure that what you end up with is, in fact, a complete multimedia PC.

An Overview of Multimedia Components

There are four primary components to multimedia hardware—CD-ROM, sound, MIDI, and video. Each component performs its distinct role, yet together they work in harmony. In a good multimedia system, all parts are cohesive, not adhesive. The parts work together rather than just being stuck together.

CD-ROM Delivery

If you were to attribute the sudden proliferation of multimedia to any one component, it would be CD-ROM drives. The actual disc is commonly called a CD.

Developed in 1982 by Sony and Philips, CD-ROM drives offered a medium for storing a large amount of data in a small amount of space. One CD can store slightly more than 600 megabytes (M), or 600 million individual characters—this is 1/3 the size of the average hard disk (200M). If you were to place 600 million characters side-by-side, they would cover a distance of 1,000 miles. Now imagine compressing all those characters into one tiny disc measuring 4 1/2 inches across.

Because multimedia requires a large amount of data, the CD became the preferred medium due to its high capacity, low cost, and compact size. Figure 1.2 is a CD. With the 600M capacity, multimedia applications and presentations can be distributed easily. Accomplishing the same capability without CDs is not feasible.

Fig. 1.2

One CD can store over 600,000,000 characters; this is ideal for the large storage requirements of multimedia.

Note

If you want to have the storage capacity of ten CDs on your system without CD technology, you need 6 gigabytes (G) of hard disk space (that's 6 billion bytes). Currently, 6G hard disks are not available; therefore, you have to buy three 2.8G drives and connect them together. Each drive costs about $3,000. Your total hard disk cost is around $9,000. There are other problems, too. It takes over 4,000 3 1/2 inch floppy disks to load the data. Even if you compressed the files 80 percent, you still need 833 disks. Supposing that you can load one disk every minute, it takes you 14 hours to load 6G.

It is little wonder why many attribute the success and sudden proliferation of multimedia directly to the advances in CD-ROM technology. With an investment of only a few hundred dollars, you can provide your computer with a tremendous storage resource.

Just as you need a CD player to listen to your favorite music CD, you also need a CD-ROM drive to access data on a CD. The data stored on a computer CD can contain pictures, sounds, and computer instructions; conversely, the data stored on a music CD is for sound only.

> **Note**
>
> You will find that playing a music CD in your computer is quite enjoyable. You also will find that playing a computer CD in your home stereo is quite annoying and could damage your stereo equipment.

> **Caution**
>
> Playing a computer CD in your home stereo could create low frequency or high frequency sounds that might damage speakers.

Sound's Good

It takes a significant amount of data to store recorded sound on a computer. This is because sound, by nature, is in the form of a sound wave. A sound wave is *analog.* Computers are *digital* (see fig. 1.3). Trying to make a computer understand analog is like of speaking Greek to someone who doesn't know Greek.

Fig. 1.3

A computer must convert analog signals to digital signals. An analog signal is a continuous fluid motion; its settings vary like a dial. A digital signal is solid and discrete, like a switch.

Analog signals must be translated into digital samples (measurements of sound at specific time intervals) before the computer can understand them. The hardware that performs this translation is a *sound board,* which is made up of electronic components that receive analog signals and convert them into digital samples. Analog signals enter the computer via a *microphone* or other audio device (such as a cassette recorder, a stereo, or a CD player). Conversely, digital signals can be converted into analog signals and be sent out to *speakers* or other audio device (such as an amplifier, a cassette recorder, or a mixer). Therefore, the three essential pieces of hardware necessary for multimedia sound are:

- *Sound board.* Converts incoming sound waves (from microphone) from analog to digital and converts outgoing sound samples (to speakers) from digital to analog.

- *Speakers.* Produces sound waves based upon analog signals generated from the sound board.

- *Microphone.* Captures sound waves and sends the corresponding analog signals to the sound board to be converted into digital samples.

Converting analog sound waves (signals) into digital data results in a significant amount of data. The reason that quality sound is now available on PCs is, again, partly due to the storage capacity available with CD-ROM technology. CD-ROM storage provided the means to store a large amount of data on a compact, affordable medium.

Sound is essential to multimedia. With sound technology you can reproduce music, sound effects, and even life-like human voices. When used effectively, sound becomes the emotion of multimedia. It's interesting to see a whale swim gracefully in the water. It is quite a different effect to actually hear the sounds of the whale in an aquatic atmosphere. Or consider sharks. How could you possibly understand the true meaning of sharks without the theme of Jaws playing in the background. You can even use your computer CD-ROM drive to play music CDs. If you have the right equipment you can please the ears of even the most critical audiophiles.

MIDI

Music is another significant component of multimedia. Instruments have been associated with music for a very long time.

MIDI (pronounced *mid-ē*) is the acronym for Musical Instrument Digital Interface. MIDI is a standard that defines how to connect instruments to computers. MIDI also establishes a standard language for sending data and instructions into, out of, and through instruments, synthesizers, and other music equipment.

MIDI is very effective at controlling instruments. So good, in fact, that it also is being used to control not only musical instruments but also theatrical devices (stage, lighting, pyrotechniques, and so on).

Another benefit of MIDI is the size of its data files. MIDI is a language; therefore, it has its own syntax. Rather than being digital samples of an analog wave form, MIDI is a sound command. This MIDI command is much smaller in size than a digitally sampled wave form. Less data is needed to make a MIDI sound than a digital wave sound (see Chapters 4 and 5 for details on Sound and MIDI).

Sound and music are good, but sound alone is not sufficient for a computer system. More is needed. In addition to audio, multimedia also addresses visual mediums.

Video: Picture That

To get the complete effect of multimedia, you need more than just sound. Images are also necessary. There are four basic types of images that apply to multimedia:

- *Still images*. A still image does not move. A picture of a face is an example of a still image. A still image is a graphic image.

- *Text*. Letters are a necessary part of multimedia because without them we couldn't write words, sentences or paragraphs. Numbers also are essential. These are displayed on-screen and are considered a part of video. However, text is an inherent part of most every application. Text really doesn't require much further explanation, so the more essential elements of multimedia will be stressed.

- *Full-motion video*. Multimedia includes the capability to view and record live video on your PC. This includes watching TV or playing a VCR tape. Full-motion video is considered life-like images moving at life-like speed.

- *Animation*. Although animation has advanced to the point where it can appear life-like, it is different from video in that it typically deals with inanimate objects. Whereas a video of a live bird flying would be considered full-motion video, a cartoon of a flying bird is considered animation.

All of these images are used separately and together in multimedia presentations. Text may flash across the screen while a full-motion video is playing. You may have an animated character dancing on the beach shore; the beach shore can be a still image. These are just a few examples. There are many options available, which go beyond the context of our discussion. For now let's focus on video hardware.

Many technological advancements have been made in video hardware. Better computer chips have resulted in better video. Photo-realistic images can easily be displayed using current computer technology with relative ease. Due to the increased speed at which computers can process information, video images can be presented so fast that the effect of life-like motion is achieved.

Video hardware for multimedia consists of two elements—a video card and a monitor. Both of these elements are discussed in detail in Chapters 2 and 6. For now a basic understanding is sufficient.

Similar to sound waves, video is produced by light waves, which are analog signals. The video card converts digital data from the computer into analog signals for the monitor. The monitor mixes different intensities of three colored light beams (red, green, and blue) to produce up to 16 million colors. Multimedia demands all these colors to produce all the different types of images discussed at the beginning of this topic.

To manipulate and present computer images in the manner required by multimedia, you need a high performance system. Without advances in technology, multimedia could not be an option today. Fortunately, these advances did occur and further advances are being made. The widespread availability of multimedia has driven the costs down significantly. This is beneficial since it makes quality, high-performing technology more affordable. Now we can justify multimedia for personal use or for small businesses.

Making a Hobby of Multimedia

Multimedia as a hobby is certainly acceptable. Children and adults of all ages find multimedia to be very entertaining. Some forms of multimedia entertainment have already been mentioned. There are several others:

- Have you ever wanted to paint like van Gogh? Just create your painting and tell the computer to simulate the brush strokes of van Gogh.

- Did you ever want to create your own cartoon? Now you can use tools that until recently were only available to professional animators.

- Have you ever wanted to create a rock video? Now you can using special sound effects and trick photography.

- Did you always want to have your own rock band? Now you can play the drums, keyboards, electric guitar, oboe, flute, tuba, xylophone, harpsichord, and so on. You can even apply special sound effects like incoming helicopters or a choir of a hundred voices all saying "Ah" in unison. You can even sing and record your own voice. If it sounds bad, just take your voice out.

- Would you like to learn to fly a jet airplane? Using a flight simulator you can land at the Los Angeles International Airport during a cloudy day.

- What about composing music? All you need to do is type in the score and have the computer play it back. You can even take a score from your favorite musical and scan it directly into a computer.

- Do you like to watch nature channels? With multimedia you can have a comprehensive nature library at your fingertips. You can even play back the sounds different animals make. Now you will be able to identify the species of bird that keeps waking you up early in the morning.

- Do you like theater? You can study classical literary accomplishments. See parts of plays reenacted. You can even become a playwright.

- Have you always wanted to try karaoke but have been too afraid to go in front of everyone and do it? Now you can. With the music playing and the words scrolling across the screen, you can hear how good you sound. Or how bad you sound and, therefore, how much you need to practice.

- Do you know what it takes to be a professional mountain biker? Now you can learn techniques from the pros. You can even see them in action.

It doesn't matter what your hobby is or where your interests are—there is a multimedia CD title for you. There are even CDs that list all of the CDs that are available.

Typically multimedia enthusiasts do not need to spend a lot of money to thoroughly enjoy their hobby. As you read through each section, you will notice that the needs of the enthusiast are addressed first. Then, as the topic continues, more sophisticated hardware and software is specified. If you become more involved in your hobby, there is nothing preventing you from purchasing more advanced technology.

Making a Career of Multimedia

The multimedia industry is relatively new, with many opportunities available. Technology that was once sold for $50,000 can now be purchased for $1,000 at your local computer store. With a relatively small amount of money you can start a full-service production business, recording studio, or even become a multimedia consultant. There are several professional opportunities available:

- Compose music for interactive games.
- Develop multimedia presentations for local businesses.
- Open a production studio and create video presentations or documentaries.
- Write jingles for advertising firms using songs, music, and sound effects.
- Open a MIDI studio and help local bands compose their first CDs.
- Become an author and develop your own CD title.
- Work with lawyers to create multimedia exhibits for their clients.
- Work with architects, and design simulated walk-through models for their planned developments.
- Develop educational materials for schools, colleges, and universities.
- Start a consulting service that creates CD photo albums for individual families.
- Become a photographer and create your own CD title of pictures you've taken.

The faster you respond, the more established you will become. Since the multimedia industry is new, there is plenty of business available. However, this will not always be the case. Each day you don't start your business is one more day that your competition will be in business.

From Here...

By now you should understand the foundation of a multimedia system. This foundation is built by knowing *when* to buy and *what* to buy. Basically, you buy when you've clearly assessed your personal/business needs. What you buy is the hardware that meets your needs. The major categories of multimedia hardware that you will be buying include a CD-ROM drive, a sound board (with a microphone and speakers), MIDI instruments (optional), and a video card & monitor.

The following chapter explains each of these components in detail.

■ Chapter 2, "Basic Computer Requirements," helps you assess the basic computer requirements of multimedia. You learn how to assess the strengths and weaknesses of your current PC. Topics discussed include the type of computer you should have, the operating system you should use, how much memory you need, and what type of video display is adequate.

Chapter 2

Basic Computer Requirements

You need to know basic computer requirements before you start disassembling your computer and purchasing multimedia products. This chapter provides an understanding of the basic requirements of a multimedia computer. The MPC standard is described and components of a computer system are clearly defined. All types of computers are discussed, from desktops to portables. You'll find answers to the following questions:

- What is the difference between BIOS, RAM, ROM, EPROM, CMOS, SIMMs, SIPPs, and flash memory?

- What is the difference between 8088, 8086, 80286, 80386, 80486, and Pentium CPUs?

- Do I need a math coprocessor?

- What is an OverDrive chip and how does it differ from CPU upgrade chips?

- Which bus should I use: ISA, EISA, MCA, VL-Bus, PCI, or VMC?

- Should I use an IDE or SCSI drive?

- What do the terms *resolution, refresh rate, dot pitch,* and *pixel* mean?

- Do I need a graphics accelerator?

- Should I get an interlaced or non-interlaced monitor?

As you can see, a lot of issues are covered. Each topic is presented at a general level and then discussed in more detail. Don't worry if some concepts are vague in your mind. They will clear up as you progress through the book.

Should You Upgrade or Buy a New Computer?

Building a multimedia PC can be expensive. When you understand why you need a computer and how it can benefit you, it's much easier to justify the cost. You'll also know what is beneficial to you.

Do you need a new computer, or should you upgrade your current one? You must answer this question yourself. Because of the cost of upgrading some systems to multimedia, you need to look at the system you have and determine whether it's too out-of-date to upgrade. Most newer systems should have an adequate Central Processing Unit (CPU), adequate Random Access Memory (RAM), and enough expansion slots (areas in your PC where you can plug in new adapters) to make upgrading to multimedia practical and cost-effective.

Because computer needs among individuals vary, you should also consider whether your present computer will meet your other computing needs (not multimedia-related) for the next few years. If you think it will, then upgrading for multimedia makes sense. If not, you should strongly consider buying a completely new system.

> **Tip**
>
> Try to buy computer equipment that meets your needs now and can do the same in the future (even though it may be more expensive) to avoid getting stuck with outdated equipment quickly.

In general, you should buy a new system instead of upgrading if:

- Your CPU is outdated (80386SX, 80286(AT), or an XT). For more details refer to "Choosing the CPU You Need" later in this chapter.

- Your motherboard does not support newer bus technology (VL-Bus, PCI, VMC, etc.). Refer to "The Motherboard" section for more details.

- There are no available expansion slots. The section "Understanding Expansion Buses and Adapters" later in this chapter will provide more details.

- SIMM or SIPP RAM chips are not supported (old DRAM chips should be avoided). For more details refer to "Installing More Memory" in this chapter.

Understanding the MPC Standard

As a general rule, look for reliable companies and equipment following predominant standards (word-of-mouth advertising by satisfied customers or experienced users is a good resource). Although standards change and even large companies disappear, you can be certain that someone else will service the needs of the masses. Once you've identified reliable standard equipment, you can base decisions on performance, quality, and features. Where multimedia is concerned there is a predominant standard—MPC.

In 1990, the Multimedia PC specification (MPC) version 1.0 was announced. This specification established the minimum hardware requirement for multimedia PCs. Although this minimum requirement is not ideal, it did set a standard that hardware and software vendors could use to base their products on. It also gave consumers a good starting point.

For a vendor's product to be MPC-compliant it must meet or exceed those standards. Adherence to the standard allows the vendor to display the MPC logo (refer to fig. 2.1). To display the MPC logo, the vendor must agree to independent testing to ensure compliance.

Fig. 2.1
Any multimedia product you purchase should have the MPC logo clearly visible to ensure compatibility.

A second specification was issued in 1993. MPC level 2 achieved a higher level of performance and consequently has a separate certification and logo.

> *"The nice thing about standards is ...there are so many to choose from!"*
>
> *-anonymous*

Understanding the two different MPC specifications will help you assess the strengths and weaknesses of your PC. The following table identifies the computer system requirements for each specification. Later in the chapter, elements such as CPU and RAM are discussed in more detail.

Table 2.1 Multimedia PC Marketing Council Specifications		
	Level 1(11/1990)	**Level 2 (05/1993)**
CPU	386SX	486SX
	16 MHz	25 MHz

(continues)

Table 2.1 Continued		
	Level 1(11/1990)	**Level 2 (05/1993)**
RAM	2M	4M
Magnetic	30M hard disk	160M hard disk
Storage	1.44M floppy	1.44M floppy
Operating System	Windows with Multimedia extensions	Windows 3.1
CD-ROM	1X single speed	2X double speed
	150K/sec	300K/sec
	1 second seek time	400 ms seek time CD-ROM XA ready multisession capable
Sound	8-bit digital	16-bit digital
Card	8-note polyphony	8-note polyphony
	6 melody	6 melody
	2 percussion	2 percussion
	MIDI playback	MIDI playback
	11.025 KHz sampling	44.1 KHz sampling
	Microphone input	Microphone input
	Speakers/Headphones	Speakers/Headphones
Video	VGA	Advanced VGA, SVGA
	640 x 480 resolution	640 x 480 resolution
	16 colors	65,536 colors (High Color)
	64K buffer	64K buffer
Input	101-key Keyboard	101-key Keyboard
	Two-button mouse	Two-button mouse
	(serial/bus)	(serial/bus)
I/O Ports	MIDI I/O ports	MIDI I/O ports
	(in/out/thru)	(in/out/thru)
	Serial port	Serial port
	Parallel port	Parallel port
	Joystick port	Joystick port

Products that meet the MPC Level 1 specification will display the MPC logo. Products that meet the criteria established for MPC Level 2 display the MPC2 logo.

Tip

The MPC standards are backward compatible. This means that MPC level 1 applications will work with MPC level 2 (MPC2). However, MPC2 applications are not compatible with MPC level 1.

Your goal should be to achieve, at bare minimum, MPC Level 2 (MPC2). Although you can get by with MPC Level 1 (MPC), this level is rapidly becoming obsolete.

> **Note**
>
> Seventy-five percent of all multimedia PCs will be upgraded from level 1 to level 2 by the end of 1994, according to the MPC Marketing Council.

Hopefully your current system meets the MPC2 specifications. If not, you'll need to identify specific areas where it's lacking and develop a plan for upgrading to MPC2.

Calculating the Cost

It's recommended that you calculate the cost before you begin upgrading your system. It may be less expensive to purchase a system already configured to MPC2 standards. For example, consider this upgrade scenario. Suppose you purchase a multimedia upgrade kit for $500; add the cost of a few hundred dollars to upgrade your RAM ($300), a 17-inch monitor ($1,000), and a video accelerator card with 4M RAM ($700). The total cost of this upgrade scenario would be approximately $2,500. Now, compare this to purchasing a new system and you quickly realize that you can get a powerful computer with all the features just mentioned, in addition to a modern motherboard, a state-of-the-art CPU, and a warranty for the same amount. The new system can also be pre-configured, which will save you a lot of time and frustration. Again, before you buy several upgrade components, make sure you compare the total of the individual costs to the cost of purchasing an entirely new PC.

If You Decide to Buy a New System

A new system, chosen wisely, will offer you many benefits you may not have considered:

- More upgrade options are available that may include an OverDrive socket that will double your computer's speed.

- You can buy a multimedia system that has already been configured.

- Expansion buses on newer systems can offer the latest technology (such as VL-bus, PCI, or VMC).

- A warranty is good insurance should anything go wrong.

Before you buy a new system or begin to upgrade your current PC you should be aware of current technology. You need to know what you have, what you need, and what's available.

What's in a Computer System?

In its simplest form, a computer receives input, processes it, and produces output. A multimedia PC isn't different in this respect. Basic system configurations, as shown in figure 2.2, include input, processing, and output devices (keyboard, system unit, and video monitor).

Fig. 2.2

A multimedia PC starts with basic PC components.

The system unit is comprised of several essential elements, each one with its specific job function clearly defined:

- *Case*. Makes the computer either a desktop or portable unit.

- *Motherboard (also called logic board)*. A printed circuit board that is essentially an electronic highway system. The CPU, memory chips, and expansion buses are affixed to the motherboard.

- *CPU*. The computer brain where all processing is performed.

- *RAM*. Random Access Memory used as a temporary storage area.

- *ROM*. Read Only Memory that can't be written over or changed. There are some things the computer can never forget, even when the power is turned off. For example, the computer must always remember how to start itself when the power is turned on. These instructions are stored in the ROM computer chip.

- *Expansion slots*. A connecting point onto the motherboard where you plug in expansion boards (adapter boards). Plugging in expansion boards increases the functionality of your computer.

- *Power supply*. Supplies the computer with Direct Current (DC). The power supply converts standard AC (alternating current) into DC for the computer's use.

- *Operating system*. Software that manages the computer's operations and lets you control the computer.

Desktops versus Portables

The two general types of computers are desktops and portables (which includes laptops and notebooks). The MPC standard doesn't state what type of computer you should have. It does, however, specify that a multimedia PC should operate at a minimum capacity and be equipped with certain components. The type of computer you have may limit your ability to add the MPC required components.

Desktops

You probably have a desktop computer. It may even resemble one of the computers in figures 2.3 and 2.4. The very name "desktop" makes it obvious that these computers are designed to sit on top of your desk and remain stationary. Because some people don't want a computer on top of their desk, they purchase *tower* computers. They are both basically the same computer, one just lies flat on your desktop (horizontal) and the other stands up vertically on the floor next to your desk. Since desktops and towers are the same they can both be referred to as desktops.

Fig. 2.3
Three computer configurations are desktop, notebook, and laptop.

Fig. 2.4

The ALR Express Series offers many options and uses little desk space. Available in 33-MHz 486SX, 50-MHz 486DX/2, and 66-MHz 486DX/2, the system can come multimedia-equipped. Photo courtesy of ALR, Irvine, CA.

Desktops come in sizes ranging from giant/tall to mini/small. Figure 2.5 is a mini–tower. The size and orientation of your computer isn't as important as growth potential. Without any room for growth it's going to be difficult, if not impossible, to upgrade your PC to multimedia.

Room for Upgrading. Upgrading usually involves adding new internal components and adapter cards to your system. If you don't have any available expansion slots or expansion bays in your PC you can either buy a new case (refer to Note), buy external components, or buy an entirely new computer.

Note

When purchasing a computer case, look at the fastening screws. Ideally you want screws that can be fastened and unfastened with your fingers. If a screwdriver is required, make sure the screw-holes are threaded. Least desirable are self-tapping screws. A self-tapping screw cuts its own threads. As self-tapping screws are removed and replaced, they become less secure; this results in more vibration and rattling.

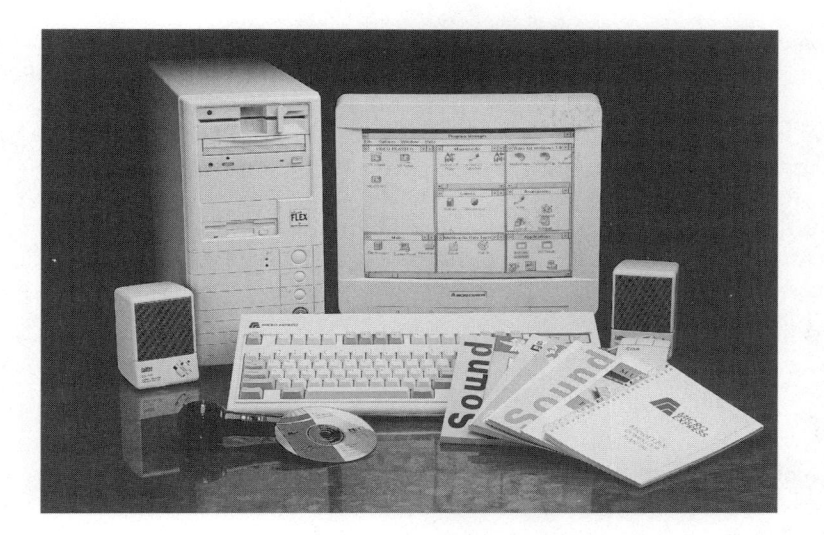

Fig. 2.5
The MicroFLEX-VL/66/Multimedia computer is a "mini-tower" that can be placed either on the desk or on the floor. Photo Courtesy of KPR.

For example, a full tower can have a total of five expansion bays (or openings for drives such as disk, ROM, or tape) accessible from the front. Each of these bays are *full-height* (1 1/2 inches). This may appear more than the average person needs, but the cost of a full tower is minimal compared to the cost of expansion when you run out of room.

If you've decided that buying a new case would be your best alternative, there are some things you must consider. First, make sure all components in your current system are transportable, including the motherboard, power supply, and disk drives (hard and floppy). Also, make sure you buy plenty of room for expansion, otherwise you'll be repeating this process later.

Purchasing external devices is another alternative, although it can be very costly. Typically, external devices are more expensive since they require their own casing and power supply. The cost of an external device can often exceed the cost of buying a full tower case.

Portables

If you're thinking of upgrading or purchasing a portable computer rather than a desktop, then you need to consider a few additional items. These computers fall into the portable category:

- ■ *Transportable computers.* Usually the most powerful of the portable family. They don't have a battery and must be plugged into a power source.

- ■ *Laptop computers.* Powered by an external source and a battery. With a fully charged battery you can work on the laptop wherever you are. All you need is a place to put it—your lap, for instance.

■ *Notebooks*. Smaller than laptop computers, they, too, are powered externally and by batteries. There are even computers that are smaller than notebooks—palmtops, handhelds, and Personal Digital Assistants (PDAs). These smaller systems are usually not powerful enough for multimedia applications. Installing add-on boards for sound, MIDI, graphics and CD-ROM drives isn't an option.

Expansion Options. To upgrade your portable for multimedia, you generally need to add the following components. To do so, you need an expansion slot (where adapter boards connect to your motherboard) or receptacle for each:

■ CD-ROM drive

■ Sound card

■ Speakers

■ Adequate video display

The CD-ROM drive, sound card, and speakers will need to be connected to your portable. Depending upon the manufacturer, you can use standard connections on the laptop (serial and parallel ports) or you can use advanced connectors, if available (PCMCIA SCSI port, adapter boards). Different combinations can be used based upon available ports. Another alternative is to upgrade to a PCMCIA SCSI port and daisy chain the individual devices into one SCSI chain that connects into one SCSI port.

The video display on your portable should meet the guidelines stated later in this chapter (refer to "Adding a New Video Monitor" later in this chapter and Chapter 6, "Upgrading Your Video"). If the display is substandard, you can purchase an external monitor. Most portables come with a standard connector for an external monitor; however, it's better to have an adequate display as part of the laptop. This is better than lugging an external monitor around.

Adding peripherals (such as an external CD-ROM drive) requires expansion slots. Portables are very limited when it comes to expansion slots. An alternative is to use external parallel or serial ports rather than expansion slots.

Full-size expansion slots aren't common to portable computers because they were designed for desktops, not portables. There are exceptions, such as the Toshiba T6600C illustrated in figure 2.6. Traditional adapter boards consume a lot of power, and they take up a lot of space. Since portables are limited on space and can run off batteries, space and power are two critical areas. In an effort to provide the same kind of expandability available to desktop computers, the Personal Computer Memory Card International Association (PCMCIA) established a new standard for portable computer expansion cards.

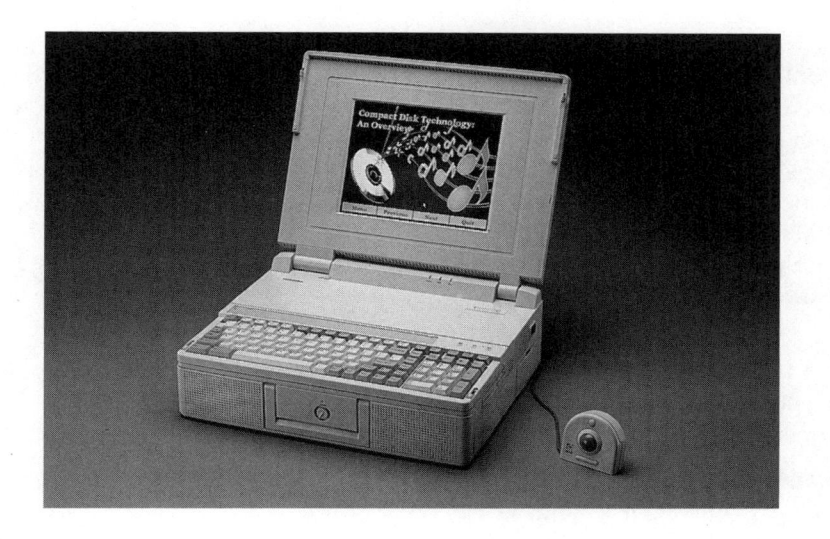

Fig. 2.6
The Toshiba T6600C offers the ability to add a full-size video card and is fully-equipped for multi-media. Photo courtesy Toshiba, Irvine, CA.

The PCMCIA expansion cards are similar in size to credit cards. The types of PCMCIA cards available include fax/modems, Local Area Network cards, memory cards, and SCSI adapters. The four types of PCMCIA standards are:

- *PCMCIA Type I.* The original standard designed specifically for memory expansion cards. Type I cards are 3.3mm thick.

- *PCMCIA Type II.* Specified a 5mm card allowing more PCMCIA functionality beyond just memory expansion. The size of the card needed to be increased to allow for more expansion capabilities. Type I cards are compatible with Type II expansion buses.

- *PCMCIA Type III.* Offers more functions with the ability to expand. The primary use of Type III PCMCIA slots is for removable hard disks, although Types I and II cards also can be used. Type III devices are 10.5mm thick.

- *PCMCIA Type IV.* To improve on the capacity of the removable hard drives. Type IV cards are larger than Type III devices.

There are problems with the PCMCIA standard. The following list identifies the problem areas you need to be aware of when buying a PCMCIA card.

■ *Functionality and Compliance with Standards.* The different PCMCIA standards were established to provide greater functionality and compliance. Improvements in functionality were required since the original Type I standard was limited to memory expansion. Improvements in compliance were necessary because not all manufacturers were complying with the PCMCIA standards. You do risk the chance of purchasing a non-compatible or non-compliant card. Before you buy a PCMCIA card, make sure the card is in compliance and is compatible with the configuration of your portable system. Ask your salesperson or contact the manufacturer of the card for this information.

■ *Cost.* PCMCIA cards are typically twice as much as a traditional desktop expansion card. The reason for this is the technology is considered new and is not purchased in a volume sufficient to drive the costs down; however, as PCMCIA cards become more widespread, the cost will become more economical.

■ *Memory Management.* The age-old problem of memory management with DOS becomes more of an annoyance with PCMCIA. This is because PCMCIA cards can dominate specific areas of memory. If other software or hardware is competing for the same area in memory, try readjusting available settings so they don't conflict. If conflicts can't be resolved, sacrifices must be made. Either return the PCMCIA card (always make sure you have a money back guarantee) or use the card in lieu of another device.

■ *Available Ports.* Although PCMCIA helps resolve the expandability problem with portables, it's not a complete solution. The number of PCMCIA slots is usually limited to one or two. When compared to desktops, which easily have five or more expansion slots, you can see the limitations of the portable. This is compounded with the multi-peripheral requirements of multimedia.

Docking Stations. If you only need multimedia while at home or in the office, you can use a docking station for your portable, as shown in figure 2.7. A docking station is an external case that makes your portable act more like a desktop system. It has connectors for a full-size monitor, keyboard, and adapter boards (may vary among the different manufacturers). Make sure you're aware of the docking station options available with your portable computer. Refer to the documentation that came with the station.
A portable computer can get very expensive. When you total the cost for a docking station, external keyboard, external monitor, batteries, PCMCIA cards, and adapter boards, you realize you could have purchased a high-powered desktop for significantly less. Although very convenient, you pay a premium for portables.

On-The-Road: A Case For Presentations. If you want to use a portable to give multimedia presentations, make sure you have an adequate screen. At minimum it must support color (65,536 colors) and a minimum resolution of 640 x 480 (refer to "Adding a New Video Monitor" later in this chapter; also, Chapter 6, "Upgrading Your Video"). The technology used for laptop screens is much different from desktop video monitors. Purchasing a portable with comparable video capabilities will cost several hundred dollars more.

Fig. 2.7
Toshiba offers a series of portable computers that provide full multimedia capabilities while in the docking station, including the T4800CT.

Typically, the display on a portable computer is too small for people to gather around. If you're presenting your multimedia production to a large audience, you're going to need an external monitor or projection device. If you do decide to purchase an external monitor, make sure the graphics capabilities of the external monitor match the requirements outlined later in the section, "Adding a New Video Monitor". Lugging around all of this extra stuff defeats the purpose of having a portable.

Portable Presentation Alternatives. There are alternatives to upgrading your portable to multimedia for portable presentations. The Kodak PhotoCD Player is an ideal tool for traveling presentations. When you get to the client location, all you need to do is connect your portable PhotoCD player into the client's computer monitor or into a television monitor. The PhotoCD is useful for presentations that use still images and sound. The presentations can be created at your office or home. Also, some companies provide the service of converting your presentation into a CD-ROM.

Another alternative is to purchase a PhotoCD recorder and create your own CDs. This will cost you several thousand dollars and isn't usually an option for the casual user. If you can't justify the cost of a CD recorder, you can resort back to the service provider, which is more than adequate.

Do you need to travel as much? If you had an effective presentation on a CD you may not even need to travel at all. All you need is to provide your client with the CD. If they don't have access to a multimedia system, you may rent one for them. That would still cost you less than an airline ticket. Plus, all the other hidden costs of travel (such as lost travel time, hotel, car rental, and per diem) would disappear.

A Case For MIDI. If the primary use of your portable is for MIDI (Musical Instrument Digital Interface), the video monitor won't be as much of a concern. You should be more concerned with conductivity to SCSI devices, synthesizers, sound cards, and controllers. The expandability of the portable is the key issue—portables aren't as expandable as desktop systems. Again, you're going to pay a premium for expandability, and even at a premium you may not have the same quality or performance that a desktop would deliver.

Tip

If you're interested in using a portable computer to handle your MIDI needs, don't get overly concerned with battery operated computers. Remember, your instruments are not battery operated.

The Motherboard

The computer's electronic components are organized and attached to a circuit board. The mother-of-all-boards is the *motherboard*. There are elements on a motherboard you want to be concerned with when you upgrade your PC:

- CPU
- RAM
- BIOS
- Expansion slots

The CPU is the brain of the computer and is the most important component of your PC. The other components work for the CPU.

Everything going to the CPU and coming from the CPU must travel across the motherboard. Data travels across the motherboard on buses. The number of lanes you have determines how much traffic can flow at a time. There are either 8, 16, 32, or 64 bit buses. Buses will be discussed in more detail later in the section, "Understanding Expansion

Buses and Adapters." For now just note that the size of the bus is important, especially where multimedia is concerned. The size of the bus determines the amount of data that can flow across it simultaneously.

When data flows across an expansion bus it's destined for the CPU. However, since the CPU can't do everything at once, it needs a temporary workspace. This workspace is called Random Access Memory (RAM).

RAM attaches to your motherboard. When you upgrade your PC, make sure you have enough RAM. Although MPC level 2 standards call for 4M of RAM, this isn't adequate. Your minimum goal should be 16M; the more RAM you have the better off you are. Your PC can access RAM faster than other forms of storage (for example, a hard disk). With more RAM, your PC can handle more tasks simultaneously.

The final item to consider is the BIOS. The Basic Input Output System (BIOS) is like a traffic cop—it manages the flow of data. The BIOS plays an important role, so you should know the type and version of your BIOS. This should display when you *power-on* your computer (American Megatrends (AMI) or Phoenix Technologies have reputable BIOSes; refer to the Buyer's Guides in Part III for more sources).

As stated before, the CPU is the most important component you can upgrade. Everything eventually traces back to the CPU, so we need to explore it in detail.

Choosing the CPU You Need

Common CPU models include the 386, 486, and 586. These refer to the Intel chip model number (80386, 80486, and 80586 (Pentium)), respectively. Intel isn't the only manufacturer of CPUs. Other manufacturers include Advanced Micro Devices (AMD), IBM, Cyrix, and NexGen. The CPU connects directly onto the motherboard. The motherboard is the structure that supports the electrical network that leads to and from the CPU, and interconnects all other components and peripherals.

When you turn your computer's power supply on, the CPU comes to life. The ROM supplies the CPU with all the instructions needed to successfully start itself. RAM is used as a temporary storage area as instructions go to and come from the CPU. With the computer up and running, you're now able to give it instructions on how to process your data. The result is computer-generated output derived from your processed data. Table 2.2 shows the input/output cycle.

Table 2.2 Device Categories		
Input	**Processing**	**Output**
Keyboards	CPU	Monitor
Mouse	Math coprocessor	Printer
Digitizer	Graphics coprocessor	Speakers
MIDI Keyboard		Headphones
Microphone		
Scanner		

The CPU for You: 486 or Better. The first few generations of CPUs were the 8086, 8088, and 80286. These CPUs don't have the necessary capabilities for multimedia computers. The MPC level 1 standards start with a 386SX, which is also quickly becoming outdated. If your CPU is a 386, 286, 8086, or 8088, you need to upgrade to MPC level 2 standards (refer to table 2.1). If your motherboard doesn't allow you to upgrade the CPU chip, you'll need a new motherboard. Conversely, if your motherboard does allow a CPU upgrade make sure the motherboard can adequately support the new CPU and multimedia in general. Provided a CPU upgrade is possible and will result in an adequate system, you'll want to upgrade to a 486 or better. Given these considerations, don't forget to always calculate the cost of upgrading versus purchasing a new system. If your PC requires extensive upgrades you will, no doubt, be better off purchasing new.

To be satisfied with your upgrade you want to start out with a 486DX or better.

The Intel486 multiprocessor is an ideal starting point for multimedia. There are five members of the Intel486 microprocessor family:

- *DX4*. High-end processor that is well-suited for multimedia.
- *DX2*. Includes Intel's speed-doubling technology and is well-suited for multimedia.
- *DX*. Doesn't have speed-doubling, but will satisfy the basic multimedia needs.
- *SL*. Used for portable computers, it saves space and power and is available in each member of the 486 CPU family.
- *SX*. Low-end model that doesn't include a math coprocessor and is slower than other models.

The 486 CPUs use *RISC* (Reduced Instruction Set Computing) technology. RISC operates on the premise that a computer can do a lot of smaller tasks quicker than it can do a smaller number of larger tasks.

Measuring Microprocessors. The two key aspects for evaluating microprocessors are:

1. Megahertz (MHz): How fast can it go?
2. Bus Width: How many bits can it handle?

How fast a computer can go is based on clock speed represented by megahertz (MHz), or *millions of cycles per second*. A 25 MHz computer runs at 25,000,000 cycles per second. MPC level 2 requires a minimum of 25 MHz. If you want acceptable performance, upgrade to 50 MHz or better. Current technology goes beyond 100 MHz. Get as much as you can afford; you won't regret it.

The second aspect is based upon its *bit* capacity. The 486 CPUs have 32-bit internal and external buses. Basically, data comes in and is processed 32 bits at a time. Current technology is moving towards 64-bit buses. Purchasing 64-bit technology is an investment for the future. Don't worry if funds are tight—32-bit technology will be around for awhile.

Note

You may come across the term, "wait-state". A *wait-state* slows down a CPU because it forces the CPU to wait until it is re-synchronized with other system components. Try to get a CPU with zero (0) wait-states.

Upgrading the CPU. If upgrading the CPU chip is more economical than buying a new PC, or if it's the most effective way to upgrade your PC to deliver the processing power you will need for multimedia, then you need to determine how the existing CPU chip is attached to your motherboard. There are basically three types of CPU sockets:

- *Soldered.* Some CPU chips can be upgraded even if they're soldered onto the motherboard. This is accomplished by *piggy-backing* the chips (physically placing a chip on top of the existing CPU). If you have an *SX* chip that runs at 20 or 25 MHz, it's more likely it can be upgraded. If, however, it runs at 16 MHz, your upgrade may be limited. Also, the existing chip must utilize a float pin. The *float pin* is part of the chip design that allows the chip to be disabled when a newer model is added.

- *Removable chips.* It is common for *DX* chips to be *removable*, or upgraded. A removable chip can be detached from the motherboard by gently prying the chip upward from the corners. Upgrading this chip amounts to removing the chip and replacing it. Usually a tool is provided when you purchase an upgrade chip, although you would need to confirm this. It is common to upgrade 16, 20, 25, and 33 MHz chips. You may be prohibited from upgrading a 40 MHz, or faster, chip.

- *Upgrade sockets.* A chip designed to be upgraded usually is seated in a socket that allows the chip to be removed easily. The two sockets, discussed above, are ways to work around a problem, whereas a chip designed to be upgraded is physically manufactured and connected to the motherboard in a manner that provides an easy way of removing and replacing the chip. This may be in the form of a separate socket (like an OverDrive socket) or a Zero Insertion Force (ZIF) socket, or a combination of the two.

Note

There are a few considerations you should be aware of when considering a CPU upgrade: if you have a math coprocessor, you need to know when was it manufactured—mid 1991 and prior may create problems; what is the speed of the RAM chips installed in your PC—some upgrade chips only work with chips at 85 nanoseconds or faster (remember the larger the number the slower the chip; 90 ns is slower than 85 ns).

> ### Tip
>
> If you install a new chip and it doesn't work, try reseating it. Sometimes a film builds up over connecting points. Reseating the chip scrapes off the film.

The manufacturers of upgrade chips can usually determine if your CPU can be upgraded. Cyrix, for example, has an 800 number that is easy to remember (1-800-46-CYRIX). Their technical support is helpful and they may even provide you a system disk that tests the upgrade compatibility of your PC.

If you can upgrade your CPU, the installation process is relatively simple. It amounts to the following steps:

1. Remove the cover to the PC. Make sure all cables are unplugged. Also, discharge any static electricity by touching the PC chassis before you touch any internal components.

2. Next, locate the existing CPU. Once the CPU is located, you can begin the physical replacement of the chip.

3. Replace the current chip. If the chip piggy-backs onto the existing chip, you simply snap it on top. If you must replace the current chip, gently pry on the corners of the existing chip until it lifts up from the socket. Then remove the chip and replace it with the new one. If you have a ZIF socket, you lift the lever back to unsecure the chip; then you remove and replace it. If an empty upgrade socket is available, simply place the new chip into the empty socket.

4. With the new CPU installed, before you put the cover back on the PC, carefully reattach all the cables and turn on the PC. Complete the installation by running any software provided by the manufacturer. If no problems are encountered and the tests are complete, reassemble the PC.

If you run into any problems during the installation, you may need to retrace your steps, ensuring that each one was properly carried out. As mentioned earlier, you may also need to reseat the chip since connection is not always made by each pin on the chip. The documentation provided with the upgrade chip should offer additional troubleshooting steps.

Adding a Math Coprocessor. The CPU is ideal for administrating system resources, but it's weak when it comes to performing mathematical functions. Math coprocessors were developed to strengthen this weakness.

A math coprocessor performs all floating point operations for a CPU (see fig. 2.8). An FPU (Floating Point Unit) is synonymous with a math coprocessor. The CPU is much faster because it is relieved of floating point operations. The math coprocessor outperforms the CPU where floating point arithmetic is concerned. Figure 2.9 shows how to seat the coprocessor.

Building a Foundation

Fig. 2.8
A math coprocessor improves the performance of multimedia PCs.

> **Note**
>
> You may think you don't need a math coprocessor because you're only going to use your computer for multimedia. Remember the computer uses math to process graphics, video, and sound. Therefore, a math coprocessor, although not mandatory for MPC2, will make your multimedia applications run faster. You'll do yourself a disservice if you don't have a math coprocessor.

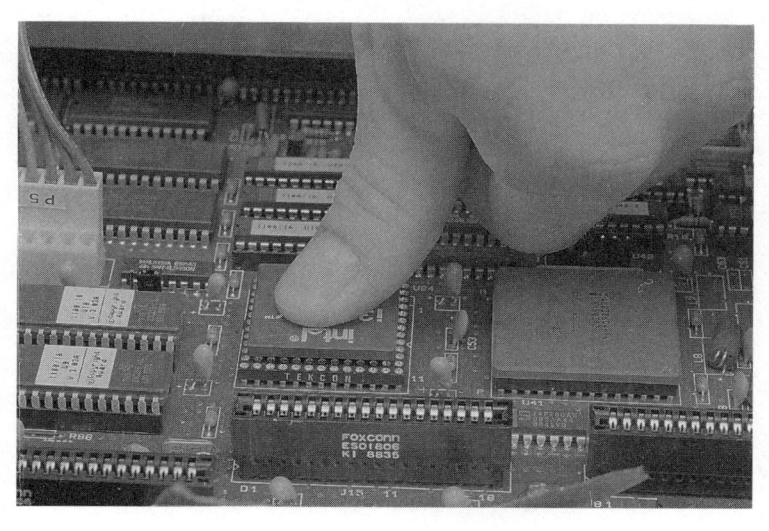

Fig. 2.9
Using your thumb, gently push the coprocessor down until it is firmly seated. Watch your motherboard—if it's bending under pressure, give it proper support.

Adding an OverDrive Chip. Intel offers speed-doubling technology via its OverDrive processor technology (see fig. 2.10). DX2 and DX4 models have this technology. If you have a CPU model lower than a DX2, it may be possible to buy an OverDrive chip to put on your motherboard. With an OverDrive processor, the CPU can operate internally at twice the clock speed.

Fig. 2.10
The raised surfaces on the top of this Intel OverDrive processor chip allows heat to dissipate.

Installing an OverDrive processor is similar to installing a new CPU chip. The process is simple, especially if you have a *Zero Insertion Force* (ZIF) socket available (see figs. 2.11 and 2.12). You need to verify that your motherboard has an OverDrive socket before going ahead with this. You may also be able to physically remove the existing CPU and replace it with an OverDrive chip. Check with your salesperson, refer to the documentation that came with your PC, or contact the manufacturer direct.

Fig. 2.11
A Zero Insertion Force socket makes adding chips easy. Locate the socket and then align the chip's pins directly above the insertion points.

Fig. 2.12
Pulling the ZIF lever over and down will slide the chip into place.

> **Tip**
>
> Considering upgrading your 486 to a Pentium? You also should consider an OverDrive processor chip. This will give you a performance boost at a much lower cost.

You don't have to be running high-end scientific and engineering applications to benefit from an OverDrive processor. Microsoft Word for Windows is estimated to run 54 percent faster with an Overdrive processor; Microsoft Excel is estimated to run 72 percent faster.

> **Note**
>
> The faster the CPU runs the hotter it gets. The 486 chip can actually exceed 185°F. A product called a *heat sink* literally attaches to the top of a 486 and maintains a safe temperature around 85° - 90°F.

If you're serious about multimedia, get a 486DX or better. If you have a DX and need more power, consider an OverDrive processor. If you need even more power than that, consider the next generation of processors, called Pentium.

Choosing a Pentium. If you have the budget and want nothing but pure processing power, then the Pentium may be the answer. Intel's Pentium processor can perform over 100 MIPS (Millions of Instructions per Second). The Pentium microprocessor chip almost doubles the speed of the 486DX2.

The Pentium is designed around *superscalar architecture*. This architecture has been used on high-end mainframe computers and allows your CPU to process several instructions at the same time.

> **Note**
>
> The Pentium's operating speed actually generates a significant amount of heat. An overheated Pentium processor can cause random system errors and shorten its life span. The *PentaCool* is a device specifically designed to mount onto the Pentium and keep it cool. You may need to install one if you upgrade to a Pentium.

There are several other technological improvements in the Pentium. The 64-bit data bus is twice the size of any of its predecessors. Also, the Pentium has a larger page size for memory management. The Intel 486, for example, has a 4,000 (4K) page size compared to the Pentium's 4,000,000 (4M) page size.

Paging is important because it divides memory into smaller pieces that the CPU can process. Until the Pentium, page sizes were only 4K. Now with 4M page sizes, the Pentium processor is capable of dividing memory into 4M pages.

Processing graphics data and sound wave files requires extensive CPU resources. The size of the graphics data files alone can easily overburden a CPU. The Pentium's larger page sizes better equip it to handle graphics and sound files, making it ideal for multimedia computing.

Understanding Expansion Buses and Adapters

When IBM Personal Computers were introduced in 1981, they included five expansion slots. Each slot interfaces with three motherboard buses:

- *Data bus*. Carries data to and from memory and the CPU.

- *Address bus*. Carries the data's destination address.

- *Control bus*. Carries specific control signals, such as an interrupt (IRQ).

When you buy an adapter board (a circuit board that enhances the functions of your PC) and plug it into an available slot, it makes a connection to these three buses on the motherboard (see fig. 2.13). You have to make sure the adapter boards you buy can connect to compatible expansion slots on the motherboard (the next several paragraphs will provide more details).

Fig. 2.13
Expansion slots provide adapter board access to the expansion bus. The expansion slot interfaces to the data, control, and address buses.

Compaq used IBM's established bus technology when it introduced its first IBM computer clone in 1982. The bus's design, including the data, address, and control bus, became the Industry Standard Architecture (ISA).

ISA Bus Architecture. The ISA bus architecture is the most prevalent standard today. There are, however, limitations. For example, the architecture can only handle a bandwidth of 16 bits. *Bandwidth* refers to the width of a data channel. If you have a 486 CPU, it's capable of handling a bus bandwidth of 32 bits. An ISA architecture can become a bottleneck.

This is only a concern when the expansion board you plan on installing demands high performance. A modem, for example, would be happy with a 16 bit bus because it can outperform the modem. A video or hard disk card, however, needs more bandwidth than ISA can offer.

EISA and MCA Bus Architectures. The EISA and MCA bus architectures are a level above ISA. IBM developed the Micro Channel Architecture. EISA was developed by a consortium of IBM-PC compatible computer manufacturers. MCA was too restrictive and is only common on IBM PCs. EISA became more of an established standard than MCA because it was less restrictive and offered upward compatibility.

The main benefit of EISA and MCA was the increased bandwidth of 32 bits. The address and control buses were also expanded so that more data could flow to more addresses with better control.

EISA and MCA expansion buses are easier to configure than their ISA predecessor (see figs. 2.14 and 2.15). Less board level configuration was required. ISA is more difficult to configure given the following considerations:

- *Interrupt Request (IRQ).* Boards can use interrupt requests to get the CPU's attention.

- *I/O Address.* Points to a specific location on the expansion bus and is used to make sure data finds its way back to the proper expansion bus.

- *Direct Memory Access (DMA).* Provides a quick way for data to flow between an expansion bus and memory. DMA completely bypasses the CPU, which keeps the CPU free to perform other necessary tasks.

EISA and MCA buses attempted to incorporate technology that automatically configured new boards. However, the technology was at times rigid and often required manual changes. The ISA bus was updated to offer true plug-and-play technology that wasn't rigid. This is currently offered as an option though, not as a standard feature among ISA boards.

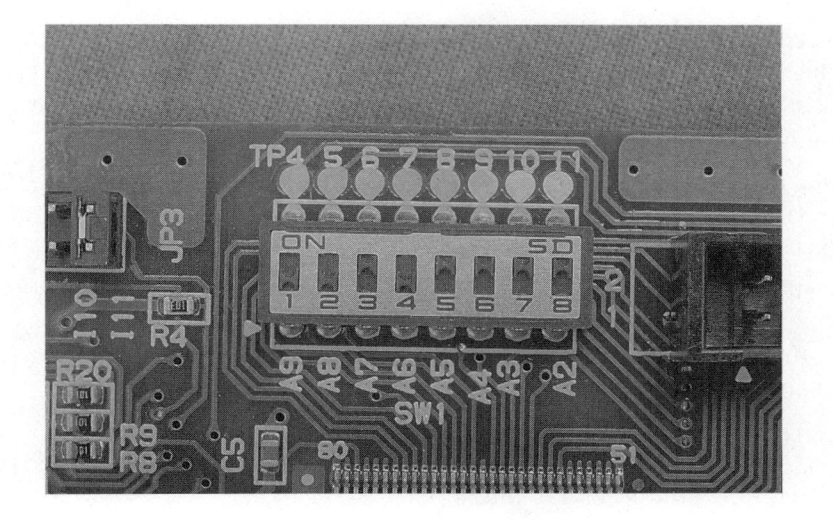

Fig. 2.14
DIP switches (Dual In-line Package) are used to change adapter board settings. New technology calls for making these switches more accessible or removing them entirely.

Fig. 2.15
Exposed DIP switches are more accessible and can be set without removing the PC cover.

VESA-Local Bus. One of the drawbacks with ISA and EISA was the 8 MHz limit imposed by the BIOS. A new bus technology was engineered to overcome this limitation. This new bus standard is the VESA local-bus (VL-BUS) developed by the Video Electronics Standard Association (VESA).

Operating as a local bus, the VL-Bus is synchronized with the CPU clock speed. The VL-Bus standard uses a Micro Channel connection to the motherboard. Only the MCA connector is used. Although VL-Bus uses an MCA type connection, it's not a part of MCA.

The VL-Bus can talk directly to motherboard components without having to go through BIOS, allowing it to achieve higher performance levels. You can think of VL-Bus as cutting out the middle-man. Another reason for the performance increase is the separation of video and audio into their own respective buses.

The VL-BUS easily outperforms ISA and EISA. The VL-BUS standard is one of the fastest performing bus architectures available. For a short while VL-Bus was the best. That all changed with the introduction of Intel's PCI bus.

Personal Computer Interface. The Personal Computer Interface (PCI) standard provides capabilities above and beyond those provided by current bus architectures. These new innovative features are:

- *Automatic configuration.* The board configures itself based upon your current PC environment (plug-and-play).
- *Platform independence.* Compatible among different hardware platforms.
- *Concurrent processing.* Can simultaneously perform several functions.

Note

Know the requirements and limitations of your peripherals before you spend money on VL-Bus or PCI adapter boards. If you have a slow disk drive, for example, you won't get better performance even if you pay a premium for a VL-Bus/PCI drive interface card. It would be better to get a faster drive.

What Bus Should You Take? The current PCI bus width is 32 bits. However, this limitation will soon be broken by a 64-bit bus version which is twice the size of the EISA but equivalent to the width of the VL-Bus. Table 2.3 helps identify the different characteristics between buses.

Table 2.3 Bus Comparisons		
Bus Architecture	**Bandwidth**	**Notes**
PCI Local Bus	32 current	Plug-and-Play
	64 future	Platform independent Concurrent processing Operates at CPU speed
VESA Local Bus	32	Separates video and audio buses Automatic configuration
EISA	32	Automatic configuration Platform independent Limited to 8 MHz
ISA	16-bit	Requires manual settings Limited to 8 MHz

It's best to have a variety of buses available (refer to the documentation that came with your PC to know which buses are on your motherboard). Your motherboard should offer a couple of high-end buses (VL-Bus or PCI) and some entry-level buses (ISA or EISA). Since EISA is compatible with ISA, it may be better to have EISA, unless the cost is a factor and you're sure you won't need EISA boards.

Tip

Be aware of the available expansion buses on your computer. If you don't have a VL-Bus or PCI expansion bus, you can't use a VL-Bus or PCI adapter board.

Note

EISA, VL-Bus and PCI are all backward compatible. You can put an older generation card in a newer generation expansion bus if it's backward compatible.

Look at your motherboard and identify the expansion bus types you have. Look for small boards plugged into a large expansion slot. You may be able to free up a VL-Bus slot or PCI slot by shuffling your adapter boards.

> **Note**
>
> ISA & EISA expansion buses are the ones you will likely find on your motherboard. You can distinguish between them by the size of their plug-in slots. ISA has the smallest plug-in slot, followed by EISA and then VL-Bus and PCI. PCI and VL-Bus are the largest expansion slots available and they also have the most connecting points within the connecting slot. If all the slots look the same on your motherboard, and they don't vary in size, you probably don't have any PCI or VL-Bus slots. They're probably all EISA. Older motherboards may have all ISA slots.

No matter what bus you have, remember that a bus is simply a path to another destination. You have to make sure you have adequate capacity to store and process the volume of data traveling along the bus. Ultimately the CPU is the determining factor, but don't underestimate the power of memory.

The Operating System

A computer operating system is software that talks to hardware. The operating system translates your software requests into hardware instructions.

Microsoft DOS (Disk Operating System) is the most common PC operating system. Microsoft Windows is a graphical operating environment that enhances DOS. Instead of DOS commands, Windows uses a more friendly graphical interface. Windows was introduced in 1985 and has become the standard graphical interface for PCs, not to mention establishing itself in the multimedia arena.

You need Windows 3.1 to adhere to the MPC standards. Recognizing that Windows is currently dependent upon DOS, you must also have DOS. You should upgrade to a current version of DOS (5.0 or 6.0).

Apple computers have been employing multimedia a lot longer than PCs. Even today some of the Apple computers use state-of-the-art sound and graphics technology. You may think it would be better to go with the Apple computers since they've been doing multimedia longer, right? Well, again you need to consider the market share and predominant standards.

It didn't take long for Windows-based PCs to become the dominating force in the multimedia industry. Some industry analysts estimate that Windows owns nearly 75 percent of the entire multimedia market. Windows is installed on over 55 million PCs, with two million more added each month.

Microsoft established itself as a viable multimedia player when it introduced multimedia-based extensions for its Windows operating environment (Microsoft Multimedia Extensions to Windows 3.0). Subsequent to multimedia extensions, Microsoft also developed a Media Control Interface (MCI). With MCI, Windows users can control audio and video devices, including recorders, laser disc devices, and others. Windows 3.1 included the multimedia extensions, device drivers, and MCI.

> **Tip**
>
> Although you can purchase multimedia extensions for 3.0, you should upgrade to Windows 3.1. Using the extensions is a quick-fix whereas Windows 3.1 provides a more cohesive solution.

Installing More Memory

There are two categories of memory: Random Access Memory (RAM) and Read Only Memory (ROM). RAM memory is like a pencil and paper. You can write, erase, and re-place what you have written. ROM is like pen and paper. Once it is written on it does not change. Both RAM and ROM are essential to your computer. When you upgrade your PC memory, you will be most concerned with RAM. RAM gives your computer a temporary workspace so your computer can do its job.

Installing Random Access Memory increases the memory capacity of your computer. There are three types of RAM chips available:

- *DRAM*: Dynamic RAM
- *SIMM:* Single In-line Memory Modules
- *SIPP*: Single In-line Pin Packages

Whereas DRAM consists of a single chip, SIMM and SIPP memory are tiny circuit boards with several chips installed on-board. DRAM is the original type of memory, but isn't commonly used. SIMM is the most common form of memory used today. Each memory chip is illustrated in figures 2.16, 2.17, and 2.18.

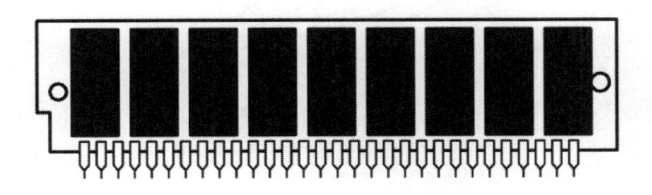

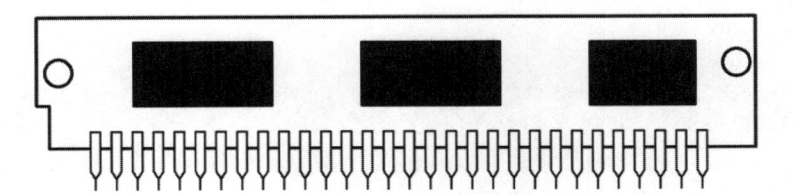

Fig. 2.16
A DRAM (Dynamic RAM) chip was used in older computers.

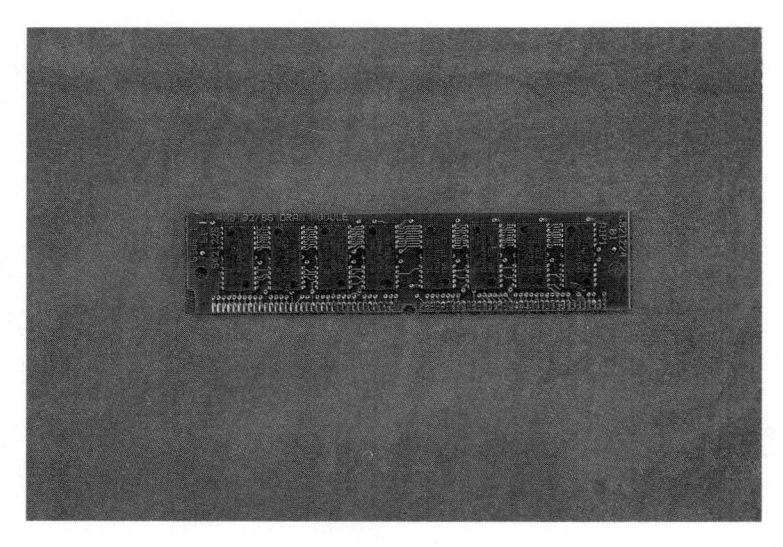

Fig. 2.17
SIMMs are Single In-line Memory Modules used to upgrade RAM.

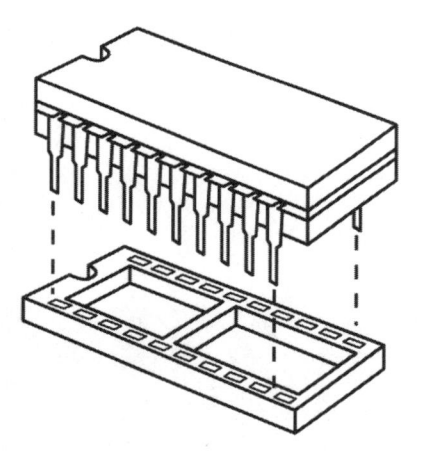

Fig. 2.18
SIPPs are Single In-line Pin Packages used to add memory. A SIPP connects differently than a SIMM via a series of pins.

> **Note**
>
> CMOS (Complementary Metal Oxide Semiconductor) is a special type of memory. CMOS stores system information about drives (hard & floppy), memory configurations, video parameters, math coprocessor information, and date and time. Although CMOS memory can be changed, it does not disappear when the power on your computer is turned off. CMOS relies on an internal battery to maintain its memory contents.

Another category of memory is Read Only Memory (ROM). BIOS, for example, is made of ROM memory. Unless a BIOS upgrade is necessary, ROM is not a significant concern when upgrading to multimedia.

There also are two other types of ROM—EPROM and Flash. EPROM (Erasable Programmable Read Only Memory) requires special equipment to reprogram, or update. Flash memory requires special software from the manufacturer. It's easier for you to upgrade flash memory because it's unlikely that you have an EPROM programmer device.

Intel has network cards that use Flash memory. With these cards you can update the system-level programs automatically. Flash memory is a more recent generation of EPROM-like memory.

Note

Even though EPROM and Flash are ROM, you can change their contents. Updating BIOS is an example of changing ROM.

Increasing Memory Size

Multimedia places a lot of demands on your computer. Where RAM is concerned you need to make sure your computer is capable of providing the temporary RAM workspace it desperately needs. Even though MPC level 2 states a minimum of 4M, you should have at least 16M of RAM. As previously mentioned, 4M is inadequate and you'll need to upgrade.

Adding RAM is much easier than it was in the past. If you have SIMMs, all you do is just plug the SIMM into its corresponding socket on the motherboard (refer to the documentation provided with your PC). SIPPs are easy to add, too. You just have to be a little more careful because SIPPs use a series of pins. Align all the pins properly into place or they may break.

Before you buy memory, make sure you know the type of memory your computer uses. To find the specific type of memory used on your PC, ask the salesperson or manufacturer, or check your documentation. Also, know the characteristics of the RAM you already have installed. Avoid using different types of chips. Although you can meet or exceed the speed capacity (60ns are faster than 80ns) of chips, you want to try to keep the same types of chips, especially when installed in the same memory bank. When you consider the potential problems, frustration, and wasted time, you really don't save anything by mixing and matching chips. Keep them consistent even if it requires replacement of old chips.

If you have DRAM your motherboard is most likely outdated. Newer motherboards use SIMM or SIPP memory. To install SIMM or SIPP memory follow these steps:

Building a Foundation

1. Adding SIMM memory involves placing the module into an available SIMM bank. You must put the module in the same orientation as other modules (refer to your documentation if no other modules are installed). Once the module is put into an available bank, gently press it at an angle in the direction of the securing brackets until the module is firmly seated.

2. Adding SIPP memory requires a little more precision. They too, must be installed in the same orientation as other SIPPs (refer to your PC documentation if no other SIPPs are installed). Align the SIPP pins with the corresponding holes in the socket. Once aligned, press the SIPP down until all the pins are secure. It may take a little pressure to press the SIPP down into place.

Upgrading Your Disk Drives

There are two types of disk drives—hard and floppy. For your computer to be complete you need both types of drives, which you probably already have.

You should have at least one of each type of floppy drive (see fig. 2.19). You can purchase a *dual-floppy drive* which can read 3.5 inch and 5.25 inch disks, although only one at a time. This usually doesn't create a problem.

> **Note**
>
> When referring to magnetic storage you should use "disk." When referring to optical storage you want to use "disc."

Fig. 2.19
Floppy disks come in two sizes: 5.25 inch and the more common 3.5 inch.

> ### Note
>
> Always have a *boot disk* safely stored away for emergency purposes. The boot disk should be for-
> matted as a *bootable* or *system disk.* Use the same version of the operating system that is on your
> hard disk. The boot disk should contain your CONFIG.SYS and AUTOEXEC.BAT files. You also
> should copy SYS.COM from your DOS subdirectory, and *.INI files from your Windows sub-
> directory. Always keep these files current with those on your hard disk.

Hard disks and floppy disks are similar in nature. The main difference is that a hard disk
is enclosed within an airtight case and provides a much larger capacity. Multimedia PCs
need a large hard disk capacity.

MPC established 160M as the minimum entry level hard disk size. You should buy as
much hard disk capacity as you can afford. Your minimum goal should be close to 500M.
Anything less will limit you; anything more will benefit you.

Hard Disk Advances

Hard disk capacity has drastically increased over the years. A hard disk is actually made
up of several platters with the same composition as a floppy disk. Figure 2.20 is an illus-
trative view of a hard disk.

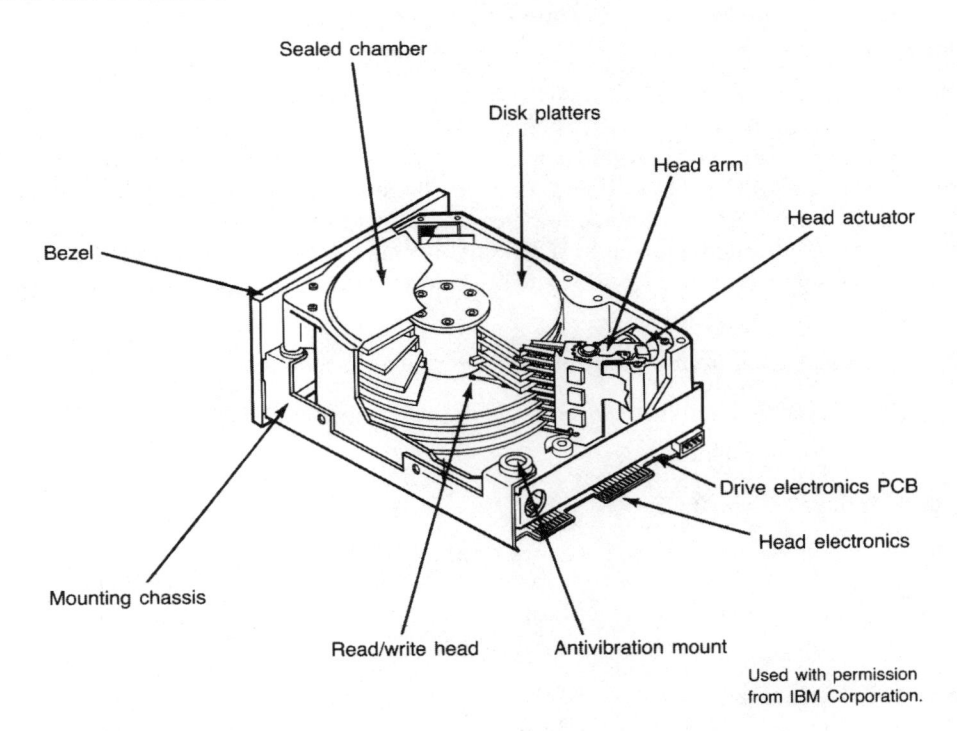

Used with permission
from IBM Corporation.

Fig. 2.20
This illustrates the components of a hard disk drive.

Multimedia files take up a lot of disk space. Consider, for example, that one picture file can be 20M or more. Sound wave files, too, can eat up a significant amount of disk storage. A file holding only a few seconds of full motion video can eat up 80M. Multiply these files by the number of different versions you'll keep and you've quickly exceeded disk capacity.

> ### Caution
>
> Don't be fooled by disk compression. A compressed multimedia file may end up larger than an uncompressed version. The nature of sound data does not lend itself to algorithms that squeeze disk space.

The cost of a hard disk is based upon capacity, speed, and interface. Capacity is measured in megabytes—500M should be your multimedia goal. Speed is measured in access time and data transfer rate. Interface protocol specifies how the drive connects and talks to the computer; IDE and SCSI are examples of interface protocols.

IDE vs. SCSI

There are two predominant disk interface standards: IDE and SCSI. Another interface standard, ESDI, is rapidly becoming obsolete, so you should focus on the two prevalent standards (IDE and SCSI).

Until multimedia, IDE (Intelligent Drive Electronics) drives were common. However, IDE has a limited capacity of 1.7G. Also, IDE is dependent upon the computer BIOS. All data flowing to and from an IDE hard disk must be handled through the computer's BIOS. This can create a bottleneck. Although there are enhancements that are being discussed, such as PRIDE and EIDE, these technologies are not yet available. To overcome these limitations, people are migrating to SCSI (Small Computer System Interface). SCSI (pronounced scuzzy) is rapidly becoming the preferred standard for interfacing hard drives to computers.

SCSI is well-suited for multimedia and offers you several benefits:

- Up to seven SCSI devices can be daisy-chained together.
- SCSI-2 allows for 14 devices.
- SCSI bypasses the BIOS
- SCSI is the common interface connection for CD-ROM drives

It's important to understand the performance differences between the two interface protocols.

Hard Disk Performance (IDE vs. SCSI)

When upgrading your PC, you want to select products that offer the best performance at a reasonable cost. IDE and SCSI drive performance is related to two basic principles: how fast data can move to/from the drive, and how much demand is placed on the CPU. Reading data is accomplished by copying it from the hard disk and placing it into RAM. Writing data to a hard disk follows the same path, just in reverse. Writing data consists of moving it from RAM to the hard disk.

One of the major bottlenecks with transferring data is the mechanical movements of the hard disk. The time it takes for the hard disk to physically locate data is called *Drive Latency*. SCSI and IDE drives are both bound by this limitation. There are differences, however, between SCSI and IDE when you consider the other aspects of disk I/O.

More overhead is required to initiate SCSI data transfers. Once established, however, large amounts of data can be transferred while freeing up the CPU. Conversely, IDE constantly interrupts the CPU each time it reads a sector on the disk. Small data transfers require fewer IDE based interrupts. However, the larger the file the more interrupts you will encounter. SCSI interrupts the CPU a few times at the beginning and once at the end of the transfer. Between SCSI interrupts, the CPU is left alone, even if the file being transferred is large.

SCSI works best with large data files. When you consider the large amount of data processed by multimedia applications, it's obvious why people like SCSI. The fact that you can interconnect several SCSI devices is also a benefit. If you are going to upgrade your hard disk, SCSI is the preferred choice.

Permanently storing data on a hard disk should be an understandable concept to you now. Data gets to and from the hard disk by the expansion bus. The hard disk is connected to the bus either by a SCSI adapter board or an IDE compatible adapter board. The only question left unanswered is how can you get the data into your computer in the first place.

Choosing a Keyboard

People often skimp on the keyboard. Not to be confused with the MIDI keyboard, a PC keyboard is used for typing. You have more physical contact with the keyboard than with anything else.

Caution

Although smart keyboards can be useful, sometimes conflicts arise with incompatible software.

The ability to configure your keyboard is another item you should consider. For example, the OmniKey/ULTRA keyboard by Northgate Computer Systems allows you to remap keys. This is especially beneficial if you are left-handed. It may be more convenient for lefties to reposition certain keys, like [Caps Lock], [Shift], or [Ctrl]. You don't have to be left-handed to prefer keys in different locations. Although a minor issue, its convenience may keep you from performing acrobatic feats with your hands.

MPC specifies the standard 101-key keyboard (see fig. 2.21). There are newer keyboards that are ergonomically designed to fit to your wrists, hands and arms. Instead of being rectangular they are shaped like a "V". This is a significant change in keyboards, especially when you consider that the 101-key keyboard has been a standard for several years now.

Fig. 2.21
Pictured here is a common keyboard with function keys, control keys, a number pad, and standard alphanumeric keys.

Tip
When purchasing a keyboard, remember the motto: *Try it before you buy it!*

There are some keyboards that are completely different from the standard layout that touch-typists are familiar with. In the late 1800's the QWERTY standard was established. The QWERTY standard was developed to slow people down. They were typing too fast and were jamming keys in the old style typewriters. The QWERTY standard is what most people use today. The original typing method, Dvorak, was a much quicker typing method.

With the advent of word processors, mechanical typewriters became obsolete. Now we can use the Dvorak method, which is a faster way of typing. You just have to un-learn QWERTY and learn Dvorak. Some people have already done this and they recognize noticeable improvements in their typing speed.

Some companies have completely redesigned the keyboard. For example, there is one keyboard design that uses only seven keys. By pressing different combinations of keys, or *chords,* you can type letters. Since only one hand is required, you can keep your other hand on your mouse.

> **Note**
>
> People with disabilities can greatly benefit by using one-handed keyboards. Infogrip offers the BAT Personal Keyboard in left-handed and right-handed models. The remaining free hand can operate a mouse or other pointing device.

If you decide to purchase a non-standard keyboard, make sure it can simultaneously support the standard 101-key keyboard. This will provide you with the additional features you sought in the non-standard keyboard, yet still keep your computer MPC compatible.

Input Pointing Devices

Some keyboards include pointing devices. They may have a trackball integrated. This is popular with portable computers. You always have the option of selecting from the plethora of pointers:

- *Mouse.* Two- or three-button. The mouse is the most common of all input devices. It is not as precise as a digitizer.

- *Trackballs.* A common input device that is moderately accurate.

- *Touch screens.* Used in kiosks and as a general pointing device. Touch screens are not a precision input device.

- *Touch pads.* Similar to a digitizer but without a stylus. Not as precise as other pointing devices but useful for non-precision input.

- *Styluses for pen-based computers.* Moderately accurate, styluses are ideally suited for pen-based computers. The screen surface acts as the contact point of the stylus.

- *Digitizers.* Ideal for precision drawings or general art work. Especially useful are pressure-sensitive digitizers that react to the pressure of the stylus on the surface of the digitizer pad.

An example of the various pointers is the DrawingSlate by CalComp. It's a pressure-sensitive pointing device that can be used with Fractal Design Painter.

The DesignSlate's stylus is battery-operated. If your battery dies, so does your pointing ability, but there is a battery-saving feature. However, it causes a delay which can be annoying. An alternative is the Wacom Art-Z tablet. The Wacom stylus doesn't require a battery which saves money, avoids possible down time, and results in a much lighter stylus.

The future looks graphical. GUI (Graphical User Interface, pronounced *gooey*) appears to be indefinite. When you operate in a GUI environment you need a pointing device. Sound technology is opening up another facet: voice commands. Voice-activated commands will become more prevalent, but today a pointing device is considered the norm.

Adding a New Video Monitor

It's likely that your PC's video capabilities are not at par with multimedia specifications. This is especially true if you've had your monitor and video card for any length of time. MPC level 2 standards require the following:

- Advanced VGA (VGA+)

- 640 x 480 resolution

- 64,000 Colors (High Color)

- 64K buffer

A good monitor is only as good as your video card (see fig. 2.22). It's your video card that actually generates the image, and your monitor simply displays what the video card tells it to display. Your objective is to have a monitor that meets or exceeds the capabilities of your video card. There are four things to consider:

- *Color depth.* Color makes images look life-like. The human eye can distinguish 16 million colors—this is a maximum goal. Since this affects performance you will probably use 65,000 (high color) on a day-by-day basis. *Color depth* is commonly expressed in bits: 8-bit = 256 colors; 16-bit = 65,000, or *high color;* and, 24-bit = 16 million (human limit).

- *Resolution.* An image is made up of thousands of dots. The total number of available dots is the *resolution.* The MPC minimum is 640 x 480, but 800 x 600 is probably what you'll use. You should be able to display 1024 x 480.

- *Refresh rate.* A monitor has to constantly illuminate the image on the monitor. A fast refresh rate (70 Hz or more) will produce a stable, non-flickering image that won't strain your eyes.

- *RAM.* Video cards have their own RAM, which is faster than RAM on the motherboard. You want a minimum of 1M of video RAM; 2M is preferable.

The distance between the individual dots on a monitor is called *dot pitch.* The smaller the distance the more crisp your image will be. Common ranges are from .28 to .31mm. A .28 dot pitch should be your goal. Anything less will simply be more crisp.

You may know the type of monitor you have by its generation acronym (see table 2.4). Based upon what you just learned, you should start at the SVGA level. Make sure your video card can produce SVGA images; then make sure you have a monitor that can keep up with your video card.

Fig. 2.22
The monitor plugs into the video card; in turn, the video card plugs into an expansion slot on the mother board.

Table 2.4   Seven Generations of Monitors

Generation	Resolution	Colors
Monochrome[1]	720 x 350	1
CGA: Color Graphics Array	320 x 200	16
EGA: Enhanced Graphics Array	640 x 350	16
VGA: Video Graphics Array	640 x 480	256
SVGA: Super VGA[2]	800 x 600	16,000,000
UVGA: Ultra VGA2[2]	1024 x 768	16,000,000
XGA: IBM's version	1024 x 768	16,000,000

1) Hercules graphics adapters provided graphics capabilities to monochrome monitors.
2) VGA is commonly used for SVGA and UVGA. Their resolutions are the distinguishing factor.

The size of your monitor has a bearing on what modes you can operate. Although they can be very expensive, you should try to get a monitor that has a 17-inch screen or more. A large monitor makes you more productive by allowing you to see more at a glance. If you have a small monitor you are constantly scrolling around for an icon, or you're switching between different applications. The more involved you become in multimedia the more multitasking you do. In this situation, a large monitor becomes an essential tool.

Interlaced monitors alternate between two images to trick the human eye into believing there is only one image. The technique was developed to cut an image into two pieces to compensate for slow technology. Interlaced monitors result in a less stable and less ergonomic image than a non-interlacing monitor.

Tip

The first three numbers on the FCC label identify the monitor's manufacturer. Learn the three-digit FCC code to determine the original equipment manufacturer.

The monitor's value depends heavily on the video card. For this reason, you should give special consideration to the video card.

Standard, Accelerated, and Coprocessor Video Cards

There are three flavors of video cards. Unlike the early days when you didn't have many options, today you have options, sub-options, and features to choose from. The three basic categories are:

- *Standard.* The standard video card simply creates images of various color depths and resolutions. Windows pushes the capacity of standard video cards to the limit, due to its intense use of graphics. Video accelerators were developed to accommodate these new demands.

- *Accelerators.* In addition to displaying standard graphics, accelerators also have common Windows commands programmed directly into their components. This reduces the need for the CPU to perform all functions. Things such as resizing and moving windows are examples of Windows functions. Another solution was created for those who required even more power and performance.

- *Coprocessor.* Graphics coprocessors completely relieve the CPU from graphics processing responsibilities. Whereas the graphics accelerator assists the CPU by performing some functions, graphics coprocessors relieve the CPU of all graphics processing tasks. A coprocessor can be thought of as a special purpose computer within a computer. It processes data and commands in coordination with the CPU.

A graphics accelerator is recommended since Windows is your common working environment and the accelerator has certain Windows functions built in. If your multimedia requirements are beyond what an accelerator can provide, you should get a coprocessor. Before you buy, make sure you have a compatible expansion slot on your motherboard. High-end video cards require sophisticated expansion buses like VESA Local-bus, PCI, or possibly VMC.

VESA Video

The standard for video was established by the Video Electronics Standards Association (VESA). Prior to VESA there were no standards, and this created a lot of confusion.

VESA established standards for video, including how the adapter boards were to connect to the motherboard and functional specifications on the component itself.

As demands for more sophisticated graphics increased, so did the standards for video. VESA was instrumental in delivering the VESA Local Bus (VL-bus) standard. This allowed video data to be exchanged at a rate of 32 bits at a time (32-bit bandwidth). Also, the VL-bus could operate at the same clock rating as the CPU. Prior to the VL-bus you were limited to a maximum of 8 MHz with the EISA and ISA standards.

The VL-bus offered a tremendous resource to adapter boards. The VL-bus started being used for more than just video. The demand for VL-bus began to increase significantly. The VL-Bus offered advantages to everyone, even users of non-video adapter boards.

Video PCI

Attention is good, but it encourages competition. Competition is good, as long as you can compete. Well, VESA got attention, and not just from clients. VESA also got the attention of Intel.

When you have clients begging for something, you want to make sure *you* have the solution, not your competition. Intel developed the PCI interface to compete with the VL-bus. They got VESA's attention by developing a standard that outperforms the VL-bus.

Although PCI has taken the lead, it hasn't eliminated VL-Bus. The VL-Bus is currently being improved to compete with PCI. EISA and ISA haven't been completely eliminated, either. There are now more options both for demanding professional use and for economical personal use. And yet another bus has entered the picture, the VMC.

VESA Media Channel

The VESA Media Channel (VMC) is a dedicated video channel between your video peripherals. Currently the VMC is a connection on the video card. In turn, the video card connects to your motherboard via an expansion slot. The VMC was designed to focus on multimedia applications in the way it was designed.

Multimedia brings new technologies into your computing realm. With multimedia components you can capture video and play it back—not just video but sound, too. Due to the size of video data, compression is required. Some companies offer specialized boards that perform functions such as MPEG playback. With a VMC all of these peripheral components can work together and share video data.

VMC allows you to daisy-chain components. Videologic offers the 928Movie graphics adapter that comes with a VMC connector. You could take this card, for example, and plug it into the appropriate slot on your motherboard. Then you could take an external peripheral component and plug it into the VMC on the 928Movie adapter. The benefit is that you're not taking up expansion slots inside your computer, and you can add other components to the chain.

The design of the VMC also allows you to achieve higher levels of performance. Components that don't support the VMC have their own video buffer. This requires the video memory to be duplicated from the video card onto each applicable peripheral. The VMC allows sharing of the video buffer. All the peripherals can access the video RAM directly, completely bypassing the processor on the video card.

The VMC is a new technology with a lot of promise. The direction multimedia is headed is congruent with the VMC: video capturing, video playback, video teleconferencing, and sound capabilities. In fact, the VMC may become competition for PCI. This isn't true now because the VMC doesn't reside on the motherboard; rather, it's part of the video card. If manufacturers start placing the VMC on their motherboards, they will become more competitive with the PCI and even the VL-bus, even though the latter is from VESA, too.

If you need to upgrade your video card, you should give the VMC consideration. Although it isn't prevalent now, it appears to be gaining momentum and supporters. Video is very important, especially with multimedia.

Assessing Your System's Video Capabilities

You need to assess your computer system and identify its current level of technology. Here are some items to consider regarding your current video capabilities:

- Does your video card meet MPC2 standards? It should produce minimum resolutions of 640 x 480 with 65,536 (64K) colors. This is also called *high color* or 16-bit color.

- If your video card meets MPC2 standards, is it adequate? You should determine the amount of RAM you have on the card. Do you have 2M? Also, determine the speed of the video card, as assessed by bandwidth and refresh rate.

- If your video card doesn't support MPC2 standards, what levels of performance must a new card achieve to meet your demands? Do you need an accelerator or a graphics coprocessor? Unless your demands are beyond normal use you probably need an accelerator.

- How much can you budget for a new video card?

- If you're going to purchase a new video card, what type of expansion bus is required (PCI, VL-Bus, EISA, ISA)? Does your motherboard support that type of expansion bus? Your goal should be PCI or VL-Bus, but also consider VMC.

- What is the speed of your CPU? Can the video card deliver its stated performance without consuming more than 40 percent of the CPU bandwidth given a sustained transfer rate of 150K/sec.? In other words, is your video card too much for your CPU? If yes, then you need to lower your video standards or increase CPU power (consider a new computer, a CPU upgrade, an OverDrive chip, or possibly a math coprocessor).

- How much are you going to budget for purchasing a monitor?

- Can you afford a 17-inch monitor?

- Have you considered other areas of needed system improvement? Before you buy any component, make sure it's a priority and will deliver the best return on your investment.

These questions are focused on your current PC. If there are limitations in any area, you need to resolve those limitations. Before you make any definite decisions, you should consider the information contained in Part II.

From Here...

With the basic requirements of your PC understood, and with an understanding of what needs to be upgraded on your PC, you can proceed into the next part.

The following chapters identify the components of multimedia:

- Chapter 3, "Adding a CD-ROM Drive," describes the components needed to update your system with a CD-ROM drive.

- Chapter 4, "Adding Sound to Your System," describes the current sound tools and how to choose them.

- Chapter 5, "MIDI: Music to Your Ears," shows you how MIDI can benefit your multimedia productions and how to install the correct hardware and software required.

- Chapter 6, "Upgrading Your Video," discusses how to improve your video and specific characteristics of multimedia monitors.

Part II

Multimedia Components

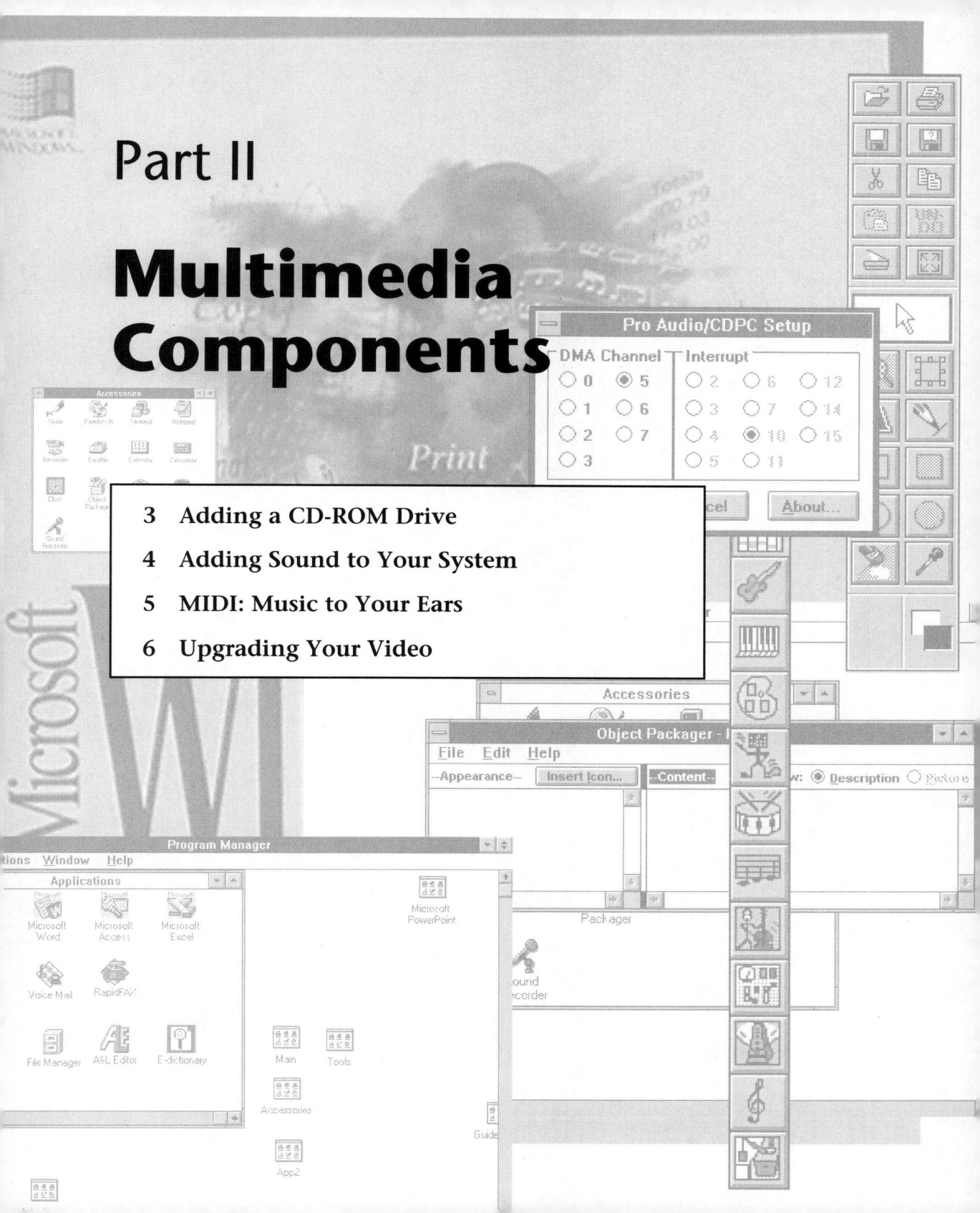

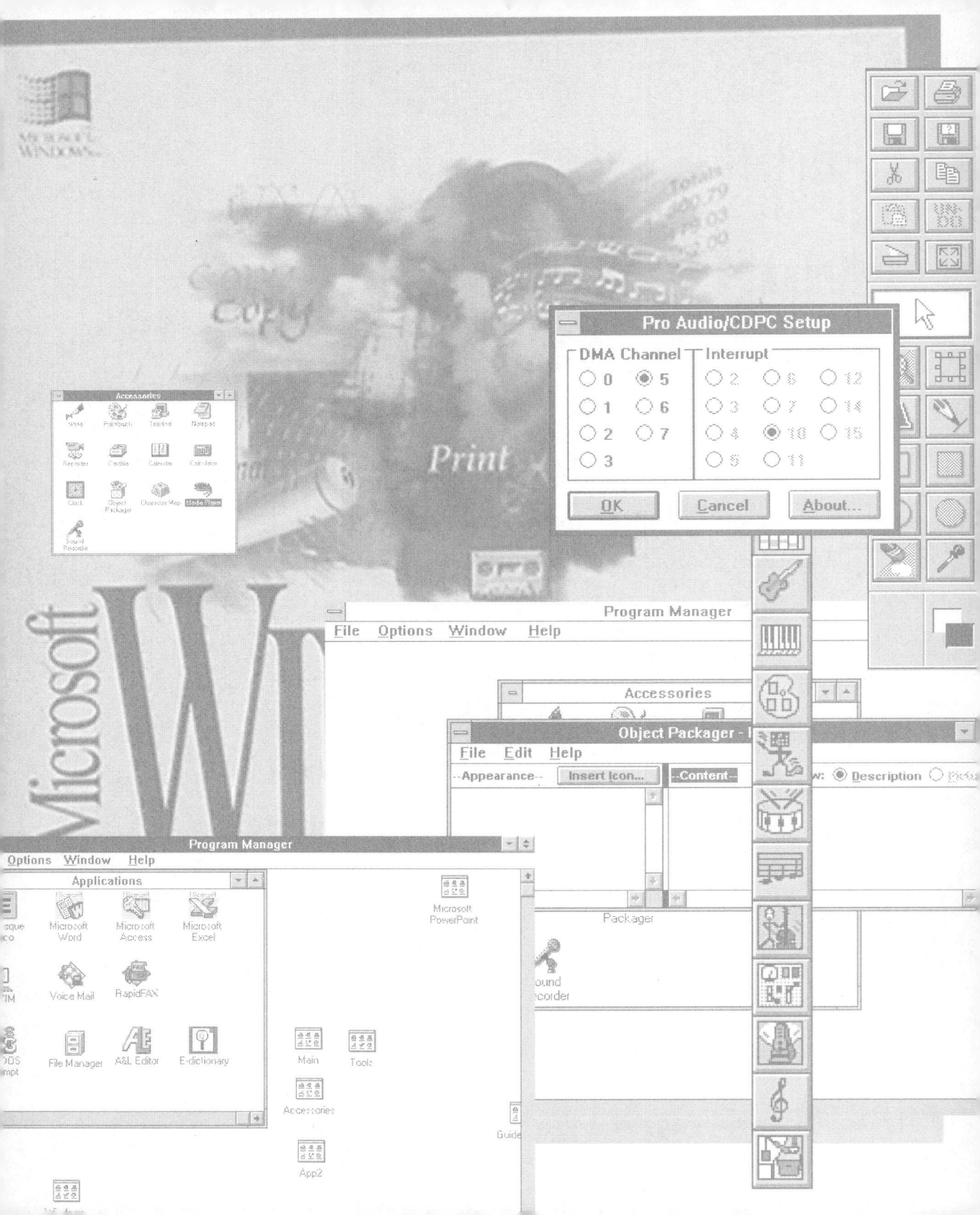

Chapter 3

Adding a CD-ROM Drive

Compact discs (CD) have become an ideal medium for storing large amounts of data. Initially used for audio, these 12 centimeter discs are now used for storing audio, video, and text. Because multimedia uses all of these mediums, the CD is a natural component of a multimedia PC.

Upgrading your PC to make it CD-compatible is not a difficult task. This chapter briefly discusses what a CD is, how it works, what to buy, and how to install a CD-ROM drive.

What Is A Compact Disc?

To equip your computer with CD capabilities you need three things:

- A CD-ROM drive
- Interface connection to PC
- A CD

The CD contains the data. The CD-ROM drive reads the data on the CD and sends the information to the interface connector (expansion board) attached to your computer motherboard. The information then travels to the CPU for processing to make video, text, or sound.

A CD is different from a hard disk. You can write to a hard disk multiple times, but once data has been written onto a CD it can't be changed.

How a CD Works

Let's quickly view how a CD works. CD technology is based upon reflecting and deflecting a laser beam. A smooth mirror-like surface (land) on the bottom-side of the CD reflects the drive's laser beam. A pit (opposite of land) on the bottom-side of a CD will deflect the laser beam. A CD-ROM recording unit (see fig. 3.1) is the device that writes data onto a blank CD by creating pits (deflective area) and ignoring lands (reflective area).

Fig. 3.1
Sony's CDW-900E CD recorder is a double-speed CD Write Once subsystem that gives multimedia developers the power to produce, prototype, and pre-master CD applications for low-volume distribution, beta testing, or for input to a mastering and replication facility.

As the laser is positioned along the surface of the spinning disc, a strobing laser is created. The strobe is translated by a photo detector into binary computer signals (0s or 1s). As mentioned earlier, different types of data can be stored on a CD. This includes audio, video (still images and animation), and sound.

The types of CDs that you've seen have probably been either CD-DA (music CDs) or a standard computer CD-ROM. There are also *Magneto Optical* and *WORM* CDs.

Magneto Optical
Magneto Optical (MO) drive technology is very promising. It offers a large amount of read/write storage. You can't write to a CD-ROM, but you can write on a MO disc. It is unlikely that you will be purchasing this technology soon, especially if you are just starting out. It's simply too expensive to justify the cost, but it will become more prevalent in the future as the costs are driven down. It may be beneficial for you to understand the basics of how it operates in case you want to add a drive of this type to your system later on.

A MO drive uses a laser to write and read an MO disc. Reading a MO disc is similar to the standard CD-ROM; reflecting and deflecting the laser beam creates a strobing light that the photo detector intercepts and passes along to be converted into binary data.

The laser is used for a different purpose when writing to the disc. A laser heats the surface of a MO disc which loosens up a solution that reflective metal particles reside in. When heated, the metal particles are mobile. When not heated, the metal particles are stationary. To change the value of a specific bit on the disc, the laser heats the area and a magnet changes (polarizes) the orientation of the microscopic metal pieces. This orientation is either positive or negative. When in a *positive* position the metal pieces reflect more light. When in a *negative* position less light is reflected. The photo detector on the

MO drive can sense these variations of the reflected/deflected laser beam. You can heat and re-heat the solution many times, in the same manner you can read and write to a hard disk multiple times. That is what makes MO so appealing—more appealing than CD-ROM or WORM technology.

WORM

WORM (Write Once Read Many) is a technology with capabilities between CD-ROMs and MO discs. You can read and write to a WORM disc; this is similar to MO. You can only do it once, which is more like the CD-ROM. The way WORM data is written is similar to MO, however, because data can only be written once you find that WORM drives and discs have different applications.

When it comes to storing large volumes of data, WORM technology is well-suited, and you should consider adding a WORM drive to your system. Conversely, if your information is constantly changing, you will need to consider MO or a very large hard disk, depending upon your storage requirements.

Back to CD Basics

Most likely you are interested in a CD-ROM drive. A MO drive may be a little advanced and too expensive for your current needs. You may have a basic understanding of CD-ROM, but not enough to make an educated purchase. Before you buy a CD-ROM drive you need to know some of the basics.

Buying A CD-ROM Drive

When you purchase a CD-ROM drive, you must make sure it is MPC level 2 compliant (see fig. 3.2). This will ensure you meet the basic minimum requirements for upgrading to multimedia. There are two primary issues regarding minimum requirements:

- *Speed.* Double, triple, or quad

- *Format.* ISO-9660, Kodak PhotoCD, eXtended Architecture (XA)

Fig. 3.2
Sony's low-cost, double-speed CD-ROM drive conforms to MPC-2 guidelines for multimedia applications.

How Fast Will it Go?

Speed is a big concern with CD-ROM drives. A CD-ROM drive is about 15 times slower than a hard disk. Whatever it lacks in speed, however, it makes up in capacity.

The speed of the data transfer rate for CD-ROM drives started out at 150 Kbps (thousand bytes per second). This was the rate recommended initially by MPC. This speed also is referred to as *single-speed*, *1x,* or *one-speed*. One-speed was then doubled to 300 Kbps. You may have heard the term *double-speed* (2x)—this implies 300 Kbps. *Triple-speed* (450, or 3x) and *quad-speed* (600, or 4x) also are available. The faster the better, but the expense increases along with the speed.

To be MPC level 2 compliant you need to start with a double-speed CD-ROM drive. This is acceptable for the average user, one who is using multimedia as a hobby or for basic entertainment. If you are more than just the casual user, then you can consider the triple or quad speeds (450 and 600 Kbps, respectively). This is ideal for professional applications or applications that demand an extreme amount of resources. The price triples and quadruples along with the speed. This extra cost will help you decide how much you really need the increase in performance.

A term related to drive speed is *multispin*. Basically, you can think of multispin as a drive that has multiple speeds. A drive that has multispin capabilities can vary the turning rate of the CD. This deals with physical movement (mechanics) of the actual drive. Faster speed is required for video and computer data. Audio data is not quite as demanding, therefore it works fine at the lower rates. Multispin drives adjust accordingly based upon the type of data. For example, a drive operating at one-speed can jump to double-speed for video or data. Again, it's the same drive; it just spins at different rates (multispin).

Another important mechanical parameter to compare is *access time*, which is the amount of time it takes the drive to locate and provide requested data. Your goal should be to achieve an access time of 280 ms, or less. The reason access time is important is because it considers more than just the speed, or spin rate, of the disc. The access time is derived from the following parameters:

- *Latency.* The drive must mechanically position itself at the proper location. This physical movement is called *latency*.

- *Seek time.* Once the *read head* is in place, the data must be located. The time it takes to locate data is called *seek time*.

- *Spin rate.* The drive is limited to the speed at which the disk turns. Mechanical movements are much slower than the speed of electricity, or because we're dealing with lasers, the speed of light. The spin rate of the drive affects the seek time.

It is common to have the spin rate published for different drives. The other two parameters (latency and seek time) are not always made available. Sometimes this information may be hidden to cover a less than optimal value for one of the parameters. This is why you want to have the access time. Again, the access time is a calculation based upon the three key parameters. It is a better way to access the drive, overall.

> **Caution**
>
> Be careful not to mix up your values. A high number for your data transfer rate is good, whereas a high number for your access time is bad. Just as 100 miles-per-hour is good, 100 hours per mile is bad. Know your values.

A CD-ROM drive by a well-known manufacturer (see Chapter 8, "Buyer's Guide To CD-ROM") meeting MPC level 2 standards, specifically the double-speed requirement, will provide you with a good entry-level drive. Make sure the interface is not proprietary, and is supported by your PC. Also make sure the access time is at par with the competition. Follow these guidelines, and you will end up with a good drive.

Choosing between XA and PhotoCD

The second issue is format compatibility. There are three key terms you want your drive to support:

- *ISO 9660.* This format is derived from the *High Sierra* (a format developed in an attempt to establish a standard; however, it was limited). High Sierra only allowed ASCII text. Therefore, ISO 9660 was developed to offer more capabilities. This is the predominant basic format.

- *CD-ROM/XA (eXtended Architecture).* This format allows video, text, sound, and system control data to be interleaved and replayed at optimal performance. To optimize space, data is compressed using ADPCM (Adaptive Differential Pulse Code Modulation). Special software is required for this format.

- *Kodak PhotoCD.* This format is a multi-session format. With a multi-session disk, you can append data by adding more sessions to the original disk.

If your drive supports all of these formats, you are in good shape. New drives typically support all of them, or they support PhotoCD and allow upgrades to XA. Try to get all three and be leery of products that promise future upgrades. Upgrading usually costs more then buying new, and the performance doesn't meet new standards. When you purchase a product that offers future upgrade options, remember that it is usually more expensive to upgrade than it is to purchase current technology. Also, upgraded products usually don't perform at the same levels as current technology.

You also may hear other formats mentioned: red book, yellow book, green book, orange book, and so on. If you want to understand these format standards, see table 3.1. Otherwise, ensure your drive supports ISO 9660, XA, and PhotoCD formats.

II

Multimedia Components

Table 3.1 CD-ROM Formats		
Format Name	**Synonyms** *Derivatives*	**Description**
Red Book	CD-DA	The first CD standard developed. Describes the format for storing audio data. This is the format for all music CDs.
Yellow Book		An extension of Red Book, this format includes the ability to store computer data. Most CD-ROM formats follow the Yellow Book structure.
	High Sierra	Created in 1985 to make CDs compatible among different systems. This format was too limited.
	ISO 9660	An updated version of the *High Sierra*, *ISO 9660* is the standard CD-ROM format for DOS and Windows PCs.
Green Book	CD-I	Built upon Red Book and Yellow Book, the Green Book, or Compact Disc Interactive (CD-I), is dependent upon a specific hardware and software platform. CD-I discs can't be read by any other CD-ROM drive. *Multisession PhotoCD and CD-ROM/XA* use parts of the Green Book standard, but are not CD-I compatible.
Orange Book	CD-R	Compact Disc Recordable (CD-R) is a data recording format used to manufacture CD-ROM discs.
White Book		The White Book format is specific to video CDs.

Don't get lost in the details of all the different CD formats. Keep it simple by focusing on the three keys (ISO 9660, XA, and PhotoCD) and you should have no problems. In addition to CD-ROM drive format compatibility, you should be aware of other options and features such as CD caddies.

CD Caddies

Some CD-ROM drives require a disc caddy. This is a protective case you place the disc into before inserting it into the drive. If the drive requires a caddy, you don't have a choice unless you choose another drive. Some users prefer caddies because they protect the discs. It's logical that a disk in a protective case is less likely to be damaged. This is especially true if you have children. Also, some of the high-performance drives use caddies. Therefore, the inconvenience of a caddy can possibly be offset by the improvement in performance.

Some find caddies to be a nuisance because you have to constantly put the CDs in the caddy. You can buy multiple caddies; possibly one for each of your most commonly used CDs. However, don't let the caddy be the deciding factor for purchasing a drive. Choose the drive based upon speed and format compatibility first. Then, if the option of caddy vs. no-caddy is available, simply choose the option you prefer.

Always make sure you handle your CDs in a proper manner. This applies to drives with and without caddies. Also, pay attention to the doors opening up to the CD-ROM drive. Dust inside the drive can be more damaging than dust on a disc. Look for double-doors and doors that seal tight. More important than caddies and double-doors is how the CD-ROM drive connects to the computer.

The CD Interface Adapter Card

All CD-ROM drives require that you install an adapter card in an expansion slot so the drive can interface with your computer. Some drive kits include an interface card, others require you to purchase one separately. If you purchased a bundled multimedia package, then the sound card will most likely have a connector for the CD-ROM drive. Whatever the case, you must make sure that all three components are compatible: your CD-ROM drive, your adapter card, and your PC. You also should have a basic understanding of your PC, including the characteristics of the expansion slots.

In Chapter 2, "Basic Computer Requirements," the issues concerning disk drive interface standards were introduced. There are two key standards that you will have to choose from: IDE (Intelligent Drive Electronics), and SCSI (Small Computer Systems Interface). The IDE standard is predominant where hard disks are concerned. In fact, 95 percent of the PCs available today use the IDE standard. This is different for CD-ROM drives, which primarily use SCSI.

Some manufacturers create their own proprietary interface connection. CD-ROM drives with a proprietary interface connection from the expansion board to the drive should be avoided. It is best to follow industry standards rather than a specific manufacturer's proprietary interface. SCSI-2, for example, is the current standard that is preferred.

Make sure the expansion board is compatible with your PC. Refer to your documentation or consult the company where you bought your PC. If they can't guarantee compatibility, then make sure you have a money-back guarantee; or, call the manufacturer of each component, independent of the other, and verify compatibility. It may take a little extra time in the beginning but it will save a lot of time, money, and frustration later.

Multimedia Likes SCSI Better than IDE. SCSI is the most popular standard for CD-ROM drives. Actually, SCSI-2 is the preferred standard for connecting CD-ROM drives. There are several reasons for this. Multimedia requires a lot of additional peripherals, and SCSI allows several peripherals to be chained together. This daisy chain allows access to multiple peripherals without sacrificing performance or available expansion slots. SCSI also is a better performer when there are large data volumes. This is because SCSI was designed to send large amounts of data without constantly interrupting the system (CPU).

The original IDE specification had limitations that have become an issue with the advent of multimedia. The 1G limitation, for example, didn't originally concern too many people, most people had hard disk capacity under 200M. Then multimedia, with its video and sound requirements, introduced a new set of standards: now you need a minimum of 500M. For these reasons, SCSI became the preferred choice for multimedia peripherals. To compensate for deficiencies, IDE was enhanced to better compete with SCSI.

II

Multimedia Components

Enhanced IDE Competes with SCSI. Enhancements have been made to the original IDE standard to make it more competitive with SCSI. Western Digital introduced the Enhanced IDE (E-IDE) specification. This new specification offers features that appeal to users of CD-ROM drives and other multimedia peripherals; also, the data transfer rate for the E-IDE specification is up to 11.1 Mbps. The 1G barrier also has been broken.

The E-IDE specification looks promising especially because of its economical cost. Even though it is a new standard, many will associate IDE and E-IDE simply because of IDE's name recognition; again, recall that 95 percent of all PCs have IDE.

The Interconnection Best for your CD-ROM Drive. The impact that E-IDE will have is uncertain. What is certain, however, is that CD-ROM drives you purchase today are geared to the SCSI specification. It is possible that E-IDE or possibly another standard will arise and take SCSI's place. The safe bet now is SCSI-2 or CD-ROM drives. However, make sure it is *true* SCSI, and not some proprietary interface.

The SCSI standard is not always strictly adhered to. This may present a problem when you decide to daisy chain several SCSI devices (connect one device to another). You should first make sure each device is compatible with the chained component. This will require a little homework on your part, but will be well worth it. Corel makes a SCSI interface kit that alleviates this concern. It is worthwhile to review this kit if you're planning on daisy chaining your multimedia peripherals.

If you feel inclined to pursue E-IDE, do a little more research on the specifics that will benefit you. If you're unclear and just want a safe answer, go with SCSI; however, make sure the SCSI expansion board is fully compatible.

Internal vs. External

You can buy an internal or an external CD-ROM drive. The *right* drive for you is based upon your budget and current PC configuration. There are pros and cons to buying both internal and external drives (see table 3.2).

Table 3.2 Internal vs. External CD-ROM Drives

Issue	Internal	External
Installation	(-)More difficult	(+)Easy
Impact	(-)Takes up an available system bay	(-)Takes up desk space
Operation	(-)External buttons limited to CD-ROM drive face (-)Difficult to access inside case	(+)Some models include external buttons for easy operation (+)Easy access while on top of your desk
Cost	(+)Less expensive	(-)More expensive

The external drive is easiest to install because the only thing that goes inside your computer is the interface expansion board. With an internal drive you also have to install the drive itself. If you want more details on the installation process, see the next section, "Installing Your CD-ROM Drive."

If you don't have any drive bays available in your computer, you will probably have to go with an external drive. If you do have available bays, you can save some money by purchasing an internal drive.

The main difference between the actual drives is that an external drive has its own case and power supply; an internal drive uses your PC's case and power supply. The same drive can be used in both internal and external configurations; therefore, you don't have to worry about sacrificing any performance for either type. Again, it is based upon your budget, your PC configuration, and your personal preference. Both types need an interface connection to your motherboard.

Purchasing Summary

After you have examined all of the possibilities, you are ready to purchase. Again, here is a quick view of the items to look for:

- *MPC level 2.* Fully compliant
- *Multisession PhotoCD* and *CD-ROM/XA upgrade options.*
- *Data transfer rate.* Double-speed (>= 300 Kbps)
- *Access time.* <= 280 ms
- *Cache.* A 64K buffer will improve performance by holding recent data in memory and avoiding physical movements necessary for accessing storage.
- *Interface board.* Fully compatible with CD-ROM drive and PC. Interface type should be *SCSI* or *E-IDE* (after you research it further)
- *Caddy vs. no-caddy.* Your preference
- *Internal vs. external.* Your decision based upon budget, current PC configuration, and your preference

With all items accounted for, it is time to purchase the CD-ROM most compatible with your needs. After a successful installation you're on your way to multimedia.

Installing Your CD-ROM Drive

Installing an internal drive differs from an external drive. For this reason, two different installation examples are provided. In the first example you'll walk through the installation of a Sony CDU-33A CD-ROM drive. This drive was provided in a multimedia upgrade kit. The second installation applies to Media Vision's Memphis multimedia upgrade kit.

II

Multimedia Components

There are some preliminary steps that apply to any hardware upgrades. They are important to note before you proceed with specifics:

1. Have a work area with plenty of room.

2. Components should be out of reach of pets and children.

3. Have an adequate set of tools (see fig. 3.3).

4. Avoid static electricity, which can easily damage components. Get into the practice of grounding yourself before touching any components. An anti-static wristband can be used, or simply touch the metal on the power supply.

> **Tip**
>
> You can purchase an anti-static wristband at most major computer retail stores.

5. Make sure you have a current backup. Each time you install a device or expose the innards of your PC, you risk the chance of damage. Always have a current backup before you perform an installation or upgrade.

6. Keep a bootable disk handy. The disk should include current system files: CONFIG.SYS, AUTOEXEC.BAT, SYSTEM.INI, and WIN.INI.

7. Keep a list of current devices and their IRQ, DMA, and address settings. If you don't have such a listing, it is a good idea to create one now while the system is running.

8. Inventory all items to ensure you have everything you need.

> **Tip**
>
> The Microsoft Diagnostics program is provided with DOS (version 6) and Windows (version 3.1). Running MSD from the DOS prompt or within Windows gives you valuable system settings. Make a hard copy printout of the full report and file it.

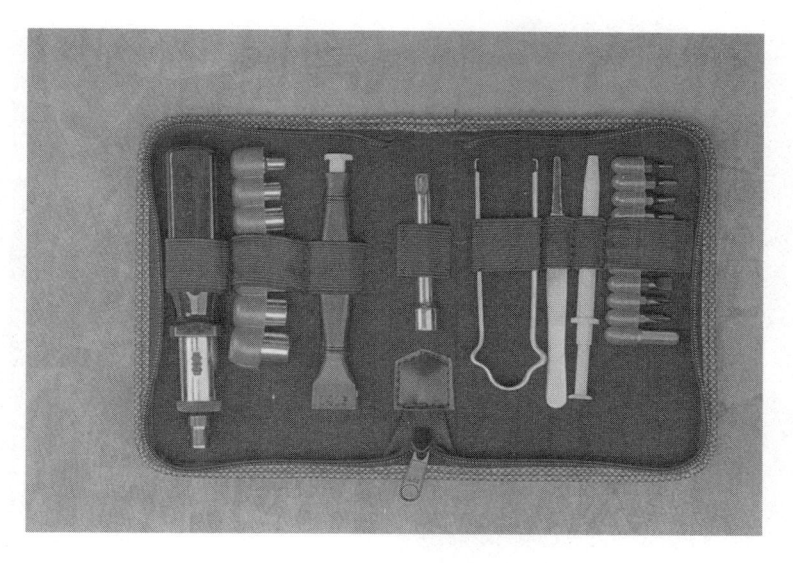

Fig. 3.3
Spending a little money on the right tools will save frustration, time, and components. Here is a basic computer tool kit.

Installing the CD-ROM Adapter Card

With all eight of the above items accomplished, you can begin to follow the directions in your CD-ROM installation documentation. Typically you are given a pre-installation check-list, possibly similar to the eight items you just read. To avoid problems rather than create them, you should read the instructions first.

1. You usually begin your installation by removing the PC's cover, as shown in figures 3.4 and 3.5. First, you want to remove all cables attached to your PC; this includes the keyboard, monitor, mouse, and especially the power.

> **Tip**
>
> You may want to sketch a diagram of the back of your computer, and then properly label each cable location.

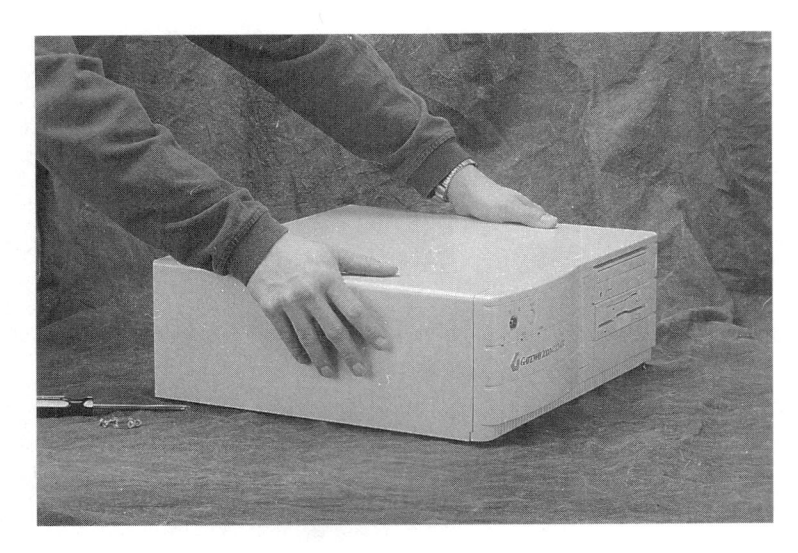

Fig. 3.4
After removing cables and screws you can begin removing the PC cover.

Fig. 3.5
The PC cover typically slides back and is then lifted up and off of the case frame. This depends upon the case type (tower or desktop) and the manufacturer's design.

2. Next, remove all the screws that fasten the cover to the case. Lift off the case and set it out of the way. Familiarize yourself with the inside of your PC. Specifically,

you are looking for an available slot for the interface board. Once you find an open, compatible slot you can verify the settings on the interface board.

3. Refer to the documentation on current system settings. Verify that the standard factory settings for the jumpers or DIP switches on the CD-ROM adapter card don't conflict with the settings for other components of your PC. Each component must have a unique IRQ and address. Table 3.3 shows common settings that may be similar to the settings on your PC. If you have a *plug-and-play* card you won't have to worry about this step. Your PC will automatically assign resources upon startup. If you don't have a card that automatically configures itself, you must select non-conflicting settings.

Table 3.3   Common Resource Settings

Device	IRQ	Address	Example Device Type
NMI parity check	NMI	—	
*CMOS clock (timer interrupt)	0	0008	
Keyboard	1	0009	
*Interrupt controller (cascade to IRQ9)	2	000A	Network, mouse, scanner
*COM2 or COM4	3	02F8 or 02E8	COM2, COM4, network, mouse, fax/modem, scanner, tape drive, video
*COM1 or COM3	4	03F8 or 02F8	COM1, COM3, mouse, CD-ROM, fax/modem, scanner
*LPT2 or hard disk	5	0278	LPT2, mouse, sound card, fax/mode, scanner, tape drive
Floppy disk controller	6	03F0-03F7	Tape drive
*LPT1	7	03BC	LPT1, network, mouse, sound card, scanner
Real-time clock	8	0070	
Cascade interrupt	9	0071	SCSI adapter, scanner
*Available	10	0072	Network, mouse, SCSI adapter, sound card
*Available	11	0073	Sound card, mouse, scanner, tape drive
*Available	12	0074	SCSI adapter, motherboard, mouse port, mouse, scanner, video

II

Multimedia Components

(continues)

Table 3.3   Continued

Device	IRQ	Address	Example Device Type
Math co-processor	13	0075	Mouse
*Hard disk	14	—	SCSI adapter, IDE adapter
*Available	15		SCSI adapter, mouse

Settings available to you

4. You may have to physically change the settings on the board. Two common methods for changing board-level settings are jumper blocks or switch banks. A *jumper block* consists of pins, usually in pairs. Figure 3.6 illustrates a common jumper block with four pairs of pins. *Shorting blocks* are shown in front of the jumper block. Repositioning the shorting blocks will alter the board level settings. It is best to use a pair of needle-nose pliers to change the shorting block positions.

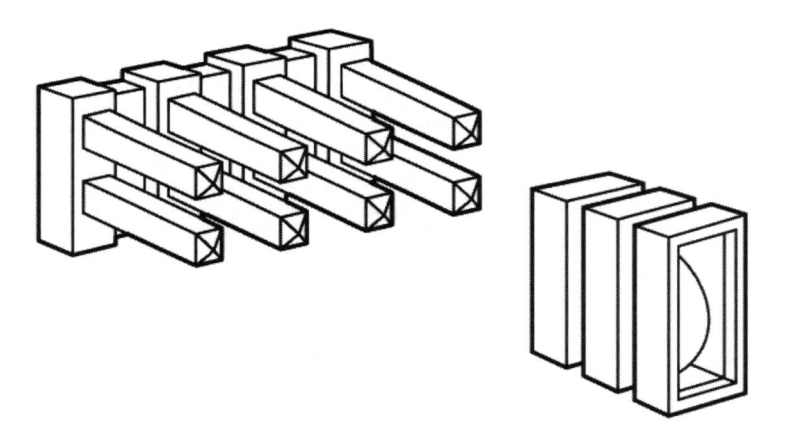

Fig. 3.6
Jumper block pins are selected by sliding the shorting block over pin pairs.

A *switch bank* is the second method used to change board-level settings. Figure 3.7 shows a switch bank. The actual switches are either rocker or slider type switches. The ON/OFF positions are usually clearly identified.

Fig. 3.7
Switch banks are used to change board-level settings. Slider or rocker switches are used to set ON/ OFF combinations.

5. With the expansion slot identified and the interface board properly configured, you're ready to install the board. First, remove the metal plate covering the expansion slot (see fig. 3.8). This plate is screwed into the case. You'll use the screw for the new board; also, you should keep the metal plate should you need it in the future.

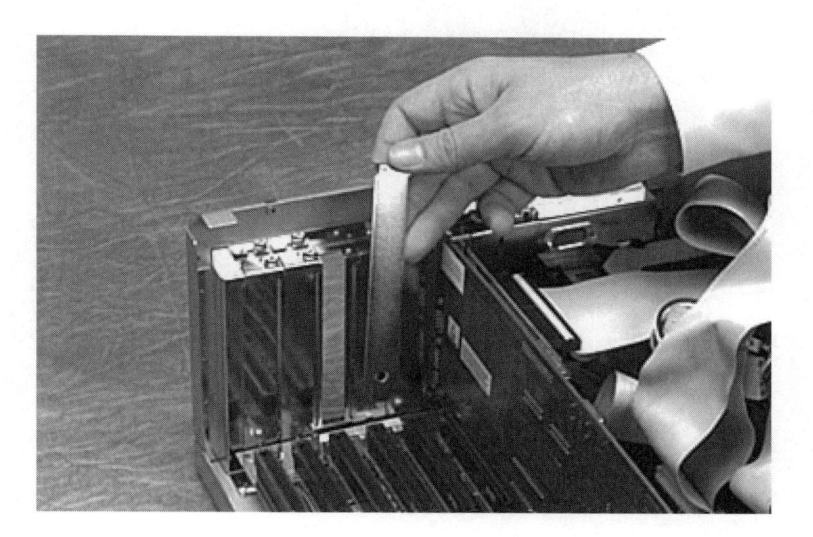

Fig. 3.8
Metal plates cover unused expansion slots. They must be removed before expansion boards can be installed.

II

Multimedia Components

> **Note**
>
> Grounding yourself before touching any computer boards will avoid damage. Simply touch the metal case of the power supply or the chassis frame of the PC. Another alternative is to purchase a wristband from a computer retail store.

6. After you have grounded yourself to discharge any static electricity, pick up the expansion board by the metal backing. Position it above the expansion slot as shown in figure 3.9. Gently rock the board back and forth until the card is firmly seated (see fig. 3.10). With the card properly in place, gently tighten the screw, fastening the board to the case frame, as shown in figure 3.11.

Fig. 3.9
You must properly position the interface board above the expansion slot.

If you are having difficulty seating the board into place then follow these steps:

1. Make sure the board is compatible with the slot. By tilting the board sideways with the gold connectors at the entry-point of the slot, you should be able to verify compatibility.

2. While holding the board at a 45-degree angle, slide the back corner (the corner opposite the chrome face) into the slot.

3. While keeping pressure on the back corner, gently press the front of the board (chrome face) down into the slot.

4. When the board is horizontal with the motherboard, press both corners together until the board is seated properly (see fig. 3.11).

Fig. 3.10
Gently pushing the board downward, and rocking it front and back, should seat the board into place.

This may take a couple of tries. If the card still does not fit, try adjusting the angle in step 2 (down 30, 20, or up 50, 60 degrees). Be patient and don't apply excessive pressure.

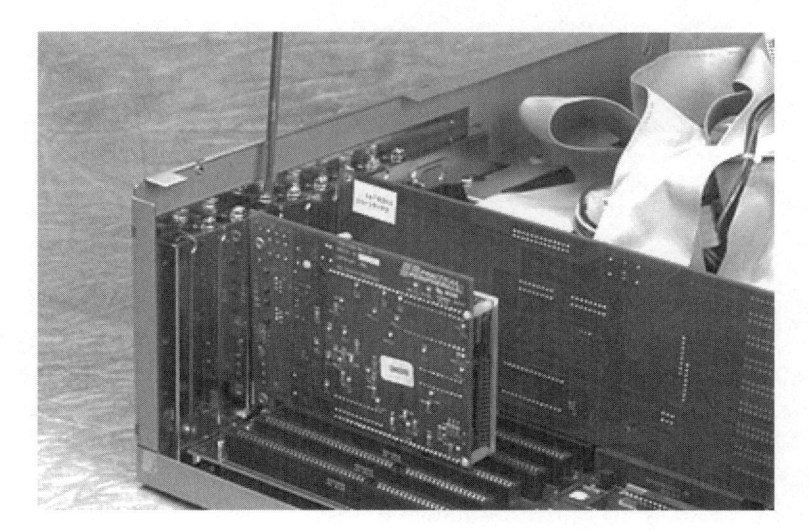

Fig. 3.11
Once the interface board is properly seated, tighten the screw gently into place.

With the board properly installed, you are ready to proceed. Now come the differences between the internal and external CD-ROM drives. An internal drive is connected using internal cables and power sources. An external drive will have its own power supply and will attach externally to the back of the computer. Since you have the computer case off

II

Multimedia Components

you will continue with the internal drive. Then you'll review the installation of an external drive.

Continuing to Install an Internal CD-ROM Drive

Installation of an internal drive is more involved than an external drive. You may purchase a multimedia upgrade kit that contains an internal drive and a sound card that includes a CD-ROM drive connection (see fig. 3.12). The primary difference you encounter when installing an internal drive is that after you install the adapter card, you must mount the drive in one of the PC drive bays. The number of available bays varies among case types and manufacturers. Plastic plates cover the bays.

Fig. 3.12
A multimedia upgrade kit is offered by QuickShot. Here is the QS818 Sound Machine CD Pro 16. Included with the kit is a Sony CDU-33A CD-ROM drive that is MPC level 2 compatible.

1. Before you install your CD-ROM drive, you must first remove the blank plate covering the drive bay opening. This is a usually a piece of plastic that snaps into place. You can typically remove the plate by pushing from behind the plate's backside. A screwdriver may also be used; be careful not to damage the surfaces adjacent to the plate by using undue force. (Keep the blank plate; it may be needed in the future.) With the plastic plate removed, you can slide the drive into the empty bay.

2. Sometimes mounting rails are required; this is true if the drive is too small for the expansion bay. Mounting rails are usually provided by the manufacturer. If not,

you can purchase them from a computer retail store. If your drive needs mounting rails, simply bolt them onto the side of the CD-ROM drive. Use the screws provided with the rails to avoid damaging the drive. With the rails secured onto the drive, slide the drive into the drive bay.

3. Before you secure the drive onto the PC's chassis, make sure you connect all the cables. Sometimes it's difficult to connect cables; the ability to slide the drive forward and backward may make it easier for you to make the connections. The cables you connect internally include power, audio (optional), and the data cable. The *data cable* is a ribbon cable that has one stripe. This stripe is to be matched with pin 1 on the drive and on the board, unless your documentation instructs you otherwise.

4. You will notice a lot of cables coming from your power supply. At various locations, connectors are attached to the power cable. Some connectors are already attached to devices, others are not. Attach an available power connector to the drive. After all connections are made, slide the drive into place and secure it by tightening the screws.

5. Once everything is connected, you can put the case cover back on. Before you bolt down the cover, however, proceed with the installation to ensure everything works properly. You can bolt down the case after the upgrade is successful.

An external CD-ROM drive is much easier to install than an internal drive. This will become more clear in the next section.

Continuing to Install an External CD-ROM Drive

An external drive is easier to install because you don't have to connect internal power sources or audio cables. A good example of an easy-to-install external drive is MediaVision's Memphis system, as shown in figure 3.13. To illustrate how easy it is to install the Memphis system, see figure 3.14. There are four steps:

1. Install the interface card.

2. Connect the card to the Memphis system with the supplied cable.

3. Plug in the speakers.

4. Plug in the power.

This is all that is required to install the Memphis system.

II

Multimedia Components

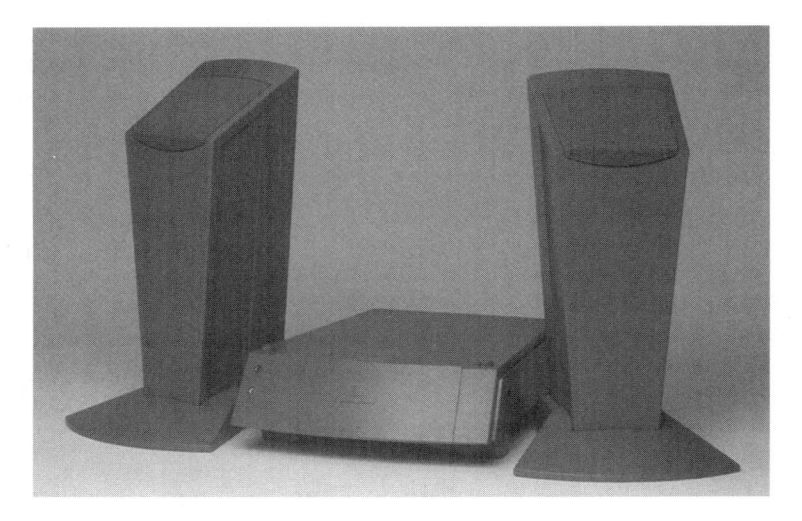

Fig. 3.13

MediaVision's Memphis product is a multimedia upgrade system. It is easy to install and offers many features including an integrated, quality sound system.

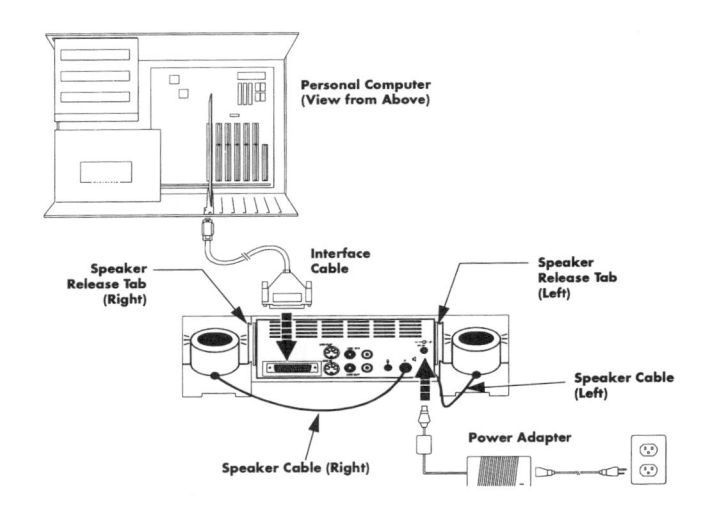

Fig. 3.14

Memphis installation is easy since the software automatically selects hardware settings.

Installing Software: The Final Step

Installing software makes your PC aware of the hardware just installed. Also, it provides your PC the ability to talk to the hardware. The software installation phase is the final step that makes all of the appropriate system-level changes. Both internal and external CD-ROM drives require software to interface with the rest of your system.

Your CD-ROM should come with the software that you need to install. In general, you need to insert the disk in a drive of your computer, log on to that drive if needed, and then run the install program, usually INSTALL.EXE from the DOS prompt or SETUP.EXE for Windows. (Check the documentation that comes with the CD-ROM kit to find out the exact name of the installation program to run.) As with other software installation routines, numerous prompts will appear, asking you for responses such as specifying a directory on your hard drive to install the software to. Simply follow the prompts. As you work through the installation program, it copies new files to the hard drive that your CD-ROM needs to operate and alters existing system files that control your computer. These are described next.

New Files Installation. Certain files are needed by hardware to operate properly. These files are installed onto your hard disk so they are always accessible when your PC is turned on. There are three files that are required when a CD-ROM drive is installed:

- *MSCDEX.EXE: MS-DOS CD-ROM extension.* Allows MS-DOS to access CD-ROM as a logical disk drive. This command is entered in the AUTOEXEC.BAT file.

- *ASPI: Advanced SCSI Programming Interface.* Originally developed by Adaptec (AdaptecSPI), this became an industry standard method for controlling SCSI devices and communication. Also, performance is increased by ASPI's method of loading BIOS from ROM into RAM. This driver is added to the CONFIG.SYS file. If you're not using SCSI, this file does not apply.

- *Device Drivers.* Specific to individual manufacturers. These drivers will be included as files and transferred during software installation. Driver files usually have a *.SYS or *.DRV extension. They appear in your CONFIG.SYS file.

Updated System Files. The install process typically changes four key files and one directory on your computer. These five areas are:

- *Subdirectory.* Files are transferred from the floppy disk onto the computer's hard disk. A new directory is usually created by the installation software. Sometimes you are prompted for the subdirectory name. A default name is usually provided; it is recommended that you use the default.

- *CONFIG.SYS.* this file is located at the root level of your hard disk (C:\). Device drivers and other system configuration parameters are contained within this file.

- *AUTOEXEC.BAT.* DOS commands that should be run each time the computer is started are contained within this file, which is located at the root level (C:\). Sometimes the PATH statement is updated to allow the system to locate the newly installed files. Also, hardware specific commands or environment variables may also be set within this file.

- *SYSTEM.INI.* Located in the Windows System subdirectory (C:\WINDOWS\SYSTEM), this file initializes the system settings for Windows based upon installed hardware, software, and your preferences. Settings for device specific variables can also be found in the SYSTEM.INI file. Changes to this file are made by the installation software, Windows, and Windows Gurus.

II

Multimedia Components

■ *WIN.INI*. Also located in the Windows System subdirectory (C:\WINDOWS\SYS-TEM), this file sets general user preferences such as colors, sounds, screen savers, and so on. Also, file extensions and their association with applications is set within the WIN.INI file. Changes to this file are made by the installation software, Windows, and Windows Gurus.

The files that may require manual changes are your DOS system files (CONFIG.SYS and AUTOEXEC.BAT). You probably will never need to manually edit your Windows system files (SYSTEM.INI and WIN.INI). Instead, your Windows system file settings are usually changed via the Control Panel located in the Windows Main program group.

Setting Driver Options via Windows

The CD-ROM software installation program usually makes all necessary changes for you and installs the correct driver files, based upon responses you entered during the installation process. If the configuration does not work, or you need to change settings, then you can use the Driver applet located in the Control Panel of the Windows Main program group. The Drivers applet is located within the Main program group of the Windows Program Manager. Figure 3.15 shows the Drivers applet.

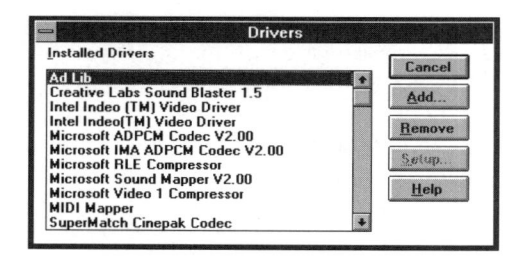

Fig. 3.15
Drivers lets you add, remove, and change system drivers.

The first window that appears is relatively easy to understand. The buttons appear as follows:

■ *Cancel*. This button will return you to the Control Panel without any changes taking affect.

■ *Add*. Pressing this button will allow you to add one of the listed drivers. Unlisted drivers also can be added once the button is pressed. You may be prompted to insert the installation disk with the driver file, so have it handy.

■ *Remove*. This allows you to remove installed drivers.

■ *Setup*. Press this button to change settings of an installed driver. This is a commonly used function.

■ *Help*. On-line help is provided. Pressing the Help button will make Help available to you.

The installation program has already added the driver. If you want to change the settings due to conflict or preference, press the Setup button. This, in turn, will display the window shown in figure 3.16.

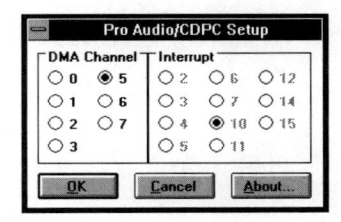

Fig. 3.16
Setup allows you to change device-specific settings.

Having good documentation will make this portion of the installation process much easier. In fact, if you initially selected non-conflicting settings (IRQ, DMA, Addresses), you may not even need to run the Drivers applet.

With everything installed and running, you are ready to begin using your CD-ROM drive. You resolved one major component of multimedia.

From Here...

This chapter provided you with the information you need to purchase and install a CD-ROM drive. By following the standards and the recommendations on speed and supported formats, you will be much happier with your investment. Refer to the following chapters for more information:

■ Chapter 4, "Adding Sound to Your System," discusses aspects of multimedia sound.

■ Chapter 8, "Buyer's Guide to CD-ROM," provides additional tips and sources for purchasing CD-ROM drives.

II

Multimedia Components

Chapter 4

Adding Sound to Your System

PC-based sound has grown from games that buzzed and beeped to computers with CD-quality music, voice, and sound effects in just the last few years. Thanks to multimedia advances on the Macintosh, Amiga, and Atari platforms (among others), owners of PC-compatibles have found computerized sound doesn't have to sound computerized.

Now, sound is popping up in every aspect of computing—music and multimedia, of course, as well as training, on-line help, communications, and business applications. With the current technology, you can do any of these things and more:

- Listen to music through your computer—with or without hooking up a CD player.

- Send an electronic mail message to an associate across the country, and include spoken instructions in your own voice.

- Create CD-quality music with full orchestration—without ever touching an instrument.

- Play games with Hollywood-quality sound effects, where the on-screen characters speak with real actors' voices.

- Use a microphone to tell your computer to open documents, save files, or perform any other action you normally perform with your keyboard.

You won't even have to mortgage your computer to pay for it all—you can make your PC noisy, regardless of your budget. The cheapest solutions are free. But if you're serious about your sound quality, you could easily spend $1,000 or more. Most multimedia users do very well with about $200 (or less) in sound equipment.

This chapter shows you how to select and work with some of the current sound tools—hardware and software—for Windows. It also explains the vocabulary of digitized sound. If the earlier mention of creating CD-quality music caught your eye, you'll also want to check out Chapter 5, "MIDI: Music to Your Ears." But read this chapter first—it gives you the basics you'll need before you move on.

> **Note**
>
> This chapter covers *digitized sounds*, which are electronic representations of real sound waves. You can make a digitized sound file out of a passing train, a thunderstorm, your voice, a tree falling in the forest, or anything else that you can hear. *MIDI* (Musical Instrument Digital Interface) is a system of digital commands used to control electronic instruments, such as keyboards. MIDI commands tell the instrument which sound to make, how long to make it, and what volume to use, among other things—sort of like an electronic version of sheet music that only MIDI instruments know how to read.

Do You Need to Add Sound?

Multimedia and sound are inseparable. A true multimedia presentation needs more than words and pictures (even if the pictures move)—it needs music, voices, and/or sound effects to grab your attention and become a complete multimedia experience.

To bear either of the Multimedia PC logos (MPC Level 1 or Level 2), a personal computer must not only support graphics, but also a set of basic sound capabilities. These are the MPC level 2 sound requirements:

- 16-bit sound
- 8 note synthesizer
- MIDI playback
- CD-ROM/XA audio capability
- Support for the IMA-adopted ADPCM algorithm
- MIDI I/O port
- Joystick port
- Double-speed CD-ROM drive (which includes audio CD capabilities)

Sound complicated? It's not, really. It just looks like alphabet soup until you know the terms (and they are explained in the next section). Most of these capabilities (except the CD-ROM drive, of course) are found on *sound cards,* electronic devices you put in your PC to handle sound functions. All of these multimedia capabilities—including the CD-ROM drive—can be purchased in a multimedia kit for as little as $300. If you shop hard enough, you can assemble the basic pieces yourself for about $200-$250. Sound cards and multimedia kits are explained later in this chapter.

An Overview of Audio Technology

Audio technology is not hard to understand—you just need to know some of the terms used and then see how they apply. This section discusses the key concepts you should understand to make the right choices regarding multimedia hardware and software.

How Sound Works

Computers deal with sound differently than people do. To us, sound is whatever vibrations are picked up by our eardrums. You can describe sound as "rich," "tinny," "deep," or anything else, depending on the way it sounds to you. Sound has a fluid quality, an ability to change pitch, volume, or other qualities so smoothly that you only notice the trend, not the individual degrees of the change. It is made up of waves, which are complex, continuous structures that are almost impossible to describe completely. You can measure some of their qualities, but measurements hardly equal the actual experience. Infinitely complex things—things which can't be completely and accurately described in measurements—are *analog*. To us, sound is analog.

The way a computer "hears" sound is much different. To a computer, sound is *digital*. The computer works off electricity, not physical movements of water or air. Sound waves are literally translated from analog to digital numbers. This process is called *sampling*, which means the computer takes samples of the sound wave and measures certain qualities of the wave at given points within the sample. The computer measures two qualities:

- *Amplitude.* The volume of the sound, which increases/decreases as the wave goes up/down.

- *Frequency.* The vibration rate of the sound waves—how fast your speakers vibrate. For example. frequency is represented in *Hz* (*Hertz*, vibrations per second) or *kHz* (*kilohertz*, thousands of vibrations per second). The human ear can identify frequencies from about 20 Hz to 20 kHz.

The process of *sampling* an analog sound wave and converting it into a digital wave form is the process of converting waves into numbers. Figure 4.1 graphically illustrates how all these elements work together.

II

Multimedia Components

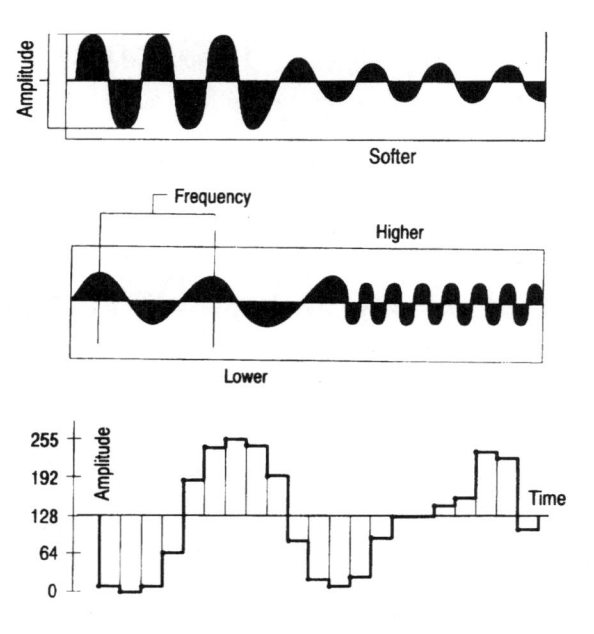

Fig. 4.1
Of these three wave sounds, the last one illustrates a sampled wave form that the computer understands. (Illustration courtesy of Microsoft Corporation)

Sampling Sound

When the computer performs sampling to convert an analog wave into numbers, it uses two internal guidelines:

1. *Sample Rate.* How often to sample the sound.

2. *Bits-per-sample.* How accurately to describe the sample.

It is important to understand these terms. They not only affect the playback quality of the sound, but also the amount of space required to store it.

Understanding Sample Rates. The sample rate is how frequently the computer measures the sound wave (refer to fig. 4.1). Sample rate is expressed in thousands of samples per second, or kilohertz (kHz), so if a sound is sampled 8,000 times in a second, it is rated at 8 kHz. A faster sampling rate will produce a more accurate representation of the wave form—up to compact disc quality of 44.1 kHz. Some cards go as high as 48 kHz, but this "improvement" over CD quality is completely imperceptible. Table 4.1 shows some common sampling rates and comparable sound quality.

Table 4.1 Sampling Rates	
Common Rates	**Sounds Like**
8 kHz	Megaphone
11 kHz	Telephone
22 kHz	Tape recorder
44 kHz	Compact Disc (CD)

Note

The highest frequency you can reproduce is half the sample rate (this is called the *Nyquist theory*, for the rabid audiophiles who might want to read up on it), and the human ear perceives sound frequencies up to about 20 kHz, so sampling at higher than around 40 kHz wastes your disk space without improving the sound quality. CD-quality sound is 44.1 kHz, which is an acceptable amount of overkill.

Understanding Bits Per Sample. The amount of data taken per sample affects the quality of the recorded sound. This is represented as *bits per sample*. Current sound cards typically use 8 bits per sample or 16 bits per sample, but you can find some high-end cards that use 32 bits per sample. The higher the bits-per-sample rating, the more true-to-life your digitized sound will be.

Note

The size of a sound file is based upon sample rate and bits-per-sample. A 44 kHz, 16-bit recording uses disk space at the rate of 5.3M per minute. An 11 kHz, 8-bit recording uses disk space at the rate of only 0.66M per minute.

Understanding Sound Cards

The sound card handles all of the audio functions for your PC. They are available in a huge range of prices and capabilities, so make sure you select the right sound card for your particular needs and budget. Understanding the design and functions of a sound card will help you make the right decision.

Dissecting a Sound Card

A sound card is similar in appearance to other adapter boards. In addition to providing audio technology, sound cards can provide the interface for your CD-ROM drive (see fig. 4.2). Using a sound card for dual purposes frees up an expansion slot for another device.

Physically, a sound card is made up of several electronic components. These include on-board processors, memory (ROM and RAM), and external ports. Table 4.2 provides more details.

Fig. 4.2
This multimedia kit includes a 16-bit sound card with an interface for the CD-ROM drive.

Table 4.2 Components of a Sound Card	
Component	**Function/Description**
Audio Control Chip	Converts sound waves from analog to digital (ADC) and digital to analog (DAC).
Digital Signal Processor (DSP)	DSPs take some of the workload off of the CPU, which helps speed up your multimedia presentations. They process sound commands and perform compression and decompression routines. Not all sound cards include DSPs.
FM Synthesis Chip	If the card includes FM synthesis instead of wavetable synthesis, it uses the formulas in this chip to reproduce sounds.
Wavetable ROM	Contains the samples—actual sounds of live instruments—used in wavetable synthesis. Most sound cards use the less-expensive FM synthesis instead of wavetable synthesis.
Audio Connector	This connection runs from your internal CD-ROM drive to the sound card, allowing you to listen to audio CDs on your PC.
CD-ROM Interface	Some sound cards have onboard SCSI interfaces (allowing them to control SCSI CD-ROM drives), but most include proprietary interfaces for CD-ROM drives from Sony, Mitsumi, Creative Labs, and/or Toshiba, among others.

Component	Function/Description
Jumpers	Used for board-level settings. This includes IRQ, DMA, and I/O address. Jumpers are also used to enable/disable certain card functions. Some cards have DIP switches instead of jumpers, while others don't need either one because they are software configurable.
External Ports	Used to connect external devices. MPC2 requires at least a MIDI/joystick port. Other possible ports include external speaker jacks, line-in (such as a microphone or external audio source), and line-out (to an external audio device or speakers).

When you start looking for a sound card, look at the specifications instead of the flashy advertisements. Know what you *really* want to do with a sound card—don't throw money away on a professional studio-quality sound processing system when you really just want to hear thundering shotgun blasts in Doom. Look for these specifications in a general-purpose sound card for multimedia:

- *SoundBlaster* (SB) and *AdLib* compatible.

- *16-bit* stereo sampling quality. If you plan to do recording, make sure this applies to both playback *and* recording. Some cards use 16-bit stereo sound only for playback, and lower-quality methods (mono or lower bits-per-sample) for recording.

- *Wavetable synthesis* (sampled sound) is the high end, which you'd only need for producing or playing MIDI-based music. It produces a rich, clear sound that's as true-to-life as you can get digitally.

- *FM-synthesis* is fine for most standard applications, and it's usually about half the cost of wavetable. Advertisements for wavetable cards call FM-synthesis "tinny," which is true to an extent. Try to find both at a computer store and listen to the difference.

- Digital Signal Processor (*DSP*) is the future direction for all sound cards. This allows for telephone (phone, fax, modem, video conferencing), real-time compression/decompression, and software upgradability. If you're doing professional multimedia presentations or music, a DSP will help speed things up, but for general use it's not necessary.

- *CD-ROM* interface. If you're buying a multimedia kit, don't worry about the sound card's compatibility with the included CD-ROM drive—the manufacturer has already matched them up. Look for a sound card that works with your existing CD-ROM drive, or a CD-ROM drive that works with your sound card's interface. SCSI is nice but expensive (both on the card and in the drive), so you may want to look at cards with proprietary interfaces for drives like Sony, Mitsumi, Toshiba, or others.

- *General MIDI (GM)* compatibility (MPU-401; 128 voices). Entry level MIDI requires 3-piece multitimbral and 6-part polyphonic. Your goal should be 16-piece multitimbral and 24-note polyphonic. (Refer to Chapter 5, "MIDI: Music to Your Ears," for more details.)

II

Multimedia Components

- IMA-adopted *ADPCM* (Adaptive Delta Pulse Code Modulation) sound file compression/decompression routine.

- Software configuration rather than hardware configuration. Some sound cards, such as those produced by Media Vision, provide software configurability—running software to change configuration options—which is much easier than changing on-board jumpers or DIP switches. This is not a requirement; it just makes the installation process much easier. Another option may be *plug-and-play* technology, which provides the same function but is more advanced.

The vast majority of sound cards connect into an expansion slot on your motherboard (see "Installing Sound Cards" later in this chapter). But if you're out of slots or working with a portable computer, you may still be able to add sound functions. The next section shows you some ways to get multimedia sound without installing a sound card.

Alternate Interfaces

Most sound cards use up a precious expansion slot in your computer, but not every computer can spare one (some, like laptops, don't even *have* them, in most cases). Luckily, you can still add high-quality multimedia sound to your PC, even without an available slot.

Some sound devices connect to your PC via the standard parallel port. Most include their own parallel port, so you can connect your printer into the other end (this is called a *printer pass-through* feature). Some, like the DSP Portable Sound Plus, even include a microphone and stereo speakers. There are some compromises in most portable sound devices (usually a higher price, if nothing else), but they're definitely a viable option if you can't spare a PC slot.

The laptop version of a PC slot is the PCMCIA slot (sometimes called a *credit-card adapter slot* because the adapters are the same length and width as a credit card). Several manufacturers now make devices—hard drives, network adapters, and even sound cards—for these tiny slots. PCMCIA cards are usually more expensive than other options, but they're super-portable (very convenient) and usually high-quality. You can even get PCMCIA adapters for your desktop computer, so if you buy a PCMCIA sound card, you can use it both at home and on the road.

The "Free" Way to Windows Sound

It's not professional-quality, but there is a way to get Windows to use your PC's speaker for some sound, and it's free. Just install the PC Speaker Driver, available from many on-line services and bulletin board systems. You'll then be able to play wave audio files through the PC speaker using standard Windows programs (see the section "Windows 3.1 Sound Software," later in this chapter).

Multimedia Upgrade Kits—Multimedia Sound the Easy Way

If you'd rather get right to work on your multimedia system instead of digging up the individual parts, you may want to consider purchasing a multimedia upgrade kit, which includes all the pieces you need in one box. You could go all out and buy a multimedia-equipped PC (see fig. 4.3), but if you were going to do that, you probably wouldn't be reading this book.

Fig. 4.3
Several manufacturers make multimedia PCs (MPCs), with the sound system and CD-ROM drive already installed.

Buying an upgrade kit guarantees that all the components will work together, and you only have one source for technical support instead of many. They're also usually cheaper than the individual components, so unless you're looking for something very specific that's not offered in a kit, a multimedia kit is a win-win proposition.

Installation of a kit is usually very easy as well, since the manufacturer's instructions can tell you exactly how to connect the specific components together. If you buy the individual pieces, you'll get instructions that try to cover all the possible combinations of third-party equipment you might add, and that usually makes for confusing reading. Some manufacturers, like Media Vision, make installation even simpler by including a step-by-step instruction video.

Even if you've never popped the top off your PC, you can install a sound card and CD-ROM drive. PC cards and drives are not the exclusive domain of educated technicians, like many believe—this isn't brain surgery, but more like snapping Legos together. The next section shows you how to install a standard sound card just like a $100-an-hour pro.

Installing Sound Cards

As you saw in Chapter 3, "Adding a CD-ROM Drive," there are a few preliminary steps to consider before opening your PC:

- Prepare a sturdy work area with plenty of room.
- Keep components out of reach from pets and children.
- Get the right tools.

> **Note**
>
> Your list of tools should include not only the hardware you'll need for the job (a screwdriver is usually all you need for sound cards, but you may need needle-nose pliers for jumpers), but also some safety measures. Make a boot disk with your system's current CONFIG.SYS and AUTOEXEC.BAT files. It's not enough to copy those files onto the disk—you'll also need to use DOS' SYS command (e.g. "SYS A:") with that disk in the drive to make the disk bootable. Make sure the disk fits your A: drive, since many systems won't boot up from the B: drive. It's also a good idea to use an anti-static wrist strap to keep from damaging the equipment with static electricity while you're poking around in the computer.

- Discharge static electricity by grounding yourself frequently.
- Make sure you have a current backup of your system.
- Keep a bootable disk handy.
- Keep a list of current devices and their IRQ, DMA, and address settings. If you haven't added any internal hardware since you bought your machine, this should be available from the manufacturer of your computer. As you add hardware, make sure you write down the IRQ, address, and DMA settings inside each of their manuals for later reference.
- Inventory all items to ensure you have everything you need.

Installation Steps

With the prerequisites covered, you're ready to begin the installation procedure. The installation instructions provided with your sound card must naturally take precedence over the instructions in this book. However, if you don't yet have a sound card, didn't receive manuals with the one you bought (second-hand, we hope), or want a second opinion, the installation steps listed here may be beneficial. The first step is the most difficult; it gets easier from there.

1. Verify on-board settings. This includes IRQs, DMAs, and I/O addresses. You must physically look at the board and verify the default settings with the documentation. If the default settings don't conflict, then you're ready to proceed to step two.

If there are conflicts, then you must change to non-conflicting settings. (The section "Resolving Installation Problems," later in this chapter discusses this further.) This applies to cards that use jumpers (see fig. 4.4).

> ## Note
>
> Key term definitions:
>
> **DMA**: Direct Memory Access channel. This is a method of linking the card directly to the computer's RAM, so it can transfer data into and out of memory without the main CPU's help.
>
> **IRQ**: Interrupt Request line. A hardware line on the motherboard that lets an expansion card signal the main CPU when it needs attention. This lets the CPU ignore the cards until they have something for it to do—otherwise it would have to check each card periodically, wasting its time if the card didn't need its attention. Each device must have its own IRQ, or the CPU doesn't know which one to work with when it gets an interrupt signal.
>
> **I/O Address**: Input/Output Address. This is how the CPU sees the location of the card within the computer—not which slot it's in, but which address it uses for data input and output. These addresses have nothing to do with the physical location of the card. Each device must have its own I/O address.

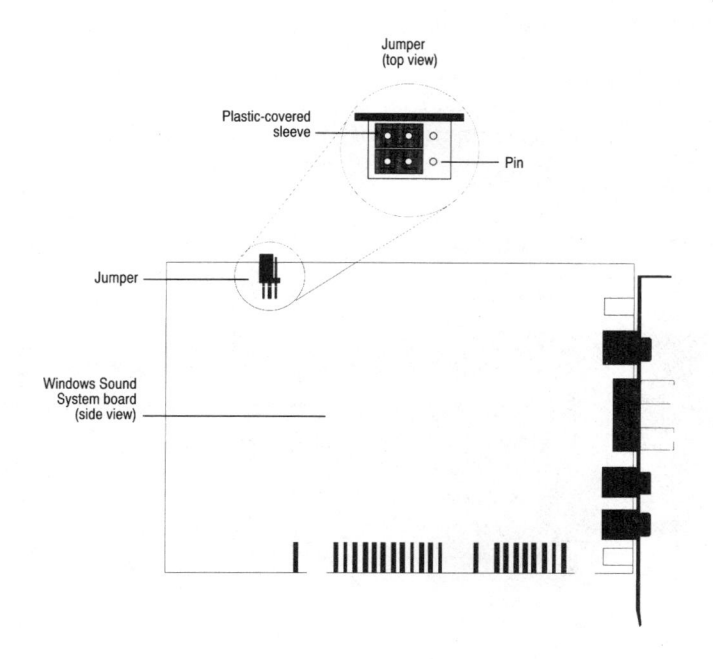

Fig. 4.4
Jumper settings can be changed by moving the plastic-covered sleeve from one set of pins to another. (Illustration courtesy of Microsoft Corporation.)

2. Remove the computer cover and the expansion slot cover (see fig. 4.5).

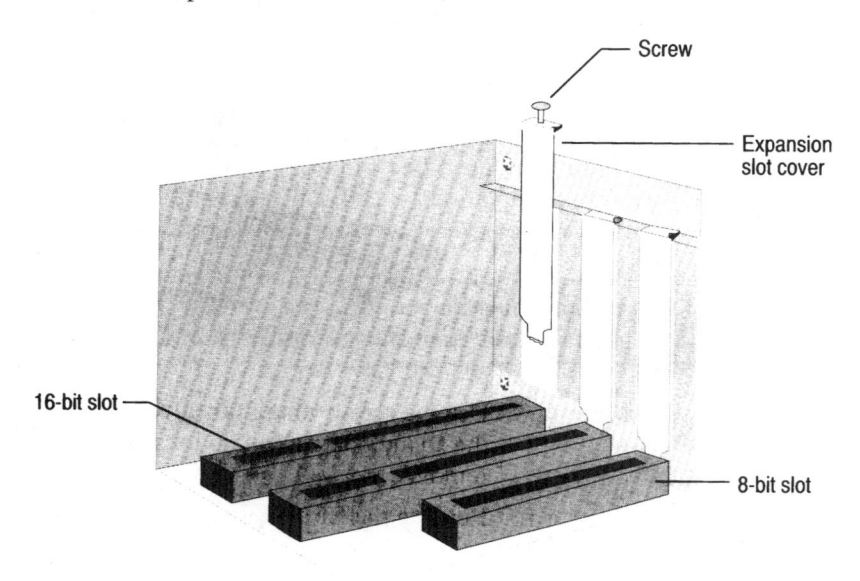

Fig. 4.5
You must remove the expansion slot cover before you can insert the card. (Illustration courtesy of Microsoft Corporation.)

3. Insert the adapter card into the expansion slot, making sure the back face plate of the card faces the back of the computer. Rocking the card may make it sit easier. Once the card is firmly in place, screw the card to the chassis (see fig. 4.6).

4. Once installed, you can attach all other components, both internal and external. If you want to listen to CD audio, connect the CD-ROM drive to the sound card using the audio connector (see fig. 4.7).

> **Note**
>
> If there is not a power connector available for the CD-ROM drive, you will need to purchase a *Y-Splitter* from your local computer store. The Y-Splitter has three connectors—one for the end of an existing power connector and two branches for other devices. Take one connector off another device, like a floppy drive; plug the middle connector of the Y-Splitter into that connector; and then run one end to the device you just unplugged and the other to the CD-ROM drive.

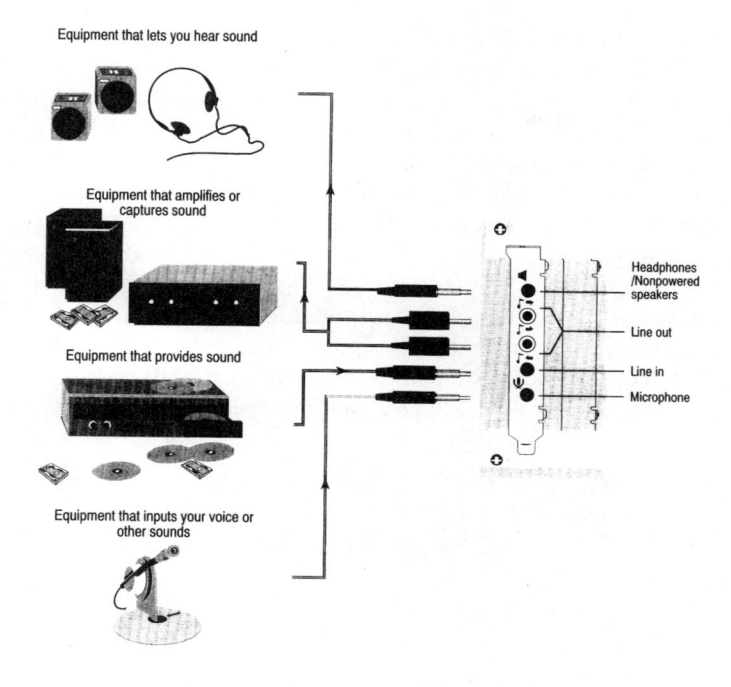

Fig. 4.6
Once the sound card is installed, you can connect external devices. (Illustration courtesy of Microsoft Corporation.)

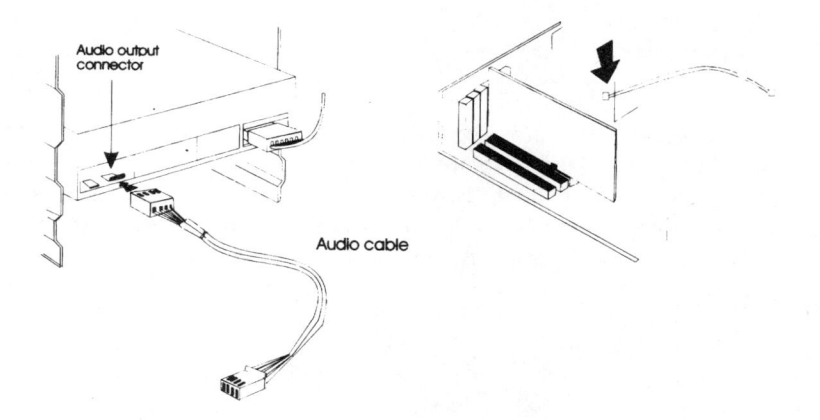

Fig. 4.7
An audio cable connects the CD-ROM drive to the sound card. This allows you to listen to CDs while working on your PC. (Illustration courtesy of Microsoft Corporation.)

5. With the sound card installed and all devices connected, plug the computer in and turn it on. While it is running with the case open, be sure to stay away from the inside of the computer! In fact, if you don't mind spending the extra time, you may want to close the case before you plug the computer back in. The reason you might run it with the case open is because you might have to get back inside to change jumper settings, and it's safe enough as long as you stay away from the inside while it's plugged in. You are ready to run the software installation program that came with your sound card. If you are fortunate, you will have a sound card that configures the IRA, DMA, and I/O settings at software installation and, there-fore, avoid board-level changes. The installation program should perform diagnostics to ensure no conflicts. If everything passes the tests, the installation program will proceed to a complete installation; otherwise, you will be made aware of any problems. Changes may be made to your CONFIG.SYS, AUTOEXEC.BAT, SYSTEM.INI, and WIN.INI files.

6. With all components fully installed and functioning properly, you are ready to put the cover back on your PC. With the PC shut off and the power disconnected, replace and secure the cover. Plug it back in, and you're done.

Resolving Installation Problems

So you plugged everything in, turned it all on, and something's amiss. You can't get the sound card to make any noise, or (worse yet) you can't get it to *stop* making noise. Maybe your modem has stopped working, or your computer won't boot up at all. Whatever happens, don't panic.

Many sound card problems are due to loose wires or improper connections. These are usually easy to spot because the symptoms are obvious—if only one speaker works, check the connection to the other. If neither works, check their connection to the card and power supply.

Watch your monitor as the computer boots up. You'll probably see the sound driver load along with the other drivers that normally load up at boot time. If there is a problem communicating with the sound card, the driver will probably put a message on-screen right after it tries to load. Each driver's failure message is different, but it should be easy to spot messages like Unable to Load or Initialization Failure.

Hardware conflicts typically become apparent early in the installation process. It is possible, though, for the sound card to work well, but another peripheral (such as the modem or scanner) to stop working. If this occurs, revisit the IRQ, DMA, and I/O settings. If your sound card is software configurable, try different IRQ, DMA, and/or I/O settings in its setup software before changing anything about the conflicting peripheral.

It is possible to share DMA channels (necessary only when all have already been assigned), but not recommended. You might get away with putting two devices on the same channel if you're absolutely certain you won't need to use those devices at the same time.

One problem that occurs frequently is when a 16-bit card is using an 8-bit DMA. When this occurs, the resulting sound is scratchy or noisy. To resolve the problem, just select a 16-bit DMA (DMAs 5 and above are 16-bit).

You also must rely on the troubleshooting tips provided in your sound card manual. If all else fails, you can call the manufacturer's technical support department, consult a guru, or get on-line help (see Appendix A for on-line resources).

Choosing Speakers

Speakers are probably the easiest audio component to work with—you don't have to load special software drivers, and their connection to the sound card is fairly self-evident. The main concern with speakers in multimedia isn't troubleshooting or conflicts—it's choosing the right ones in the first place.

It's not unusual to see someone invest in a quality sound card with all the features, and then slap a cheap pair of speakers on it. The disappointing sound quality shouldn't be a surprise. This illustrates one of two problems: the person either paid too much for a sound card or too little for speakers to meet their needs. Use the following guidelines when purchasing speakers to avoid disappointment:

- *Magnetically shielded.* This one is a must with computers. Not only do unshielded speakers pose fatal threats to your disks (big magnets, remember?), they screw up your monitor's picture and even damage the monitor.

- *Built-in amplifier.* The line-out on sound cards usually produces mediocre power levels (though some higher-end cards are amplified). Buying speakers with their own amplifiers is a good idea regardless of the sound card's output. As a general rule, internally-amplified computer speakers range in watts from 1 to 30. The more watts you have, the louder your sound system will be.

- *Frequency range.* The human ear can distinguish frequencies from about 20 Hz to 20 kHz. The frequency range of a professional level speaker system exceeds these ranges. The narrower the range, the lower the quality. You want as wide a range as possible.

- *Efficiency.* An efficient speaker driver responds well to the amplifier. An efficient speaker can produce quality sound at lower watts; an inefficient speaker requires more watts to produce the same sound.

- *Personal preference.* The most important criteria is what sounds best to you.

Note

Speaker technology uses the term *drivers* to refer to internal components (such as a woofer or tweeter). Don't confuse a *speaker driver* (hardware) with a *software driver* (software).

> **Note**
>
> Raw numbers (watts, frequency range, and so on) should only be used as an indicator. There are other unspecified factors that are just as important. This includes speaker construction, efficiency, watts per channel (versus total watts), frequency range, and the acoustics of your environment. Always *try before you buy*. If you're buying high-end speakers, you may be able to try the speakers at your workplace or home before you buy them. Otherwise, make sure you get a money-back guarantee to guard against disappointing results once you get the speakers home.

Most speakers perform well when high frequencies are involved. However, they often lack bass. Some systems include a subwoofer for frequencies below 100 Hz. A fine example is the Bose Acoustimass-3 (see fig. 4.8). For most applications, a professional system like this is overkill, but you wouldn't believe how Rebel Assault sounds through this set. You can get much cheaper units (some with subwoofers) that do an impressive job with games, multimedia presentations, and even music.

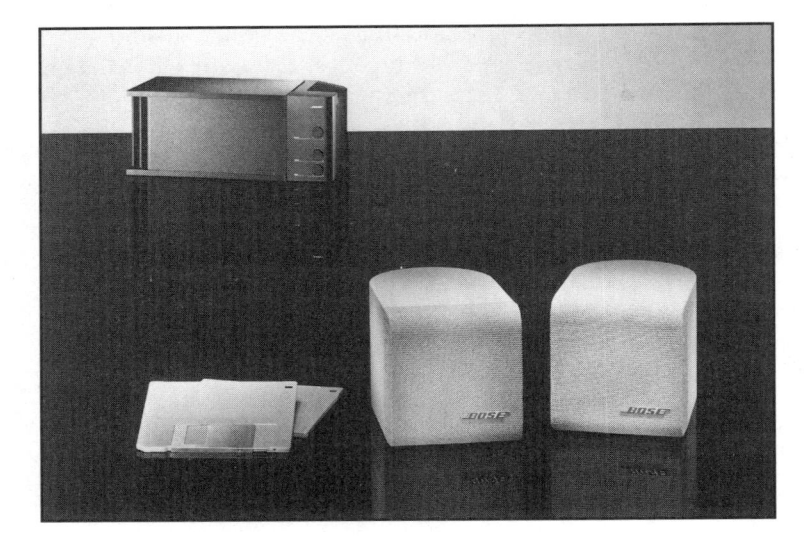

Fig. 4.8
The Bose Acoustimass-3 offers a 50-watt bass amplifier and two 25-watt amplifiers for midrange and treble.

Other points you want to consider when selecting speakers include the following:

- Type of connectors. Bare wire or RCA-type connectors (sometimes called "phono plugs") are preferred.

- Accessible controls that allow you to adjust bass/treble, volume, balance. This feature is common on even very low-priced units—don't settle for less if you have the option.

■ Available audio jacks on the speakers. Since multimedia speakers are usually positioned close to the listener, it is more convenient to plug a set of headphones into a speaker than into the back of your PC.

■ Battery-powered speakers, which are useful for portable computers.

■ Compact speakers, which occupy less desk space. You might be able to mount them to a shelf or the sides of your monitor to get them out of the way. The exception is a subwoofer, which you can set under a desk, behind a couch, in a wall, or elsewhere.

And don't forget that you can use the line-out jack on your sound board to send PC audio directly to your home stereo system. If you're going to invest in high-end speakers, you might as well buy them for the home stereo rather than using them exclusively for the PC.

Selecting a Microphone

Microphones for multimedia recording are probably as important as speakers, and they're just as often overlooked by the multimedia buyer. If you want quality recording (or accurate voice recognition), buy a quality microphone. If you'll only be using the sound card's recording functions occasionally for very informal uses, you can get by with a cheaper microphone.

Professional musicians and multimedia developers may want to consider concert-quality microphones, which can cost $500 or more. Most users can get by with a good $20-$40 microphone from the local electronics or music store.

For business uses, like changing voice annotations to memos and electronic mail, a standard-quality microphone is fine. In fact, most business-oriented applications will record your voice at a low sampling rate (low quality sound) to save disk space, so a high-quality microphone would be wasted.

Several multimedia upgrade kits and sound systems include microphones. Media Vision's Memphis system includes a tiny microphone that you can affix to a convenient location with double-faced tape. The Microsoft Sound System has a microphone that can either be affixed to the side of your monitor or placed in a stand that is provided.

Headphones and Headsets

As with the other audio components, headphones come in a huge range of prices and quality. You can find simple Walkman-type headphones and ear buds at the discount store, or $200+ professional headphones with all the trimmings—it's completely up to your personal preference. There is no magic quality beyond good sound reproduction that makes a set of headphones especially good for multimedia, except possibly a long cord—you may have to run the cord to the back of your PC after all.

If you require a lot of voice commands, telephony, or privacy, then you may want to consider a headset that includes headphones and a microphone.

If you are a professional multimedia developer or MIDI composer, then a high-quality headset or headphones will be worth the investment. Otherwise, you can run to your local electronics store and buy an inexpensive one. Again, personal preference is the most important criteria.

Software to Make It All Work

The software drivers that come with your sound card just set it up to work with other software. In addition to those drivers, you'll need software applications to perform functions like playing digital sounds, recording new ones, and editing them.

There are dozens of shareware or freeware digital sound players available on bulletin board systems, on-line services, and through shareware distributors. There's even one included in Windows 3.1 (see the section "Media Player," later in this chapter). The most common file type for digital sound on the PC is the Windows Wave format (these files have the extension .WAV), so most of the currently-available Windows sound players support that format. You may also find players for other types of digital sounds—a DOS-based program called ReMac even plays sounds intended for use with a Macintosh.

Tip

If you're doing your own recording, the application you use to record will also be able to play back sounds, so you won't need a dedicated sound player application.

Where do You Find Digital Sounds—Legally?

If you use on-line services, you'll find that digital sound is very popular—you can find digital snippets from just about every television show, movie, or other recording. Be aware, however, that in most cases this recording is done without the original artists'/publishers' permission, so it infringes on their copyrights—which is *illegal*. The practice is very widespread, but artists and publishers are starting to work against it with lawsuits and injunctions against offending on-line services. The moral: don't get caught with unauthorized samples when the Software Publishers Association drops by the office for a visit.

Several publishers (like Microsoft) sell authorized (legal) sound collections, including a few collections from Star Trek—one of the most popular targets for unauthorized sampling. Check a multimedia or computer-oriented magazine for sources.

Shareware wave recording and editing software is also widely available on computer bulletin board systems and on-line services. Before you hunt down a dedicated recorder, though, you should know that Windows 3.1 includes a simple wave recorder (see the section "Sound Recorder," later in this chapter). If you want to do high-quality recording, you can find recording software that will let you control just about every aspect of the process.

Editing software (which usually includes more advanced recording functions) is worth seeking out, since Windows' sound editing functions are minimal. Two very functional shareware wave editors are GoldWave and WaveEdit. Both allow you to select sections of your wave file and cut and paste them via Windows' clipboard. You can use these features to mix sections of wave files together into a new file, or delete unwanted pieces (like long blocks of silence) from existing files. They both provide some special-effects processing as well, allowing you to add echoes to your sounds or filter out unwanted frequencies. GoldWave also lets you "mechanize" the sounds (make them sound like they're coming out of a computer in a movie from the 60s), transpose them to a higher or lower pitch, and pan between the sides of a stereo track.

Windows 3.1 Sound Software

Most sound cards come bundled with some sound software (especially if you buy them as part of a multimedia kit). Even if no additional software is provided with your sound card, however, Windows 3.1 provides some basic sound software right out of the box. The small applications (applets) that come with Windows let you do basic recording, playback, and system configuration.

> **Note**
>
> Don't confuse Windows' included sound software with the term "Windows Sound System," which is a completely separate product, also from Microsoft.

The following sections show you how to use Windows' sound applets, and some other options for playing, recording, and editing digital sounds in Windows. If you're more interested in MIDI than digital sound, you should still read the sections on the Drivers applet and the Media Player before you skip to Chapter 5, "MIDI: Music to Your Ears."

Sound Recorder. The Windows Sound Recorder is used to record and play sound files. It also includes some basic editing functions. Figure 4.9 shows the Sound Recorder window. If you have not installed sound hardware properly, you will not be able to run the Sound Recorder.

The Sound Recorder operates like a common tape recorder, with buttons for fast-forward, reverse, play, stop, and record. When you start the Sound Recorder, you can create a new sound file from scratch or you can open an existing file. To create a sound file you need to provide an input source, typically a microphone or audio input connected to your sound card. Select the button that looks like a microphone to begin recording, and select it again to stop.

Fig. 4.9
With the proper sound hardware installed you can record, edit, and play sounds using the Windows Sound Recorder.

Sound Recorder comes with some basic mixing functions, as well. You can link sounds together end-to-end (with the **E**dit menu's **I**nsert File command), or mix them together so they play simultaneously (with the **E**dit menu's **M**ix with File command). You can use these features to add sound effects to a sound file or overlay different musical instruments together.

Sound Recorder also lets you apply some basic effects to your sounds. With the options on the Effec**t**s menu, you can manipulate the sound's volume and speed, and add a simple echo effect. If you make a mistake in editing, you can use the **F**ile menu's **R**evert command to change the sound back to its original form—the way it was before you started making changes.

Media Player. Media Player is a more basic applet than Sound Recorder, but it does allow you to playback MIDI files as well as digital sounds—if you've got a MIDI driver installed, that is. The functions in Media Player change with the multimedia drivers you install in your system. If you've got a Video for Windows driver installed, for example, Media Player lets you play Video for Windows movies, and if you've got an audio CD driver for your CD-ROM drive, Media Player will control it as well. The key word is *Player*—Media Player doesn't record but only plays multimedia files. Select its Play, Pause, or Stop buttons to control the current wave file.

Setting up Windows for Sound
Windows is very multimedia-friendly, but it doesn't do *everything* for you—you still have to do some tweaking to get it to perform like you want. You may want to change settings for your sound drivers, install new sound drivers, or change the sounds Windows uses for system events (like error messages or new mail messages). This section shows you how to use the Control Panel to configure your sound drivers and sounds for system events.

Drivers. As you saw earlier, you need sound driver software to make your sound card work. In addition to the DOS-based drivers that load in your DOS system files (CONFIG.SYS and AUTOEXEC.BAT), you'll need Windows-based drivers to tell Windows how to work with your sound card. If you're lucky, the Windows drivers will be installed and configured by your sound card's installation program, but if you get a new driver from an on-line service or bulletin board system, you'll most likely have to install it manually. Use the Control Panel's Drivers utility (see fig. 4.10) to make any changes or additions to your driver setup.

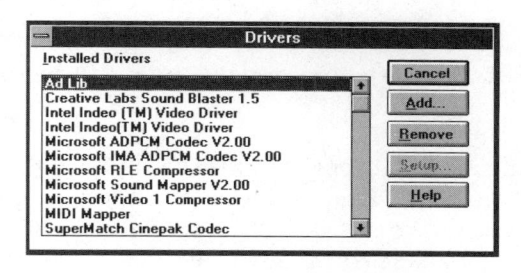

Fig. 4.10
The Drivers dialog box allows you to add, remove, and change multimedia device drivers.

The first dialog box that appears is relatively easy to understand. Its buttons perform these functions:

- *Cancel.* Returns you to the Control Panel without making any changes.

- *Add.* Allows you to install a new driver.

- **Remove.** Deletes the selected driver from the Windows setup.

- *Setup.* Some (but not all) drivers have options that you can set. If you highlight the driver and press this button, you'll be able to set those options within the driver. If the selected driver doesn't have any options, this button is grayed out.

- *Help.* Displays the Control Panel's Help system, which can guide you through some general procedures, such as installing or removing a driver. This button doesn't help you with the specific driver you have selected; it just helps you with the Drivers dialog box in general.

To install a new driver manually, follow these steps:

1. Select **A**dd. You'll see a list of drivers Windows knows about (ones that have been installed and disabled, along with some that appear by default). If the driver you want isn't listed, select the first option: Unlisted or Updated Driver.

   You can type the path to the driver in the Install Driver text box, or choose **B**rowse to see a standard Windows file selection box, which lets you click the different drives and directories until you find the directory with the driver you want to install.

2. Choose OK to select the drive and directory with the new driver. If you see a message that says a file (usually OEMSETUP.INF) can't be found, check to make sure the driver and the vendor-supplied OEMSETUP.INF file are in the chosen directory. If the files are in a different directory, select the correct directory and choose OK again. Otherwise, check with the vendor to get the right files.

II

Multimedia Components

3. When you have selected a drive and directory with the correct files, the names of the drivers in that directory appear in the Add Unlisted or Updated Driver dialog box. Select one you want to install and choose OK. If you're installing an update to an existing driver, you'll see the Driver Exists dialog box, which lets you choose the driver already installed in the system or the new one.

4. Select **N**ew (the default), Cu**rr**ent to keep the current driver, or Cancel to abort the installation.

Once you have a driver installed, it appears in the Drivers list. If the driver has options you can change, the **S**etup button is enabled when you select the driver; otherwise the button is disabled (grayed out). Your sound driver will most likely have some options that you can set, so select it and select the **S**etup button to see what you can configure. In most cases, you'll be able to change the hardware settings (IRQ, I/O address, and DMA), and you may be able to set other options as well, such as what type of emulation to use.

Sound. Windows 3.1 lets you associate sounds with different system events. It can welcome you to work when you start up Windows, for example, and wish you good night when you exit Windows. The sounds Windows uses for different system events are set up with the Sound option in the Control Panel (see fig. 4.11).

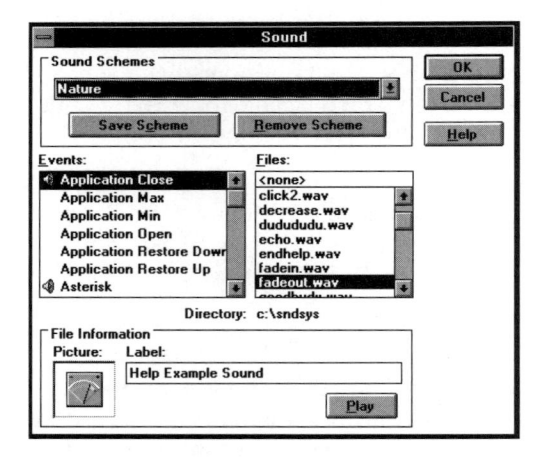

Fig. 4.11
The Control Panel's Sound dialog box.

The left side of the Sound dialog box lists all the system events (your list may be different, as applications you install can add system events to Windows). You can associate each event with a different .WAV file by selecting the event, and then selecting the .WAV file from the file selection box in the middle of the dialog box. If you choose Windows Start (from the bottom of the Events list) and associate it with the TADA.WAV file, you'll hear that wave file each time you start Windows. If you don't know what a particular wave file sounds like, click it in the file selection box and choose the **T**est button. The file will play through your sound device.

> **Caution**
>
> If you're easily irritated, don't choose long wave files for common system events. You may not realize how often you hear the 1/2-second beep in Windows when you make a mistake, but if you associate the Asterisk, Default Beep, and/or Exclamation events with long .WAV files, it'll get old in a hurry.

From Here...

This chapter covered the basics of digital audio on your PC. It explained the vocabulary you need to work with digital audio, and showed you how to choose the right hardware (sound cards, input devices, speakers). For the heart of the sound system—the sound card—this chapter provided step-by-step instructions for installation. Since even the best sound hardware is silent without the right software, some of the sound-oriented programs included with Windows 3.1 as well as some shareware sound editors were covered. For more information about sound, see the following chapters:

- Chapter 5, "MIDI: Music to Your Ears," explains MIDI hardware and software. Check it out if you're interested in making music with your multimedia PC.

- Chapter 7, "Buying Advice," and Chapter 9, "Buyer's Guide to Sound" will help you buy a sound card or other equipment.

- Chapter 10, "Buyer's Guide to MIDI," covers some of the MIDI hardware currently on the market.

- Appendix A, "Additional Resources," lists some other sources of information— clubs, books, magazines—and help on multimedia topics.

Chapter 5

MIDI: Music to Your Ears

Musical instruments have evolved from noise makers into intelligent electronic devices. Today a single computer can create the sounds that it took an entire orchestra to create in the past.

How can one computer play several different sophisticated instruments, each with its own sound characteristics, at the same time? The answer is MIDI (Musical Instrument Digital Interface). Many recognize MIDI as one of the most profound and influential technologies music has ever known. MIDI is to music what the automobile is to transportation.

Besides musical instruments, MIDI also can control other electronic devices—lighting panels, pyrotechnic controllers (fireworks), video equipment, and others—as long as they speak the MIDI language.

MIDI is the medium for multimedia music. Multimedia uses sound, including music, in addition to other mediums (video, animation, and so on). MIDI complements multimedia because it's designed to produce professional music. Realizing this capability, MPC level 2 requires MIDI compatibility.

Advancements in technology have made quality equipment available to the masses. Prices drop as more people buy, resulting in a growing appetite among consumers for professional quality technology.

In this chapter you explore the details of MIDI and get answers to the following questions:

- What is MIDI, in detail?
- How can MIDI benefit my multimedia productions?
- What hardware do I need?
- How do I install MIDI hardware?
- What type of MIDI software do I need?

You may think you don't need MIDI because you can't play a musical instrument and you're only interested in playing the latest multimedia games. However, once you learn the benefits of MIDI, even if you're just playing games, you may quickly change your mind. Let's start by defining MIDI in general, and then discuss some of the specifics.

What Is MIDI?

MIDI (Musical Instrument Digital Interface) is the standard language spoken among musical instruments and computers. MIDI is a command protocol that gives one intelligent device the ability to control another.

MIDI tells an instrument or other MIDI device what to do—*play this note; do this effect; turn up the volume; turn on the projector.* It's important to realize that MIDI isn't an audio signal. Some people incorrectly reason that MIDI is for making music; therefore, it must be an audio signal. This is false. Sound does not travel over the MIDI cables. What does travel over the MIDI cable is an instruction, or command, for a MIDI instrument or device to make sound or perform some other action. Since MIDI is capable of controlling remote devices, it is being used for more than just musical instruments. More applications for MIDI are being recognized; because of this, MIDI is exceeding original expectations.

You can use MIDI to control lighting and other special effects. Essentially, you can take an entire rock concert, including special effects, and program it into a computer via the MIDI standard. At precise moments, or upon certain events, the computer can send MIDI instructions to switch on lights, launch fireworks, or replay videos on large screens. Multimedia also is promoting MIDI because of the advantages it offers to multimedia (the advantages will be discussed in a moment).

As you can see, MIDI is very powerful. Most likely you won't be using MIDI at its full capacity. The multimedia applications you use will handle the MIDI details for you. Your main interest will probably be in using MIDI for playing back music or for basic MIDI music composition.

A Quick MIDI History

MIDI was developed in 1983 by manufacturers of electronic music equipment. They wanted to define a standard way to make synthesizers work in harmony. During the 1970s, musicians had found that a richer, fatter sound could be produced by playing more than one keyboard at a time (a technique known as *layering*).

To meet client demands, equipment manufacturers began developing synthesizers that could be interconnected to produce these layered sounds. Each manufacturer developed its own standard, and the resulting incompatibility created frustration and confusion. Then MIDI came to the rescue with a standard that defined how to communicate (*data format*) and how to connect devices (*cabling*).

With the MIDI standard, musicians and non-musicians alike can interconnect multiple synthesizers and play them with only one keyboard, computer, or other device.

MIDI Today

Most electronic instruments and multimedia adhere to the MIDI standard. Three reasons why MIDI is beneficial to multimedia are:

- *Smaller files.* MIDI stores the command that produces sound, not the literal sound wave. This makes the file much smaller.

- *Easier to edit.* It is easier to edit commands rather than sound waves.

- *Background music.* MIDI music can play music simultaneously with other mediums (video, graphics, voice). This allows background music to continually play through different phases of the multimedia presentation.

Multimedia presentations that use MIDI are more professional sounding and easier to create. They also are more efficient because the file sizes are smaller and therefore require less resources to process the files.

MIDI Hardware

The PC needs a MIDI interface to translate MIDI data into binary data. You can upgrade your PC to MIDI capability with these options:

- MIDI-Capable Sound card

- Internal MIDI card

- External MIDI interface

Just because a component says it's MIDI compatible doesn't necessarily mean you have full MIDI capabilities. Some PCs can play MIDI files but can't control other MIDI devices. If you only want to play games but want quality sound, all you need is a MIDI-only card. If you want to compose music or control external devices via MIDI, your PC's MIDI component has ports, which are discussed in the section "Installing MIDI Hardware" later in this chapter.

> **Tip**
>
> MIDI files are easily identified by their filename extension (*.MID). Stick to this standard when you name your files.

Along with the physical aspects of the MIDI standard, there also is the command or language protocol level with even more capabilities.

Understanding the Language

MIDI is more than just cables and ports. MIDI also includes a comprehensive data structure. The data structure allows devices to exchange instructions and signals to all devices (globally) or to specific devices (individually).

Like cable TV's capability to provide several stations with only one cable attached to the TV, MIDI also has several channels on one cable.

MIDI standards specify 16 channels. You can assign different devices to these channels. So, along with the IN, OUT, and THRU ports, you also can control a device by assigning it to a specific channel. Specific channel data is embedded within the MIDI data format. Each device reads the MIDI data and determines if it should perform the command. If not, the device simply ignores the command and allows it to pass THRU.

As everyone began assigning devices to channels, they all came up with their own way of doing things. This created problems not only with channels, but with other user configurable MIDI parameters. To resolve these conflicts the General MIDI specification was created.

The General MIDI Specification

General MIDI is a standard within the MIDI standard. There are still 16 channels you can configure; however, General MIDI (GM) does specify that channel 10 is dedicated to drums. GM also assigns 128 specific voices. The term voices refers to individual MIDI sounds. The acoustic piano, for example, is always voice 01. Tables 5.1 and 5.2 list General MIDI specifications for voices.

Table 5.1   General MIDI Voice Settings

Voice #	Voice Name
001	Acoustic Piano
002	Bright Acoustic Piano
003	Electric Grand Piano
004	Honky-tonk Piano
005	Electric Piano 1
006	Electric Piano 2
007	Harpsichord
008	Clavinet
009	Celeste
010	Glockenspiel
011	Music Box
012	Vibraphone
013	Marimba
014	Xylophone
015	Tubular Bells
016	Dulcimer
017	Drawbar Organ
018	Percussive Organ
019	Rock Organ
020	Church Organ

Voice #	Voice Name
021	Reed Organ
022	Accordion
023	Harmonica
024	Tango Accordion
025	Nylon Stringed Guitar
026	Acoustic Guitar (Steel Strings)
027	Electric Guitar (Jazz)
028	Electric Guitar (Clean)
029	Electric Guitar (Muted)
030	Overdriver Guitar
031	Distortion Guitar
032	Guitar Harmonics
033	Acoustic Bass
034	Electric Bass
035	Picked Bass
036	Fretless Bass
037	Slap Bass 1
038	Slap Bass 2
039	Synth Bass 1
040	Synth Bass 2
041	Violin
042	Viola
043	Cello
044	Contrabass
045	Tremolo Strings
046	Pizzicato Strings
047	Orchestral Harp
048	Timpani
049	String Ensemble 1
050	String Ensemble 2
051	Synth Strings 1
052	Synth Strings 2
053	Choir Aahs
054	Voice Oohs
055	Synth Voice
056	Orchestra Hit
057	Trumpet
058	Trombone
059	Tuba

II

Multimedia Components

(continues)

Table 5.1 Continued	
Voice #	**Voice Name**
060	Muted Trumpet
061	French Horn
062	Brass Section
063	Synth Brass 1
064	Synth Brass 2
065	Soprano Saxophone
066	Alto Saxophone
067	Tenor Saxophone
068	Baritone Saxophone
069	Oboe
070	English Horn
071	Bassoon
072	Clarinet
073	Piccolo
074	Flute
075	Recorder
076	Pan Flute
077	Blown Bottle
078	Shakuhachi
079	Whistle
080	Ocarina
081	Square Wave Synth
082	Sawtooth Wave Synth
083	Synth Calliope
084	Chiff Lead
085	Charang Lead
086	Voice Lead
087	Fifth Lead
088	Bass and Lead
089	New Age Pad
090	Warm Pad
091	Polysynth Pad
092	Choir Pad
093	Bowed Pad
094	Metallic Pad
095	Halo Pad
096	Sweep Pad
097	Rain FX

Voice #	Voice Name
098	Soundtrack FX
099	Crystal FX
100	Atmosphere FX
101	Brightness FX
102	Goblins FX
103	Echo Sweep FX
104	SciFi FX
105	Sitar
106	Banjo
107	Shamisen
108	Koto
109	Kalimba
110	Bagpipe
111	Fiddle
112	Shanai
113	Tinkle Bell
114	Agogo
115	Steel Drums
116	Wood Block
117	Taiko Drum
118	Melodic Tom
119	Synth Drum
120	Reverse Cymbal
121	Guitar Fret Noise
122	Breath Noise
123	Seashore
124	Bird Tweet
125	Telephone Ring
126	Helicopter
127	Applause
128	Gunshot

(Table courtesy of Turtle Beach Systems)

As you can see, General MIDI (GM) includes sounds other than instruments. These can add special appeal to multimedia presentations. For example, *applause* can be played after a feature of a presentation is revealed. Also, a *gunshot* can be sounded for items in a *bulleted list*, as each item appears. The *bird tweet* can be used to add a soothing atmosphere. It was stated earlier that music and sound can create emotion. From the examples just given, you can begin to see how MIDI voices can be used as emotion inspiring sounds.

II

Multimedia Components

Table 5.2	Channel 10 General MIDI Voice Settings
Voice #	**Voice Name**
27	High Q
28	Slap
29	Scratch Push
30	Scratch Pull
31	Sticks
32	Square Click
33	Metronome Click
34	Metronome Bell
35	Acoustic Bass Drum
36	Bass Drum 1
37	Side Stick
38	Acoustic Snare
39	Hand Clap
40	Electric Snare
41	Low Floor Tom
42	Closed High Hat
43	High Floor Tom
44	Pedal High Hat
45	Low Tom
46	Open High Hat
47	Low-Mid Tom
48	High-Mid Tom
49	Crash Cymbal 1
50	High Tom
51	Ride Cymbal 1
52	Chinese Cymbal
53	Ride Cymbal Bell
54	Tambourine
55	Splash Cymbal
56	Cowbell
57	Crash Cymbal 2
58	Vibraslap
59	Ride Cymbal 2
60*	High Bongo
61	Low Bongo
62	Mute High Bongo
63	Open High Bongo
64	Low Conga
65	High Timbale

Voice #	Voice Name
66	Low Timbale
67	High Agogo
68	Low Agogo
69	Cabasa
70	Maracas
71	Short Whistle
72	Long Whistle
73	Short Guiro
74	Long Guiro
75	Claves
76	High Woodblock
77	Low Woodblock
78	Mute Cuica
79	Open Cuica
80	Mute Triangle
81	Open Triangle
82	Shaker
83	Jingle Bells
84	Belltree
85	Castanets
86	Mute Surdo
87	Open Surdo

* Drum sound is Middle C on the keyboard.

(Table courtesy of Turtle Beach Systems)

MIDI devices act as a slave or a master device. A *slave device* is configured to receive MIDI commands on a specific channel. The devices know when a command is intended for them when it's received on a channel specified to them (IN or THRU port). If you configure a slave to channel 3 and send a command down channel 4, the slave will ignore the command. Send the same command down channel 3 and the slave will respond. A master device issues commands to slaves from the OUT or THRU port. Several devices can be daisy-chained together via the THRU port. Along the chain of devices, slaves respond to the MIDI instructions of their corresponding masters, and masters control the subservient slave devices.

Tip

Roland was the first company to produce a GM sound module, and it eventually became the standard. Look for MPU-401 compatibility when purchasing a General MIDI interface to avoid incompatibilities.

II

Multimedia Components

Adhering to the GM standard assures you that music will sound the same on any GM system. Although the sound quality may differ, based upon the synthesizer, pianos will be pianos and drums will be drums.

Beyond General MIDI

A MIDI command involves more than just playing a specific note. The device also must be commanded on *how* the note was played. This includes the following:

- *Delay.* The amount of time to delay before a note is played.

- *Attack.* How to increment sound to full volume.

- *Hold.* How long to hold the volume.

- *Decay.* The amount of volume loss after the hold.

- *Sustain.* How long the sound remains.

- *Release.* How to stop the sound.

MIDI commands aren't limited strictly to music notes. *System exclusive (sys-ex)* command is used exclusively by equipment manufacturers for system specific instructions primarily dealing with the sound programming of a device. A common example for using a sys-ex command involves *bulk dumps*. You can configure a keyboard and bulk dump the configuration to your PC. Whenever you want that specific configuration, you can perform a bulk dump from the PC back to the keyboard.

MIDI is very functional and very flexible, too. Using different commands and channels you can create elaborate productions. Computer games use channels to create moods with music. Because a mood can instantly change in a game, you need to have the MIDI data readily available. Multimedia producers separate moods into different channel groups. For example, Group A channels may contain relaxing music and group B channels may contain suspenseful music. Alternating between groups A and B can change moods from relaxed to suspenseful, respectively.

You also may come across Standard MIDI, Type 1, or Type 2. For now, just focus your attention on GM, the MPC standard.

MPC and MIDI

Multimedia places additional requirements on MIDI components. For MIDI to be MPC level 2 compliant, it must meet certain criteria.

In addition to General MIDI (GM), MIDI devices for MPC2 must be able to play three voices at a time. Each voice must be able to play six notes simultaneously. Also, the percussion channel must support five notes each, simultaneously. In MIDI lingo these terms are referred to as multitimbral and polyphonic.

- *Multitimbral.* Number of instruments (voices) that can be played at the same time.

- *Polyphonic.* Number of notes that can be played at the same time.

If you want professional level multimedia MIDI sound, you should exceed the MPC2 standard and get 16 piece multitimbrance with 24 note polyphony. The multitimbral ranges currently found on synthesizers range from 11 to 32.

Tip

It's best to purchase MIDI products that meet MPC level 2 standards. This assures you that the hardware meets the minimum requirements and the software can run successfully on the hardware.

Understanding MIDI Hardware

A MIDI PC can be very simple and economical, or very sophisticated and expensive. A MIDI system can be as simple as a sound card or as elaborate as a system including several synthesizers, sound modules, keyboards, wind controllers, mixers, and PCs running a plethora of software.

Whatever your requirements are, you need one of three things to produce MIDI sound:

- Sound board
- Synthesizer
- Sound module

Table 5.3 provides details on each of these components.

Table 5.3 Components that Produce MIDI Sound	
Component	**Description**
Sound Board	Common on multimedia PCs, low-end sound boards use FM synthesizer computer chips. More advanced sound boards use wavetable synthesis chips. A sound board is used essentially for playing back MIDI music and is mandatory.
Synthesizer	Keyboard devices equipped to produce sound, synthesizers can be FM or wavetable. Wavetable synthesizers are used to produce professional quality sound. A synthesizer is necessary if you plan on creating music via a keyboard. A synthesizer is optional.
Sound Module	A synthesizer without a keyboard. Commands are received from another MIDI device (master device). Since a sound module does not have a keyboard, it is only used for playback. Sound modules are used to improve the playback quality of sound, which would otherwise be reproduced via the lower-quality sound board. A sound module is optional.

II

Multimedia Components

> **Tip**
>
> If you purchase a sound board, make sure it's MCI compatible. MCI is the Media Control Interface in a standard part of the Windows Multimedia extensions.

If you have a sound card that uses FM synthesis you may be able to upgrade to a wavetable synthesizer. For example, the Memphis multimedia system has an FM synthesizer, and can be upgraded with the Maui Wavetable Synthesizer. See table 5.4 for the MIDI configuration used with this example to help you understand how all the parts work together.

Table 5.4   Example MIDI Configuration

Component	Function
Memphis multimedia system by MediaVision	Multimedia upgrade kit
Porta Tone PSR-510 by Yamaha	Keyboard synthesizer
WT11 Wind Tone Generator and Wind MIDI Controller by Yamaha	MIDI wind instrument
Maui Wavetable Synthesizer by Turtle Beach Systems	Upgrade to wavetable synth
*Cakewalk Professional (2.0) by Twelve Tone Systems	Sequencing software
*Wave SE (2.0) by Turtle Beach Systems	Sound editor
*Power Cords Pro by Howling Dog Systems	Fretboard based sequencing

For more details, refer to the section on MIDI Software later in this chapter.

Cakewalk Professional lets you record, edit, play, and print music. Wave SE lets you record and edit waveform sounds. The Maui Wavetable Synthesizer upgrades the FM synthesizer included in Memphis to a wave table synthesizer. Maui also lets you create and store your own MIDI voices (sounds) using Wave SE. The Yamaha keyboard and wind controller are examples of the instruments you could play. Finally, with Power Cords Pro you can easily create a rhythm section.

MIDI Synthesizers

MIDI sound is only as good as the synthesizer. The two basic types of synthesizers you will encounter are:

- Frequency Modulation (FM)
- Wavetable or Sampled Sound

FM synthesizers try to copy a sound. Wavetable synthesizers are actual originals. Although many synthesizers are FM, more people are beginning to buy wavetable synthesizers because the quality is significantly better (sounds live rather than reproduced).

FM Synthesizers. FM synthesizers have been around since the 1970s and were developed by John Chowning of Stanford University. Yamaha has exclusive rights to this license and
produces microchips using this technique. The two common Yamaha synthesizer chips are OPL-2 and OPL-3.

The MPC standards don't require these synthesizers. If you have a sound board, you may have a different FM synthesizer. Roland, for example, used a technique called linear arithmetic, but have since migrated to wavetable technology. Yamaha is also working on a new technology based upon physical-modeling synthesis called *Virtual Acoustic Synthesis,* that will produce a better sound than FM synthesis. All this new technology doesn't mean FM synthesis will disappear overnight.

FM synthesizers are used because of their availability and affordable prices. The most common FM synthesizer, OPL-3, uses four sine waves to copy an instrument sound. This sound may be adequate for low-end, semi-professional multimedia systems. However, if you're using multimedia for business presentations or music composition, you'll need to upgrade to wavetable synthesizers.

Wavetable synthesizers. Wavetable synthesizers use digitally recorded samples of actual instruments. Rather than reading a sine wave (like FM), digital numbers reproduce the actual waveform of the instrument. These waveform originals are stored on-board, in memory (RAM or ROM).

The technology used for processing digital signals (Digital Signal Processing, or DSP) is used for more than just producing MIDI music. The professional quality of DSP technology is also used in the telephone industry (phones, answering machines, fax/modems, video conferencing, and so on).

The Best Synthesizer for You. The best available technology is wavetable. If you're only going to be playing games and have a limited budget, you may be satisfied with FM synthesis.

Purchasing your synthesizer is a matter of personal preference. Certain instruments may sound better on one synthesizer rather than another. One synthesizer may have good sounding woodwinds but terrible sounding strings, or visa versa. This applies even to digitally sampled sound. The key to success is to listen to different synthesizers before you buy, and select the one you prefer.

> **Note**
>
> Don't forget the speakers. Synthesizers, sound boards, and sound modules require speakers. Typically, output from different components go to a mixer that combines all of the individual signals into one stereo signal. For more details, refer to Chapter 4, "Adding Sound to Your System."

Another option to consider is a *keyboard controller*. A keyboard controller does not have a synthesizer. It only generates MIDI commands. A sound module or sound board is required to actually produce sounds based upon a keyboard controller's MIDI commands. Some individuals prefer keyboard controllers because they can select a professional quality keyboard apart from a sound module. Therefore, to improve the quality of the sound, all that is needed is another sound module. You don't have to re-familiarize yourself with a new keyboard. Also, as a general rule, keyboard controllers are typically manufactured to be professional quality keyboards; they look, act, and feel like a genuine piano keyboard.

> **Note**
>
> If you're purchasing a keyboard, make sure it can produce aftertouch and velocity. *Aftertouch* signifies the pressure a key is depressed. *Velocity* signifies the impact at which the keys hit the sensor. Without aftertouch and velocity you wouldn't be able to produce realistic sounding music. Every note you play will be identical, no matter how hard/soft (aftertouch) or how fast/slow (velocity) you press the key.

There are a variety of MIDI instruments available—wind instruments, guitars, keyboards, pianos, drums, and so on. If you play any of these instruments, you may want to purchase its MIDI equivalent. Some instruments, guitars for example, have MIDI upgrade kits. You don't even have to play an instrument to compose music. All you need is a PC, and the PC keyboard and mouse become your instrument.

Consider how you use your system to help you decide what system you may need. If you conduct traveling presentations, you may want an MPC laptop equipped with a wavetable synthesizer. Some MIDI interfaces connect via serial ports; this would be ideal. Sound modules are also a good choice (some are equipped with MIDI interfaces). It's more difficult to carry a keyboard synthesizer than a sound module.

> **Note**
>
> Don't forget MIDI cables to connect devices. Depending upon your configuration, each device can have up to two MIDI cable connections (IN, OUT, or THRU combinations). Physically, MIDI connectors are all the same. At issue is how many cables you will actually need. One recommendatio: Get colored cables to let you quickly identify what cable goes where.

If you're building a studio, you may need to meet a higher degree of standards. Some MIDI interface modules have multiple ports allowing several sound modules to connect into one device, instead of daisy-chaining several devices together. These devices are typically more expensive and only offer benefits to high-end MIDI users.

Installing MIDI Hardware

Installing MIDI hardware primarily deals with connecting MIDI devices. The one exception is installing a sound board (refer to Chapter 4, "Adding Sound to Your System").

General Guidelines

There are a number of different scenarios that you can create with MIDI. That is part of the beauty and frustration. Here are some general guidelines:

- *Know your "slaves" and "masters."* Having a clear understanding of what device acts as the master (issue commands) and what device acts upon the commands (slave) is the key issue. Once you understand this, it's a matter of configuring your devices accordingly.

- *Keep good documentation.* Since there are so many areas where settings can be made, it's vital that you keep good documentation. Documentation includes parameters set in your sequencing software, hardware settings, drivers used, and mappings.

- *Develop a standard.* It's better to have a standard rather than selecting tracks, channels, and voices ad hoc. This standard isn't General MIDI or MPC2—it's your own personal standard that relates to how you set up your MIDI working environment. You can discuss strategies with MIDI gurus. If you don't know any, you may want to research some of the MIDI magazines; you may have to refer to back issues. You also can check on-line sources such as Internet or CompuServe. There are MIDI forums swarming with MIDI gurus.

Making the Connection

Understanding how MIDI devices are interconnected is probably the most important hardware installation concept you can learn. Specifically, there are three types of ports used for interconnecting MIDI hardware: IN, OUT, and THRU. Table 5.5 shows the function of each port. A standard 5-pin DIN cable attaches to either of the three ports (see fig. 5.1). Devices can be interconnected to form a daisy-chain of MIDI devices. Depending on how a device is connected and configured, it will act as a master device, a slave device, or both.

Table 5.5 MIDI Ports		
MIDI Port	**Role**	**Function**
IN	Slave	Commands are received IN from other device.
OUT	Master	Commands are sent OUT to other device.
THRU	Both	Commands are received IN and can be sent OUT. If a MIDI command is intended for this device it will respond. Otherwise, the command will pass THRU to the next device. Commands originating from this device will also be passed THRU.

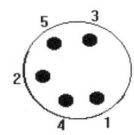

Fig. 5.1

With standard 5-pin DIN cables, signals can be sent and received simultaneously.

A *master* device gives commands. A *slave* device responds to commands from a master. This is a simple MIDI connection, as illustrated in figure 5.2. Because devices can be daisy-chained, you could have two keyboards interconnected, both as masters and slaves (see fig. 5.3). Playing a note on the master keyboard would simultaneously play the same note on the slave keyboard. You also could form a complex interconnection with multiple devices, as shown in figure 5.4.

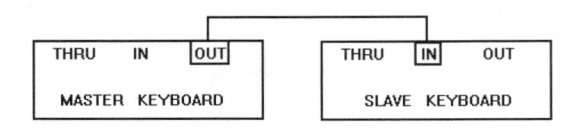

Fig. 5.2

In a single configuration, one master device controls one slave.

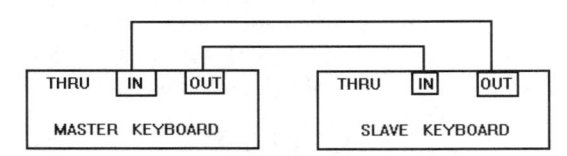

Fig. 5.3

One device can have two roles. Here both devices serve as masters and slaves to the other device.

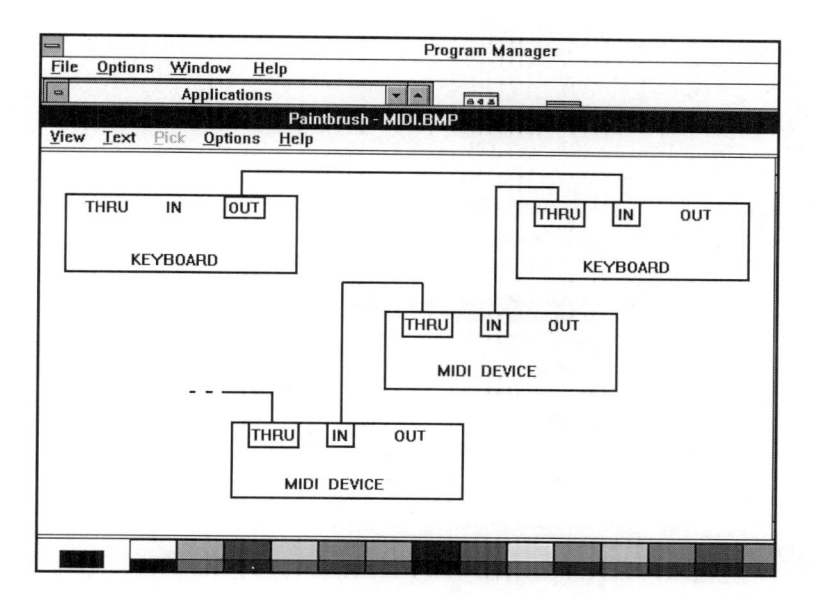

Fig. 5.4
A daisy chain can include several devices acting as masters or slaves, depending upon how they're configured.

Being able to interconnect different MIDI devices allows a lot of room for creativity. Software is required to capture and record the sound produced from these different scenarios.

Installing the MIDI Software You Need

MIDI software will include a standard installation program. The basic procedure is to insert the installation disk in a drive on your PC. Once inserted, log on to that drive, if needed, and then run the install program, usually INSTALL.EXE from the DOS prompt or SETUP.EXE from the Windows Program Manager (**F**ile **R**un). The installation instructions should confirm the procedure used. Once the installation program begins, you will be prompted several times to provide responses. One common example is the prompt to accept or alter the default director on your hard drive to install the software to. The prompts should be self-explanatory. As you proceed through the installation, new files will be copied onto the hard disk and existing files will be altered. This procedure is common for installing software.

MIDI software is usually purchased separately from MIDI hardware. The software provides additional functionality beyond the basics provided by the hardware. Windows includes special purpose applications specifically for MIDI (MIDI Mapper). With Sequencing programs you can compose music. There are also programs that allow you to create and edit actual MIDI voices.

II

Multimedia Components

MIDI Mapper

The *MIDI Mapper* applet allows you to customize the way Windows plays MIDI data. You should use extreme caution when using MIDI Mapper. Changing settings can be an involved process and can result in a configuration that produces no sound, due to improper settings. Because this can become quite involved, this section focuses on a general understanding. Figure 5.5 shows the screen that appears when you select the MIDI Mapper icon from the Control Panel in Windows.

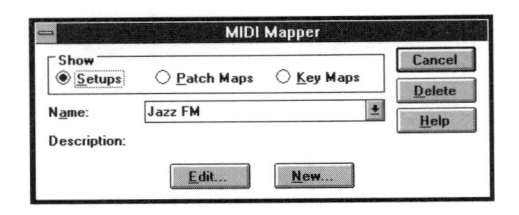

Fig. 5.5
Customize your MIDI setup using the Windows MIDI Mapper.

The MIDI Mapper relates to a sound device and allows you to create a new setup or change an existing one. Some of the changes you can make are:

- Edit Key Maps
- Edit Patch Maps
- Edit Channel Mappings

You need to be familiar with MIDI concepts before you make changes to settings in the MIDI Mapper. You need to know what effect each change will make on your system. Knowing the effect of changes becomes more apparent when you become more proficient with MIDI. As an example, however, recall the discussion of slave devices and how specific channels are assigned to them. Remember, a slave device looks for instructions on the channel it's assigned. If you reassign a slaves channel via MIDI Mapper, the slave will stop responding because it will assume that since the command is on a different channel it does not apply. The slave will ignore the commands until it's reconfigured to look at a different channel or until the channel is changed back to its appropriate setting.

MIDI is a powerful interface standard with a lot of flexibility. Because of this power, you're responsible for knowing what you're changing. It's also helpful to have an understanding of the characteristics of the sound device that the MIDI Mapper will interface with.

You also can perform similar functions and more with sequencing software, described next.

> **Note**
>
> Most sound boards are GM compatible. When you run the installation software provided with sound boards, a special Windows MIDI file is replaced on your system. This file (MIDIMAP.CFG) contains the MIDI map configuration on your PC. If you want to retain the old MIDI map configuration you must copy and save the MIDIMAP.CFG file before you run the installation program. Some programs will rename the current MIDIMAP.CFG file to MIDIMAP.OLD, and then subsequently install the new MIDIMAP.CFG file.

Putting Music into Sequence. The best analogy to describe MIDI sequencer software is a word processor. A sequencer is to MIDI what a word processor is to text. It allows you to record, edit, play, and print music as you would create, edit, and print words with a word processor. You can even perform functions like the standard cut and paste.

You'll have no trouble finding available sequencing software (see Chapter 10, "Buyer's Guide to MIDI" for help). Two programs, for example, are Cakewalk Professional for Windows and Power Chords Pro. Both are Windows compatible.

Cakewalk Professional. Cakewalk by Twelve Tone provides professional level sequencing capabilities. If you're an entry-level user you'll find Cakewalk easy to use. As you become more sophisticated you can begin using more advanced features.

You can record up to 256 tracks. For example, you can record a piano on track one, a cello on track two, a violin on track three, and a tuba on track four. When played back you have a quartet unlike any other you've ever heard. Figure 5.6 illustrates the Cakewalk interface.

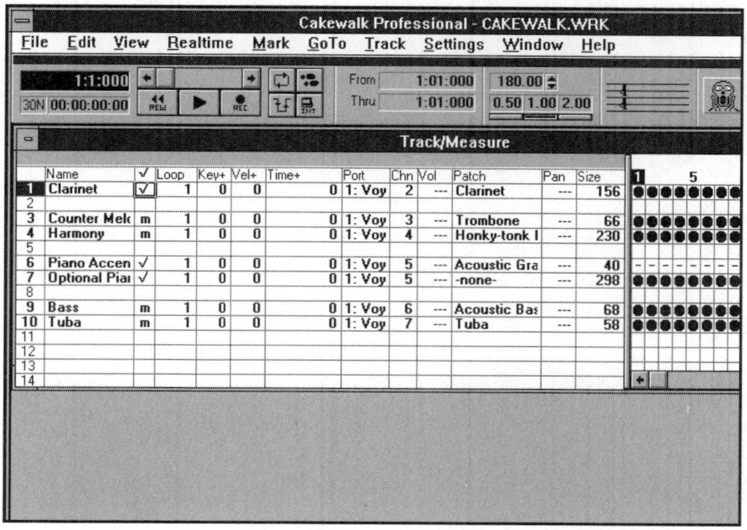

Fig. 5.6
The Track/Measure view is Cakewalk Professional's main window and is displayed automatically each time you start the program.

There are other views in addition to the Track/Measure view—piano roll, event list, controllers, and staff view. You can have multiple views open simultaneously. As the music is played, each view is synchronized as the movement progresses.

Power Chords Pro. If you've had prior experience creating MIDI music, then you realize that guitar and drum pieces are not easy to compose. Keyboards and wind controllers don't quite do the job. Power Chords Pro by Howling Dog Systems provides a solution to this problem (see fig. 5.7). You'll find Power Chords Pro especially useful if you're a guitar player.

By treating parts of music as objects, it's easy to compose an outstanding rhythm section that includes a chord part, drum part, and a bass line. A melody also can be created using any of the MIDI voices. Because it's compatible with other major sequencers, you can create a piece in Power Chords Pro and send it off to another sequencer, and vice versa.

Sometimes you need the ability to do more than just sequence software. You can get software that lets you actually create a new instrument (MIDI voice). Essentially, you need a waveform editor.

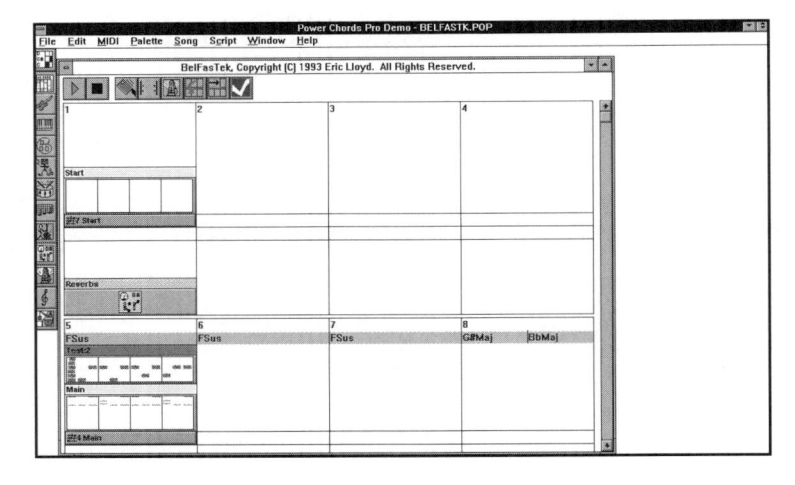

Fig. 5.7
Power Chords Pro keeps music parts intact and treats them as individual objects.

Making Waves. You don't need special software to create waveform files. Included in Windows 3.1 is the *Sound Recorder* that provides basic recording and editing functions. However, if you want more functionality, you should consider third-party software such as Wave SE by Turtle Beach Systems (other sources are provided in Chapter 10, "Buyer's Guide to MIDI").

Making a waveform file lets you create your own MIDI voices. If you have a synthesizer, sound module, or sound board that lets you load your own sounds, you can replay personalized MIDI voices using your MIDI hardware. The Maui Wavetable Synthesizer by Turtle Beach Systems has this capability.

With Wave SE, you can record, edit, and process waveform audio. Running in a Windows environment, Wave SE uses a graphical interface. Wave includes the basic functions of record and playback, in addition to many other sophisticated sound processing algorithms. Some of these include the following:

- Three-dimensional analysis (see fig. 5.8)
- Mixing of up to three partial or complete soundfiles
- Graphic waveform drawing and editing
- Crossfading, gain adjustment, and muting
- Time reversal and amplitude inversion
- Time compression and expansion
- Sample rate and channel conversion
- Import and export to a wide variety of file formats

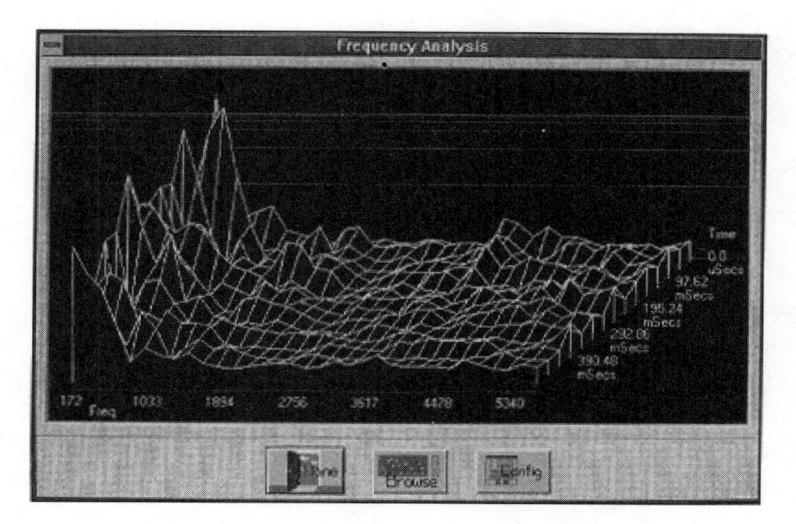

Fig. 5.8
Frequency Analysis uses Fast Fourier Transformation (FFT) to determine the frequency content for portions of the music.

Wave SE is easy to install and use. The interface is similar to a tape deck. Besides MIDI, Wave SE can be used to edit or record waveform files that can be used throughout Windows. You can capture these files using a sound board and a microphone. For example, you can record your own sounds that play based upon certain Windows events. Refer to Chapter 4, "Adding Sound to Your System," for more details on sound technology and Windows.

Waveform recording and editing is used to make your own MIDI voices. If you need this capability, a program like Wave SE will be useful.

From Here...

The discussion of MIDI within this chapter provids you with a basic understanding of MIDI and guidelines for installation of both hardware and software. To learn more about multimedia video, see the following chapters:

- Chapter 6, "Upgrading Your Video" discusses types of multimedia visuals (animation, still images, and so on), video hardware, video software, and installation procedures.

- Chapter 10, "Buyer's Guide To MIDI" provides additional tips and resources for buying MIDI hardware and software.

Chapter 6

Upgrading Your Video

Multimedia is the result of several different mediums working together. Until now, you've explored individual elements. This chapter looks at multimedia on a global level.

Topics not yet discussed include animation, full-motion video (playback and capture), still-images, graphics processing, and authoring software. The last topic, *authoring software*, encapsulates multimedia into a presentation. At the presentation level, individual mediums are combined and delivered simultaneously. Still images and graphics become dazzling slides; animation and full-motion video breathe life into the computer; and sound accentuates and stirs emotion. The capability to combine and deliver these mediums is what makes multimedia alluring, effective, and entertaining.

This chapter begins by discussing animation. Building on the knowledge you obtained from Chapter 2, "Basic Computer Requirements," specific characteristics of multimedia monitors are discussed. Next, the process of capturing and creating video is defined—how it's done, what hardware is needed, and what software is needed. Finally, a summary helps you recall key items.

Real Animation

All children enjoy cartoons. To children, they are more real than life. In fact, the word *animate* means to make alive. Animation is still a very effective communication tool, even for mature adults. Many people are actually investing in the original cells of their favorite cartoons. These *cells,* (transparent celluloid sheets), are becoming rare and therefore more valuable because computer animation is replacing the old way of doing things.

Cartoons the Hard Way

Rather than drawing the same picture over-and-over, transparent cells were created. The animated portion of the cartoon was drawn on a cell and overlaid onto a static background. Therefore, you didn't have to redraw the background each time, just the animated portion. However, this was still difficult and required a new cell for each movement of the animated characters.

Cartoons Today

Current computer technology uses a technique similar to a transparent overlay on a static background. The difference is that digital images can be overlaid without the need of celluloid sheets. Also, the computer can mathematically animate sequences between key frames. A *key frame* identifies specific points. A bouncing ball, for example, can have three key frames—up, down, and up. Using these frames as a reference point, the computer creates all the images in-between, producing the effect of a smoothly bouncing ball.

Technology also has advanced to the point that computer art can look identical to hand-drawn art. Using a pressure-sensitive tablet and a program like Fractal Design Painter, you can create images that look like they were drawn free-hand, as shown in figure 6.1. (For more details, see the section "Video Software," later in this chapter.)

Fig. 6.1

You can create images that look like they were drawn free-hand using Fractal Design Painter and a pressure-sensitive tablet.

You may ask why you would use a computer to draw images that look hand-drawn? The answer is simple. Although it may take you longer at first, after you become proficient at using animation software, you will be more productive. The computer offers tools to assist you. It doesn't take away your creative expression; it simply enhances it. A common example of computer-assisted animation is morphing.

Morphing

The process of *metamorphosis (morphing)* is easily performed on a computer. You can take one image and then *morph* it into another. This imaging technique is becoming commonplace. Figure 6.2 illustrates this by morphing a little girl into a cat.

Fig. 6.2
Morphing animates the transformation of one form to another. You can do this using software such as CorelMOVE! (provided with CorelDRAW!).

To this point you have learned about 2D (two-dimensional) graphics. A 2D image has no depth—only width and height (x,y). In multimedia, you also can use 3D (three-dimensional) graphics.

3D Animation

A computer looks at 3D graphics differently from 2D. The third dimension is depth (z). From a computer's perspective, a 3D object is a mathematical model. Shadows can be applied by establishing a virtual light source that projects onto the 3D object. Shadows are cast opposite the light source when an object crosses the path of the light source. This creates a more realistic effect.

1,2,3D. Three-dimensional animation has three basic steps. First, you create a *wire frame* (mathematical model), which is made up of points in space (*vertices*) interconnected with straight lines (*edges*). When edges and vertices connect, they form flat surfaces—a triangle, for example. These flat surfaces are called *polygons*. A triangle is a polygon made up of three vertices (points) interconnected to form three edges (lines). A complete 3D model is made up of several polygons (see fig. 6.3) which appear as an elaborate wire frame.

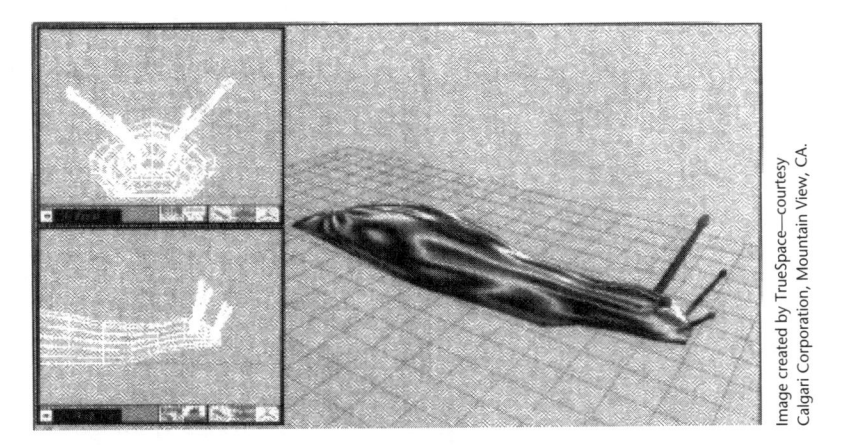

Image created by TrueSpace—courtesy Calgari Corporation, Mountain View, CA.

Fig. 6.3
Pictured here is a wire frame of a slug with a surface rendered to provide a 3D effect

To make a *wire frame* appear realistic, you need to add a surface texture (*rendering*). When you render a 3D-object (wire frame), you are asking a lot from the computer. Depending on the options you select, a texture can reflect light, refract light (like beveled glass), or cast shadows. The movie *Terminator 2: Judgment Day* contains a good example of a 3D-model rendered with a texture that reflects light, refracts light, and casts shadows, giving the illusion of liquefied metal. *The Abyss* is another movie you may recall that contains the 3D illusion of a being formed out of water.

When you work with 3D images, you have two basic methods for animation:

- Path animation
- Cell animation (like 2D)

Cell animation is basically a series of still images that, when replayed, provides the effect of animation. With *path animation,* you can actually draw a path that your 3D-object can follow (see fig. 6.4). Other techniques also are provided that allow your model to change size and rotate while in an animated sequence (see fig. 6.5).

This may be very entertaining, but is it useful in a business presentation? The answer is YES!

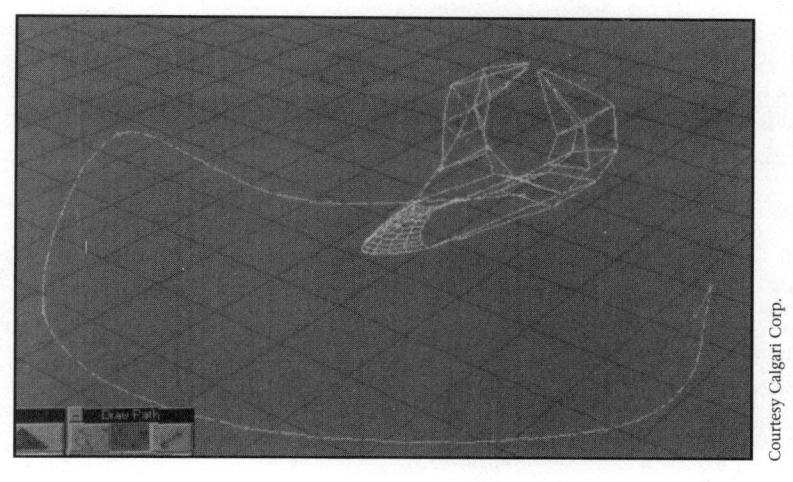

Courtesy Calgari Corp.

Fig. 6.4
Pictured here is a 3D wire frame spaceship and an animation path. Selecting PLAY moves the
spaceship along the path.

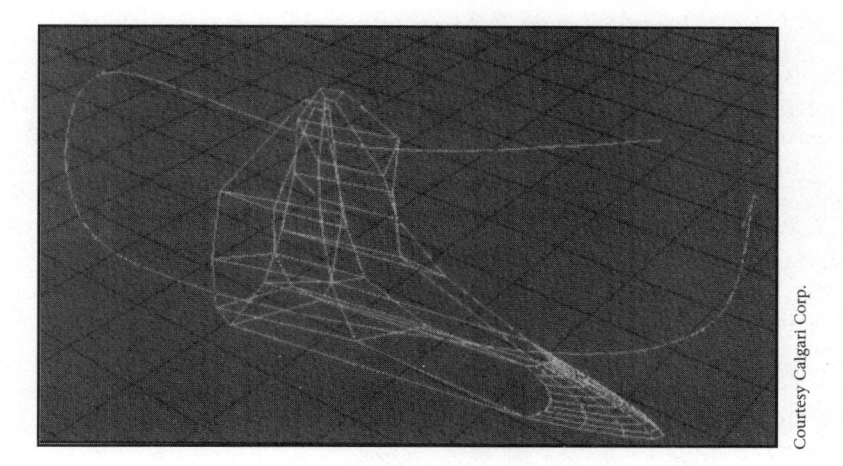

Courtesy Calgari Corp.

Fig. 6.5
The spaceship rotates to a side-view as it follows the animation path.

Business Applications for 3D. Corporate logos can be rendered in 3D and animated.
Instead of having dull text, you can have a company (or client) logo come flying out
from the distance, flip over a couple of times, and then instantly stop, perfectly centered
on-screen.

II

Multimedia Components

Another example is in the environmental sciences. With 3D animation you can create a *real-world* illustration that graphically depicts how a hazardous waste problem began. Most importantly, by running through different scenarios you can illustrate the most effective way to resolve a problem, or to keep a problem from occurring. A 3D animation can be used to prove innocence or to establish guilt. This is great stuff, but it comes with a price.

Price and Performance Costs of Animation

If you are serious about animation, you will have to spend approximately a few thousand dollars ($2,995 to be exact) for a program like 3D Studio by Autodesk. Less expensive programs are available, such as Calgari's TrueSpace, for only a few hundred; this may be adequate for your needs. However, if you do not get 3D Studio, make sure that the 3D animation software you get supports 3D Studio file formats (both import and export).

Three-dimensional animation places strong demands on hardware. An entry-level system that delivers acceptable performance exceeds the specifications of MPC2 (486DX/66 or better, 16M RAM, 500M Hard Disk, 17-inch+ monitor, advanced bus graphics accelerator with 2M VRAM). The more power, RAM, storage, and screen real estate you have, the better off you are.

More people are realizing the benefits of 3D animation. Prices are dropping and technology, once available only to high-end workstations, is now available on PCs. One example is the 64-bit graphics accelerator offered by Matrox Graphics. What makes this graphics accelerator card unique is the on-board 3D rendering engine—Vesa Media Channel (VMC) option also available. This allows smooth, photo realistic 3D images (*Gauraud shading*) to be performed on a PC level at speeds exceeding low-end workstations. This is accomplished by dithering between the flat surfaces (polygons) of the wire frame. Some other features of Matrox's 64-bit graphics card are as follows:

- Instant zooms (two to four times normal size)
- Virtual desktop (ideal for desktop publishing)
- Double buffering (simultaneously process and display)

Other 64-bit graphics cards are available (refer to Chapter 2, "Basic Computer Requirements"). Currently, only Matrox offers a 3D rendering engine, although competitors will no doubt have alternatives by the time you read this book.

Don't underestimate the power and application of animation. It is a very effective communication tool for multimedia. Remember, however, that it requires an investment in both hardware and software. Also, keep your power/performance standards balanced. If you buy a high-end 3D graphics accelerator, make sure that you have a monitor capable of presenting the images the card can produce, at performance levels that meet or exceed those of the card.

Multimedia Monitors

Upgrading your video card and monitor are two of the most significant upgrades you can make to equip your PC for multimedia. When you do it, you should do it right. Here are a few pointers:

■ Get a large monitor—17-inch minimum; preferably 20- to 21-inch.

■ Make sure that your monitor can keep up with the video card, including resolutions, refresh rates, and color depths. Also, make sure that you have a crisp, clean image (dot pitch <=.28). The monitor should also have multiscan capabilities (multisync is another term used but is an NEC trademark). Avoid multi-mode; whereas a multiscan monitor can change scan frequencies *on-the-fly*, a multi-mode monitor requires manual settings and is a standard below multiscan.

■ Your video card should be a *graphics accelerator* with DSP (Digital Signal Processor) technology. It should be a 32-bit or 64-bit card that interfaces to an advanced bus (VL-bus, PCI, VMC). The resolutions, refresh rates, and color depth should be up to par: 1024 x 786; 72 Hz (or more); and 16 million, respectively. The monitor should be non-interlaced. The card also should have or be capable of upgrading to at least 4M of VRAM.

Note

Certain chips are common to graphics accelerators. The chip typically indicates quality/performance. Common chips are: Matrox MGA, AGC 98032, Weitek P9000, S3, ATI, C&T F82C481, Cirrus Logic GD5428, and Tseng ET4000/W32i. These are listed in a relative order of importance with Matrox representing high-end chips and Tseng representing economical low-end chips. This can be used as a general assessment criteria.

Follow the preceding guidelines to have an adequate system—a good configuration that should satisfy your needs. It won't be easy sifting through all the products available. Specifications can be confusing or inaccurate (sometimes deliberately). The best advice is to do your homework and follow these tips:

■ Finish reading this chapter.

■ Prepare a list of your applications (software) and your hardware configuration and keep it handy. Note any anticipated future upgrades—hardware and software.

■ Ask friends, gurus, clients, and so on what they prefer.

■ Check multiple on-line sources and reviews in magazines. Compare among different sources. The top performers usually surface above any bias.

■ After you select the monitor/video card, call each manufacturer. If incompatible, have them recommend alternatives.

II

Multimedia Components

The purpose of acquiring all this technology is to make your multimedia applications perform well and have a quality appearance.

Looking for Quality Images

The quality of an image displayed on the monitor is determined by how precise each individual dot appears on-screen. Your monitor is made up of thousands of little dots; the dots are so many and so close together that they look like one solid picture.

Every color seen on a computer screen is based upon the three primary colors of red, green, and blue. Different combinations and intensities of these three colors produce the 16 million other colors the human eye can see. These thousands of multicolored dots (pixels) make up a monitor image.

A Pixel's Worth 1,000 Words. The smallest element of a computer screen, as far as humans are concerned, is called a *pixel* (short for *picture element*). A good monitor will be calibrated so that rays of red, green, and blue light hit their targets (individual phosphor dots) precisely. If they don't, then you have what is referred to as bad *convergence*. This is apparent when edges of lines appear to illuminate with a specific color. If you have good convergence, the colors will be crisp, clear, and true, provided there is not a predominant tint in the phosphor.

To get real picky, you can assess the quality of a monitor's phosphor. Good phosphor is white. Looking at a screen with a lot of white space is the best way to determine phosphor quality. A noticeable tint (yellow or blue) indicates poor quality. If a screen has a pure, white appearance, then it is considered good and clean, just like your finished laundry.

In addition to what an image looks like, you also want to consider how much you can see. Because a screen image is made up of pixels, it's only logical to conclude that the more pixels you have, the more information you can display. The number of pixels available equates to a monitor's *resolution*.

Resolution. A monitor's resolution is expressed by two numbers indicating how many pixels there are horizontally and vertically (x, y). You frequently see the monitor specifications such as 1024 x 768 or 800 x 600. This is the number of pixels horizontally (x) and the number of pixels vertically (y). When you multiply these numbers, you get the total number of pixels on-screen. For example, $800 \times 600 = 480,000$ pixels.

The MPC standard for video monitors is 640 x 480 VGA (Video Graphics Array). You definitely want to go above this resolution. You most likely will operate at 800 x 600. This is good for multimedia because video images appear more realistic at this resolution (this is because 800 x 600 offers more colors, which makes an object look more realistic to the human eye). However, you see less on an 800 x 600 screen than you do on a 1024 x 768. Sometimes, you may want to change settings to operate at a resolution higher than 800 x 600. If you're fortunate, you will have a card that has *instant mode switching* capabilities (Matrox offers instant mode switching of up to four commonly used resolutions); this enables you to change resolution settings on-the-fly. If you don't have instant mode switching, then you have to restart Windows after changing monitor settings.

Another factor is the actual size of the display. As mentioned earlier, a 21-inch monitor is ideal because higher resolutions have bigger images on a 21-inch monitor. Trying to run at this resolution on a 14-inch monitor would be the equivalent of trying to read microfilm with the naked eye. Higher resolutions and larger monitors enable you to see much more information comfortably. Basically, you want a great deal of screen real estate.

Screen Real Estate

Screen real estate is how much available space you have on your screen. A 14-inch monitor at low resolution is like a square foot of land, whereas a 21-inch monitor at a high resolution is like an acre of land. Actually, you can view over 35 percent more with a 21-inch monitor than with a 17-inch. Get the picture?

A high-resolution monitor can display more information than a low-resolution monitor because the pixels are more compact. When you display an image using compact pixels, the image also becomes compact, or tiny. That's why you need a large monitor. It displays the higher resolution over a broader space; therefore, it becomes a larger display of a higher resolution (see fig. 6.6). A higher resolution will show more data (see fig. 6.7).

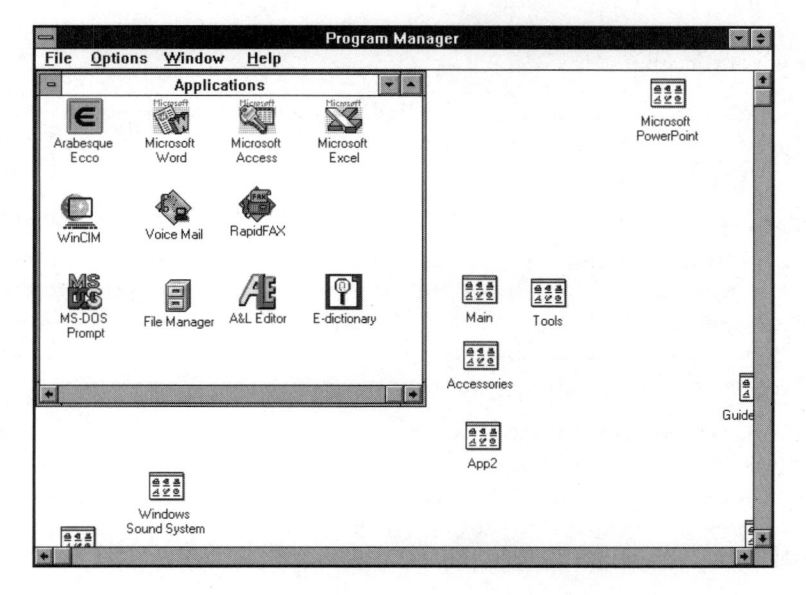

Fig. 6.6
The resolution setting for this display is 640 x 480. A higher resolution shows more data.

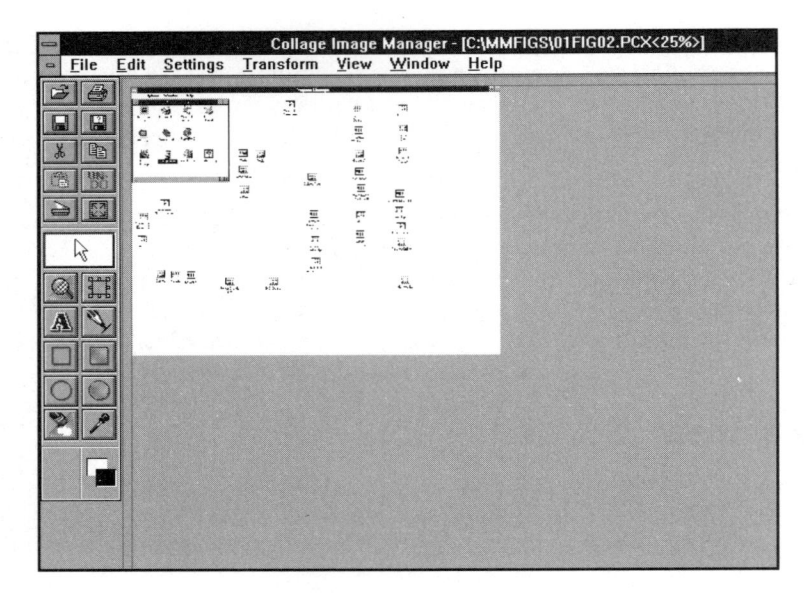

Fig. 6.7
You can see more with higher resolutions, but the image becomes smaller. Here, 1280 x 960 displays the entire MS-Word window adjacent to available icons.

More isn't always better. An 800 x 600 resolution, for example, displays a better motion video than a 1024 x 768 screen for two reasons. First, the image is bigger. Second, you can display more colors at a faster rate. Resolution makes an image look sharper; color makes an image look more life-like. Therefore, you need to achieve a good balance of color, speed, and resolution.

Not everything concerning graphics is dictated by the monitor. You also have to make sure that your video card is capable of providing the graphics to your monitor at compatible speeds and resolutions.

Video Chain Links
As just stated, a close relationship exists between the video monitor and the video card. A close relationship also exists between the video card and the expansion bus and the available RAM on the video card and on the motherboard. Buying a monitor is like buying any other device; you're not just buying a monitor, you're also buying an adapter card that lets your monitor talk to your computer.

If you have the world's best monitor and the world's best video card, then you also need the world's best expansion bus to plug it into. High performance video cards typically require a top-of-the line expansion bus, like VL-bus or PCI. Your motherboard, therefore, must have one of these expansion buses available. Assume that your motherboard does have an available compatible bus. Now you have to make sure that you have sufficient memory to store the volume of data required to fill your monitor's screen (larger, higher resolution screens require much more data). You need a great deal of RAM.

Limited RAM overtaxes the CPU. Without available RAM, the CPU must depend on hard disk storage, which is slow because of its mechanical nature.

VRAM versus DRAM. The RAM on a video card used to be identical to the RAM used on your motherboard (DRAM). This was slow and didn't meet the needs of graphics processing. A new type of RAM was developed called Video RAM (VRAM). With VRAM, you can simultaneously write and read data, which results in a performance boost. Most new cards use VRAM.

After you get your RAM up to par, you must make sure that your CPU can support the duty of processing such a large amount of video information. Performance and quality are only as good as the weakest component.

Note

If you plan to produce top-quality video, you also should consider the type of cables you need. Low-quality cables can cause crosstalk between signals. *Crosstalk* occurs when one signal interferes with another.

Good cables are shielded to prevent crosstalk and electromagnetic interference (EMI). Gold is a good conductive metal and is preferred. Consider solid connections and try to avoid long cable runs. The longer the cable, the more likely *attenuation* (loss in signal quality over distance) or *distortion* (interference such as crosstalk or EMI) will occur. Finally, try to keep your cable away from other electronic devices.

For example, consider the following video monitor and card configuration (an Orchid Fahrenheit VL-Bus video adapter card). The monitor is a MAG 17-inch MX17H. Given this scenario, the following question needs to be answered: is the monitor compatible with the Orchid Video card?

To find the answer, Mark Mayer of MAGtechnical support was contacted. Mark has been in the video industry for over 22 years. He gave the following advice: "The video card capabilities will be the main factor in determining which refresh rates are available for a given resolution....A refresh rate that pushes the monitor to the limit of its horizontal frequency should be avoided." After all, he claims, "if you drive your car with the gas pedal floored, you are bound to wind up in trouble."

The video card was compared to the monitor to ensure compatibility. Fortunately, specifications are provided in both the MAG and Orchid documentation. These specifications were merged and are presented in table 6.1.

II

Multimedia Components

Table 6.1 Fahrenheit Video Card versus MAG MX17H Preset Monitor Modes					
Resolution	**Card Colors**	**Monitor Horiz.**	**Vert.**	**Horiz.**	**Vert.**
800 x 600	16	35.2	56	35.2	56
800 x 600	16	37.8	60	37.8	60
800 x 600	256	48.8	72	48	72
800 x 600			85	56.5	85
1024 x 768			44	35.2	43.5
1024 x 768	16	48.4	60	48.9	60
1024 x 768	16	56.5	70	56.5	70
1280 x 1024*	256	47.0	43.5	64	60

indicates interlaced

First, compare the horizontal and vertical ratings (Hz) for the video card (per table 6.1). Then compare these values to corresponding monitor values. The monitor value should meet or exceed the value of the video card. Preferably, the monitor will exceed the capacity of the video card. The video card is what drives the graphics. When a monitor can't keep up with a video card, then you have problems.

Some card specifications exceeded the monitor's, so there was some concern that it wouldn't be able to keep up with the card. Running the Orchid utility program tested the configuration and detected no problems with the monitor. Most importantly, the image is acceptable, and the performance is good for the requirements in this scenario. This is the most important criteria. After all things are considered you must ask yourself, "Do I like it?" To answer that question, you have to test the monitor yourself.

The technical support staff at Orchid recommends that you use the FSCAN utility program to select supportable modes. They indicated that user preference is most important; therefore, select the supported mode you prefer most. They also warned against blindly following the specifications provided by monitor manufacturers. The specifications of the manufacturer can be in error, either intentionally or unintentionally. By using FSCAN you can verify the monitor's capability to support a specific mode. This takes precedence over any manufacturer claims.

The Orchid card used to be considered state-of-the-art. Now, some video cards are much more capable. Current video card technology can support up to a 64-bit bus. Orchid has the Kelvin, and several other good video cards are offered by other companies (refer to the Video Buyers Guide near the end of the book for more details). You have several options, too, when you consider upgrading your video card.

Not only can you display video, you also can record it. The next section describes the necessary details for recording video for multimedia applications.

Recording Video

When video technology was first introduced, it was based upon television. There is a difference, however, between the signals a television uses and the signals used by a computer. In the United States, color television standards were established in 1953 by a committee. This committee and the standard it established is called the *National Television System Committee (NTSC)*. Some countries, such as Japan, followed this standard; other countries in Europe developed more sophisticated standards (Phase Alternate Line, PAL; SEquential Couleur Avec Memoire, SECAM). Table 6.2 illustrates the difference between standards.

Table 6.2 Television versus Computer Monitors				
Standard	**Yr.Est.**	**Country**	**Lines**	**Rate**
Television				
NTSC	1953 (color)	U.S., Japan	525	60 Hz
	1941 (b&w)			
PAL	1941	Europe#	625	50 Hz
SECAM	1962	France	625	25 Hz
Computer				
VGA*			640 x 480@	72 Hz

England, Holland, West Germany

* VGA is based upon pixels whereas Television standards use lines. Gen-locking is used to lock pixels into lines and synchronize computers with TV standards.

Based upon table 6.2, you will notice that not only must a computer work at a faster rate (72 Hz), a computer image also is made up of more lines (640). Another factor is the number of possible colors. You already learned that a computer can display up to 16 million colors; the NTSC standard only allows for approximately 32,000.

Another interesting point is the longevity of the NTSC standard. Many technological advancements have occurred since 1941/1953. Originally, technology was not up to par with the standards. A big demand was placed on the older technology. To create the illusion of movement, it was necessary to show a series of progressive still images. To compensate for lagging picture tube technology, a technique called *interlacing* was devised.

Note

Both television and computer refer to an individual image as a *frame*. The difference is that a television frame is expressed as lines (525 lines = 1 frame); a computer image frame is expressed as total pixels (640 x 480 pixels = 1 frame).

Interlacing

Interlacing is the process of dividing a frame into two pieces (even lines and odd lines). By displaying all even lines as a frame and then all odd lines, the television can successfully deceive the human eye and, at the same time, cut the frame load in half.

Because television is dynamic—constantly moving—interlacing produces an acceptable image. This is not acceptable, however, for static computer images. Old computer monitors used interlacing, but the flicker caused headaches. Today interlacing computer monitors is avoided. However, some monitors may use interlacing at higher level resolutions; this is acceptable as long as the mode you constantly operate in is not interlaced.

Digital Video versus Analog Video

Because television video is analog and computers use digital video, an *analog-to-digital* (AD) conversion must occur. Conversely, when data from a computer is sent to a television, it must be converted from digital to analog (DA). The differences between TVs and computers require special hardware and software to effectively convert the images.

Conversions slow down processing. To compensate, computers use *compression* and *decompression (codec)* techniques. Also, the actual screen size may be reduced to one-fourth the computer monitor size. These limitations, however, are quickly being resolved by graphics accelerators, faster computers, and new codecs. This is especially true with hardware based upon Digital Signal Processors (DSP). DSPs are designed specifically for video and audio. They are also software upgradable and, therefore, can incorporate new advancements in technology, such as new codec algorithms. Another benefit is that DSPs are multitasking; they can perform multiple tasks simultaneously.

Compression and Decompression

Considering the fact that full-motion video can consume massive quantities of disk space (0.5 seconds = 15M), it is apparent that compression is needed. Compression and decompression (codec) applies to both video and audio. Not only does a compressed file take up less space, it also performs better; there is simply less data to process. When you're ready to replay the video/audio, you simply decompress the file during playback.

Two types of codecs are hardware-dependent codecs (hardware codecs) and software-dependent codecs. Hardware codecs are typically better; however, they do require additional hardware. Software codecs don't require hardware for compression or playback, but they typically don't deliver the same quality or compression ratio. Two of the major codec algorithms are as follows:

- *JPEG (Joint Photographic Experts Group)*. Originally developed for still images, JPEG can be compressed and decompressed at rates acceptable for nearly full-motion video (30FPS). JPEG uses a series of still images, which is easier for editing. Typically *lossy* (but can be *lossless*), JPEG eliminates redundant data for each individual image (*intraframe*). *Lossy* compression "loses" details of the original image, therefore the term *lossy* is used. Compression efficiency is approximately 30:1 (20:1 - 40:1).

- *MPEG (Moving Pictures Expert Group).* Because MPEG can compress up to 200:1 at high-quality levels, it results in better, faster videos that require less space. MPEG is an interframe compressor. Because MPEG stores only incremental changes, it is not used during editing phases.

Additional considerations between JPEG (motion JPEG) and MPEG have not been discussed. For example, MPEG is asymmetrical; it takes more time to compress video than it does to decompress. JPEG is symmetrical; compression and decompression take equivalent amounts of time. The best codec to use varies among different scenarios. Determination is based upon a few key considerations, including the following:

- *What hardware platform will be used?* This is especially true for hardware-dependent codecs because compatible hardware is needed to play back the presentation. The speed at which the hardware can operate also is a consideration; some codecs can synchronize their playback speed automatically.

- *What is the software's availability?* Cinepak and Indeo are good examples of available codecs.

- *What level of quality are you trying to achieve? Can you use lossy* or *is lossless acceptable?* What should the result look like? Is a full-screen image necessary or will a partial-screen suffice (this is also related to performance)?

- *What are your storage limitations?* This relates to the compression ratio (1:1, 20:1, 200:1, and so on). A good compression ratio is said to have a high *efficiency.*

- *What level of performance is satisfactory?* This includes compression performance and decompression performance.

- *Is a full-screen image necessary or will a partial-screen be acceptable?*

If you will be capturing, compressing, and playing video, you will need Microsoft Video for Windows (VFW). The following codecs are provided along with VFW:

- *Cinepak (also called Compact Video Coded (CVC)).* Although Cinepak can take longer to compress, it can produce better quality and higher compression than Indeo.

- *Indeo.* Can outperform Cinepak and is capable of real-time compression (Intel Smart Video board required for real-time compression).

- *Microsoft Video 1.* Developed by MediaVision (MotiVE) and renamed to MS Video 1, this is a DCT-based post-processor; a file is compressed after capture.

A compression algorithm type can be an indicator of a codec's quality or performance. Common terms you will encounter include the following:

- *DCT (Discrete Cosign Transform).* This looks at an image in discrete 8-pixel x 8-pixel blocks. This can result in artifacts.

- *DWT (Discrete Wavlet Transform).* This looks at the entire image; therefore, artifacts are avoided. DWT is used for high-end, professional level quality.

II

Multimedia Components

- *Fractal.* This is extremely asymmetrical. A 30-second clip could take up to seven hours to compress. However, the resolution independence, efficiency, and reproducibility make this algorithm ideal in certain situations.

Tip

Joining the WINMM forum (Windows Multimedia) in CompuServe enables you to receive the VFW Software Developer's Kit (VFW SDK) for free. (Refer to Appendix A for information on joining CompuServe).

Note

A Digital Video Test Suite (DVTS) was developed by *"The Envisioneering Group."* Their goal was to establish a standard methodology for assessing codecs. This includes EVD (decompression) and EVC (compression) benchmarks. This may be a good resource for determining the best codec for your needs.

It's impossible to mention every codec, its pros and cons, and other esoteric nuances within this chapter, or book for that matter. There is simply not enough room, and I couldn't tell you even if I wanted to. The knowledge you now possess gets you started in the right direction. You now need to understand the hardware side a little better.

Video Hardware

The type of video hardware you need is based upon what your intentions are. If you don't want to record any video images, you won't necessarily need any hardware beyond MPC2 specifications. However, if you want to record video, then you will need additional hardware.

You can record to and from the following different video sources:

- TV (to)
- VCR (to/from)
- Video camera (to/from)
- Laser disk (from)
- Computer (to/from)

You need to decide how you will be recording. If you will be creating video on your PC, then you can purchase hardware that simply sends video signals from your PC to the corresponding video device. Conversely, if you also need to capture video from your video device (TV, VCR, or video camera), then you need a different type of hardware. The more simple scenario is discussed first.

> **Note**
>
> Many manufacturers offer boards and devices to present or capture video. I frequently refer to AITech because these are the products I'm most familiar with. Making reference to AITech products is for example only. It is wise to consider other souces. Refer to Chapter 11, "Buyer's Guide to Video."

Presenting Onto a Television

When your only requirement is to present to a television, you don't need a video capture or digitizer board. All you need is the capability to encode computer signals (VGA) to TV signals (NTSC). When you can successfully present images from your PC to your TV, you're done.

Computer-To-Video Encoder. If the only function you require is to either present to a television screen or record onto a VCR, all you need is a computer-to-video encoder. If your TV can understand a standard signal, it's logical that a VCR can record these very signals. AITech's MultiProCTV computer-to-video encoder provides this capability.

Installation is straightforward. No adapter boards are required. The MultiProCTV interconnects to your computer via a standard 15-Pin VGA (DB-15) connector. A few options are available to connect the video device: 4-pin mini DIN circular S-VHS connector; RCA connector; or RF cable connector.

The MultiProCTV is also useful for traveling presentations or demonstrations. If you don't need to travel, then you can purchase an internal card that accomplishes the same function. AITech also offers the AudioShow, which provides this capability. In addition, the AudioShow also functions as a sound card and offers multiple CD-ROM interfaces that support Sony, Mitsumi, and Panasonic drives via proprietary interfaces.

If you need to actually record from video devices onto your computer, then you need a video capture board.

Video Capture. Actually, capturing and recording video from external sources and saving the files onto your PC requires special technology. What you need is a video capture board, also referred to as a video digitizer or video grabber.

AITech offers the WaveWatcher-TV. Included with the board is the Audio Visual Recorder for Windows by In:Sync. The WaveWatcher-TV (WW-TV) enables you to literally watch television on your computer. In addition, incoming TV signals can be digitized and stored as AVI files.

II

Multimedia Components

AVI is the Windows 3.1 standard file format for compressed audio and video data. Microsoft Video for Windows runtime extensions are required for the Audio Visual Recorder. When the board is installed, video devices connected and the Audio Visual Recorder software loaded, you're ready to begin recording.

Video can come from a variety of sources: TV, VCR, video camera, or a laser disc player. When an animation file is recorded, it can be saved in a variety of different formats as follows:

- AVI—Audio Video Interleave
- FLI—320 x 200 pixel animation file
- FLC—an animation file of any size

These files can then be incorporated into a multimedia presentation using authoring software such as Icon Author from AIMTECH; or you can include the animated files as OLE objects to be used with MS-Word, Excel, Access, or other OLE-compliant applications.

Installing Video Hardware

Installing video hardware is similar to installing a sound card; however, depending upon the manufacturer and the specific product model, the installation can become quite involved.

The general guidelines regarding IRQs, DMA channels, and I/O addresses apply to video hardware just as they do to sound cards. Also, the instructions in the video hardware manuals take precedence over instructions provided within this book. Refer to Chapters 3 and 4 for detailed instructions on installing sound cards. (Many sound cards include CD-ROM connections—that's why Chapter 4 is mentioned.)

The most complex part of installing video hardware is making sure that you have the right cables and that they're attached properly. Some manufacturers include all the cables and connectors; others don't. Before you purchase any product, make sure that you're properly informed. This way you will know if you should purchase cables or if they're included.

When connecting video devices, you should use the S-Video (S-VHS) connector whenever available. This cable provides the best signal because separate signals are used for color (*chroma*) and brightness (*luma*). Otherwise, you have to use *composite video,* which mixes luma and chroma, resulting in a lower quality signal. The better your signal, the better your video quality.

With your hardware properly installed, your next step is to install the software. This is covered in the next section.

Video Software

If your only purpose is to play back multimedia presentations, software selection is easy; simply select the software you want, and you are basically done. Conversely, if you want to create multimedia presentations, software selection becomes a little more involved.

Your goal should be to have a balance of the right tools. Not having the right software tool to do the job is like trying to fix a car with only a hammer. Having six hammers doesn't benefit you either; you don't want to have six software applications that accomplish the same task. Granted, some redundancy will occur; in some situations, having a certain program can get you more work. Obviously, in these scenarios, the cost is justifiable. The key is to use your discretion.

One of the most important issues is file compatibility. You don't always have to buy name brand software; just make sure that your software is compatible with the file formats of the name brands. Standards and market share are very important—especially with file formats. If the software you're using is capable of importing and exporting standard file formats, you probably will only encounter small problems.

Find out what your friends, clients, and co-workers are using. Magazine articles (reviews, top ten lists, and so on) also provide a good resource. On-line services like CompuServe, Internet, Prodigy, and America Online are extremely good resources (refer to Appendix A for more details). I'll give you a starting point by describing software I currently have.

> **Note**
>
> Many software descriptions are based upon the introductory statements found within the actual documentation. This provides a good overview of the applications, stressing the aspects the software vendors feel are most important and useful to you.

Fractal Design Painter

Fractal Design Painter is a paint program that simulates natural-media tools and textures and gives your PC special image-editing capabilities. In Painter, you find all the supplies you're used to working with when not using your computer—from felt pens, charcoal, and colored pencils to water color and oils. As image-editing software, Painter provides many powerful options that enable you to sharpen, soften, and distort scanned photographs; apply marbling; or make your image appear as if it were viewed through glass (see fig. 6.8). To process graphic images successfully, you need a quality scanner (see fig. 6.9).

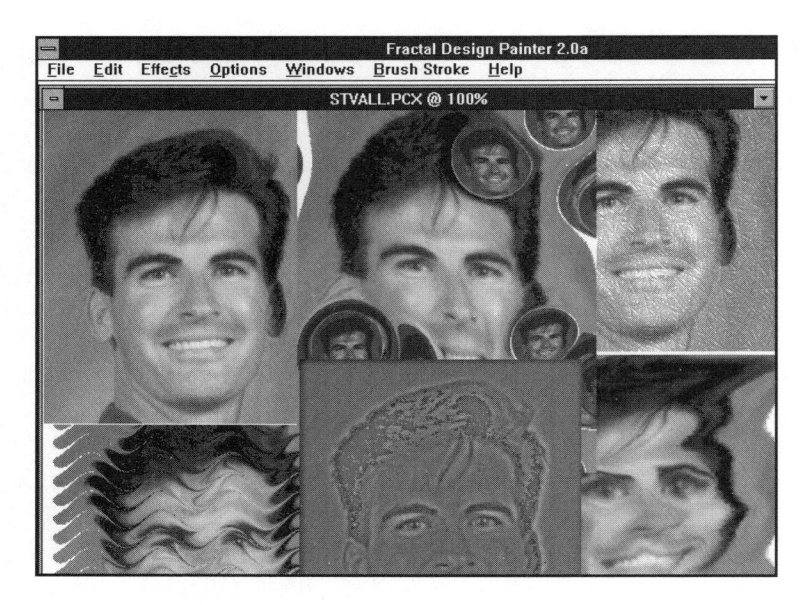

Fig. 6.8
With Fractal Design Painter, you can create different effects and apply various textures.

In figure 6.8, starting in the upper-left corner is a scanned image. Next, the "blob" effect was applied. Another effect is applying paper textures, such as rice paper. At the lower-left, you can see a marbling effect. Next is the "highpass" effect, which introduces stark shifts between brightness levels. The final effect is in the lower-right; the "liquid" tool was used to smear the image.

You need a pressure-sensitive tablet to gain the full effect of Painter's natural-media tools. I've used both the DesignSlate by Calcomp and Wacom's ArtZ Graphics Tablet (refer to Chapter 2, "Basic Computer Requirements," for more details).

To show you how serious they are, Fractal Design Painter is packaged in a paint can. For more information, contact Fractal Design Corporation, Aptos, California.

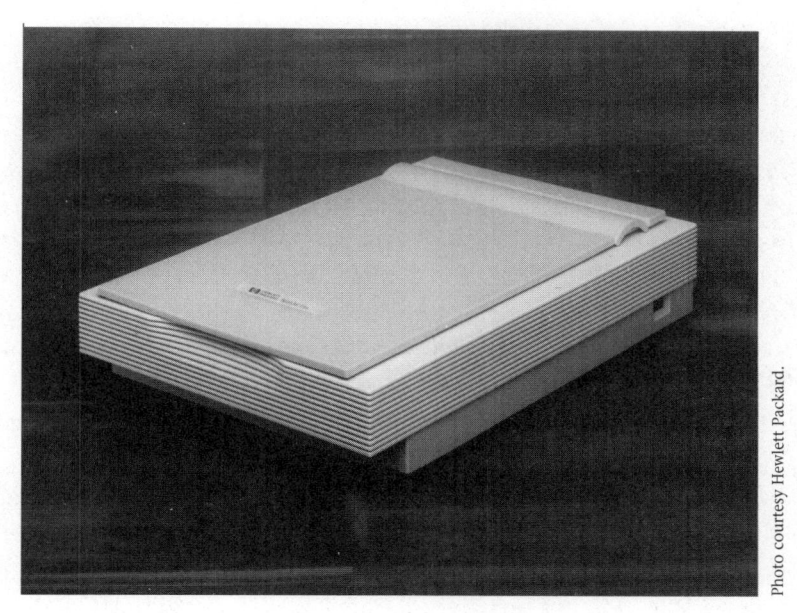

Photo courtesy Hewlett Packard.

Fig. 6.9
Scanners are an essential tool for graphics processing. The HP ScanJet IIc, pictured here, is a premiere flatbed, full-color scanner.

CorelDRAW!

CorelDRAW! 5 is a premiere PC graphics package that endeavors to provide you with the ultimate all-in-one graphics package. CorelDRAW! 5 is complete with powerful, yet easy-to-use drawing, charting, painting, and presentation tools. Included are the following applications:

- *CorelDRAW!*. This vector-based drawing program has extensive text handling and precision drawing features that make it an ideal tool for virtually any design project—from logos and product packaging to technical illustrations and advertisements.

- *Corel VENTURA!*. A full-featured page layout and document composition system, CorelVENTURA! enables you to create typeset documents by combining text and graphics from many popular word processor and graphics programs.

II

Multimedia Components

- *CorelPHOTO-PAINT!*. This powerful paint and photo retouching application features numerous image enhancing filters for improving the quality of scanned images, and special effects filters that can dramatically alter the appearance of your images.

- *CorelCHART!*. This is a charting program for building charts and graphs of all types—from simple bar and pie graphs to 3D area and pictographs. You can enter chart data from scratch into the program's Data Manager, or import files from several popular spreadsheet and database programs.

- *CorelMOVE!*. This animation program enables you to create both simple and complex animations. Used on their own or in CorelSHOW!, animations you create in CorelMOVE! can turn a dull presentation into a spectacular event.

- *CorelTRACE!*. This program converts bitmap images into vector graphic images.

- *CorelMOSAIC!*. CorelMOSAIC! enables you to view entire subdirectories of images on-screen before opening one. You can use it to store images in compressed libraries and perform batch operations such as printing and exporting on groups of files.

- *CorelSHOW!*. This program enables you to assemble printed or on-screen presentations using objects from CorelDRAW!, CorelCHART!, CorelPHOTO-PAINT!, CorelMOVE!, and other programs that support Windows OLE.

- *CorelQUERY!*. This is a data query facility that enables you to gather information from various data sources, such as spreadsheets and databases, and combine the information into tables you can sort, search, and link to other applications and print.

- *Ares FontMinder*. This font management program has a drag-and-drop interface that makes organizing and managing your font library a simple task. FontMinder also improves Windows and application start-up times.

- *TagWrite*. An autotagging application, TagWrite can modify "tags" or "codes" and deals with such elements as the structure, format, and content of your file. TagWrite can be configured to support almost any coding system, including Standard Generalized Markup Language (SGML).

Corel also offers professional photo CD-ROM titles. The photos are provided via Kodak PhotoCDs. Each title contains 100 royalty free photographs. Although they are purchased separately, a limited edition sampler was provided with the release I have (CorelDRAW! 5). For more information, contact Corel Corporation, Salinas, California.

Although CorelMOVE! performs animation, it does not replace a 3D animation software application.

Calgari trueSpace 3D Animation

With trueSpace, you can design 3D objects with many different tools, apply colors and textures to their surfaces, and render them as solid objects with millions of colors. You also can animate objects by moving them along paths that you draw, rotating and scaling them, and shaping them like putty. You can maneuver efficiently through the program's interface, quickly accomplishing your modeling, rendering, and animation goals without having to stop to wonder if you performed specific tasks. (See the section, "Real Animation," near the beginning of this chapter.) For more information, contact Calgari Corporation, Mountain View, California.

IconAuthor: The Best For Last

IconAuthor is an authoring tool used to create interactive multimedia applications that combine text, graphics, animation, full-motion video, and audio. You can use it to create any kind of multimedia application. IconAuthor is well-suited for computer-based training courses, self-service terminals, interactive desktop presentations, and point-of-sale systems. IconAuthor's intuitive graphical interface enables you to instruct a computer to perform tasks that previously required the expertise of a trained computer programmer. Almost anyone can learn to create exciting, appealing, and informative applications with IconAuthor.

IconAuthor uses *icons* (small pictures) to represent the flowchart or structure of an application. The application development process is completed when "content" is added to each of the icons in the structure through a series of user-friendly dialog boxes. IconAuthor comes with the following major components:

- An authoring system used to author an application
- A presentation system used to run the applications that you create with the authoring system
- The SmartObject Editor for all your object-oriented, text editing needs
- IAScope, a utility program designed to help you visually debug your IconAuthor applications
- A graphics editor that enables you to create colorful graphics to be used as still images or images in motion
- IconAnimage, an animation editor that enables you to build scripts to display your graphics in motion
- A video editor that enables you to preview analog and digital video that you plan to include in your applications
- RezSolution, a graphics utility that enables you to change the resolution of your bitmap graphics to accommodate different systems in which your applications can be used
- The Resource Manager, a utility that enables you to organize and distribute your IconAuthor applications

Choosing the Right Equipment

Choosing the right video hardware platform makes upgrading your PC to multimedia much more enjoyable. The end results will meet your expectations.

This requires a little homework, however. You need to understand your needs and then select hardware and software based upon your needs. You also must upgrade in a balanced, methodical order. Individual components should all operate at compatible levels of performance and capacity. This is especially true with video cards and monitors. First, you must select a video card that meets your processing needs. Second, purchase a monitor that meets or exceeds the capacity of the video card.

How you will use multimedia determines the level of hardware and software required. If you are simply using multimedia in a playback mode, the requirements are not as stringent. Conversely, if you are going to create multimedia titles and presentations, then you need the right combination of hardware and software that results in a professional quality presentation.

A balanced suite of software applications provides the necessary tools to get the most out of your hardware and produce the best results. Of key concern is compatibility among the software you're using; specifically, you want to ensure the capability to import and export compatible files. This is especially true with authoring software.

Authoring software encapsulates the world of multimedia into a single package. Make sure that all your mediums (video, audio, animation, still images, MIDI compositions, and so on) can be brought into your authoring application. Otherwise, it will be like trying to write a book without words.

Now you should be ready to purchase multimedia hardware and software and upgrade your PC. The final part of this book provides guidance in a reference format. A word of caution—once you start, it's hard to stop. Enjoy!

From Here...

The following chapters provide more information on video equipment:

- Chapter 7, "Buying Advice," presents a complete rundown on what to look for when upgrading to multimedia.

- Chapter 11, "Buyer's Guide to Video," presents specific information about purchasing video equipment.

Part III

Investing in Multimedia

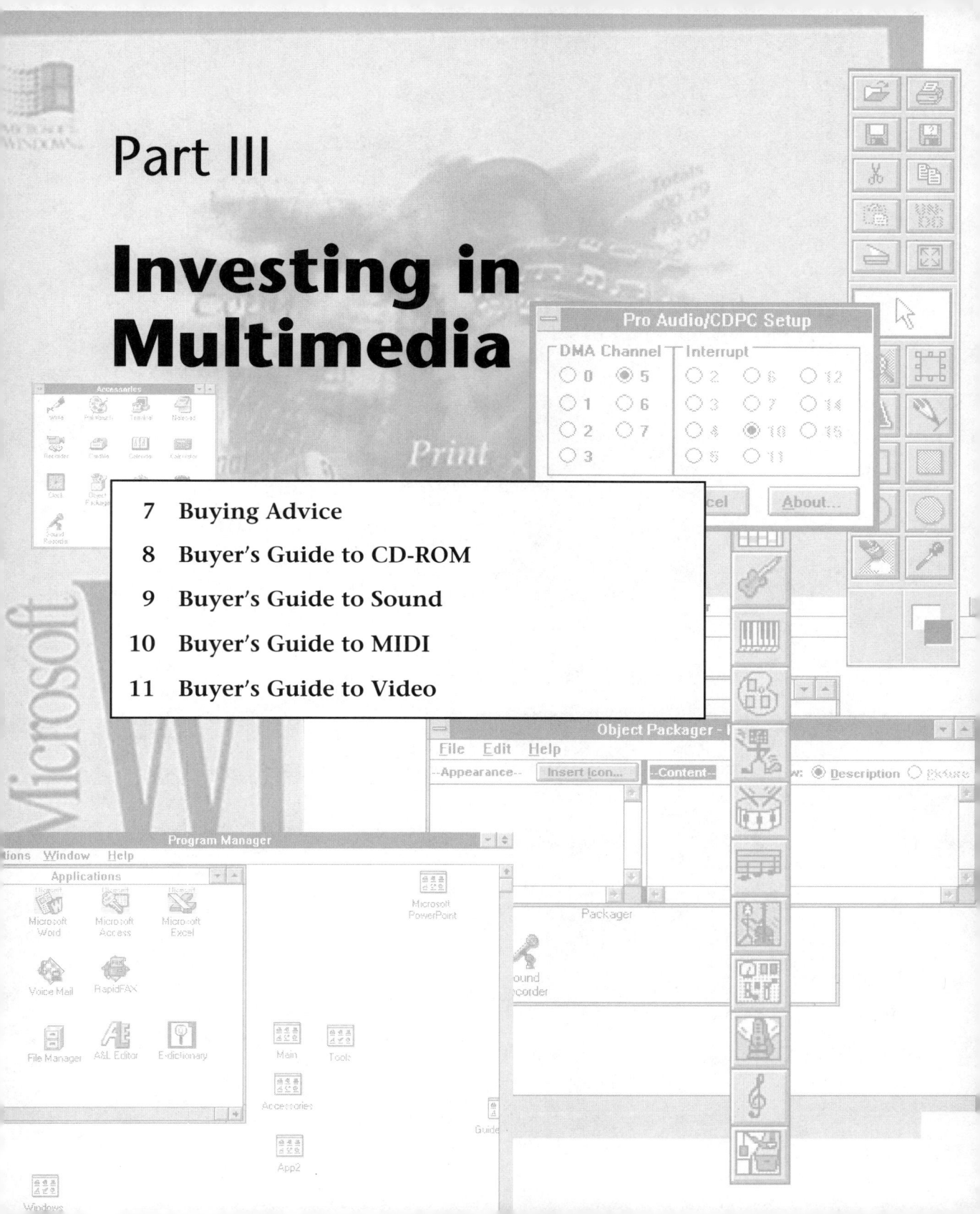

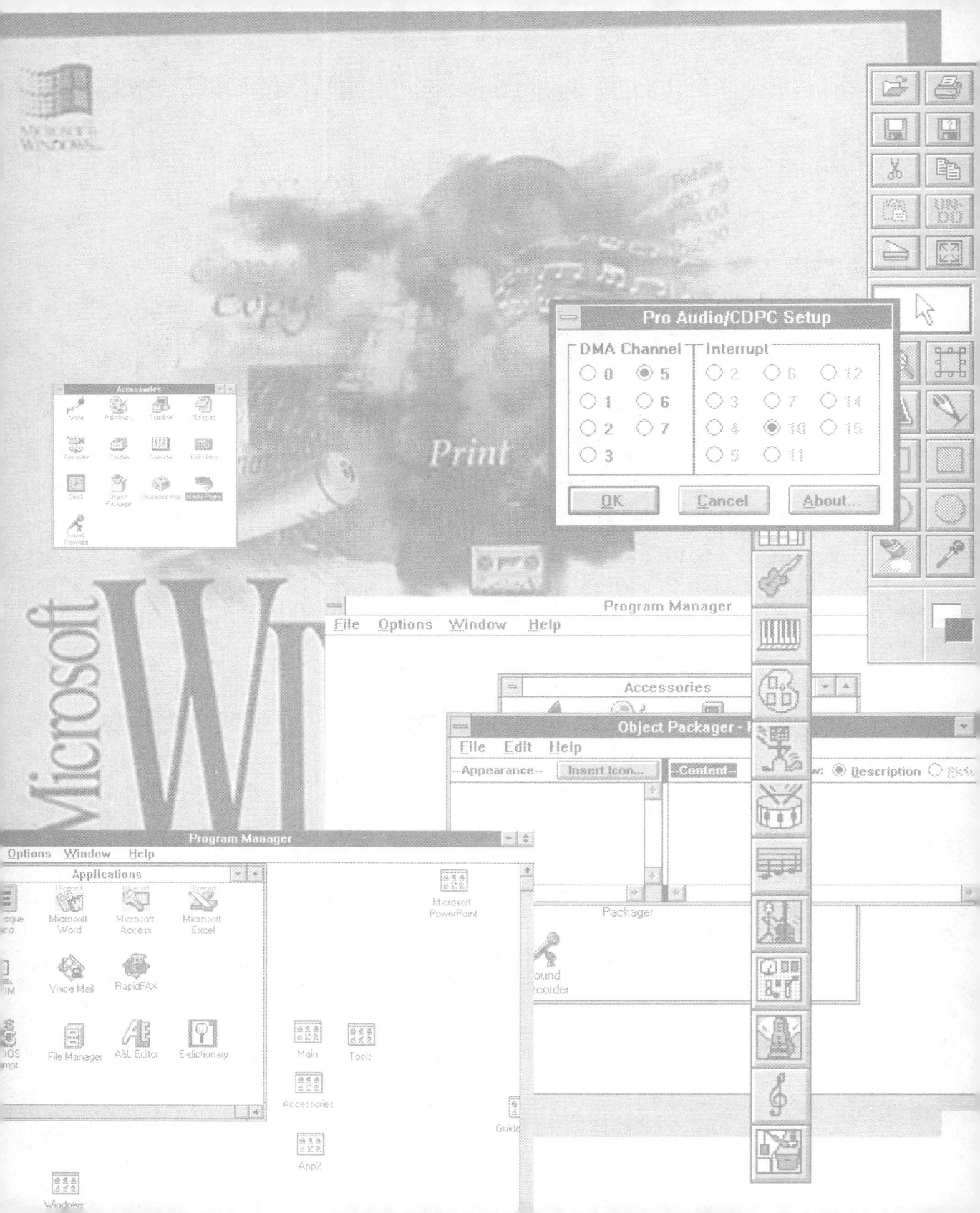

Chapter 7

Buying Advice

The multimedia upgrade. Few things strike terror in the hearts of computer users more than the thought of undergoing a multimedia upgrade well-known for hair-pulling installation procedures. But adding multimedia capabilities is one of the most important upgrades you'll ever make, because it opens your computer to the new world of video, sound, and diverse multimedia software.

The previous chapters have highlighted the various components of multimedia: CD-ROM drives, sound cards, MIDI components and video hardware. From this foundation, you can proceed to develop your own multimedia PC (MPC).

You should have a strategy when upgrading your PC. It's not a matter of getting your PC to "do multimedia." Like traveling, you can elect to take a bus, car, plane, or subway. You may even decide to walk. What's the difference? It all depends on how far you have to go, how much money you wish to spend, and how quickly you want to get there. For example, you could purchase a sound card that lacks MIDI capabilities, but only if you know you won't be needing those capabilities later. Or you could buy a triple-speed CD-ROM drive if you know you'll later need the perkier performance.

Multimedia Upgrade Kits

If you need both a CD-ROM drive and a sound card, consider a multimedia upgrade kit (see fig. 7.1). These bundled kits add multimedia capabilities to 80386- and 80486-based microcomputers. (Of course, you need an 80486SX PC to be a true MPC.)

> **Tip**
>
> A multimedia upgrade kit can save you money by bundling everything you need to turn your PC into a multimedia system.

Upgrade kits include at least a sound card and CD-ROM drive. Many also include a microphone, headphone, speakers, MIDI software, CD-ROM titles, CD-ROM interface cord, and software applications. A few even include options for expanded MIDI tone generators and video support.

Multimedia upgrade kits provide one-stop upgrade solutions. Buying a kit instead of purchasing a CD-ROM and sound card separately ensures that each component is well-matched. Also, kits give you the extras you need—cables, integrated installation software, and often extensive bonus CD-ROM libraries. Best of all, quality multimedia kits are now available for less than $500, giving you a much better value than if you were to buy the components separately.

Before buying a multimedia kit, make sure your PC can handle the upgrade. As a bare minimum, your PC needs to have one empty ISA expansion slot, a vacant drive bay, the necessary mounting rails, and free power connectors for powering the CD-ROM drive.

> **Tip**
>
> Ensure that your PC has extra power cables to operate a CD-ROM drive and an expansion slot to accommodate the sound card.

The Multimedia PC Marketing Council, formed in 1991 to set PC standards for the multimedia industry, stipulates the minimum system requirements for a PC to be equipped for multimedia. A manufacturer may license the use of the MPC logo on its products, indicating adherence to these standards. Some upgrade kits are compliant with the original MPC Level One (MPC-1) specification, although most support the updated Level Two (MPC-2) specification. The MPC trademark now signifies tested compliance with the specifications, and can be found on the packaging of many upgrade kits.

Most games and CD-ROM titles are written for MPC-1 machines, but many hardware components are now made in accordance with MPC-2 specs. You should buy an MPC-2 compliant kit because within one to two years, virtually all software releases will require the enhanced performance MPC-2.

Pros and cons for buying a multimedia upgrade kit are listed in table 7.1.

Table 7.1   Pros and Cons of Upgrading to Multimedia

Pros

- You get all your multimedia equipment in one purchase
- The components are selected to work well together
- You receive complete installation instructions
- You receive several CD-ROM titles provided at minimal cost

Cons

- You may be distracted by the number of included CD-ROM titles
- The overall quality of the individual components, such as speakers, may be of average quality
- You can't customize your multimedia system to your individual needs

CD-ROM Drive in Kits

The CD-ROM drives included with most multimedia kits are typically lackluster. They usually have the MPC-recommended 64K buffer, which perks up access. However, an exemplary drive may include a 256K cache. Most drives' data transfer rates hover around 300 Kbps, although some may exceed this. Some high-end upgrade kits may include triple-speed and quadruple-speed drives. At such speeds, data transfer rates will be at 450 Kbps and 600 Kbps, respectively.

Tip

A 256K cache in a CD-ROM drive is one feature to look for in an upgrade kit's drive.

Note

Many upgrade kit vendors who list their "own" CD-ROM drives are actually repackaging units manufactured by others. Try to find out who really makes the CD-ROM drive. Then, you can discover the strengths and weaknesses of that particular drive.

Sound Cards in Kits

When evaluating the sound card in a kit, consider the *sampling resolution*. This indicates the largest sound samples the sound card can play back. Most existing CD-ROM titles and games use 8-bit samples, but newer releases support enhanced 16-bit sounds.

Since most DOS games and CD-ROM titles were designed to be SoundBlaster compatible, you should ensure your kit's sound card supports this.

Many upgrade kits bundle software packages for MIDI sequencing, sampling, and recording. To clarify your MIDI hardware options, double-check with the sound card manufacturer or your local retailer.

Tip

If you intend to do MIDI music, look for a kit's sound card to include wavetable synthesis or an upgrade path to it.

Most kit sound cards do not offer wavetable MIDI support. However, some multimedia kits offer a wavetable upgrade path.

In terms of the bundled speakers, the single most important factor in audio performance is to try to audition your kit's speakers. Adjust the bass and treble controls to check the tonal response. Also, turn up the volume to see at what level the sound becomes

III

Investing in Multimedia

distorted. Buying a speaker is an individual affair; find one that sounds "good" to you. One popular model found in multimedia upgrade kits is the Labtec CS-550 speakers.

> **Note**
>
> Some multimedia upgrade kits use a sound card that has a CD-ROM interface. By using this interface, the kits require only one expansion slot instead of two—an advantage if you are short on slots.

Bundled Extras

Some kits offer additional equipment such as speakers, microphones, headphones, or joysticks. You will find that speakers are included as an extra quite often, while other kits rarely include joysticks or a microphone.

> **Note**
>
> Most multimedia upgrade kits use inexpensive speakers, joysticks, and other accessories. Add the standalone prices of the individual components in a kit before making your decision. You may be better off buying separate components that are of better quality than accepting the bundled accessories.

Often, several CD-ROM titles are included with a kit as an added bonus. The titles included with a particular kit often change frequently. By getting CD-ROM titles with your kit, you can save a considerable amount of money compared to buying the titles after the fact. However, be sure to evaluate the components in these kits one by one. Don't let anyone slip you a slow CD player by enticing you with good CD-ROM discs.

> **Tip**
>
> Don't be distracted by a plethora of CD-ROM titles. Instead, consider kits that have the titles you want or think you will use.

Easier to Install?

Typically, piecing together a multimedia system may force you to spend spare hours rummaging through boxes and manuals. You may find yourself adjusting IRQ (interrupt request) settings and racking up time on tech-support calls. However, the multimedia upgrade kit reduces these problems. Installation is often easier, although installation procedures and policies differ from kit to kit.

> **Note**
>
> Some multimedia kits even include an instructional video tape. The Reveal Multimedia FX-04 kit includes a 15-minute video, which addresses many commonly asked questions.

Still, a multimedia upgrade kit can be a challenge to install, especially if your PC already has several cards in use. The basic problem is that your PC's system resources (IRQs, memory and port addresses, and DMAs) may already be assigned to other peripherals. Be sure to set aside a block of uninterrupted time to perform your upgrade.

> **Note**
>
> See Chapter 3, "Adding a CD-ROM Drive," for information on upgrading to a CD-ROM drive and Chapter 4, "Adding Sound to Your System," for information on upgrading to a sound card.

Selecting the Right Kit

Deciding which kit is the best value for you depends on what type of multimedia functions you intend to perform. If you plan to work primarily with data CD-ROMs, such as phone directories or maps, then consider a kit with a speedy CD-ROM drive.

If you intend to get involved with MIDI, then consider a sound card that has wavetable MIDI or at least a wavetable upgrade path. Similarly, try to get a kit with good speakers.

If you don't want to invest in CD-ROM titles, try to find a kit that has the types of titles in which you are interested. For example, if you like computer games, you may be interested in those kits that offer Doom, Stellar 7 and ChessMaster on CD disc. If you are concerned about having educational materials available to yourself or your children, look for those kits that bundle encyclopedias and atlases. Don't be misled by a kit that includes several titles. You may find that all those titles may simply collect dust in a corner or consume several megabytes of valuable disk space. Instead, consider kits that include titles you will actually use.

Avoiding Trouble

Even if you follow your multimedia upgrade kit's instructions to the letter, you still may run into trouble. Here are some common multimedia installation problems and tips on solving them.

The most common problem for multimedia devices is that they fight with other devices installed in your PC. You may notice your sound card or CD-ROM simply doesn't work or cannot be found by your software, the sound card repeats the same sounds over and over, or it causes your PC to freeze in Windows or DOS. This situation is called a *device*, or *hardware, conflict*. What are they fighting over? The same signal lines or channels used for talking to your PC. Even though your kit's installation software can scan your system for available resources, it can only advise you of hardware conflicts, not eliminate them.

III

Investing in Multimedia

You might have to reset some jumpers on your cards to get them to work.

The sources of conflict are threefold:

- *Interrupt requests (IRQs)*. IRQs are used to "interrupt" your PC and get its attention.

- *Direct memory access (DMA) channels*. DMA channels are a way to move information directly to your PC's memory, bypassing your PC's central brain. DMA channels allow sound to play while your PC is doing other work.

- *Input/output (I/O) addresses*. An I/O address in your PC is used to channel information between your sound card and your PC. Usually the address mentioned in a sound card manual is the starting address. Actually, your sound card may require several addresses, which together are called an *address segment*.

Multimedia troubles begin with the weakness of the PC's design. When installing video-capture boards, sound cards, and CD-ROM controller cards, each must be configured manually to avoid these conflicts.

> **Note**
>
> CompUSA reportedly suffers a 25 percent return rate on multimedia products because users just can't install them.

Your potential for problems is doubled or tripled since many sound cards also use an IRQ, DMA and I/O address for the Sound Blaster-compatible or MIDI portions of their cards. For example, the Pro AudioStudio 16 by default uses DMA 5 and IRQ 7 for its "native" mode and DMA 1 and IRQ 5 for Sound Blaster compatibility. Also, you can have separate DMA and IRQ settings when your sound card is used with Microsoft Windows.

Because the industry-standard ISA bus—unlike EISA, MCA, and PCI—does not allow for automatic or software configuration of new cards, often the card's hardware must be reset, forcing users to manipulate tiny jumpers or DIP (dual-inline pin) switches to allocate IRQs, port and memory addresses, and DMA channels. This can translate into hours spent tinkering, calling tech support, and perhaps finally throwing your hands up in despair.

The best way to find your hardware conflict is to locate all of the documentation for your PC and its various devices, such as a tape drive interface card, CD-ROM drive, and so on. How do you find which device is conflicting with your sound card? Temporarily remove all of your expansion cards except your sound card and other essential cards (such as your video card). Then, add each removed card one at a time until your sound card no longer works. The last card you added was the troublemaker.

> **Note**
>
> Hardware conflicts may become an anachronism with the new Plug and Play (PNP) specification from a consortium led by Compaq, Intel, Microsoft, and BIOS-maker Phoenix. As its name implies, PNP's purpose is to make sure installing a new card is simply a matter of plugging it in and at most loading a device driver.

Here are some other problems you might encounter:

- *No audio.* If you don't get any audio at all, check to see that power, data, and audio cables are seated properly, and the data cable between the sound card and CD-ROM drive is seated with pin 1 aligned between the cable and the two connectors. Pin 1 is colored on one side of the cable and marked by an arrow or 1 on the board and the drive. Also check that the audio cable between the CD-ROM drive and the sound board is connected. Finally, verify that the speakers are connected to the output, not input, jack of the sound board.

- *Can't play an audio CD.* Most likely, Windows' CD Audio driver is not installed. Use the Control Panel to add this driver. Afterward, make sure you exit Windows or reboot so that the new driver changes are recognized.

- *Volume too loud or soft.* If there is a volume control on the back of the sound board, rotate it halfway between minimum and maximum volume. On many sound cards, maximum and minimum volume positions aren't marked—setting the control to the halfway point ensures that at least some output is occurring. Then use controls on the DOS or Windows mixer utility to raise volume levels for CD-audio, WAV, or MIDI playback. If output still isn't loud enough, adjust the control to maximum gain.

- *No audio in recording.* Make sure that the Play/Record button or similar control in your recording utility is set to Record, not Play. Conversely, make sure your audio source (CD-ROM, line-in, or microphone) is set to Play, not Record.

- *Memory problems with DOS applications.* Because your CD-ROM's drivers are loaded when your system boots, you might find the driver constrains your system's conventional memory. In this case, create an edited version of your AUTOEXEC.BAT and CONFIG.SYS start-up files with all references to CD-ROM and sound card drivers disabled. Then create a batch file that swaps normal and edited configuration files to your root directory. You also can use DOS 6.0's boot menu abilities to load only certain lines of your CONFIG.SYS and AUTOEXEC.BAT.

Selected Multimedia Kits

Several computer resellers offer "multimedia upgrade kits," which are often just a combination of CD-ROM drive, sound card, and speakers thrown together. Tables 7.2 through 7.8 list a few true multimedia upgrade kits.

> **Note**
>
> The prices and configurations of multimedia kits change frequently. Call your local retail store or mail-order company for up-to-date information before making a buying decision. You can also call the manufacturers listed later to find out if their kits' retail prices have dropped; the reductions eventually are passed onto the buyer.

Often, multimedia kits from the same manufacturer vary little. The primary differences may be the number of CD-ROM titles that are included in the kit. Sometimes, one kit may be targeted more for computer game players or students. For example, a game-oriented kit, such as Creative Labs' Game Blaster 16 CD, may include a joystick and game titles.

> **Note**
>
> One rule of thumb is that the more titles included in a kit, the more likely the CD-ROM drive or sound card component is less than adequate. (Manufacturers hope to gloss over any deficiencies by including some sizzling titles.)

Table 7.2   Aztech Labs Inc. Products

Maker	Aztech Labs Inc.		
Kit Name	Sound Galaxy Asteroid Multimedia Kit	Sound Galaxy Voyager Multimedia Kit	Sound Galaxy Explorer Multimedia Kit
List Price	$349	$399	$499
Sound Card Model 16-bit	Sound Galaxy Nova 16	Sound Galaxy Nova 16	Sound Galaxy Pro 16L
CD-ROM Drive	CDA 268-01A double-speed	CDA 268-01A double-speed	External CD-ROM drive
Data Transfer Rate	340 Kbps	340 Kbps	340 Kbps
Access Speed	380 ms	380 ms	380 ms
Buffer	64K	64K	64K
Caddy Required	No	No	No
Supplied Speakers	Amplified stereo	Amplified stereo	Amplified stereo
Microphone	Yes	Yes	Yes
# of CD-ROM Titles	4	7	10
Warranty	1 year	1 year	1 year

Aztech Labs Inc.
46707 Fremont Blvd.
Fremont, CA 94538
800-886-8779 or 510-623-8988
Fax: 510-623-8989

Table 7.3   Apple Computer Inc. Products

Maker	Apple Computer Inc.
Kit Name	CD Multimedia Kit for PCs
List Price	$600-$700
Sound Card Model	Media Vision Pro Audio 16
CD-ROM Drive	Apple Macintosh AppleCD 300i double-speed
Data Transfer Rate	300 Kbps
Access Speed	295 ms
Buffer	256K
Caddy Required	No
Supplied Speakers	AppleDesign Powered Speakers
Microphone	No
# of CD-ROM Titles	6
Warranty	1 year

Apple Computer Inc.
20525 Mariani Ave.
Cupertino, CA 95014-6299
800-776-2333; 408-996-1010
FAX: 408-996-0275
Tech support: 800-767-2775
Tech support BBS: 800-877-8221

Table 7.4   Cardinal Technologies Inc. Products

Maker	Cardinal Technologies Inc.
Kit Name	Cardinal Sensory System I
List Price	$599
Sound Card Model	Digital Sound Pro 16
CD-ROM Drive	Sony CDU33A double-speed
Data Transfer Rate	300 Kbps
Access Speed	370 ms
Buffer	256K
Caddy Required	No
Supplied Speakers	Labtec CS-150
Microphone	No
# of CD-ROM Titles	6
Warranty	1 year

III

Investing in Multimedia

Cardinal Technologies Inc.
1827 Freedom Rd.
Lancaster, PA 17601
717-293-3000
Direct sales: 717-293-3049
FAX: 717-293-3055
Tech support: 717-293-3124
Tech support BBS: 717-293-3074

Table 7.5 Creative Labs Inc. Products

Maker	Creative Labs Inc.	
Kit Name	Game Blaster CD 16	Discovery CD 16
List Price	$549	$549
Sound Card Model	Sound Blaster 16	Sound Blaster 16
CD-ROM Drive	Panasonic double-speed	Panasonic double-speed
Data Transfer Rate	300 Kbps	300 Kbps
Access Speed	320 ms	320 ms
Buffer	64K	64K
Caddy Required	No	No
Supplied Speakers	Creative Labs CT-38	Labtec CS550
Microphone	No	Yes
Joystick	Yes	No
# of CD-ROM Titles	9	5
Warranty	1 year	1 year

Table 7.6 Media Vision Inc. Products

Maker	Media Vision Inc.	
Kit Name	Family Deluxe Multimedia Kit	Super Deluxe Multimedia Kit
List Price	$399	$499
Sound Card Model	Pro AudioSpectrum 16	Pro AudioSpectrum 16
CD-ROM Drive	Sanyo CDRH93MV	Sanyo CDRH93MV
Data Transfer Rate	306 Kbps	306 Kbps
Access Speed	320 ms	320 ms
Buffer	64K	64K
Caddy Required	No	No
Supplied Speakers	Labtec CS550	Labtec CS550
Microphone	No	Yes
Joystick	Yes	Yes
# of CD-ROM Titles	9	15
Warranty	3 year	3 year

Creative Labs Inc. (subsidiary of Creative Technology, Ltd.)
1901 McCarthy Blvd.
Milpitas, CA 95035
800-998-1000; 408-428-6600
Direct sales: 800-998-5227
FAX: 408-428-6611
Tech support: 405-742-6622
Tech support BBS: 405-742-6660

Edutainment CD 16	Digital Edge 3X
$599	$995
Sound Blaster 16	Sound Blaster 16
Panasonic double-speed	NEC triple-speed
300 Kbps	450 Kbps
320 ms	195 ms
64K	256K
No	Yes
Creative Labs CT-38	Creative Labs CT-38
Yes	Yes
No	No
9	19
1 year	1 year

Premium Deluxe Multimedia Kit for PC	Pro Deluxe Multimedia Kit	Memphis Multimedia System
$599	$799	$899
Premium 3D	Premium 3D	Pro AudioSpectrum 16
Reno Portable CD-ROM player	NEC 510	OEM
306 Kbps	450 Kbps	306 Kbps
180 ms	195 ms	320 ms
64K	256K	64K
No	No	No
Labtec CS550	Labtec CS550	Labtec CS550
Yes	Yes	Yes
Yes	Yes	Yes
15	15	2
3 year	3 year	3 year

Media Vision Inc.
47300 Bayside Pkwy.
Fremont, CA 94538
800-348-7116; 510-770-8600
Direct sales: 800-845-5870
FAX: 510-770-9592
Tech support: 800-638-2807
Tech support BBS: 510-770-0527

Table 7.7 MediaMagic Products

Maker	MediaMagic (division of IPC Corp. Ltd.)	
Kit Name	ISP-16 Sound System	MediaMagic DSP-16 Plus Sound
List Price	$429	$829
Sound Card Model	MediaMagic ISP-16 Plus	MediaMagic DSP-16 Plus
CD-ROM Drive	Sony CDU-31A/03	Toshiba XM3401
Data Transfer Rate	300 Kbps	330 Kbps
Access Speed	320 ms	200 ms
Buffer	64K	256K
Caddy Required	No	No
Supplied Speakers	Labtec CS-150	Labtec CS-150
Microphone	No	No
# of CD-ROM Titles	4	4
Warranty	1 year	1 year

Table 7.8 Reveal Computer Products Inc. Products

Maker	Reveal Computer Products Inc.	
Kit Name	MFX01 Explorer	MFX02 Prestige
List Price	$299	$479
Sound Card Model	SoundFX Pro 16	SoundFX Pro 16
CD-ROM Drive	Reveal CDD12	Reveal CDD12
Data Transfer Rate	300 Kbps	300 Kbps
Access Speed	320 ms	320 ms
Buffer	64K	64K
Caddy Required	No	No
Supplied Speakers	RS250 speakers	RS250 speakers
Microphone	Yes	Yes
Joystick	No	No
# of CD-ROM Titles	5	9
Warranty	1 year	1 year

MediaMagic (division of IPC Corp. Ltd.)
10300 Metric Blvd.
Austin, TX 78758-9846
800-624-8654; 512-339-3500
FAX: 512-454-1357

Reveal Computer Products Inc.
6045 Variel Ave.
Woodland Hills, CA 91367
800-326-2222; 818-713-1400
FAX: 818-340-3671

The Multimedia Core

Preconfigured multimedia systems provide an attractive alternative to hard-to-install multimedia upgrade kits, but don't settle for cheap bundled components. Look for a double-speed CD-ROM drive, a 16-bit sound card, and external stereo speakers.

Ensure your sound card is compatible with major brands, particularly Creative Labs' Sound Blaster, so it can use the widest variety of multimedia and game programs. Some MPC computers have speakers built into the case or monitor. Often, these bundled PC speakers produce a questionable quality of sound. It's a better idea to buy a bundled system with external speakers you can replace later, opposed to paying extra cash for a custom case with built-in speakers, which are usually the same cheap speakers in a more expensive setting.

MFX04 Ultra	MFX06 Elite	MFX08 Quantum
$599	$699	$799
SoundFX Pro 16	SoundFX Pro 16	SoundFX Wave32
Reveal CDD12	Reveal CDD12	Reveal CDD12
300 Kbps	300 Kbps	300 Kbps
320 ms	320 ms	320 ms
64K	64K	64K
No	No	No
RS250 speakers	RS250 speakers	RS380 speakers
Yes	Yes	Yes
No	Yes	Yes
13	20	37
1 year	1 year	1 year

III

Investing in Multimedia

Service with a Smile

Whatever the components you buy in a new system, be sure to determine what levels of service and support you can expect from the seller. One-year parts and labor warranties are the minimum, with two-, three-, and five-year warranties on the rise.

On-site service policies for the first year, often free but sometimes at a slight extra charge of $35 to $100, are also increasingly common. If on-site help is essential, be sure to get all the details—for example, the provider of the service and the process for activating it. Most consumer protection agencies advise that extended warranties are not worthwhile; instead, rely on the manufacturer's or store's standard warranty and your own good sense to take care of your multimedia system.

Several direct-market firms offer 24-hour, seven-day toll-free technical support by phone, though you may find you are placed on hold or forced to leave your number for a call-back.

> **Note**
>
> If you're concerned about technical support, ask about the sellers' average call-answer times and perhaps even try calling technical support to see how long it takes to get through.

Some vendors offer facsimile support lines where you can fax a description of your problems to receive a faxed or callback answer. Several companies offer automated fax systems for common problems: you call on a touch-tone phone, choose from a voice-mail menu of common system glitches, enter your fax number, and soon receive a fax bulletin covering the problem specified.

For additional help, a company may have its own on-line bulletin board service or user forums on major on-line networks such as CompuServe, Prodigy, and America Online.

Types of Vendors

You could rush out to buy some multimedia components or computers. However, you should do some further research. Besides this book, seek help from computer magazines, which often have reviews of many products. Some good examples are *Computer Shopper*, *PC Magazine*, and *PC World*. These magazines are often on the shelves at bookstores and most grocery store magazine racks.

You also can get help from on-line services, such as the Prodigy service's Computer Club and the many forums on CompuServe and America Online. Thousands of people from across the country use these services to share their experiences about improving their PCs. Locally, you can join a PC users group. Usually, such a group gets together once a month to discuss general questions and to learn in detail some new product from either another member or a company official.

Now that you know what type of multimedia system you need to buy or upgrade, it's time to find a place to buy your system. Multimedia computers and components are available from three major sources:

- Local computer dealers (check your yellow pages)
- Large chain or wholesale stores
- Mail-order vendors

With so many different places to buy a PC, how do you decide where to go? You need to evaluate three criteria:

- *Price.* How much is the MPC or multimedia upgrade kit going to cost, including shipping, taxes and any other charges?
- *Service.* What happens if something breaks? Besides backing up a warranty, will the vendor answer your questions about how to use the multimedia system?
- *Support.* What happens when you need help or don't understand how to use something?

You'll need to judge how each computer vendor stacks up in these three areas before you buy. The right mix of price, service, and support can greatly reduce your frustration.

Local Computer Dealers

Look for local computer dealers in your phone book, typically under "Computers, Dealers." Some bigger names include computer superstores CompUSA and Computer City. You also can get some rudimentary help from the salespeople at PC stores like Egghead Software and Software Etc.

Typically, computer dealers offer fair prices. They usually have better trained sales, service and support staff. Also, it is much easier to get your multimedia system serviced by a local store than elsewhere. Computer dealers often specialize in several applications. If multimedia is one of them, you've found your multimedia source.

Large Chain or Wholesale Stores

Mass market and wholesale stores usually have pricing that's competitive with mail-order vendors. One benefit of such stores is that you can see, touch, and test the merchandise before you buy.

These stores typically rely on third-party service companies to provide warranty service, or they make you ship your PC back to the manufacturer for service. Shipping an MPC is expensive and the delays can be interminable. You get little support from a large store. Often, the staff may be no more knowledgeable than yourself.

Mail-Order Mania

Buying by mail is attractive—if you know what you want. Mail-order firms have the best prices available because they don't have to invest in the overhead of a storefront.

III

Investing in Multimedia

Mail-order companies often provide 30-day money-back guarantees (except on software). If price is your hot button, look no further.

Mail-order firms have had to work hard to earn trust serving customers from afar. Some mail-order companies rely on many of the same third-party service providers as mass merchant stores. Again, this service is only as good as the local service firm. Support at mail-order companies varies widely. Some companies are willing to answer questions. Others may not support anything, shuffling you off to the manufacturer.

When buying by mail, don't spend a lot of time paging through every magazine or even the 900 pages of *Computer Shopper*. Rather, jot down the prices of about five vendors. Statistically, the lowest price in that list is probably in the ballpark. *Computer Shopper*, by the way, has a wonderful advertiser index of mail-order computer products. They even have a section that lists multimedia add-on kits, listed by manufacturer.

If you do buy by mail, make sure you definitely want what you are ordering. If you return opened merchandise, you may be hit with a 10 to 20 percent "restocking" fee. Also, watch out for exorbitant shipping and handling fees. You should avoid companies that tack on a surcharge when you use a major credit card.

> **Note**
>
> When buying by mail, use a major credit card. This provides an important protection because a buyer can go to the credit card company and dispute the charge if the product is unsatisfactory or the company goes out of business. Avoid companies that do not accept credit cards or that charge the card before shipping the purchase.

From Here...

In the next four chapters, you will examine some buying criteria and specific products.

- Chapter 8, "Buyer's Guide to CD-ROM," recommends CD-ROM drives, accessories, and some CD-ROM titles.

- Chapter 9, "Buyer's Guide to Sound," lists sound cards and the software that makes the most of them.

- Chapter 10, "Buyer's Guide to MIDI," lists criteria for purchasing a MIDI system, including keyboard synthesizers and related software.

- Chapter 11, "Buyer's Guide to Video," describes video and video capture/playback cards that allow you to build and present a top-notch multimedia show.

Chapter 8

Buyer's Guide to CD-ROM

The real "information highway" is not some seemingly distant Internet you may never access (or care to access). Instead, the information revolution is under your nose and your computer's hood.

The *CD-ROM* (compact-disc, read-only memory) drive provides a way to distribute hundreds of megabytes (666M, to be exact) of information on a small 4.75-inch silver disc. This chapter describes information needed to purchase the correct CD-ROM for your system.

The CD-ROM is no longer read-only. With a CD-Recordable (CD-R) drive, you can "press" your own CD-ROM discs. Fill a single blank disc with more than 600M of data, hand it over to Federal Express, and you can absolutely positively bring a regional office up-to-date overnight—for less than $20. No other optical or magnetic storage system is as cost-effective, and it would take 12 hours to send that much information over a standard phone line.

Buying Criteria

Unless you missed the multimedia revolution, you already know that you need a CD-ROM drive. How else can you get massive libraries of data on a single disk, as well as vast clip collections of stereo sound, high-color graphics, full-motion video—and great games?

But what do you need in a CD-ROM drive for your multimedia system? A drive that meets the following Multimedia PC Marketing Council Level Two specifications is a good start:

- Capable of sustaining a data transfer rate of 300K per second, while claiming no more than 60 percent of your PC's attention

- Capable of 150K per second data transfer rate requiring no more than 40 percent of your PC's attention

- An average seek time of 400 milliseconds (ms) or less

- Capable of reading multisession and Kodak Photo CD discs
- Upgradable to CD-ROM XA
- A recommended buffer of 64K

Selected Models

CD-ROM drives are the heart of any multimedia PC, so researching your purchase is a smart investment. The end of this section lists contact information for each manufacturer and provides a comparison table.

Note

Like multimedia kits, the prices and configurations of CD-ROM drives change (that is, drop or become discontinued) frequently. Call for up-to-date information before buying.

Internal and External Drives

The most popular CD-ROM drive configuration is internal. Unless you need to share a CD-ROM drive between computers or have no room for an internal drive, an internal model is ideal.

Tip

An internal CD-ROM drive also can be shared by users on a computer network. For example, Windows for Workgroups 3.11 allows you to share a CD-ROM drive among users.

NEC MultiSpin 74-1 and MultiSpin 84-1. NEC Technologies' MultiSpin CDR-84 provides a good value for a double-speed drive (300Kps). It supports SCSI or SCSI-2 interfaces and includes a 256K cache and an average access speed of 280 ms.

The MultiSpin 84 features a motorized eject button, and an inward-swinging door protects the mechanism from dust and debris. The drive also includes a second, outward-swinging door, presumably for extra protection, but the stiff spring makes it a challenge to insert a caddy with one hand.

NEC MultiSpin 3Xi. NEC's MultiSpin 3Xi is a triple-speed internal drive with a blazing access time of 195 ms. At the time of this writing, the 3Xi provides the best balance of performance versus price.

This drive, like most NEC drives, does not include an interface kit, which can cost between $60 and $150. If you do not purchase NEC's $125 ISA host adapter ($150 for the

MCA model), you may have to purchase a separate cable to attach the 3Xe to a SCSI adapter. The 3Xi can read all standard CD-ROM disks, including multisession Kodak Photo CDs and CD-ROM XA disks. New design features include a rotating external door for switching disks and the capability to play standard music CDs without special software.

NEC MultiSpin 4X Pro. NEC Technologies has brought out its MultiSpin 4X Pro, a quadruple-speed CD-ROM drive with an average access time of 180 ms and a data-transfer rate of 600Kps (see fig. 8.1). NEC was the first company to introduce a 4X drive, but was soon followed by other manufacturers, including Panasonic, Philips, Pioneer, and Sony. The 4X Pro is only available in an external model. It is compatible with multisession Photo CDs and is designed to provide smooth full-motion video for developers.

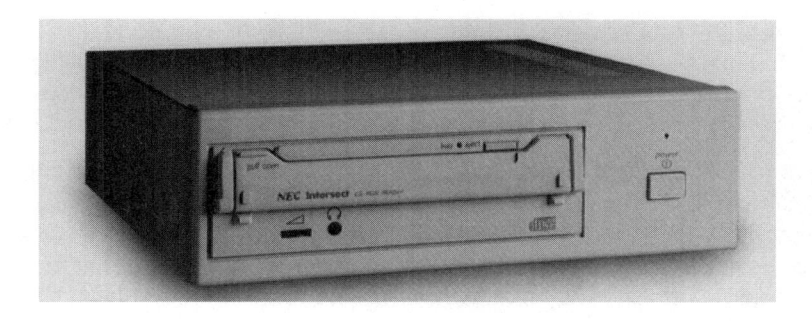

Fig. 8.1
The NEC MultiSpin 4X Pro is one of the fastest CD-ROM drives available.

Surprisingly, the 4X Pro is only a bit faster than the 3Xe in real-world use, despite its faster rotational speed. These external units sport a rotating half-drum dust door and front-mounted miniature headphone jacks and volume controls. The rear panels have pairs of phono stereo-out jacks. Each unit comes with a 16-bit SCSI interface kit using the Trantor SCSI-2 card. Installation is fairly easy.

SONY CDU-7811. SONY Corporation of America's CDU-7811 is available with and without an interface kit. This double-speed drive is a high-end, heavy-duty unit that offers substantial construction, but not necessarily better performance. Despite a 256K cache, its multimedia performance is somewhat poor, suffering from muddy audio and video frame dropping. The drive has a rated data transfer rate of 300Kps and an average access time of 295 ms.

The small case has a volume control, headphone jack, power/busy indicator, and eject button on the front panel. Sony supplies a Future Domain 8-bit SCSI controller, which seems somewhat slow.

Toshiba XM-3401B and TXM-3401E1. Toshiba's XM-3401B CD-ROM internal drive offers solid construction and good ergonomics as well as high-quality audio. The drive's 200-millisecond average seek time is one of the fastest available and is backed up by a 256K cache. The drive finds data quickly, but is slowed down by its double-speed mechanism, which is rated at 330Kps. The 8-bit Future Domain SCSI adapter uses DOS installation software and is fairly easy to set up. The TXM-3401E1 is the external model of this drive.

Pioneer DR-U104X and DR-S104X. Hot on the heels of triple-speed CD-ROM players, the Laser Optical Systems Group of Pioneer New Media Technologies unveiled its DR-U104X, a half-height internal CD-ROM reader running at four times the standard transfer rate (614Kps).

The DR-U104X uses Pioneer's Quadraspin technology, SCSI interface, and a 256K data buffer. It supports multisession Kodak Photo CD and full-motion video. The rated speed is 300 ms, slower than other quadruple-speed drives. The DR-S104X is the external version of the DR-U104X.

Another Pioneer product that uses Quadraspin technology is the DRM-1804X, a SCSI-2 desktop minichanger system that holds 18 CD-ROM disks. It uses three separate six-disk magazines, offering an overall capacity of 12G of data when fully loaded. (See the section, "Jukeboxes: Changers for a Song," later in this chapter for more information.)

Plextor DM-3028 and DM-5028. Plextor's DM-3028 DoubleSpeed Plus CD-ROM drive is a reasonably priced internal drive. It has a 335Kps data transfer rate and an average access time of 240 ms. Although it only has a 64K buffer, its performance is outstanding; video clips play back smoothly, and audio quality is excellent. Unfortunately, the Plextor drives must insert the CD caddy manually—a design Plextor says results in fewer jammed loading mechanisms. A Trantor 16-bit SCSI host adapter and Trantor drivers are bundled. The external model of the DM-3028 is the DM-5028.

TEAC CD-55A Super Quad. Teac Corp.'s TEAC Super Quad is another quadruple-speed CD-ROM drive. TEAC Super Quad drive uses the regular AT IDE interface, and SCSI will be available as well. It provides a 600Kps data transfer rate and a 195-ms seek time. It supports both the multisession Kodak Photo CD format and the CD-ROM XA format.

External (Portable) Drives

You may not need to bring a CD-ROM drive on every business trip you take, but sometimes playing a CD on the road is mission-critical. Some CD-ROM drives plug into a parallel or a PCMCIA port. Can you really take multimedia on the road? The short answer is yes—if you're willing to accept some compromises. A portable CD-ROM drive that uses the parallel port is sluggish. Playing AVI (audio video interleaved) clips from a parallel-port CD-ROM drive, for example, results in choppy video and even audio dropouts. Adding a second device to the parallel port only makes the problem worse.

PCMCIA-based CD-ROM drives skirt some of the problems associated with parallel ports but introduce hassles of their own. You may have troubles getting the PCMCIA card and your external SCSI drive to work. The current state of PCMCIA is best described as converging on a standard rather than actually being a standard. Also, PCMCIA drivers can take up more memory than you might be willing to spare. You may have trouble freeing enough conventional memory to run your CD-ROM application. Still, having a portable CD-ROM drive is better than having no drive at all.

Media Vision Reno Personal CD-ROM Player. Media Vision introduced its Reno Personal CD-ROM player in early 1994 (see fig. 8.2). The drive is so small and light (1.2 pounds) that it can double as a portable audio CD player.

This double-speed drive offers a 306Kps data-transfer rate and an access speed of 180 ms. It supports SCSI-2 and includes a 64K cache. Reno also supports Eastman Kodak's Photo-CD format. It includes an AC adapter and can run on nickel cadmium batteries for about two hours.

> **Note**
>
> The Reno drive may go by another name—the Premium Portable CD-ROM Player.

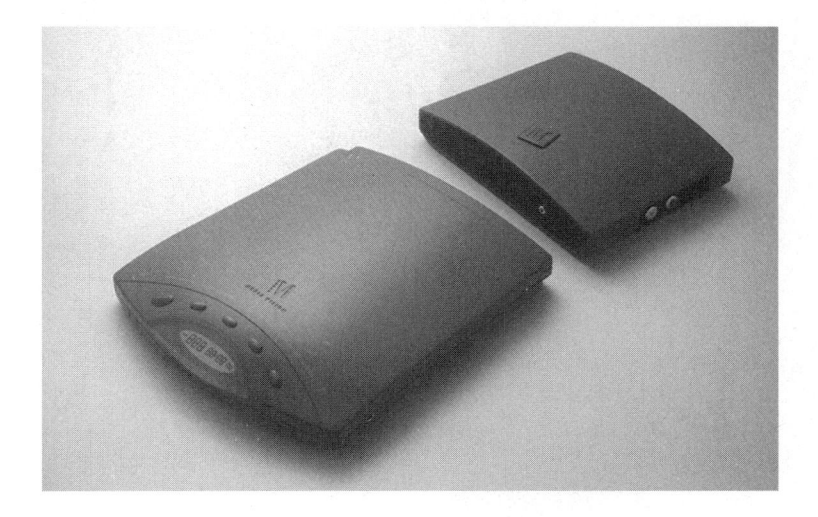

Fig. 8.2
The Reno Personal CD-ROM Player is a portable drive for people on the go.

NEC 3Xp. NEC Technologies Inc.'s 3Xp is a portable external drive (the "p" stands for personal). The 3Xp is small enough to fit in your briefcase. This SCSI/SCSI-2 drive provides triple-speed but a mediocre access time of 250 ms. A 256K cache provides smoother viewing of images and photographs.

CD-Friendly Laptops. Recent advances in laptops make it easier to have CD-ROM drives work with your laptop computer.

Although no one has yet figured out how to fit a 5 1/4-inch CD-ROM drive into a notebook, Toshiba, Texas Instruments, IBM, and others have taken a step toward multimedia portables. Texas Instruments, for example, includes a 16-bit stereo sound chip and stereo output jack in their TravelMate 4000M line of portables.

III

Investing in Multimedia

CD-ROM drives are appearing in *docking stations*. A docking station provides a laptop with a "home base" that provides add-in slots or larger hard drives. Texas Instruments' docking station includes a double-speed CD-ROM drive, built-in speakers, Microsoft headphones, and microphone (see fig. 8.3). IBM's Dock I docking station extends the multimedia capabilities of the popular ThinkPad laptops. The Dock I provides built-in SCSI support, two speakers, one ISA expansion slot, and an empty drive bay that's typically used to house a CD-ROM drive.

Fig. 8.3
The Texas Instruments T4000M series of laptops attach to an optional CD-ROM docking station.

Jukeboxes: Changers for a Song

Do you have too many CD-ROM discs to handle? Pioneer's 6- and 18-disc CD-ROM changers pour multiple silver platters into your PC. Unfortunately, there is only one read mechanism, so you can only access one disc at a time. (It takes about five seconds to switch between discs.)

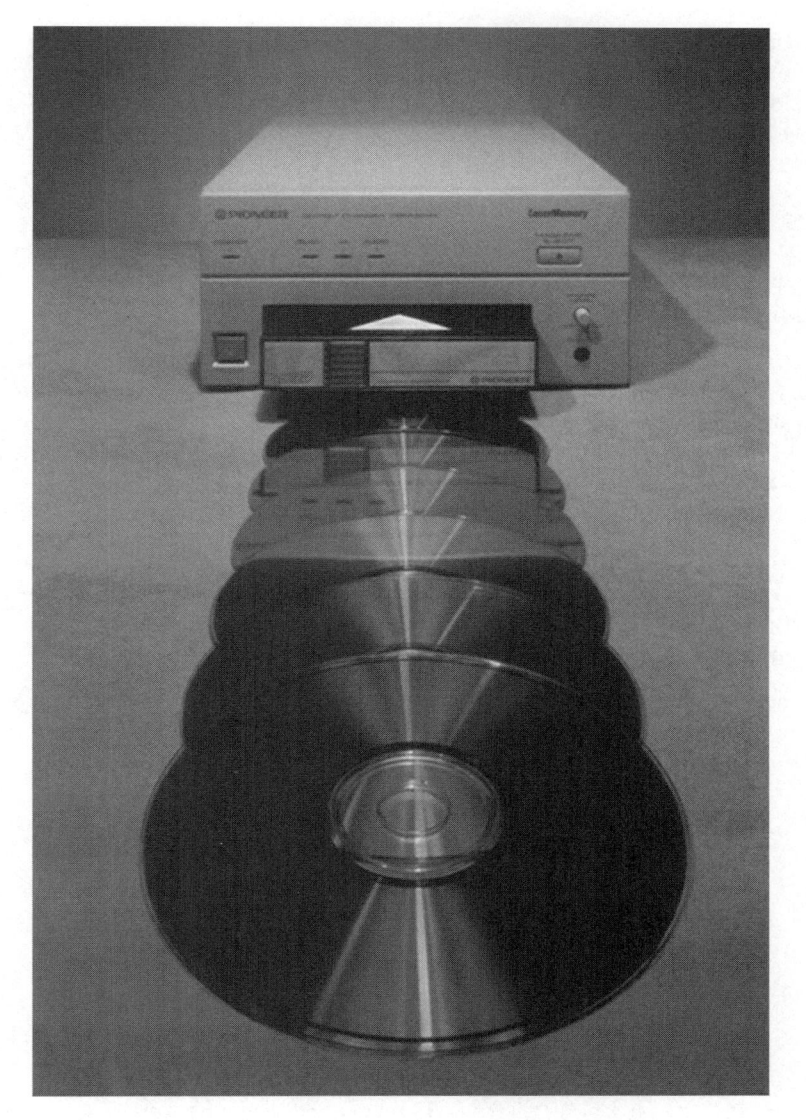

Fig. 8.4
The Pioneer DRM-604X Minichanger enables you to have six CD-ROM discs at your fingertips.

Pioneer New Media Technologies Inc.'s DRM-604X Minichanger (see fig. 8.4) is a quadruple-speed, six-disk CD-ROM player that is SCSI-driven. It features a 128K buffer, 610-Kps data transfer rate, and a 300-ms access time. The six-disk magazine makes changing disks quick and easy and eliminates the need to insert disks separately each time a new one is needed. The DRM-604X is best suited for small offices that use large databases.

The DRM-1804X Minichanger also is a quadruple-speed CD jukebox, but holds 18 discs rather than six. Like the DRM-604X, this drive switches discs quickly, but cannot access two discs simultaneously. The drive's transfer rate is up to 600Kps, twice as fast as typical double-speed drives. The DRM-1804X includes a 256K cache, 610Kps data transfer rate, and a 300-ms access time.

Publishing Your Own CD-ROM

You may be interested in CD publishing. You can put just about anything on a custom CD-ROM, such as a regularly updated product catalog, up-to-the-minute service manual, or a disc full of digitized forms.

Desktop CD-recordable (CD-R) technology is bringing CD-ROM publishing to the masses. Just a few years ago, producing CD-ROMs required the services of a commercial mastering and replication plant, with typical charges of $1,500 to $5,000 for the mastering process and a minimum run of 1,000 CDs at $2 apiece. In 1989, Sony and Yamaha introduced the first desktop CD-recordable devices, but with list prices close to $30,000 and media that cost $100 per disk, creating a CD was still an expensive proposition.

Today's CD-R drives, just like basic desktop CD-ROM drives, can run at dual-speed. But hold on to your hats, because Eastman Kodak is about to introduce its PCD Writer 600 (see fig. 8.5), which is six times faster than a standard CD-ROM drive and can fill a CD in just over ten minutes.

Fig. 8.5
The Eastman Kodak PCD Writer 600 can publish a CD in just ten minutes.

The cost of CD-R publishing overlaps with the cost of traditional replication at somewhere between 40 and 100 copies of a single premastered image, depending on the price you pay for CD-R media, the services you would require from a replication plant, and the value of your time. That, combined with CD-R's hefty storage capacity (as much as 666MB per disk), makes CD-R economical for distributing a large amount of data to a limited number of users.

You need a premastering software package, such as QuickTOPiX/Windows and Simpli-CD. CD-Gen for DOS is one package that provides a fine degree of control. Some CD recorders come with proprietary software; conversely, many premastering packages work only with certain CD-R drives.

Besides falling prices, one trend in CD-R drives is increasing speed. Single- and double-speed recorders—which take about 70 and 35 minutes, respectively, to record 650M of data—are likely to be supplanted by quadruple-speed and faster recorders as they become available. One quadruple-speed recorder, the Yamaha CDE100, includes a 512K buffer. It has an access time of 500 ms, but presents a 600Kps data transfer rate.

The premastering process consists of building an image of the CD on your hard disk, including instructions on the location of each file; translating the image to ISO 9660 format; and writing the data to the CD. Most packages also have a feature that enables you to simulate CD performance on the hard disk before actually writing data to the CD-R drive. Although the accuracy of simulation varies among software packages, you can usually get an idea of whether files need to be rearranged for better performance.

Selected CD-ROM Drive and Drive Component Manufacturers

As you shop around for a CD-ROM drive, consider models from these manufacturers. We've also assembled information about some of the most popular and powerful drives and their characteristics (see table 8.1).

NEC Technologies Inc. (subsidiary of NEC Corp.)
1414 Massachusetts Ave.
Boxborough, MA 01719-2298
800-632-4636; 508-264-8000
Direct sales: 800-374-8000 (NEC Select)
FAX: 508-264-8673

Sony Electronics Inc. (Computer Peripheral Products Co.)
3300 Zanker Rd.
San Jose, CA 95134
800-352-7669; 408-432-0190
FAX: 408-943-0740

Toshiba America Information Systems Inc. (TAIS) (subsidiary of Toshiba Corp.)
9740 Irvine Blvd., PO Box 19724
Irvine, CA 92713-9724
714-457-0777

Pioneer New Media Technologies Inc. (Optical Memory Systems Division)
2265 East 220th St.
Long Beach, CA 90810
800-444-6784; 310-952-2111
FAX: 310-952-2990

Plextor (subsidiary of Shinano Kenshi Co., Ltd.)
4255 Burton Dr.
Santa Clara, CA 95054
800-4PLEXTOR; 408-980-1838
FAX: 408-986-1010

TEAC America Inc. (Data Storage Products Division)
7733 Telegraph Rd.
Montebello, CA 90640
213-726-0303
FAX: 213-727-7652

Eastman Kodak Co.
343 State St.
Rochester, NY 14650-0519
800-242-2424; 716-724-4000

Table 8.1 Selected CD-ROM Manufacturers and Models			
Maker	**Model**	**Internal/ External (I/E)**	**Data Transfer Rate**
NEC	MultiSpin 74-1	E	300Kps
NEC	MultiSpin 84-1	I	300Kps
NEC	MultiSpin 38	E	300Kps
NEC	MultiSpin 3Xp	E	450Kps
NEC	MultiSpin 3Xi	I	450Kps
NEC	MultiSpin 4X Pro	E	600Kps
SONY	CDU-7811	E	300Kps
Toshiba America	XM-3401B	I	330Kps
Toshiba America	TXM-3401E1	E	330Kps
Pioneer New Media Technologies	DR-U104X	I	614Kps
Pioneer New Media Technologies	DR-S104X	E	614Kps
Pioneer New Media Technologies	DRM-604X	E	610Kps
Pioneer New Media Technologies	DRM-1804X	E	610Kps
Plextor	DM-3028	I	335Kps
Plextor	DM-5028	E	335Kps
TEAC	CD-55A SuperQuad	I	600Kps
MediaVision	Reno Personal CD-ROM Player	E	306Kps
Eastman Kodak	PCD Writer 600	E	???Kps

Media Vision Inc.
47300 Bayside Pkwy.
Fremont, CA 94538
800-348-7116; 510-770-8600
Direct sales: 800-845-5870
FAX: 510-770-9592

Texas Instruments Inc.
13500 N. Central Expy.
Dallas, TX 75265
800-336-5236; 214-995-2011
FAX: 214-995-4360

Access Time	Buffer	# of CDs	Retail Price
280 ms	256K	1	$550
280 ms	256K	1	$615
400 ms	64K	1	$465
250 ms	256K	1	$415
195 ms	256K	1	$465
180 ms	256K	1	$995
295 ms	256K	1	$530
200 ms	256K	1	$510
200 ms	256K	1	$640
300 ms	256K	1	$995
300 ms	256K	1	$995
300 ms	128K	6	$1795
300 ms	256K	18	$2995
240 ms	64K	1	$329
240 ms	64K	1	$439
195 ms	64K	1	$399
180 ms	64K	1	$399
n/a	2M	1	$28,995

CD-ROM Applications

After you get a CD-ROM drive, what can you do with it? Everywhere you turn, CD-ROM-based applications and titles are inundating the market—including reference information and text sources, educational and training applications, entertainment titles, and business applications and operating systems such as Microsoft Office, CorelDraw, and Windows NT. Mecklermedia's *CD-ROMs In Print 1994* lists over 5,800 CD-ROM products on the market today. The following section lists some uses of CD-ROM drives.

Simpler Software Installation

Eventually, you may see your operating system available only on CD-ROM discs. In fact, the lowly floppy disk is about to be replaced by the CD-ROM as the best way to deliver software.

Installing Microsoft Windows NT, for example, requires a CD-ROM drive. Windows NT comes with a few floppy disks and a CD-ROM disc. Simply load the CD-ROM and respond to a few menu-based questions about disk partitions and subdirectories. Because of the CD-ROM disc, installation doesn't take much more time than a full installation of Windows 3.1.

Installing CorelDRAW! is simplified by replacing 10 floppy disks with a CD-ROM disc. In fact, ordering just the CD-ROM version saves the buyer $200 over the CD-ROM/floppy disk combination ($695 versus $895). Also, the second CD-ROM provides thousands of clip-art images and hundreds of fonts.

More and More Information

Because of their capacity, CD-ROM drives can provide additional information and disk-based tutorials. A CD-ROM edition of Microsoft Publisher 2.0, for example, provides additional desktop publishing templates, images, and a tutorial.

Peachtree Software ships Peachtree Accounting for Windows in a CD-ROM edition, which incorporates several small business-oriented software packages onto a single CD-ROM. Besides Peachtree Accounting 2.0 for Windows, the user gets The Multimedia Business Library from Allegro New Media (a collection of 12 books on a variety of business subjects); CompuServe WinCIM (for navigating the CompuServe Information Service); SoftNet's FaxWorks 3.0 for fax modem owners; and Avery's LabelPro for Windows, which includes clip art and bar codes. Also included on the CD-ROM are Individual Software's Professor Windows, which is a Windows tutorial program, and Mastering Computers' Tip-A-Day software.

Perhaps CD-ROMs will save some trees. Lotus 1-2-3 Release 4 is provided on CD-ROM; no paper documentation or disks are included. The program and documentation, except for a tiny startup booklet, are all on a single CD-ROM. Lotus has also added a 40-minute audio and animated Guided Tour to using the Lotus 1-2-3 package and a QuickMovie feature that demonstrates certain concepts and functions. Because of their large sizes, these built-in tutorials would have been impossible to provide on floppy disks. Paper documentation is available for an additional $59.

Software by Phone

The hard way to buy software is to stand in line at a superstore. The easy way is to receive from a reseller a CD-ROM packed with full retail versions of the top 40 business applications (and maybe even a game or two). You browse through detailed descriptions of every program on the disk and install demo versions of any you want to try before you buy. To close the deal, call your reseller and exchange a credit card number for a secret code. Type in the code, click OK, and install the application right off the CD. (The printed documentation, if you want it, arrives in the mail a day or two later.)

Softbank, Ingram Micro Inc., Test Drive Inc., InfoNow Corp., Software Spectrum Inc., and hardware makers such as IBM and Apple Computer Inc. have released encrypted software on CD-ROM with limited results.

Edutainment or Just Plain Fun?

Games, which require both excellent graphics and sound, are best suited for CD-ROM. Games such as Myst from Broderbund are provided only on CD-ROM. Some popular games bundled with some CD-ROM drives and multimedia upgrade kits are Dynamix' Stellar 7, LucasArts' Loom, ChessMaster 3000, and King's Quest VI. Our estimates show that about one of every seven game titles is available exclusively or also on CD-ROM.

Besides games, you also can expand your skills and education. For example, the Reveal Multimedia FX-04 kit includes 13 CD-ROM titles, including Mavis Beacon Teaches Typing, United States Atlas and World Atlas, and Software Toolworks' Multimedia Encyclopedia. Mavis Beacon Teaches Typing, for example, provides a lifelike keyboard, help windows, and tempo-typing to teach you how to type. On-screen speed, accuracy, and completion meters are provided, as well as a resume writer.

You also can get specialty titles, such as J.F.K. Assassination: A Visual Investigation. This CD-ROM is brimming with video—including the famous Zapruder film of the Kennedy entourage as it motors through Dealey Plaza. This home movie taken by Abraham Zapruder is considered to be the best of several such films taken by witnesses to the assassination. Lesser-known films are on the disc as well.

J.F.K. also provides 3-D computer simulations of the shot, hypothesizing different bullet trajectories and locations of the assassin. All hypothesized shots are synchronized to different frames of the Zapruder film.

These details are complemented by massive amounts of research information. The disk is packed with data from the House Select Committee on Assassinations, the full text from the Warren Commission Report, the book *Crossfire*, and the *Complete Book of Facts* on the assassination—all with hypertext links. A number of viewpoints are presented, ranging from the single-shooter, magic-bullet theory to elaborate conspiracy theories.

J.F.K. Assassination: A Visual Investigation ($49.95)
Medio Multimedia
2643 151st Pl. N.E.
Redmond, WA 98052-5562
1-800-788-3866; 206-867-5500

III

Investing in Multimedia

Do you want to be a computer whiz? Detailed technical hardware information is now instantly available with Technical Library, a CD-ROM from Micro House International Inc. Technical Library contains often hard-to-find information on 2,200 hard drives, 1,700 motherboards, 600 network adapters, and 400 hard-disk controllers.

Micro House International Inc.
4900 Pearl E. Circle, Suite 101
Boulder, CO 80301
800-926-8299; 303-443-3388

Graphics on Disc

You can liven up your presentations with digitized photos on CD-ROM. Using a Kodak Photo CD-compatible drive, you can place images in any document. You can use two types of photography: stock photography or clip images. *Stock photography* requires you to pay fees for using each image. *Clip images*, on the other hand, are the perfect alternative. Unlike stock photos, which you can only use once, clip images are yours to use however and as often as you want. Clip image libraries, such as Corel Corp.'s Professional Photos CD-ROM ($49.95 each—see fig. 8.6) and Digital Stock Professional's offerings ($249 each) are relatively inexpensive sources of high-quality images. You also can get from several sources hundreds of fonts on a single CD-ROM.

Fig. 8.6
You can get high-quality, royalty-free photos from companies such as Corel Corp.

Corel Professional Photos Series ($24.95 for 100 images)
Corel Corp.
1600 Carling Ave., The Corel Bldg.
Ottawa, ON, CD K1Z 8R7
800-77-COREL; 613-728-8200
Direct sales: 800-836-3729

FAX: 613-728-9790

Digital Stock Professional ($249)
Digital Stock Inc.
400 S. Sierra Ave., Ste. 100
Solana Beach, CA 92075
800-545-4514; 619-794-4040

FAX: 619-794-4041

Getting the Most from Your CD-ROM Drive

You can make the most of your CD-ROM drive with the utilities and tricks discussed in the following sections. Some of these additions give your CD-ROM drive more speed or more capabilities.

More Speed

Even the fastest CD-ROM drives are slow when compared to most hard disks—about one-tenth to one-twentieth the speed! And although newer drives feature improved data transfer rates and faster access times, they still need speeding up.

Disk caching software has been used for years on hard disks and is the most effective way to improve your hard disk's performance and extend its life.

Basically, a *disk cache* is a software program you run to dynamically duplicate parts of your hard disk to your computer's memory. Once in memory, the contents can be read at top speed. DOS versions 4.x and higher and Microsoft Windows 3.0 and higher include the disk caching utility SmartDrive.

Some disk caching programs buffer, or delay, writing to your hard disk. In other words, the disk caching program saves information in its memory to your hard disk when your computer is not busy doing your other work, usually waiting no more than five seconds. This also is called *delayed writing*. This waiting period adds significant speed, but can cause information to be lost if your computer is turned off suddenly. Because of the small delay, often less than one second, this concern is minor.

Caching is now available for CD-ROM drives as well. Caching doesn't just improve CD-ROM performance; it throws it into overdrive. The improvement you see depends on your work. If you frequently reread files from the CD-ROM that are small enough to fit into the cache, the results can be impressive. Beware of the advertisements; you won't see a 60 percent improvement or more. More likely, expect faster speeds of between 10 and 40 percent, depending on how often you read the same information.

III

> **Note**
>
> With MS-DOS 6.2, SmartDrive was enhanced to cache CD-ROM drives, not just hard disks and floppy drives.

Lightning CD from Lucid Corp. is one CD-ROM cache utility that addresses the speed problem by doing what most cache programs do: watching the read requests you make from the drive and storing frequently accessed data in memory. The next time you look for the information, Lightning CD reads it from the cache rather than from the much slower drive.

Lightning CD can remember the results of searches or disk reads, and it quickly recalls the data. For example, a search of the Front-Page News CD-ROM for articles on the Federal Republic of Germany took 10.61 seconds without Lightning CD; 8.5 seconds the first time the search was performed with Lightning CD; and only 5.65 seconds after the search results were in the cache. The time it took to access the first article dropped from 12 seconds the first time it was read to a barely measurable 0.6 seconds after it was in the cache.

For games and other CD-ROM applications, the benefit of having a cache like the one from Lucid Corp. is significant. Also, Lightning CD's intelligent "read-ahead" component can anticipate the next area that will be read by the application and load it into RAM while the application is using current data. This can help reduce the pauses that normally occur when a program has to read from disk.

If you use Lightning CD, you have to forgo any other caches because it replaces Windows' SmartDrive. It acts as the only cache in the system, and it does a good job. On one elaborate Windows-based test system, Lightning CD reduced the time required to launch Windows from two minutes to 68 seconds.

The utility does require some memory tuning so that you can run large applications under Windows. Its behavior under Windows, however, yields no unpleasant surprises. You can even set up different cache profiles to fine-tune performance for each CD-ROM.

Utilities included with Lightning CD give it even more functionality. Disk Watch—a utility that flashes the drive letter on-screen whenever the system issues a read request to the hard disk—lets you know that the cache is working; LKey speeds up keyboard performance; and LScreen speeds up screen refresh on systems that aren't using ANSI.SYS.

Lightning CD also includes a tree-deletion utility that deletes the contents of a directory and all subdirectories below it. The package also includes Best of the Bureau, a CD-ROM with samples of products published by the Bureau of Electronic Publishing.

Lightning CD ($49.95)
Lucid Corp.
101 W. Renner Rd. #450
Richardson, TX 75082-2017
800-925-8243; 214-994-8100

Symantec's Norton Speedcache Plus provides similar performance to Lightning CD. Speedcache Plus dramatically shortens the time required to open and search CD-ROMs. Speedcache Plus provides an advanced cache that incorporates read-ahead and write-back caching and delayed writes. It also supports floppy drives, but goes beyond SmartDrive in its support of Bernoulli and Iomega drives.

SpeedDrive Plus uses less conventional memory than Lightning CD and contains Windows utilities that enable you to configure many cache settings by simply clicking buttons. If you're tired of waiting for your CD-ROM drive, SpeedDrive Plus is your solution.

Norton SpeedDrive Plus 4.0 for DOS and Windows ($99)
Symantec Corp.
175 W. Broadway
Eugene, OR 97401
800-441-7234

CD-Blitz is another CD-ROM caching utility. CD-Blitz features a Windows control panel that enables you to configure the cache. CD-Blitz occupies just 13K of RAM. The utility has two different caching modes: Max, which caches directory reads and CD-ROM program data, and Min, which only caches directory reads. The program can use as little as 256K and as much as 64M of extended memory to speed up seek times and data-transfer rates.

CD-Blitz ($79)
Blitz 'n' Software Inc.
33030 Mission Blvd., Ste. 212
Hayward, CA 94544
800-230-0045; 510-441-7140
FAX: 510-441-7142

CD-ROM Accessories

A CD-ROM drive often comes complete with everything you need, and few accessories are available for outfitting your drive. However, the following paragraphs describe a few additions that can give you more from your drive.

Connecting a SCSI device to your computer is now easier than ever. The T348 MiniSCSI Plus (see fig. 8.7) parallel-to-SCSI connector from Trantor Systems improves on its predecessor, the MiniSCSI. The new adapter's design builds parallel-to-SCSI conversion into a cable instead of a back-of-the-system connector. It all happens in one device.

Plug one end into your computer's parallel port and the other end into the SCSI device—you don't need additional cables. Like the MiniSCSI, the Plus includes a parallel port "pass-through" capability so that you can print while accessing a SCSI drive, without slowing performance. You can daisy-chain up to seven SCSI devices with MiniSCSI Plus.

Fig. 8.7
The Trantor MiniSCSI Plus enables you to plug a SCSI drive into any printer port in just seconds.

This Walkman-style approach is the only way to use a CD-ROM with a laptop or note-book PC, although it may not prove up to multimedia performance standards (parallel adapters aren't as fast as bus interfaces). Because the device is SCSI, you can use it for portable CD-ROM readers, hard disks, Bernoulli Box, magneto optical, floptical, Syquest, and tape drives.

Trantor also offers the T460 SlimSCSI connector for laptops with PCMCIA (Personal Computer Memory Card International Association) slots. Many laptops offer one or two slots for a credit-card sized PCMCIA card. The PCMCIA specification enables you to add additional features through a thin slot in the laptop. Using PCMCIA-compliant PC Cards, you can quickly give your laptop a modem, fax card, LAN connection, external SCSI device (such as a CD-ROM drive), and even a second hard disk. The T460 SlimSCSI is perfect for connecting a SCSI CD-ROM to your laptop.

ATA348 MiniSCSI Plus Parallel-SCSI ($189)
ATA460 SlimSCSI ($349)
Trantor Systems, Ltd. (subsidiary of Adaptec Inc.)
691 S. Milpitas Blvd.
Milpitas, CA 95035
800-934-2766; 408-945-8600
FAX: 408-957-7150

When assembling a multimedia PC from disparate sound cards and CD-ROM drives, you may find you are lacking the audio cable that goes from the back of the CD-ROM drive to your sound card. Over 600 combinations of CD-ROM drive-to-sound-board connections are possible. But unless the two devices are bundled and the patch cable is provided (as with multimedia PCs), finding a cable with the correct connectors can be difficult.

Sometimes, sound card vendors may not supply the proper cable (if at all). If so, you can contact companies that specialize in this, such as CD-ROM Access (800-959-5260) and TTS Multimedia Cables (800-887-4968). Just identify your sound board and CD-ROM drive, and they can determine the appropriate patch cable.

Caring for Your CD-ROM Drive

CD-ROM drives are relatively maintenance free. Like your computer, drives should not be used in high humidity, dusty environments, or excessive heat. Avoid direct sunlight and do not place heavy objects on them. Do not spill any beverage on the drive, and do not drop or hit the drive.

With dust protection and self-cleaning lenses built into many drives, cleaning is minimized. If you want, you can get an audio CD cleaning kit to clean your system. Otherwise, you can use a soft damp cloth with a light detergent to clean the drive's external housing. The CD-ROM discs themselves can be cleaned by wiping each with a soft cloth from the center to the edge. Like the drive itself, do not place CD-ROM discs in direct sunlight or in high temperatures.

CD-ROM Titles

Looking for some CD-ROMs that will help you begin your multimedia experience? The following tables list more than 20 of the most exciting and helpful CD titles under various categories. The most interesting ones are highlighted.

The 7th Guest

The 7th Guest is a two-CD-ROM horror game (one CD-ROM for the game plus one filled with game-based music) that lets you move through a fully rendered 3-D environment as you watch ghostly visions unfold.

The story involves a crazed toy maker, Henry Stauf, and his mystical creations. Although the toys are popular, they turn out to have a horrific effect—their owners die. Having retreated to his newly constructed mansion, Stauf invites six guests, for reasons revealed only gradually throughout the game. You play the part of Ego, a character who explores the mansion after the story is over, solving puzzles (22 in all) and attempting to figure out what happened—with the assistance of some unquiet ghosts. Although its puzzles leave a bit to be desired, The 7th Guest is a visual treat well worth exploring.

Microsoft Bookshelf '94

The Microsoft Bookshelf is a popular collection of seven volumes. Microsoft Bookshelf '94 is easier to use, more up-to-date, and more visually appealing than last year's edition. The popular multimedia reference library has an improved dictionary, book of quotations, thesaurus, and chronology of world events; in addition, the encyclopedia, world atlas, and almanac have been updated. Also new—and a real ace in the hole for anyone who writes—is the QuickShelf feature, which puts volumes of data at your fingertips. When you're creating a document in a Windows word processor and you need to flesh out an idea, highlight the word you're stuck on and click the QuickShelf tool bar. From

Table 8.2   Entertainment Titles

Title	Purpose
The 7th Guest 4.0	3-D horror game
Microsoft Golf	Play golf from the comfort of your home
Hell Cab	Save your soul during the ride of your life
Rebel Assault	Continue the Star Wars saga

Table 8.3   Education and Reference Titles

Title	Purpose
Microsoft Bookshelf '94	Seven popular reference books
Professor Multimedia	Educates and demonstrates multimedia concepts
1994 Guinness Multimedia Disc of Records	Contains world records
Random House Unabridged Dictionary, Second Edition	Complete unabridged dictionary
Small Blue Planet	Provides topographical maps for armchair astronauts
Movies on TV and Videocassette	Lists/rates movies on TV and videocassette
The Complete Guide to Special Interest Videos	Lists many non-fiction movies
Microsoft TechNet	Contains technical knowledge about Microsoft products
1994 Auto Almanac	Information on 1,500 vehicles
The Family Doctor, 3rd Edition	Information on first aid, diseases and drugs

there, you can access any work in the library for more information about the highlighted word. And since all seven volumes are linked, you can search all of them for citations—many of which have accompanying photos, sound, or video clips.

This CD-ROM isn't just for kids or students; it's a thorough reference work and a great way to experience information. For all that, Microsoft Bookshelf '94 requires just 2M of disk space.

Professor Multimedia

Want another tool to help you bone up on multimedia? Consider purchasing Professor Multimedia from Individual Software. This interactive CD-ROM guides you through multimedia terminology using sound, animation, and video. For instance, to demonstrate the importance of frame rate in video playback, Professor Multimedia shows two clips: one at 4 frames per second (fps), the other at 15 fps.

Publisher	Price	Phone
Virgin Interactive Entertainment	$79.95	800-874-4607/714-833-8710
Microsoft Corp.	$64.95	800-426-9400
Time Warner Interactive Group	$99.99	818-955-9999
LucasArts Entertainment	$79.95	415-721-3300

Publisher	Price	Phone
Microsoft Corp.	$99	800-426-9400
Individual Software	$59.95	800-822-3522
Grolier Electronic Publishing	$49.95	203-797-3500
Random House Reference and Electronic Publishing	$79	800-733-3000
Now What Software	$79.95	800-322-1954
Compton's NewMedia	$39.95	800-862-2206
Quanta Press Inc.	$49.95	612-379-3956
Microsoft Corp.	$295 per year	800-344-2121 x160
CE3 Inc.	$49.95	800-288-6347
Creative Multimedia Corp.	$79.99	503-241-1530

Wines of the World

Imagine you want to learn how to open and serve a bottle of champagne. Before you pop the cork, pop Multicom's Wines of the World into your CD-ROM drive. This multimedia guide to the great wine-producing regions and the bottles they fill can enhance your appreciation of wine, especially if you're a novice wine connoisseur.

The disc is divided into four parts: Wine Quality, Wine Appreciation, Wine Regions, and Wine Browser. The first three categories tell the story of wine from the grape to the tasting. The Wine Appreciation section describes professional ratings and teaches novices how to educate their own palates. The Wine Regions section uses maps to explore vineyards around the world.

The articles provided on each section of the disc are uniformly well-written and informative. Photographs and narrated video clips add multimedia flair and help you understand

Table 8.4 Hobby Titles

Title	Purpose
Wines of the World	Learn to appreciate and handle wine
The Exotic Garden	Explains flowering
RedShift for Windows 1.0	Turns your PC into a planetarium
Microsoft Complete Baseball CD-ROM	Contains stats on 2,500 baseball players
Sports Illustrated 1994 Multimedia Sports Almanac	1993 sports stats and news
Know Your Waterfowl	Bird fancier pictures and information
Multimedia Stravinsky: The Rite of Spring	Analyze and enjoy Stravinsky's music
ComputerWorks	Describes the inner workings of a PC

Table 8.5 Business Titles

Title	Purpose
Accumail	Updates your database with ZIP+4
Mailer's Business Database	Contains 1.3 million business addresses
11 Million Businesses' Phone Directory	Contains business phone numbers
Connect for Success	Trains employees how to deal with others
Multimedia Business 500	Information on the top 500 corporations

the process of making and selecting a wine. Through the Browser, you can search a database of more than 20,000 wines according to producer, variety, vintage, price, and other attributes.

Accumail

To keep your direct mail costs down, you need to manage your mailing list carefully. Group 1 Software's AccuMail helps by processing address lists to help you take advantage of discounted postal rates and improve the chances of your mail arriving at its desired destination.

The program performs five basic clean-up operations on mailing lists (stored in ASCII, dBASE, Alpha Four, Clipper, dBXL, or FoxPro formats). It corrects addresses with misspelled or missing components; corrects or adds five-digit ZIP codes; adds ZIP+4 codes if desired; adds carrier-route and delivery-point codes; and standardizes street addresses. These small steps reduce the amount of handling your mail requires at the post office, so your pieces get delivered faster.

Publisher	Price	Phone
Multicom Publishing Inc.	$59.95	800-850-7272
VT Productions	$49.95	408-464-1552
Maris Multimedia Ltd.	$64.95	800-336-2947
Microsoft Corp.	$79.95	800-426-9400
StarPress Multimedia	$59.95	800-782-7944
Axia Int'l.	$69.95	403-262-2942
Microsoft Corp.	$79.95	800-426-9400
Software Marketing Corp.	$79.95	602-893-3377

Publisher	Price	Phone
Group 1 Software	$295	800-368-5806
Mailer's Software	$149	800-800-6245
American Business Information	$49	402-593-4595
Wilson Learning Corp.	$69.95	800-247-7332
Allegro New Media	$49.95	201-808-1992

The Haldeman Diaries: Inside the Nixon White House

Sony Corp's and ImageSoft Inc.'s "The Haldeman Diaries: Inside the Nixon White House, The Complete Multimedia Edition" is an excellent reference tool about H. R. Haldeman's era as President Richard Nixon's chief of staff. The CD-ROM is based on Haldeman's book, published by G.P. Putnam's Sons in May 1994, but includes large amounts of additional information that could not fit into the 700-page volume. There are 2,200 pages of text, 700 photographs and 45 minutes of home movies taken by Haldeman that give users insight into the operations and strategies of the Nixon White House. The CD-ROM also includes a letter he wrote in prison trying to justify his crimes.

Jonathan Pond's Personal Financial Planner

Financial-planning correspondent Jonathan Pond is your partner in "Jonathan Pond's Personal Financial Planner," a CD-ROM-based electronic book that uses tests and quizzes to generate a suggested reading plan. Browsing through the book, you can see video clips of Pond's words of wisdom.

III

Investing in Multimedia

Table 8.6   Historic Titles

Title	Purpose
The Haldeman Diaries: Inside the Nixon White House, The Complete Multimedia Edition	H.R. Haldeman's spin on Watergate
Gettysburg Multimedia Battle Simulation	Half history, half game of Civil War battle
Normandy: The Great Crusade	Brings to life the great D-Day invasion
CNN Time Capsule 1993: 100 Defining Moments of the Year	Lists 100 major news events of 1993

Table 8.7   Personal and Financial Improvement

Title	Purpose
Jonathan Pond's Personal Financial Planner	Plans investment strategy
Kathy Smith's Fat Burning System	A 10-week multimedia exercise session
TurboTax Deluxe	Prepare your taxes more quickly

Table 8.8   Children's Titles

Title	Purpose
Putt Putt Goes to the Moon	Help a high-flying car get back to Earth
Dinosaur Safari	Track down dinosaurs for photographs

Pond's Planner generates a reading plan based on a "Wealth" test that you take at the beginning of the book. Despite its name, the test focuses more on your record-keeping practices and familiarity with financial-planning topics than your current income level. At the end of the test, you get a score and a reading plan with links to chapters on the topics that you need to learn.

By entering different values in the electronic worksheets provided, you can view the effects of different financial assumptions. For example, on the "Can You Afford to Buy?" page, varying the values of mortgage rates and terms gives you different estimates of the size of mortgage you can qualify for. For each scenario, a suggested financial strategy is displayed with sidebar links to sections of the book.

If financial planning is new to you, Jonathan Pond's Personal Financial Planner is an interesting way to learn about the subject. Navigation is easy, the video clips add a pleasant tutorial touch, and the interactive worksheets encourage "what if" investigations.

Publisher	Price	Phone
Sony Electronic Publishing/ ImageSoft Inc.	$69	800-654-8802
Swfte International	$69.95	800-237-9383
Discovery Communications	$49.95	301-986-0444
Vicarious Entertainment	$29.95	800-908-9966

Publisher	Price	Phone
Vertigo Development Group	$49.95	800-688-4750
Xiphias	$69.95	310-841-2790
ChipSoft	$99.95	800-964-1040

Publisher	Price	Phone
Humungous Entertainment	$49.95	206-485-1212
Creative Multimedia	$69.99	503-241-4351

Putt Putt Goes to the Moon

Putt Putt Goes to the Moon is simple but captivating. The concept is simple: A freak accident at a fireworks factory transports Putt Putt (a little purple car) to the moon. Your job is to get Putt Putt home again. Though geared to the preliterate set, Putt Putt is captivating for the whole family.

From Here...

- Chapter 9, "Buyer's Guide to Sound," discusses sound cards and various models. Some sound cards include built-in interfaces for controlling your CD-ROM drive.
- Chapter 3, "Adding a CD-ROM Drive," discusses CD-ROM drives and their operations.

III

Investing in Multimedia

Chapter 9

Buyer's Guide to Sound

Selecting a sound card is like buying a car. Many have the same features, but some will give you more—for a price. Like the Yugo, other sound cards provide affordability but not style or reliability. To make a decision about the car, you have to check under the hood or kick the tires. But comparing sound cards is much more difficult than comparing a Honda to a Lexus. What you hear is what you get.

In this chapter, you learn how to select a sound card, based on several criteria. You also are introduced to several models of sound cards, based on price, features and portability. Lastly, you discover software that makes use of a sound card, including screen savers, voice recognition and other software accessories.

Sound Card Criteria

Buying a sound card has become very stylish. In 1993, about 3 million sound cards were sold. In 1994, that figure will double to 6.2 million, according to market research firm Dataquest.

Telling you which sound card to get is like telling you what is good art or literature. Sound is so subjective. However, the technology you may get in one sound card is the same as that in another. Case in point: Logitech has licensed Media Vision's multimedia chip sets for its sound cards. At this time, Media Vision provides its sound technology to almost 40 companies.

What are some key features to consider when buying a sound card? Although some aspects are based simply on preference, the following are some key buying points.

Game Standards

There are no official sound card standards, but the popular Sound Blaster card has become a de facto standard. Although nearly all sound cards claim to be compatible with Sound Blaster, only those of two companies are strictly compatible: Creative Labs, the originator of the de facto standard, and IBM, which has licensed the technology from Creative Labs. The other "compatible" boards generally rely on reverse-engineered chips.

MPC Compatibility

Most sound cards support the Multimedia PC (MPC) Level 2 specifications, which allows you to play sound files in Windows and more. This compatibility encompasses many features, including those described next.

MIDI for Music. Most sound cards come with a MIDI interface, requiring you to purchase the hardware separately to hook up other MIDI devices.

The MPC Level 2 specifications insist on a MIDI interface. Many sound cards contain one or two FM (frequency modulation) MIDI synthesizer chips. Most use synthesizer chips developed by Yamaha. The least expensive sound cards use the monophonic 11-voice YM3812 or OPL2 chip. Better sound cards use the stereophonic and popular 20-voice YMF262 or OPL3 chip.

High-end sound cards include wavetable synthesis, where digital recordings of real instruments and sound effects are embedded onto read-only memory (ROM) chips on the card. The Yamaha OPL4 chip is one popular chip for providing wavetable synthesis.

The serious musician may prefer a high-end sound card, such as the MultiSound Monterey from Turtle Beach. The MultiSound uses wavetable synthesis; it contains digitized sounds of actual instruments that are preserved in ROM. The MultiSound plays genuine strings and trumpets instead of synthesized music that sounds like strings and trumpets.

Tip

If you want top-notch quality sound and may use your sound card for MIDI music, insist on wavetable synthesis on your sound card or at least an upgrade path to it through a wavetable daughtercard.

Not all wavetable sound cards are the same. The key to success is having sufficient space to store the samples. The basic waveforms for all 128 General MIDI instruments can be stored in 256K of ROM. However, devoting more space to hold more information about each sample dramatically increases the music's realism. For example, the synthesizer on Turtle Beach Systems' MultiSound, is one of the best available, holding 4M of samples. If you intend to record soundtracks and the like, you'll want a card with this serious MIDI capability, such as Roland Corporation's RAP-10.

Some sound cards allow you to later buy an add-on that provides wavetable synthesis to an otherwise bland card. For example, the Sound Blaster 16 ASP offered an optional Wave Blaster. When MIDI music is played, it looks to the Wave Blaster for any of 213

CD-quality digitally recorded musical instrument sounds. Without the Wave Blaster, the Sound Blaster 16 ASP would imitate these sounds through FM synthesis.

> **Note**
>
> Other sound cards may exclude the MIDI interface, barely falling short of the MPC specs. Budget-priced sound cards such as the Microsoft Sound System 2.0 do not provide a MIDI interface.

WAV Files. A sound card should be able to play Windows WAV files to be MPC-compatible. When recording WAV files, the most important sound card quality is its sampling capabilities. The rate at which the card samples (measured in kilohertz) and the size of its sample (expressed in bits) determine the quality of the sound. The standard sampling rates for sound cards are 11 kHz, 22 kHz, and 44 kHz, while sample sizes are often 8, 12, and 16 bits. The higher each set of numbers, the better the quality.

> **Tip**
>
> Insist on 16-bit sampling on your sound card to be compatible with the MPC Level 2 specifications.

The MPC Level 1 specification requires the card to be able to record sound at 8-bits and 11 kHz. It must be able to play back at 11 and 22 kHz. The MPC Level 2 specification requires the card to be able to record and play back at 16 bits at all three sampling rates.

Inexpensive monophonic cards generally sample at 8 bits up to speeds of 22 kHz, which is fine for recording voice messages. Some stereo-capable cards sample at 8 bits and run at speeds of 22 kHz in stereo and up to 44 kHz in mono. Other cards can sample 8 bits at 44 kHz speeds in both stereo and mono. The latest generation of cards do it all; they can record CD-quality audio of 16 bits at 44 kHz.

The Logitech AudioMan, for example, was designed as an 8-bit sound device for business users to add voice notes to their Windows work. Likewise, Compaq Computer Corp.'s original Business Audio was 8-bit quality. (It has since been replaced by 16-bit Enhanced Business Audio.)

Choosing between 8-bit vs. 16-bit sound is often simply a matter of trading sound quality for disk space. A sound sampled in 16-bit stereo at 44 kHz (CD-audio quality) takes as much as *10.5M per minute!* The same sound sample in 8-bit mono at 11 kHz takes 1/16th the space. If price but not MPC Level 2 compatibility is your primary concern, a basic 8-bit card may meet your needs.

III

Investing in Multimedia

> **Tip**
>
> Avoid using DoubleSpace or other disk compression utilities to "create" additional disk space. Your computer spends part of its processing time compressing and decompressing files when it should be working with your sound card.

If you do buy a card that supports 16-bit sampling, ensure you have plenty of hard disk space, ideally at least 100M free. The higher the resolution of sampling, the more hard disk space required to store the file. The sampling rate also affects file size; sampling at the next higher rate doubles the file size.

You'll also have to consider buying a monophonic or stereophonic sound card. Inexpensive sound cards are monophonic, producing sound from a single source. Still, monophonic cards produce better sound than your PC's speaker. However, Level 2 MPC specifications require stereo sound.

CD-ROM Connector

Most stereo sound cards not only provide great sound but also can operate your CD-ROM drive. While many cards come with a SCSI port for any SCSI device, such as a CD-ROM drive, others support only a proprietary CD-ROM interface, such as Mitsumi or Sony CD-ROM interfaces. For example, some Creative Labs Sound Blaster cards only work with Panasonic CD-ROM drives. If you own a CD-ROM drive, make sure it's compatible with the sound card you plan to buy. If you plan to add a CD-ROM drive or if you expect to upgrade your drive, keep in mind that a proprietary interface will limit your choices. You may be limited to a single CD-ROM brand or a handful of models.

> **Tip**
>
> Avoid sound cards that only provide a CD-ROM interface for a specific CD-ROM drive or a handful of drives. To be compatible, insist on a SCSI-2 interface.

For sound cards with SCSI ports, consider the level of SCSI supported. For example, the Logitech SoundMan Wave supports SCSI-1, while the Sound Blaster 16 SCSI-2 and Diamond Systems SonicSound provide SCSI-2 support. SCSI-2 provides better reliability and data throughput than the older SCSI-1 specifications.

If you're seeking to add both a sound card and a CD-ROM drive, consider *multimedia upgrade kits*. These kits bundle a sound card, CD-ROM drive, CD-ROM titles, software, and cables in an attractively priced package. A multimedia upgrade kit may save you some money over buying disparate components. Plus, you'll have the assurance that the components will work together, especially if you have proper documentation with the kit.

> **Note**
>
> For more information on multimedia upgrade kits, see Chapter 7, "Buying Advice."

Data Compression

Because recorded WAV files demand so much disk space—up to 10.5M for each recorded minute—many sound cards include a data-compression capability. Several sound card makers use ADPCM (Adaptive Differential Pulse Code Modulation) compression to reduce file size by 50 to 75 percent. For example, the Sound Blaster ASP 16 includes on-the-fly compression of sound in ratios of 2:1, 3:1 or 4:1. However, a simple fact of audio life is that if you use such compression, you lose sound quality. Because the compression quality is so poor, there is no ADPCM standard.

DSP Included

One recent addition to many sound boards is the digital signal processor (DSP). DSPs add intelligence to your sound card, freeing your computer from work-intensive tasks, such as filtering noise from recordings or compressing audio on the fly.

About half of most general-purpose sound cards use DSPs. The Cardinal Technologies Sound Pro 16 and Sound Pro 16 Plus, for example, use the Analog Devices ADSP2115 digital signal processor. DSPs allow a sound card to be a multi-purpose device. IBM uses its DSP to add a 14,400-bits-per-second modem, 9,600-bps fax, and a digital answering machine to its WindSurfer Communications Adapter.

> **Tip**
>
> By getting a sound card with a DSP onboard, you open yourself to new features, such as on-the-fly audio compression, voice recognition, and other capabilities.

Are DSPs worth the extra price? On low-powered PCs (those less powerful than a 486SX/25) or in true multitasking environments like Windows 3.1 or Windows NT, a DSP can make real-time compression possible—a feature valuable for voice annotation.

Bundled Software

Sound cards usually include several sound utilities to immediately begin using your sound card. Most of this software is DOS-based but Windows-based versions are available with some cards (see table 9.1). The possibilities include the following:

- Text-to-speech conversion programs

- Programs for playing, editing, and recording audio files

- Cards with MIDI interfaces generally come with sequencer software, which helps you compose music

- Various sound clips

III

Investing in Multimedia

Table 9.1   Sound Cards for Less than $170

Model	Maker	Record rate	Playback rate
Disney Sound Source	Walt Disney Computer Software		
ThunderBoard for Windows	Media Vision	8-bit, 22 kHz	8-bit, 22 kHz
MediaMagic ISP-16	MediaMagic	16-bit, 48 kHz	16-bit, 48 kHz
Sound Blaster Pro Value Edition	Creative Labs	8-bit, 44.1 kHz	8-bit, 44.1 kHz
AudioBlitz	Classic Genoa Systems	16-bit, 44.1 kHz	16-bit, 44.1 kHz
ARIA 16	Prometheus Wavetable	16-bit, 44.1 kHz	16-bit, 44.1 kHz

---

Tip

Don't be distracted by several software utilities or CD-ROM titles bundled with your sound card. Instead, focus on the features you want from a sound card and then the actual utilities and titles you would use.

Selected Models

This chapter provides sections for categories of sound cards, such as:

- Inexpensive sound cards
- Portable sound cards, including PCMCIA sound cards
- Mainstream stereo sound cards
- Combination video/sound cards
- High-end sound cards

Some sections also provide a table of comparative features.

Mono/Stereo Sound	AdLib/ Interface Blaster compatible (A,S)	MIDI Type	Synthesis	Retail Price
Mono	S	No	FM	$49.95
Stereo	A/S	No	FM	$169
Stereo	A/S	No	FM	$99
Stereo	S	Yes	FM	$115
Stereo	A/S	Yes	FM	$79
Stereo	S	Yes	Products	$99

Note

The prices listed in the tables are retail prices; street prices are often 20 to 40 percent less.

Sound on a Budget

Many sound cards are available for under $100 (retail price of about $170 or less). Table 9.1 lists these cards. Their sound may not be exquisite, but their price will be music to your ears. Some of these cards are monophonic, but you can get a stereo sound card in this price range.

Disney Sound Source. Trying to offer "family computing," Walt Disney Software introduced The Sound Source. This external sound device plugs into your PC's parallel port primarily to provide sound to Disney educational software. The Sound Source is supported by several game manufacturers, including Sierra, Broderbund, Interplay, and Maxis. For example, the Disney Sound Source is supported by games such as Prince of Persia 2: The Shadow and the Flame and Where In Space is Carmen Sandiego? Deluxe, both from Broderbund.

The latest rendition of The Sound Source is MPC Level 1 compatible, thereby able to play Microsoft Windows WAV files. The Sound Source is ideal for laptop users making small-scale presentations and for adding sound to a home system.

III

Investing in Multimedia

The Sound Source is the size of a small answering machine. It runs on a single nine-volt battery. Because it is plugged into your PC, you don't have to wrestle with opening your computer.

Don't expect rich sound from The Sound Source. It is designed as an inexpensive alternative for users who want better sound than what their PC speaker provides. Plus, The Sound Source does not have any way to provide audio input. In other words, there's no microphone jack for recording. The retail price of The Sound Source is $49.95.

Disney signed an agreement with Packard Bell to offer seven Disney software titles and The Sound Source audio speaker system with Packard Bell systems in the United States and Canada.

Note

ESS, the Fremont company that makes the chips for the Disney Sound Source, plans to roll out a one-chip-does-all sound solution. Supposedly, this chip will be picked up by Compaq and other computer makers that have yearned for a one-chip-does-all motherboard-based sound system for the PC. The ESS 1688 will run with Sound Blaster and Sound Blaster Pro and will act as a 16-bit 44 kHz DAC for sound sampling.

ThunderBoard for Windows. Sound card giant Media Vision is competing in the low end with its $169 ThunderBoard for Windows. The Thunder Board is a lesser version of its famous Pro Audio Spectrum sound card.

The ThunderBoard provides 11-voice mono playback by using a single 8-bit Yamaha digital-to-analog converter (DAC). The ThunderBoard includes a microphone jack, volume control, joystick port and stereo out jacks. To save disk space, it can compress sound files up to a ratio of 4:1. The Thunder Board is versatile; it is compatible with AdLib and Sound Blaster audio drivers. It can record and play back sounds up to 22 kHz.

Note

Don't expect the ThunderBoard to be around long. The ThunderBoard is being sold in Computer City stores for just $29!

ThunderBoard for Windows ($169-$179)
Media Vision Inc.
47300 Bayside Pkwy.
Fremont, CA 94538

800-348-7116; 510-770-8600
Direct sales: 800-845-5870
FAX: 510-770-8648
Tech support: 800-638-2807
Tech support BBS: 510-770-0527

MediaMagic ISP-16. MediaMagic offers its stereo ISP-16 sound card for less than $100. This sound card provides 16-bit, 44 kHz stereo recording and playback. It is both AdLib and Sound Blaster compatible. For its price, it provides FM synthesis using Yamaha's OPL3 synthesizer chip. It includes an AT CD-ROM interface.

MediaMagic ISP-16 ($99)
MediaMagic (division of IPC Corp., Ltd.)
10300 Metric Blvd.
Austin, TX 78758-9846
800-624-8654; 512-339-3500
FAX: 512-454-1357

Sound Blaster Pro Value Edition. Creative Labs' Sound Blaster Pro Value Edition provides affordable 8-bit, 44 kHz stereo recording and playback. Of course, this card is Sound Blaster compatible. Like the MediaMagic card, it uses FM synthesis using the Yamaha OPL3. It includes a CD-ROM interface for Panasonic CD-ROM drives. It also includes a MIDI, joystick, line-out, and microphone connectors. Its built-in amplifier provides four watts per channel.

Sound Blaster Pro Value Edition ($115)
Creative Labs Inc. (subsidiary of Creative Technology, Ltd.)
1901 McCarthy Blvd.
Milpitas, CA 95035
800-998-1000; 408-428-6600
Direct sales: 800-998-5227
FAX: 408-428-6611
Tech support: 405-742-6622
Tech support BBS: 405-742-6660

AudioBlitz Classic. Video card maker Genoa Systems has gotten into the sound card act. Its $79 AudioBlitz Classic (see fig. 9.1) is a 16-bit sound card that records and plays back at 44.1 kHz. It is bolstered by a 4-watt amplifier and includes a two-player joystick port, microphone, and earphones. The software that comes bundled with the card includes audio clips, a recorder, and a reminder function as well as a talking calculator and talking clock. It is both AdLib and Sound Blaster compatible and includes a MIDI interface.

III

Investing in Multimedia

Fig. 9.1
The AudioBlitz Classic provides stereo sound for less than $80.

AudioBlitz Classic ($79)
Genoa Systems Corp.
75 E. Trimble Rd.
San Jose, CA 95131
800-934-3662; 408-432-9090
Direct sales: 408-432-9123
FAX: 408-434-0997
Tech support: 408-432-8324
Tech support BBS: 408-943-1231

ARIA 16. The ARIA 16 from Prometheus Products Inc. provides affordable 16-bit stereo recording and playback at 44.1 kHz. It is Sound Blaster compatible and, surprisingly, uses wavetable, not FM, synthesis. It includes CD-ROM, joystick, and MIDI interfaces.

ARIA 16 ($99)
Prometheus Products Inc.
9524 S.W. Tualatin Sherwood Rd.
Tualatin, OR 97062
800-477-3473; 503-692-9600
FAX: 503-691-1101
Tech support: 503-692-9601

Sound on the Go
Need a sound card that is easy to add to either your desktop PC or laptop? Consider the following options.

Noisy Notebooks. Now that PC audio is less of a luxury and more of a necessity, notebook manufacturers are breaking into sealed cases and cramped motherboards to add sound components to the list of standard notebook features.

Sound is becoming essential for business presentations, and it can be used for auditing spreadsheets, annotating documents, even practicing Japanese lessons.

IBM, Toshiba, and Texas Instruments now offer notebooks with built-in sound. IBM was the first major vendor to put sound in a notebook. Its ThinkPad 750 has a DSP-based audio chip that can handle 16-bit stereo sound. Although the notebook has a single speaker, there are stereo jacks that can be used for headphones or external speakers. Toshiba's T4700 includes a color screen, a built-in microphone, and the Microsoft Sound System. It will record and play .WAV files, but can't play MIDI music files. And it's strictly monaural, but has jacks for headphones or external speakers.

Portable Sound. If you want to add sound to your notebook or desktop computer with minimal fuss, you have a few options, listed in table 9.2.

The older $199 AudioPort from Media Vision Inc. gives laptop computers plug-and-play monaural sound. Like most portable sound cards, the AudioPort plugs into your computer's parallel port. The size of a handheld calculator, the AudioPort either runs on four AA penlight batteries or with an AC adapter that is included.

The AudioPort supports both digitized sound (WAV) and MIDI files. It has a volume control and an internal speaker. Its output power is only one-fourth of a watt, but can be heard even with the volume turned down. If you want privacy, there is a headphone jack, which can be used to drive self-powered speakers. A microphone jack is included (but not a microphone) so you can make your own recordings. The AudioPort also supports MIDI.

III

Investing in Multimedia

Table 9.2 Audio Port Sound Cards

Model	Maker	Record rate	Playback rate
AudioPort	Media Vision	8-bit, 22.05 kHz	8-bit, 22.05 kHz
Port-Able Sound Plus	DSP Solutions	16-bit, 44.1 kHz	16-bit, 44.1 kHz
AudioMan	Logitech	8-bit, 11 kHz	8-bit, 22 kHz
PC Max	Gilltro-Electronics & Associates	16-bit, 8 kHz	16-bit, 44.1 kHz
JEI Soundport	Jacobs Electronics Inc.	8-bit, 11 kHz	8-bit, 25 kHz
AVerKey2 Plus Sound	ADDA Technologies Inc.	16-bit, 44.1 kHz	16-bit 44.1 kHz
MicroKey/AudioPort	Video Associates Labs	12-bit, 44.1 kHz	16-bit, 44.1 kHz

The AudioPort is not the most amazing product. It records in mono at a resolution of 8 bits and a sampling rate of 22 kHz. Other similar cards are providing 16-bit resolution at 44.1 kHz. Most likely, this doesn't matter. The end result is that the AudioPort is adequate for voice notes and an occasional game. With laptop hard disks getting fuller, the disk space required for high-fidelity recordings may be unavailable anyway.

AudioPort ($199)
Media Vision Inc.
47300 Bayside Pkwy.
Fremont, CA 94538
800-348-7116; 510-770-8600
Direct sales: 800-845-5870
FAX: 510-770-9592
Tech support: 800-638-2807
Tech support BBS: 510-770-0527

Digispeech's $198.95 Port-Able Sound Plus parallel-port sound device (see fig. 9.2) is slightly more expensive than its competitors but comes with better bundled software. It ships with a presentation package called Show and Tell for Kids, a WinReader text-reading program, and the Lotus Sound utility.

This portable sound card can produce fairly loud volumes. The Port-Able Sound Plus can also play MIDI sound effectively. The unit is suitable for office use; it has a hardware volume control and separate speaker as well as a pass-through connector for linking a printer through the device into the parallel port. One problem is the fact that the Port-Able must be turned off before the printer can operate. It can record and play 16-bit stereo audio, and is AdLib- and Sound Blaster-compatible for games.

Mono/Stereo	AdLib/Sound Blaster compatible (A,S)	MIDI Interface	Retail Price
Mono	A/S	Yes	$199
Stereo	A/S	No	$199
Stereo	—	No	$179
Stereo	A/S	No	$199
Stereo	?	No	$70
Stereo	No	Yes	$449
Mono	?	No	$295

Fig. 9.2
The Port-Able Sound Plus provides 16-bit sound through your parallel port.

Port-Able Sound Plus ($198.95)
DSP Solutions Inc.
2464 Embarcadero Way
Palo Alto, CA 94303
415-494-8086
Tech support: 415-494-8088
FAX: 415-494-8114

III

Investing in Multimedia

The AudioMan was Logitech's flagship product for its "Senseware" products designed to give human-like senses such as sight, sound, and touch to your computer. Already one of the world's largest manufacturers of computer mice and the international market leader in hand-held scanners, Logitech has entered the realm of sound cards.

AudioMan was designed to provide hassle-free addition of voice notes to Windows files. It doesn't do much else; it doesn't provide Sound Blaster-compatible sound to games and cannot work with MIDI devices. The $179 device connects to a standard parallel port but still allows you to print normally. The shaver-shaped device is powered by either two included AA batteries or an AC adapter. An audio output jack handles headphones, external speakers or other devices, and an input jack attaches to a CD player or other device.

Installing the AudioMan is simple. Simply connect it to your parallel port. The companion software requires less than a half-megabyte of disk space and is installed through either the Windows Control Panel or Program Manager. Even if you already have a sound card, you can install AudioMan. To use AudioMan, you open the AudioMan dialog box from the Control Panel. From there, you can set the volume or check the charge in your AA batteries. (There also is a manual volume control on the AudioMan itself.)

AudioMan comes with some great software. An AudioMan Setup utility lets you test output volume by ear and monitor battery level by eye. BestSpeech ReadOut lets you pick one of four natural voices to read your text. AudioPanel provides a slick graphical interface, mimicking digital sound equipment, as it lets you stack up sounds on a play list or call up an AudioEdit module. AudioAnnotator inserts sounds as objects. Logitech also stuffs a MIDI music-file player and Moon Valley Software's Icon Hear-It Lite in the box. The latter lets you attach sound files to desktop icons.

AudioMan's microphone sits on top of its 2-inch concave speaker. AudioMan records in sample rates of 8 bits (mono) at 11 kHz and plays back at sample rates of 8 bits at 22 or 44 kHz. For adding simple voice notes to business documents, AudioMan offers a simple, inexpensive solution.

AudioMan ($179)

Logitech Inc. (division of Logitech International)
6505 Kaiser Dr.
Fremont, CA 94555
800-231-7717; 510-795-8500
Direct sales: 800-732-2990
FAX: 510-792-8901
Tech support: 510-795-8100
Tech support BBS: 510-795-0408

Gilltro-Electronics & Associates offers PC MAX, which also attaches to one's parallel port. PC MAX records sounds at 13-bit at 8 kHz, suitable for voice annotation, and plays back sounds at up to 44.1 kHz. It also is AdLib and Sound Blaster compatible, and includes a microphone and two internal speakers.

PC MAX ($229)
Gilltro-Electronics & Associates
2994 Scott Blvd.
Santa Clara, CA 95054
800-GILTROX; 408-727-6422
FAX: 408-727-5508

Jacobs Electronics Inc. offers JEI Soundport for just $70. This audio port connects to the parallel port and plays and records 8-bit sound at up to 25 kHz.

JEI Soundport ($70)
Jacobs Electronics Inc.
16914 28th Dr., SE
Bothell, WA 98012
206-483-8755

ADDA Technologies Inc. offers AVerKey2 Plus Sound, an audio port that connects to the serial, not parallel, port. The AVerKey2 provides 44.1 kHz, 16-bit recording and playback. For its $449 price tag, it includes wavetable synthesis and a MIDI and line-out connector.

AVerKey2 Plus Sound ($449)
ADDA Technologies Inc.
48501 Warm Springs Blvd., Unit 109
Fremont, CA 94539
800-863-ADDA; 510-770-9899
FAX: 510-623-1803

Video Associates Labs' MicroKey/AudioPort also provides slot-free sound. The compact six-ounce unit plugs into your PC's parallel port. The $295 record-and-play version comes with a microphone (with a 9-foot cord), headphones, and AC adapter, along with drivers, editing programs, and sample sound files for both DOS and Windows. A play-back-only version is $100 less.

The device records 16-bit mono samples at sampling rates of 4 to 44 kHz. Sample size is limited only by disk space; ADPCM 4:1 data compression squeezes up to 8.5 minutes of sound per megabyte.

When working with uncompressed files, AudioPort's software can display sounds graphically for easy marking and editing. It has an auto-rewind option, and offers you the chance to audition sound files from the File Open dialog box instead of having to load each sound before you hear it. The software reads and writes WAV files and converts uncompressed VOC files to ADPCM format.

Neither AudioPort nor its headphones have hardware volume controls, so you'll have to adjust the volume through software or buy speakers with knobs or dials.

III

Investing in Multimedia

MicroKey/AudioPort ($295)
Video Associates Labs Inc.
4926 Spicewood Springs Rd.
Austin, TX 78759-8434
800-331-0547; 512-346-5781
FAX: 512-346-9407

PCMCIA. Many laptops are getting a voice through PCMCIA slots. By plugging a credit-card sized card into a PCMCIA slot, a laptop can become your sound system on the road. Table 9.3 summarizes some of the options in this category.

> **Tip**
>
> Because PCMCIA is an evolving specification, you may have some difficulties getting a PCMCIA sound card to work with your laptop. Insist on a money-back guarantee if you can't get it to work.

> **Note**
>
> PCMCIA stands for Personal Computer Memory Card International Association. Many laptops offer one or two PCMCIA slots for the addition of a credit-card sized PCMCIA card. The PCMCIA specification has three (soon to be four) versions. All three types use the same female 68-pin edge connector but differ in thickness. Thinner Type II cards can provide full Ethernet thinnet and 10BaseT and Token Ring LAN connections. On Type III PC Cards, the thickest, manufacturers such as Maxtor are able to place 100M or larger hard disks.

New Media is one of a handful of companies that offers PCMCIA audio ports. Its $399 .WAVjammer works with any PCMCIA Type I slots. It provides 16-bit, 44 kHz stereo recording and playback. It is both AdLib and Sound Blaster compatible. It uses FM synthesis and includes MIDI capabilities (but no port) and line-in, line-out, and microphone connectors.

Table 9.3   PCMCIA Sound Cards

Model	Maker	Record rate	Playback rate
.WAVjammer	New Media Corp.	16-bit, 44.1 kHz	16-bit, 44.1 kHz
Port-Able Sound PCMCIA	DSP Solutions	8-bit, 11 kHz	16-bit, 44.1 kHz
Pro Audio PCMCIA	Media Vision Inc.	16-bit, 48 kHz	16-bit, 48 kHz
Audio Advantage	Turtle Beach Systems	12-bit, 44.1 kHz	12-bit, 44.1 kHz
Temp	I/O Magic Corp.	12-bit, 44.1 kHz	12-bit, 44.1 kHz

.WAVjammer ($399)
New Media Corp.
One Technology, Bldg. A
Irvine, CA 92718
800-CARDS-4U; 714-453-0100
FAX: 714-453-0114
Tech support BBS: 714-453-0214

Turtle Beach Systems offers its Audio Advantage for $159. The PCMCIA Type I audio port provides 12-bit mono recording and playback at up to 44.1 kHz. It includes MIDI-in and MIDI-out connectors.

Audio Advantage ($159)
Turtle Beach Systems (subsidiary of Integrated Circuit Systems Inc.)
52 Grumbacher Rd.
York, PA 17402
800-645-5640; 717-767-0200
FAX: 717-767-6033
Tech support: 717-764-5265
Tech support BBS: 717-767-0250

I/O Magic Corp. offers its Tempo PCMCIA audio port. The $399 Tempo uses a PCMCIA Type II slot to provide 12-bit recording at up to 44.1 kHz and 16-bit, 44.1 kHz audio playback. It is both AdLib and Sound Blaster compatible and provides wavetable synthesis. It includes a MIDI interface, line-in, line-out, and microphone connectors.

Tempo ($299)
I/O Magic Corp.
199 Technology Dr., Bldg. 140
Irvine, CA 92718
800-607-7466; 714-727-7466
FAX: 714-727-7467

Mono/Stereo	AdLib/Sound Blaster compatible (A,S)	MIDI Interface	Retail Price
Stereo	A/S	Y	$399
Stereo	S	No	$280
Stereo	A/S	Y	$299
Mono	-	Y	$159
Mono	A/S	Y	$399

Mainstream Sound Cards

The bulk of sound cards can record and playback 16-bit, 44.1 kHz sounds in stereo—the standard MPC Level 2 requirement. Although such sounds require more disk space, you'll hear what you've been missing. Table 9.4 compares key features of these sound cards, and additional details follow.

Advanced Gravis UltraSound CD3 and UltraSound Max. With a list price of $199, the UltraSound CD3 provides a low-cost entry into the world of wavetable and three-dimensional sound. However, its lukewarm sound quality and a lack of business software limit its use to education and games. By itself, the UltraSound offers only 8-bit recording with 16-bit playback, though adding a $99.95 daughtercard gives you 16-bit recording.

Table 9.4 Mainstream Sound Cards

Model	Maker	Record rate	Playback rate
UltraSound CD3	Advanced Gravis	8-bit, 44.1 kHz	16-bit, 44.1 kHz
UltraSound Max	Advanced Gravis	8-bit, 44.1 kHz	16-bit, 44.1 kHz
Sound Galaxy Basic 16	Aztech Labs	16-bit, 44.1 kHz	16-bit, 44.1 kHz
Sound Galaxy PRO 16 Extra	Aztech Labs	16-bit, 44.1 kHz	16-bit, 44.1 kHz
Digital Sound Pro 16	Cardinal Technologies	16-bit, 48 kHz	16-bit, 48 kHz
Digital Sound Plus Pro 16	Cardinal Technologies	16-bit, 48 kHz	16-bit, 48 kHz
Sound Blaster 16 Basic	Creative Labs	16-bit, 44.1 kHz	16-bit, 44.1 kHz
Sound Blaster 16 SCSI-2	Creative Labs	16-bit, 44.1 kHz	16-bit, 44.1 kHz
SonicSound	Diamond Computer Systems	16-bit, 44.1 kHz	16-bit, 44.1 kHz
SonicSound LX	Diamond Computer Systems	16-bit, 44.1 kHz	16-bit, 44.1 kHz
Audiovation Adapter	IBM	16-bit, 44.1 kHz	16-bit, 44.1 kHz
WindSurfer	IBM	16-bit, 44.1 kHz	16-bit, 44.1 kHz
SoundMan 16	Logitech	16-bit, 44.1 kHz	16-bit, 44.1 kHz
Pro Audio 16 Basic	Media Vision	16-bit, 44.1 kHz	16-bit, 44.1 kHz
Pro AudioStudio 16	Media Vision	16-bit, 44.1 kHz	16-bit, 44.1 kHz
Premium 3-D	Media Vision	16-bit, 48 kHz	16-bit, 48 kHz
Microsoft Sound System	Microsoft	16-bit, 44.1 kHz	16-bit, 44.1 kHz
SoundWave 32	Orchid Technology	16-bit, 48 kHz	16-bit, 48 kHz

The UltraSound uses wavetable, not the cruder FM, synthesis. However, unlike most wavetable-based boards, which store digitized audio samples in on-board ROM, the UltraSound uses your hard disk to store 5.6M of supplied digitized samples. It supports patch caching, a feature of Windows 3.1's Multimedia extensions. Applications that support patch caching download only those patches required for a particular set of MIDI data to the 512K on-board RAM (upgradable to 1M). The UltraSound ships with Patch Maker software, which lets you record new sample files or edit existing ones.

Advanced Gravis has added Roland MPU-401 emulation and has updated its Creative Labs Sound Blaster emulation and Windows driver files. The UltraSound ships with Modus (a Windows MOD player), Turtle Beach Systems' Wave Lite for Windows

Mono/Stereo	AdLib/Sound Blaster compatible (A,S)	MIDI Interface	Synthesis Type	CD-ROM Interface	Retail Price
Stereo	A/S	Yes	Wavetable	No	$199
Stereo	A/S	Yes	Wavetable	Yes	$249
Stereo	A/S	Yes	FM	Yes	$169
Stereo	A/S	Yes	FM	Yes	$279
Stereo	A/S	Yes	FM	Yes	$159
Stereo	A/S	Yes	FM	Yes	$229
Stereo	S	Yes	FM	No	$199.95
Stereo	S	Yes	FM	No	$279.95
Stereo	A/S	Yes	Wavetable	Yes	$299
Stereo	A/S	Yes	Wavetable	Yes	$149
Stereo	S	Yes	Wavetable	Yes	$255
Stereo	S	Yes	Wavetable	No	$399
Stereo	A/S	Yes	FM	No	$199
Stereo	A/S	Yes	FM	No	$199
Stereo	A/S	Yes	FM	Yes	$349
Stereo	A/S	Yes	FM	Yes	$199
Stereo	A	No	FM	No	$219
Stereo	A/S	Yes	Wavetable	Yes	$249

III

Investing in Multimedia

(Windows mixer), Howling Dog Systems' Power Chords (a guitar-based synthesizer and drum machine program), Midisoft's Recording Session (sequencer software), Epic Pinball, Doom, Ultrasound Studio, a 3-D demo, and WinSoft SoundStation (Windows record and playback software). No microphone or headphones are included.

Advanced Gravis also offers the UltraSound Max. The $249 UltraSound Max is essentially the same design but includes 16-bit recording and a Mitsumi/Panasonic/Sony CD-ROM AT-style interface.

Gravis UltraSound CD3 ($199)
UltraSound Max ($249)
Advanced Gravis Computer Technology, Ltd.
3750 N. Fraser Way, Ste. 101
Burnaby, BC, CD V5J 5E9
800-663-8558; 604-431-5020
FAX: 604-431-5155
Tech support: 604-431-1807

Aztech Sound Galaxy Basic 16 & Sound Galaxy Pro 16 Extra. The Aztech Sound Galaxy Basic 16 ($137) and Aztech Sound Galaxy PRO 16 Extra ($150) offer a solid set of features and great software bundles. The Sound Galaxy Basic is a natural for entertainment or educational use; the Sound Galaxy PRO is appealing for business applications. Both products use FM synthesis and can be upgraded with a wavetable synthesis daughtercard called Wave Power ($148).

Both cards reproduce 16-bit CD-quality (44.1 kHz) audio, provide AdLib and Sound Blaster compatibility, and use a Yamaha OPL3 FM synthesis chip. Overall, the Sound Galaxy PRO 16 Extra sounds slightly better than the Sound Galaxy Basic 16. Installation is easy, especially for the Sound Galaxy PRO 16 Extra, which has a smooth, software-only configuration.

The Sound Galaxy PRO 16 Extra has an auto-adjust filtering feature that lets you filter out distortion introduced by digital-to-analog conversion, according to Aztech; you can manually override the filtering for special effects. The Sound Galaxy PRO 16 Extra supports Mitsumi, Panasonic, and Sony CD-ROM drives; a SCSI CD-ROM interface is a $39 option. The Sony CD requires an adapter ($19). The Sound Galaxy Basic 16 has a CD-ROM interface, and supports Mitsumi, Panasonic, and Sony CD-ROM drives as well. Sony CD-ROM drives need the same adapter headphone.

Both cards come with headphones and are bundled with Voyetra's AudioStation for Windows; SoundScript for both DOS and Windows; an audio calendar; Say It voice annotation; voice mail for NetWare; WinDAT sound editor; Jukebox, for playing .WAV, MIDI, and CD music in the background; an audio screen saver; a DOS command-line MIDI player; and a collection of sound tracks. The Sound Galaxy PRO 16 Extra adds CommVoice (a voice recognition program), a microphone, and a Monologue.

The Wave Power upgrade conforms to the General MIDI sound set, offering 128 authentic instrument samples and 47 percussion sounds. The output was more realistic with the add-on card installed, and the included Midisoft Studio software gave us excellent control over MIDI composition. The software lets you note music in standard notation with drag-and-drop operation on up to 32,000 tracks.

Sound Galaxy Basic 16 ($137)
Sound Galaxy PRO 16 Extra ($159)
Aztech Labs Inc. (subsidiary of Aztech Systems Pte., Ltd.)
46707 Fremont Blvd.
Fremont, CA 94538
800-886-8829; 510-623-8988
Tech support: 800-886-8879
FAX: 510-623-8989

Cardinal Digital Sound Pro 16 and Digital Sound Pro 16 Plus. The Cardinal Digital Sound Pro 16, shown in figure 9.3, and the Cardinal Digital Sound Pro 16 Plus are inexpensive, average-quality sound cards that are capable enough for games, everyday business use, and low-end multimedia. The Sound Pro 16 has a list price of $159. The Sound Pro 16 Plus, which adds a SCSI CD-ROM interface, lists for $229. Both use FM synthesis, which can be upgraded to wavetable synthesis for $59.

Installation is straightforward: Each card has only two jumpers (you can select from eight IRQ lines and two DMA channels via software), and setup menus are simple. Adding an option (such as the wavetable ROM) is a bit more complicated because the add-on configuration routines aren't as intuitive.

These two Sound Pro 16 boards are compatible with major audio standards including Creative Labs Sound Blaster, the Microsoft Windows Sound System, and Compaq Business Audio. With each card you get the Voyetra Sound Software Collection (a collection of tools for both business and audio-production applications); Voyetra's AudioStation (a software stereo system); Say It (a sound annotation utility); WinDAT and DOSDAT (recording tools); SoundScript (a multimedia authoring tool); MIDI Orchestrator (to create and play back MIDI files); JukeBox (an audio CD player); and a small collection of music clips.

Both Cardinal boards are based on the Analog Devices ADSP2115 digital signal processor. Because this DSP, unlike a fixed-function sound chip, is programmable, you can upgrade the cards' capabilities simply by buying a software upgrade. For instance, a $79 upgrade from Xing Technology Corp. (805-473-0145) allows you to add 12:1 MPEG compression and decompression capabilities to complement the cards' standard A-Law and Mu-Law compression algorithms.

These two Sound Pro 16 boards offer external mini-jacks for a microphone, speakers, line input and output, and a game port. An internal connector lets you hook up audio output from an internal CD-ROM drive. Since the Sound Pro 16 Plus's 16-bit SCSI controller is from Adaptec, most SCSI-based CD-ROM drives and utilities should work without a hitch.

III

Investing in Multimedia

Fig. 9.3
The Sound Pro 16 provides affordable sound for everyday game or business use.

Digital Sound Pro 16 ($100)
Digital Sound Pro 16 Plus ($150)
Cardinal Technologies Inc.
1827 Freedom Rd.
Lancaster, PA 17601
717-293-3000
Direct sales: 717-293-3049
FAX: 717-399-2324
Tech support: 717-293-3124
Tech support BBS: 717-293-3074

Creative Labs Sound Blaster 16 Basic Edition and Sound Blaster 16 SCSI-2. These
two Creative Labs Sound Blaster cards are not much different than their predecessors.
However, they are among the better FM synthesis boards. The Creative Labs Sound
Blaster 16 Basic Edition, which lists for $199.95, is well-suited for professional and busi-
ness audio as well as to games and education. The Basic Edition can be upgraded to the
now-discontinued Sound Blaster 16 ASP by adding a $69.95 CSP chip.

In the SCSI-2 version, the Sound Blaster 16 is available either with or without a CSP chip.
The Sound Blaster 16 SCSI-2 has a SCSI-2 interface run by an Adaptec controller instead
of the Panasonic CD-ROM interface that the Basic Edition has.

Both Sound Blaster 16 cards produce 16-bit, 44.1 kHz audio output that is good but not
stellar. MIDI playback is handled by the Yamaha OPL3 chip. For more realistic sound,
you can add the optional $249.95 Wave Blaster daughtercard, which includes the E-mu
Proteus/1 wavetable synthesizer chip and General MIDI instrument patches.

The Sound Blaster cards also share the same installation procedure and program. The installation software checks that the Sound Blaster's IRQ, DMA, and address settings aren't already in use by another device.

Both units come with Soundo'LE (an OLE-server recording utility for voice); CD, MIDI, and .WAV files; Wave Studio (a .WAV file editor); Talking Scheduler (which converts text to speech for verbal reminders of appointments); Mosaic (a tile game); Jukebox (a MIDI player); and First Byte's Monologue for Windows (a text-to-speech synthesizer). The SCSI-2 version includes Grolier's Multimedia Encyclopedia on CD, HSC InterActive SE (a multimedia authoring tool), Pacific Motion Software's PC Animate Plus (an animation editor), and Creative VoiceAssist (a voice recognition utility).

Additionally, the Sound Blaster 16 SCSI-2 comes with QSound, which downloads an algorithm onto the board's proprietary CSP to create an impressive "three-dimensional" sound effect. The on-board DSP also allows for real-time (albeit proprietary) file compression, as well as A-Law and Mu-Law compression standards on both boards.

Sound Blaster Value Edition ($149)
Sound Blaster 16 SCSI-2 ($249)
Creative Labs Inc. (subsidiary of Creative Technology, Ltd.)
1901 McCarthy Blvd.
Milpitas, CA 95035
800-998-1000; 408-428-6600
Direct sales: 800-998-5227
FAX: 408-428-6611
Tech support: 405-742-6622
Tech support BBS: 405-742-6660

Diamond SonicSound and SonicSound LX. Video card maker Diamond Computer Systems has made a promising entrance into the audio market with its Diamond SonicSound and Diamond SonicSound LX. The SonicSound LX, a basic FM synthesis board aimed at the game player or entry-level PC audio buyer, lists for $149 and has a street price of around $90 or $100. The more capable SonicSound, which lists for $299, is targeted toward the business or professional user. It offers wavetable synthesis and an on-board DSP; enhanced General MIDI capabilities and rudimentary voice recognition are a $129 option. Both cards support CD-ROM drives, include game (joystick) ports, and are Sound Blaster compatible.

Sound quality is generally above average, although the SonicSound LX has been reported to have poor bass response. Both cards rely on software controls for setting output volume. Both cards come with concise installation instructions, although documentation for the SonicSound was more extensive than that for the SonicSound LX.

The SonicSound LX is based on the popular Yamaha OPL3 FM synthesis chip but uses the Sierra chip. Its CD-ROM interface supports only drives from Mitsumi, Panasonic, and Sony. The board includes Midisoft's Recording Session and Sound Impression, plus a collection of DOS utilities that lets you record and play CD audio as well as .WAV and MIDI files.

The more expensive SonicSound uses the Sierra Semiconductor Aria chip set and a Texas Instruments TMS320C25 DSP chip. Its SCSI-2 interface supports a variety of CD-ROM drives. The SonicSound includes the same software as the SonicSound LX and adds Macromedia Action! 2.5 SE and Virgin/Trilobyte's 7th Guest.

A $129 Professional Upgrade for the SonicSound provides additional MIDI patches and comes with a passable headset with microphone. Also included is SonicSound Listener software, which lets you operate Windows software by speaking common commands. In practice, the voice recognition proved more frustrating than convenient: even after training, it was accurate about only two-thirds of the time in our testing.

A MIDI cable kit (which offers MIDI In and MIDI Out jacks) is a $39.95 option for either product.

SonicSound ($299)
SonicSound LX ($149)
Diamond Computer Systems Inc.
1130 E. Arques Ave.
Sunnyvale, CA 94086
408-736-2000
FAX: 408-730-5750
Tech support BBS: 408-524-9301

IBM Audiovation Adapter and WindSurfer Communications Adapter. The IBM Audiovation Adapter ($255) and the IBM WindSurfer Communications Adapter ($399) are aimed directly at business users. The Audiovation includes wavetable synthesis, a CD-ROM port (only on ISA), and an on-board DSP. The WindSurfer, also a wavetable synthesis board, uses its IBM Electronics DSP to double as a 14,400 bps modem (V.32bis and MNP 5-compatible), 9,600 bps fax, and digital answering machine. Both cards produce clear sound, without breaks or hissing.

Setting up the WindSurfer can be an involved task because its communications functions can cause conflicts with existing COM ports in your PC. You must also run a supplied utility to activate the board's communication features. The Audiovation's setup is unremarkable.

Tip

The WindSurfer, shown in figure 9.4, provides a combination sound card, answering machine, and fax modem in one, thanks to the digital signal processor (DSP).

The same Windows-based sound utilities, Mwave Recorder and Mwave Audio, are included for both cards. Besides the usual array of audio jacks, the Audiovation includes two connectors for Panasonic or Sony CD-ROM drives. Two additional Windows applications are standard: Talk-togPlus gives you voice control over Windows applications, and First Byte's Monologue converts text into speech.

The WindSurfer has one stereo line-in jack and one RJ-11 jack for headphone hookups. The ISA version does not include a CD-ROM interface, although the MCA version does. IBM PhoneFX, which allows you to set up a voice mail system on your desktop system, is bundled with the board, as is Trio Fax Lite software and a Prodigy membership kit.

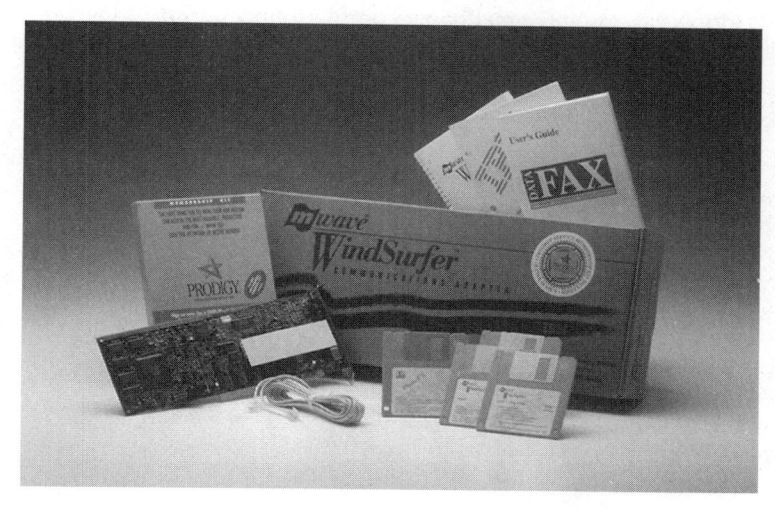

Fig. 9.4
The IBM WindSurfer provides not only a sound card but a fax modem as well.

IBM Audiovation Adapter ($255)
IBM WindSurfer Communications Adapter ($399)
IBM (International Business Machines)
Old Orchard Rd.
Armonk, NY 10504
800-426-3333; 914-765-1900
Direct sales: 800-426-7695 (IBM PC Direct)
Tech support: 800-237-5511
Tech support BBS: 919-517-0001; 800-847-7211 (OS2)

Logitech SoundMan 16. The Logitech SoundMan 16 is a low-priced package best suited for entry-level business and game applications. The SoundMan 16 hardware consists solely of the sound card, a minimalist approach that carries over to the card itself. Built around the Media Vision Pro Audio Spectrum chip set, the card offers FM synthesis with four operators; it uses the Yamaha OPL3 chip but lacks a CD-ROM interface or anything as sophisticated as a DSP, wavetable in firmware, or hardware support for voice recognition. The one extra on the board is hardware support for ADPCM data compression, an important feature for business use.

The software is lean. The DOS-level software is limited to a mixer and utilities for recording .WAV files and playing .WAV or PCM files. Windows software includes the widely-used MCS MusicRack, which provides a mixer, MIDI player, CD player, and a digital recorder, all of which use controls that will be familiar to anyone who has a tape recorder or CD player.

The SoundMan 16 also includes three somewhat whimsical utilities that let you add such options to Windows as animated wallpaper complete with sound. No business applications, such as a voice annotator, text-to-speech utility, or voice recognition software, come with the package.

The Logitech SoundMan 16 is best as a starter kit with enough quality hardware and software to be useful. It's certain to leave gaps that you need to fill in. However, it's surprisingly easy to set up, and it's inexpensive enough so that buying additional software shouldn't break your budget.

Logitech SoundMan 16 ($149)
Logitech Inc. (division of Logitech International)
6505 Kaiser Dr.
Fremont, CA 94555
800-231-7717; 510-795-8500
Direct sales: 800-732-2990
FAX: 510-792-8901
Tech support: 510-795-8100
Tech support BBS: 510-795-0408

Media Vision Premium 3-D. Media Vision's Premium 3-D is aimed directly at Creative Labs' Sound Blaster. This $199 sound card was designed for the gaming world.

An optional daughtercard, the $199 Professional Wavetable Upgrade, gives the Premium 3-D 32 synthesized voices and superior sound effects. It's compatible with the Creative Labs' Wave Blaster FM/wavetable daughtercard but relies on a ROM chip-based sound library holding digital samples. This daughtercard includes 4M of samples made up of 128 general MIDI instruments and 4 drum sets, plus reverb and chorus effects. This daughtercard not only works with the 3-D but also any Sound Blaster-compatible card that has a 26-pin connector.

The Premium 3-D includes supports multiple CD-ROM drives through its standard SCSI-2 interface. In its MultiCD version, the 3D can handle dual-speed Mitsumi, Panasonic, or Sony drives.

The Premium 3-D provides 8- and 16-bit playback and recording at sampling rates from 4 to 48 kHz, 5-channel audio mixing, and amplified lines with 4 watts of power. The card includes microphone, line-in, and CD-ROM audio jacks, and it has a volume control wheel and MIDI/game port connector.

The Premium 3-D uses a standard FM/wavetable synthesis chip (the Yamaha OPL3 sound processor), but it also has an important added audio enhancement: surround-sound technology. This 3-D sound technology adds a richness to software audio effects that really sweetens the sound experience for game players.

Media Vision's automatic DOS installation for the Premium 3-D quickly loads the list of software drivers and installs the included software, but demands 9M of disk space for the full installation. With the SCSI-2 Premium 3-D you get CD-ROM drivers, Windows 3.1 sound drivers, DOS utilities, MidiSoft's Sound Impression and Recording Session, and Monologue text-to-speech software.

The Premium 3-D is a mix of interesting technologies. While there's nothing too remarkable about the sound quality and effects presented by the Professional Wavetable Upgrade card, the surround-sound effects and the price of the Premium card itself make it noteworthy.

Premium 3-D ($199)
Media Vision Inc.
47300 Bayside Pkwy.
Fremont, CA 94538
800-348-7116; 510-770-8600
Direct sales: 800-845-5870
FAX: 510-770-9592
Tech support: 800-638-2807
Tech support BBS: 510-770-0527

Microsoft Windows Sound System 2.0. The $219 Microsoft Windows Sound System 2.0 (see fig. 9.5) may disappoint MIDI composers, game players and those with internal CD-ROM drives. However, tight software integration makes the Windows Sound System the best argument yet for business audio.

The Windows Sound System uses FM synthesis. Its sound quality won't impress audiophiles, but for speech-driven business audio applications, the system's quality is certainly adequate.

Seven basic, easy-to-use applets are included with the sound board. They are also available separately for $79 with the directional microphone. You can use the applets with an earlier version of the Windows Sound System or with compatible products from other vendors.

One of the bundled utilities, Quick Recorder, lets you make recordings at a variety of preset sampling rates and sizes—or choose your own custom parameters. You can then drag-and-drop voice annotations or music clips into any OLE 2.0 and choose an icon to mark the annotation.

A significant addition to Quick Recorder is the software-based TrueSpeech codec (compression/decompression algorithm), which compresses voice recordings while maintaining maximum fidelity. During our subjective testing, we found that Microsoft's TrueSpeech spoken-word recordings sounded better than uncompressed 8-bit, 11-kHz recordings while requiring only one-tenth the disk space. The product also supports ADPCM compression.

Among other improvements in this version of the Windows Sound System is the revamped Voice Pilot voice recognition utility, which lets you issue voice commands to software. The new version requires less training time and lets you add words and different vocabularies more easily.

The board omits an internal analog audio connector, which means you can't play back audio from standard CDs or mixed-mode CD-ROM disks. No MIDI or joystick connector is provided, either.

Fig. 9.5
The Microsoft Windows Sound System legitimized the use of sound in the workplace.

Microsoft Windows Sound System 2.0 ($219)
Microsoft Corp.
One Microsoft Way
Redmond, WA 98052-6399
206-882-8080

Orchid SoundWave 32. The Orchid SoundWave 32, from Orchid Technology, is a combination wavetable/FM synthesis sound card rich in features. The SoundWave 32 lists for $299. It supports CD-ROM drives from Mitsumi and Sony.

Based on the Analog Devices ADSP 2115 digital signal processor, the SoundWave 32 provides broad compatibility and 1M of built-in wavetable-based instrument sounds. It is suitable for both multimedia presentations and games.

The card is bundled with Midisoft's Sound Impression, a "rack-mounted" multimedia control panel. It also comes with a simplified software mixer control. If you make the mistake of having Sound Impression and the mixer open simultaneously, you'll find that the two interfere with each other—a problem that was briefly troubling during installation. Otherwise, installation proves straightforward.

Midisoft's Sound Impression, however, doesn't match the intuitive, elegant usability of Voyetra's AudioStation program, which is included with many competitors' boards. Macromedia Action! and Aristo-Soft's Wired for Sound Pro also ship with the SoundWave 32, as do a pair of small unamplified speakers and a clip-on microphone.

> **Note**
>
> A game version of the SoundWave 32 is also available. For $179, the GameWave 32 provides all the features of the SoundWave 32 except it can only play back sounds, not record.

SoundWave 32 ($299)
Orchid Technology Inc.
45365 Northport Loop West
Fremont, CA 94538
800-767-2443; 510-683-0300
FAX: 510-490-9312
Tech support: 510-683-0323
Tech support BBS: 510-683-0327

Video and Sound

If your PC's slots are crammed to the gills, you can add video and sound in one step. There are several graphics boards with multimedia capabilities. Such a board could be just what you need if you're short on expansion slots. Some graphics cards are including sound chips, while some sound cards are adding graphics. Either way, you can save money by buying two cards in one as well as an expansion slot. However, the marketplace is still unsure if such combination cards will become mainstream products or just a footnote in computer history.

A graphics-plus-sound card is inevitably a compromise; although you get the benefit of two cards' worth of hardware in one slot, you're usually giving up the full-featured power of two separate and dedicated cards. Equally important, if one function becomes technically outdated and you decide to upgrade, or if it breaks down, you're stuck replacing the entire board, including the half that still works fine.

ATI Wonder XL. ATI Technologies offers its VGA stereo FX card, which mixes VGA graphics with 8-bit, Sound Blaster-compatible sound for game players. In other words, it compromises on both graphics and sound, but for a list price of $199, you really can't expect much more.

ATI Wonder XL ($199)
ATI Technologies Inc.
33 Commerce Valley Dr., E
Thornhill, ON, CD L3T 7N6
905-882-2600
FAX: 905-882-2620
Tech support: 905-882-2626
Tech support BBS: 905-764-9404

High-End Sound

If you are interested in multimedia primarily for MIDI or for high-end multimedia presentations or productions, consider these products, which retail for more than $350. For their price, virtually all high-end sound cards provide wavetable synthesis. Their serious nature, however, may exclude any game sound capabilities, such as Sound Blaster compatibility. Table 9.5 summarizes what high-end cards have to offer.

Antex Model Z1. The Antex Model Z1 may appear to be a high-priced FM synthesis board, but it's a high-quality product that professional audio users will appreciate. The Model Z1's audio quality is excellent, in the same class as the high-end Turtle Beach MultiSound. The Model Z1 also supports SCSI CD-ROM drives and includes a DSP that handles multiple compression formats. For heavy-duty multimedia production, the Model Z1 is an excellent choice.

Table 9.5   High-End Sound Cards (over $350)

Model	Maker	Record rate	Playback rate
Model Z1	Antex	16-bit, 50 kHz	16-bit, 50 kHz
Sound Blaster AWE32	Creative Labs	16-bit, 44 kHz	16-bit, 44 kHz
MultiSound Monterey	Turtle Beach Systems	16-bit, 44.1 kHz	16-bit, 44.1 kHz
SoundMan Wave	Logitech	16-bit, 44.1 kHz	16-bit, 44.1 kHz
MultiSound Monterey	Turtle Beach Systems	16-bit, 44.1 kHz	16-bit, 44.1 kHz
RAP-10/AT	Roland Corp.	16-bit, 44.1 kHz	16-bit, 110 kHz

The Model Z1 is compatible with Sound Blaster. For serious MIDI work, Antex offers a 32-voice wavetable MIDI synthesis option called Z.WAV ($195). Based on the new Ensoniq OTTO synthesizer engine, Z.WAV offers Roland MPU-401 compatibility and MIDI buffering on top of 175 MIDI instrument samples. The Model Z1 supports 4:1 ADPCM compression. A sister card, the $595 Model Z1e, adds MPEG compression capabilities.

The card ships with DOS and Windows drivers, a demo program, and a Windows-based sound mixer utility called Antex Mixer. Voyetra Technologies' Multimedia Toolkit for Windows and DOS is also included. Programmers can use the optional SPDK toolkit ($500) to program the on-board DSP in C or the optional ADK toolkit ($750) to create BASIC programs that control the board.

Antex Model Z1 ($395)
Antex Electronics Corp.
16100 S. Figueroa St.
Gardena, CA 90248
800-338-4231
310-532-3092
FAX: 310-532-8509.

Creative Labs Sound Blaster AWE32. Creative Labs' $399.95 Sound Blaster AWE32, shown in figure 9.6, includes enhanced MIDI sampling, speech and voice processing, and special effects like 3-D surround-sound to help it compete with high-end companies like Turtle Beach Systems.

Based on the E-mu Systems EMU8000 upgradable audio DSP, the AWE32 is a full CD-audio-quality card with 8- and 16-bit recording and playback, 32 simultaneous wave-table voices, standard FM music synthesis, and 128 general MIDI samples. Its programmable DSP features compression algorithms for processing text-to-speech data and enables the card's QSound surround-sound 3-D audio, along with reverb and chorus effects.

Mono/ Stereo	AdLib/Sound Blaster compatible (A,S)	MIDI Interface	Synthesis Type	CD-ROM Interface	Retail Price
Stereo	A/S	Yes	FM	Yes	$595
Stereo wavetable	S	Yes	FM/	Yes	$399
Stereo	—	Yes	Wavetable	No	$399
Stereo	A/S	Yes	FM	Yes	$349
Stereo	—	Yes	Wavetable	No	$399
Stereo	—	Yes	Wavetable	No	$599

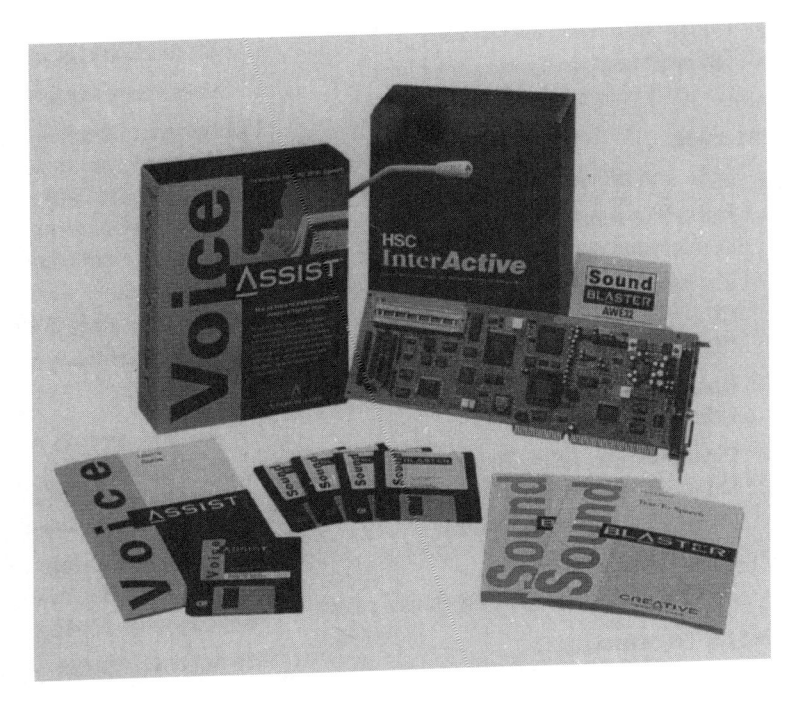

Fig. 9.6
The Sound Blaster AWE32 provides high-end sound for audiophiles.

The Sound Blaster AWE32 is fast and easy to install. Despite the half-dozen disks you have to load, it doesn't take much to get the new Sound Blaster up and running. Sound quality for the AWE32 is a close match for any card in its price range, though the sharpness of its Roland MPU-401/MT 32-compatible MIDI output remains its obvious strength.

The AWE32's 10-channel mixer handles 4-watts per channel of amplified stereo output, while its complete array of I/O jacks give you a range of sampling and playback options. These include CD-ROM interface connectors for Creative Labs (Panasonic),and Sony and Mitsumi double-speed drives. In addition, you get lines in and out for microphone, CD players, and speakers. The external MIDI port doubles as a joystick connector, too.

The Sound Blaster AWE32 includes several Windows and DOS utilities, including VoiceAssist (voice recognition), TextAssist (text-to-speech conversion), WaveStudio (WAV editing) and more.

Sound Blaster AWE32 ($399.95)
Creative Labs Inc.
1901 McCarthy Blvd.
Milpitas, CA 95035
800-998-5227; 408-428-6600
FAX: 408-428-6611

Turtle Beach Systems MultiSound Monterey. The Turtle Beach Systems' $399 MultiSound Monterey (see fig. 9.7) builds on the features of the company's original MultiSound: it adds the ability to store software wavetables and to expand on-board memory using standard SIMMs.

Fig. 9.7
The Turtle Beach Systems MultiSound has been a standard against which other cards must be measured.

The MultiSound Monterey's undisputed forte is professional-quality recording, playback, and MIDI composition. It is expensive for entertainment use, and its lack of a CD-ROM port and standard microphone input (you must use an expensive line-level mike or your own mixer) make it inappropriate for many business applications. Also, the MultiSound Monterey won't work with games that require Sound Blaster or MT-32 compatibility. But for serious music or multimedia applications, it's hard to beat.

The card's audio quality is still the best around. In fact, the audio connectors are plated in gold to prevent oxidation. Level controls provided much flexibility, with smooth volume control over their entire range.

The MultiSound uses the E-mu Proteus 1XR wavetable chip set preferred by professional musicians. With 4M of stored instrument sounds, MIDI playback sounds realistic. Turtle Beach's proprietary Hurricane Architecture uses a high-speed on-board DSP to eliminate the need for a DMA channel and reduce CPU overhead.

Installation of the hardware is straightforward. Three switches on the board select the board's port address; all other hardware requirements are selected during the installation program.

Besides some MIDI tools and other accessory programs, Turtle Beach provides Wave Lite for Windows, a "lite" version of the company's excellent Wave for Windows editing

III

Investing in Multimedia

program. Wave Lite provides basic sound-editing functions but offers no special effects or drag-and-drop capability.

Turtle Beach MultiSound Monterey ($399)
Turtle Beach Systems
52 Grumbacher Rd.
York, PA 17402
800-645-5640; 717-767-0200
FAX: 717-767-6033

Logitech SoundMan Wave. Logitech's SoundMan Wave ($299) offers the best of almost everything. It produces MIDI music that's above average, has great waveform characteristics, a SCSI CD-ROM interface, and a good software bundle.

This ISA board uses the new OPL4 chip set, which is the next generation of music synthesizers from Yamaha Corp. of America. Unlike the OPL3 chip, which offers tinny FM synthesis, this chip produces music using higher-quality wavetable synthesis, producing impressively realistic sound, except for a few guitar and piano instruments. But overall, the OPL4 chip fares well and maintains complete compatibility with its now lowly predecessor, the OPL3 FM synthesizer.

The 16-bit, 44.1-kHz card interfaces with SCSI-1 CD-ROM drives and offers 6 watts per channel of stereo amplification as well as a port for joysticks and MIDI (Musical Instrument Digital Interface) devices. Installation requires no jumpers; file decompression is hardware-based for speed, and SoundMan Wave's setup software makes installation easy.

The SoundMan Wave offers a good collection of software for tasks such as voice annotation, waveform recording, MIDI-music sequencing, and voice playback of computer text. The only area that needs improvement is installation. The problem? The SoundMan Wave works with too few IRQs, a limitation that derives from its ability to emulate the Sound Blaster, which works only with IRQs 2. 3. 4. 5 or 7. It would be helpful if the board also supported IRQs 10 to 12.

Logitech SoundMan Wave ($299)
Logitech Inc. (division of Logitech International)
6505 Kaiser Dr.
Fremont, CA 94555
800-231-7717; 510-795-8500
Direct sales: 800-732-2990
FAX: 510-792-8901
Tech support: 510-795-8100
Tech support BBS: 510-795-0408

Roland RAP-10/AT. The $599 Roland RAP-10/AT (RAP stands for Roland Audio Production) is the latest entry from a company long respected for its professional MIDI keyboards. Like the Turtle Beach MultiSound, this sound card provides high-end performance more for the professional than for the casual business audio user or game player. In fact, the RAP-10/AT entirely omits a CD-ROM interface.

When playing back MIDI files, the RAP-10/AT (see fig. 9.8) provides realistic sound, thanks to Roland's custom-wavetable-based Sound Canvas chip set and DSP. The RAP-10/AT also supports special effects such as chorus, reverb, and delay in hardware.

Fig. 9.8
The Roland RAP-10/AT leverages Roland's extensive MIDI experience.

The RAP-10/AT offers a stereo microphone input that can be switched under software control to handle a second line-level source. The board doesn't provide a power amplifier on-board, so you'll either have to use powered speakers or hook the output to an audio amplifier of your own.

Installing the RAP-10/AT means setting jumpers for the board's one required IRQ and two required DMA channels. The installation software checks the system for resource conflicts but doesn't give you a list of available resources up front.

Roland includes Roland Audio Tools, a version of Midisoft's Sound Impression software that's been specifically optimized for the RAP-10/AT. Roland Audio Tools provides convenient controls and powerful editing functions with the familiar "rack-mounted" interface. The included WaMI Mixer software lets you mix and sequence .WAV and MIDI files, too.

Roland RAP-10/AT ($349)
Roland Consumer Products Group
7200 Dominion Circle
Los Angeles, CA 90040
213-685-5141
FAX: 213-726-8865

III

Investing in Multimedia

Sound Card Applications

While the Multimedia PC specifications may tell you what you *need* for multimedia and digitized sound, the software and hardware below are items you may *want* for audio variety and just simple entertainment. Through software, a sound card offers many uses, such as:

- Adding sound effects to business presentations and training software
- Adding sound effects to Windows
- Giving a PC voice commands
- Adding voice security to your PC
- Turning a PC into a proofreader
- Turning a PC into a dictator

Voice Recognition

Some sound cards are capable of voice recognition. Imagine giving your PC voice commands from within Microsoft Windows. Voice-recognition technology is not perfect and requires a speedy computer, such as a 486DX4 or Pentium for nimble response times. Also, most voice-recognition programs are speaker dependent, working best with a single person, not multiple users.

Voice recognition software is included with some sound cards. The Pro AudioStudio 16 from Media Vision includes ExecuVoice, Creative Labs bundles its VoiceAssist with some Sound Blaster sound cards, and the Microsoft Windows Sound System includes Voice Pilot. These packages' primary problems are that they are sensitive to background noise and are harder to train. But these packages are free and serve as a basic introduction to voice recognition.

Listen for Windows. Listen for Windows is a capable, continuous-speech voice-recognition program that works with multiple sound cards. Designed for everyday use, Listen for Windows lets users interact with their computers by simply talking to them. The product runs on standard audio hardware, such as the Sound Blaster from Creative Labs. Slower systems than a 33-MHz 486DX may require the optional Verbex coprocessor card.

Listen for Windows lets a user control many of the functions that might otherwise be operated by a mouse, such as opening a program group or a file. Likewise, Listen for Windows supports the commands of some commercial applications, including Microsoft Office, Lotus SmartSuite, Quicken from Intuit, WordPerfect 5.2, The Norton Desktop, and even SimCity and SimAnt. You cannot, however, use Listen for Windows as a tool to take dictation.

Listen for Windows uses voice recognition based on continuous speech, letting you speak as you would in a normal conversation, with one word flowing into the next. Most previous speech-recognition systems have only recognized discrete speech, in which each word is separated by a brief pause.

While Listen for Windows installs easily, it first must be trained to understand how you pronounce individual words. The product includes training sessions for Windows and for the applications it supports. The product trains you by prompting you to speak words or phrases again and again until the software can recognize your voice most of the time. A series of training sessions can easily take a couple of hours and can be much longer if you train with multiple applications in one sitting.

Once trained, Listen for Windows works well. Listen for Windows keeps a list of all possible words and phrases in a small window in the lower-right corner of the screen to prevent forgetfulness. The phrase window is smart enough to load the proper context for the application that's active at any given time, so you can switch programs without having to remember to change the window.

For now, Verbex's Listen for Windows holds the lead with a product that's inexpensive, easy to use, and solidly designed. If you want to control your computer by voice and are willing to spend a couple of hours training the software, Listen for Windows is a product that's worthy of serious consideration.

Listen for Windows 2.0 ($139)
Verbex Voice Systems Inc.
1090 King Georges Post Rd., Bldg. 107
Edison, NJ 08837
800-ASK-VRBX; 908-225-5225

VoiceAssist. Creative Labs offers its VoiceAssist, as shown in figure 9.9, as a stand-alone program. The package does not, however, contain as broad a range of features as more expensive packages. The software comes with a microphone that is too large and lacks a stand.

Installation of the software is simple, and the package performs smoothly with either a Creative Labs Sound Blaster 16 sound board or a Windows Sound System board. (A 16-bit sound card is required.) Setup is complex because users must create and train new voice commands and connect them with scripts for the computer to perform.

VoiceAssist installs a short slate of 32 generic commands such as open, close, left, and right that work within all Windows applications. Go to sleep and Wake up commands are included to turn the microphone off and on. However, you cannot change these commands or add to them. The package is ready to run Microsoft Windows' File Manager, Program Manager, and applets.

You can also build custom commands in a short three-step process of naming the command, training its voice, and assigning a macro. To add the command "New document" to Microsoft Word for Windows, for example, you simply type in the name, say "New document" into the microphone, and then record the keystrokes necessary to call the File menu. Then you select New and press Enter.

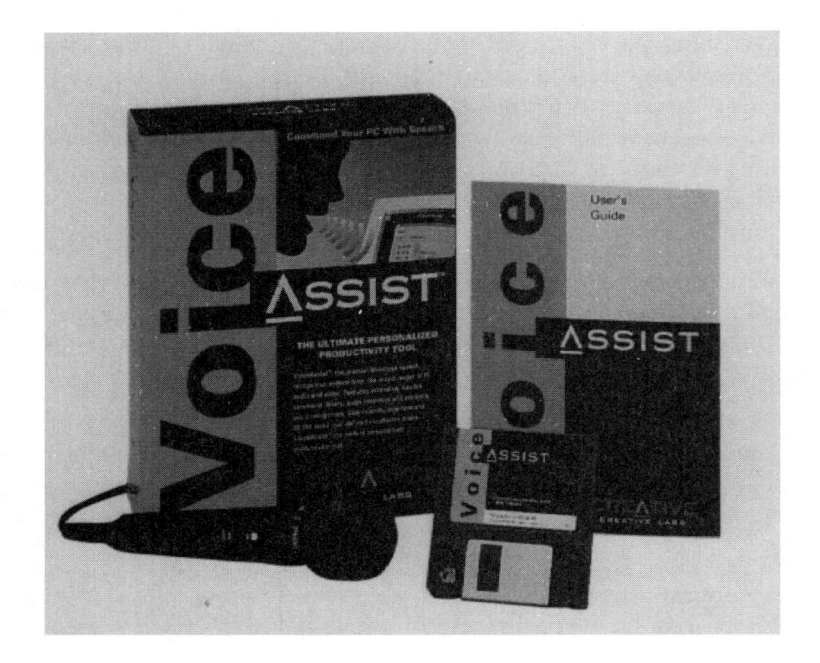

Fig. 9.9
Although included with the Sound Blaster line, VoiceAssist is sold as a separate product.

VoiceAssist lets you define multiple users, each with his or her own way of pronouncing commands; supports more than 29,000 commands per user; and makes 1,024 commands available at once. Like all voice recognition packages, VoiceAssist is almost unusable in noisy environments. Documentation is also lacking.

VoiceAssist ($99.95)
Creative Labs Inc.
1901 McCarthy Blvd.
Milpitas, CA 95035
800-998-5227; 408-428-6600

Covox Voice Blaster. Covox Inc's $119.95 Voice Blaster is an accomplished software package that allows users of Sound Blaster-compatible sound cards to issue spoken commands to application programs. Unlike other recognition programs, Voice Blaster works with DOS programs.
It doesn't do dictation, however.

Like VoiceAssist, Voice Blaster ties spoken instructions to keyboard/mouse commands, and to macros for DOS and Windows 3.1 users.

The Voice Blaster package includes an E/Q module (a printer pass-through port); a microphone headset; and DOS and Windows software. The E/Q module has three cables: one with a male plug that connects to the microphone input jack of your sound card, and two with female jacks that connect to the included headset and to an optional foot switch that can be used to activate voice recognition. All these connections are external so you don't have to open your machine.

After running the DOS installation program, the manual guides you through a helpful tutorial. The TSR DOS menu system is opened by pressing a hot key. Users record macros in their applications or through the Voice Blaster menu system's built-in editor, and then attach a voice command by speaking into the microphone. You can customize command sets for your most frequently used applications by loading and programming Voice Blaster from within your word processor, spreadsheet, database, and so on. To execute voice recognition, press a hot key or depress the optional foot pedal to tell the PC to expect a voice command.

Voice Blaster's Windows software includes a Windows version of the voice-recognition application, as well as two sound-recording programs: Sync-Recorder and Turtle Beach Wave Lite.

Voice Blaster's recognition is speaker-dependent. Training is accomplished easily by repeating a spoken command three times; if the pronunciations are too different, the program instructs you to try again. Recognition is fairly accurate, but some commands, especially one-syllable words such as "move" and "close," are frequently confused. This problem can be alleviated by retraining Voice Blaster using a lengthier synonym for the word—one with more syllables to distinguish it.

Voice Blaster ($119.95)
Covox Inc.
675 Conger St.
Eugene, OR 97402

IBM VoiceType Control for Windows. IBM's VoiceType Control for Windows also processes Windows commands. The $129 package includes software and a Sony F-VX300 microphone. You supply a Sound Blaster or compatible audio board.

Installation is simple: you just run the setup program and plug the included microphone into the mono input port on your sound card. VoiceType Control supports multiple users on the same machine, so the first step is to tell it who you are.

A quick-training option lets you teach VoiceType Control your pronunciation of the basic commands, which it calls the "always active" vocabulary. VoiceType Control is very sensitive to how the control words are pronounced.

Once the basic vocabulary is established, VoiceType Control leaves a Voicebar active on the screen. The Voicebar lets you toggle the microphone on and off, change users, and reopen the quick-training option. You can also open a window that shows the currently active vocabulary. Besides the basic commands, VoiceType Control includes vocabularies for a number of Windows utilities such as Notepad, Calculator, and File Manager, as well as for several Windows applications.

III

Investing in Multimedia

VoiceType Control for Windows ($99)
IBM PC Co.
Route 100, Maildrop 3426
Somers, NY 10589
800-426-2968.

Computer, Take a Letter

Need a personal dictator? IBM's Personal Dictation System (IPDS) includes a voice-activated interface and sophisticated software for converting speech to text.

IPDS is one of the first products to bring computerized dictation into the corporate mainstream. It requires a single adapter card that provides audio I/O and offloads dictation algorithms from the CPU using a digital signal processor (DSP). IBM recommends a system with 16M of RAM. Unfortunately, the product requires OS/2 2.1 or OS/2 for Windows to function.

The software occupies 32M of hard disk space plus 30M for training; most of the latter can be recovered once the system has learned to recognize the speaker's voice, with only 2M needed to hold voice parameters. Optional dictionaries require an additional 10 to 15M. Right out of the box, IPDS has a vocabulary of 32,000 words, which is extraordinary. As you train it, the vocabulary can increase up to about 34,000 words.

IPDS performs discrete rather than continuous speech recognition, requiring a short break before and after each word. The device can recognize a maximum of 70 words per minute. Speed is acceptable on a 33-MHz 486DX2 PC. At first, you will have to correct the system frequently, but learning takes place fairly rapidly. IBM is targeting IPDS as a general business correspondence tool; most business letters use consistent terminology and phrasing, allowing IPDS to become quite accurate over time.

IBM Personal Dictation System ($998)
IBM Corp.
Armonk, NY 10504
800-825-5263; 914-765-1900.

Proofreader in a Can

Sound cards can also be used as inexpensive proofreaders. Text-to-speech utilities can read back a list of numbers or text to you.

Monologue from First Byte Inc. ($149) is included with the Pro AudioStudio 16 sound card. This text-to-speech utility can be loaded in the background while you are using your spreadsheet or word processor. For example, you may be in Lotus 1-2-3 entering columns of numbers. By pressing a hot key, Monologue begins to read back the numbers you've highlighted. Monologue can also read back an entire file.

You can change the speed and volume of Monologue's voice. You can also change the pitch to resemble a male or female voice. You can even add words to a dictionary of exceptions in which you teach Monologue how to speak "correct" English. There are also

Windows versions of text-to-speech utilities. Monologue for Windows ($149) will read back text you copy into the Windows Clipboard.

What are the practical uses for a text-to-speech utility? Hearing a letter read aloud may reveal forgotten words or awkward phrases. Accountants can double-check spreadsheet numbers, and busy executives can have their e-mail read to them while they are doing paperwork.

Built-In Voice Authorization

You can use your sound card to add security to your PC. VoiceLock from QVoice Inc. uses your 16-bit sound card to prevent access to your Windows system until it recognizes your voice.

Like a guard dog, VoiceLock needs to be trained to recognize you before it can guard your computer. This is a simple process requiring only that you speak randomly into a microphone plugged into your sound card. VoiceLock analyzes your voice and places its unique characteristics into a voice database. It can save and recognize as many voices as you want.

To secure your computer, press the Pause key; VoiceLock displays its own screen, then shows your normal screen saver. When you resume Windows activity, VoiceLock pops up again. A new feature added to VoiceLock allows files in specified directories to be encrypted when the VoiceLock is activated. If the computer (especially a laptop model) were to be stolen, the files would be unusable to the thief.

To regain access, you speak into a microphone. If VoiceLock recognizes your voice, you can resume your work; you even can set the program to play a recording that announces that it recognizes you and is granting access. If VoiceLock doesn't recognize your voice, an on-screen message notifies you that it is denying access.

VoiceLock ($79.95)
QVoice Inc.
PO Box 645
Andover, NJ 07821
201-786-6878
FAX: 201-786-5868

Audio CDs

Microsoft Windows' Media Player has the ability to play audio CDs while you are working on something else. The music can be piped not only through a pair of speakers but also through a headphone set plugged into the front of one's CD-ROM drive. While some sound cards include a DOS- or Windows-based CD-player utility, you could use a third-party utility for superior results. These affordable utilities, which stimulate the full workings of a home CD audio player, add to your PC music experience.

All CD audio players allow you to choose between displaying time elapsed or time remaining for either the current track or for the entire disc. Minimize these players on the desktop, and they'll display the currently playing disc's time and track information with the program's icon, counting up or down in time with the disc.

III

Investing in Multimedia

They also include a simple database to let you catalog your CDs by artist, title, and track. Each takes a different approach to the fill-in-the-fields task, but is easy to figure out and work with. Once you've cataloged a disc, the programs save the description as an index file on your hard disk. When you next pop in the CD, the list of tracks displays automatically. Programming CDs to play tracks in a certain order is easier than on a home system; just point-and-click on the ones you want to move to the play list. Each also lets you shuffle or repeat selected tracks, or the entire disc.

CDMaster. CDMaster gives you some volume control independent of your sound card's abilities. With the other two packages, you use the volume controls that came with the sound card you own. Older sound boards don't support software-controlled volume. With MPC-compatible audio cards, however, you can regulate the sound output level on any of these three utilities directly, by clicking or sliding the volume buttons or slider up and down.

CDMaster includes a more powerful database: Its TitleTrax feature lets you catalog your entire audio library, including albums and tapes, and sort and print your collection by artist or title. CDMaster is actually a subset of Animotion's MCS Stereo utility, a full "virtual stereo system" that can play and edit digital audio files. Although it can't edit MIDI files, CDMaster can play them.

MCS CDMaster ($29.95)
Animotion Development Corp.
3720 Fourth Ave., S, Ste. 205
Birmingham, AL 35222
800-536-4175; 205-591-5715
FAX: 205-591-5716
Tech support BBS: 205-591-5795

WinCD. WinCD offers the highest-tech bonus of all: track sampling. WinCD can take a four-second sample of each track on the disc and record them to your hard disk. You may replay the samples at any time, without having the CD itself loaded in your CD drive. Like any digital recording, samples take up lots of hard disk space, and WinCD uses an average of 256K of hard disk space for each disc. This feature, nice as it is, seems to have little practical utility.

WinCD ($49.95)
Kinesoft Development
772 W. Algonquin Rd.
Arlington Heights, IL 60005
708-806-9562
FAX: 708-806-6538

Ultimate Sound Bites

You can order various collections of audio files to enhance your presentations or Windows sounds. For example, you can assign certain WAV files to certain Windows events, such as when Windows starts or reports an error. These audio files might include WAV files, CD audio tracks or MIDI songs. Some of the files come in the Sound Blaster VOC format, which may be played by or converted to WAV format by other sound cards. The entire group may be called "clip notes," the audio equivalent of clip art.

Microsoft SoundBits. The Microsoft SoundBits is comprised of three separate sound clip collections featuring audio clips from Hanna-Barbera cartoon characters, classic Hollywood films, and musical sounds from around the world, respectively. You can attach these digitized sounds to Windows events such as starting and exiting other software programs, error messages, and re-sizing windows.

SoundBits provides humorous one-liners, fun sound effects, and a variety of musical instruments. For example, clips from the Flintstones, The Jetsons, Yogi Bear and Scooby Doo are included. Classic dialog clips from Hollywood movies are also included, such as those of Groucho Marx, Humphrey Bogart, Cary Grant, and characters from the Wizard of Oz. Sounds from around the world provide rare cuts of international music from harmonicas and violins to African drums and Andean pan pipes.

Microsoft SoundBits ($24.95/each)
Microsoft Corp.
One Microsoft Way
Redmond, WA 98052-6399
800-426-9400; 206-882-8080
Direct sales: 800-MSPRESS
FAX: 206-883-8101
Tech support: 206-454-2030; 206-637-7098 (Windows)
Tech support BBS: 206-936-6735

Audio Clips. Sound Source Unlimited's AudioClips can replace the PC's primitive beeps with quotes from your favorite movies and TV series. With seven titles from which to choose, including "Terminator II: Judgment Day" and "Star Trek: The Next Generation," you'll never have to hear a beep again.

To run AudioClips on your PC, you'll need Windows 3.1. Some of the 75 WAV files in "Star Trek" include theme music, the "Final Frontier" intro, and sound effects for ship operations. T-2's 62 WAV files include sound effects from Cyberdyne Systems, gunshots, and penetrating metal spears. Among the Schwarzenegger snippets on the Terminator 2 disk are, "I'll be back" and "Hasta la vista, baby."

AudioClips' setup engine—like the one in Control Panel's sound engine—lets you assign specific recordings (WAV files) to system events like startup and shutdown. But unlike Control Panel's mere six events, the AudioClips engine lets you assign sounds to up to 14 system and generic application events, plus seven events for each application you choose to configure separately. Another option lets you choose an event and select Random, so the computer will surprise you with its choice of sound when that event takes place. The setup engine works with any WAV files you have, and AudioClips WAV files can be run with other setup engines such as Windows Control Panel's or Microsoft SoundBits'.

III

Investing in Multimedia

AudioClips won't save a number of "sound schemes" the way Microsoft SoundBits does, or as Control Panel Color saves color schemes. However, AudioClips stores your most recent choice of sounds in a file called WHOOP.INI in the Windows directory. To save several sound schemes, you can rename the current WHOOP.INI, and then create another by choosing different sounds.

AudioClips ($49.95 each)
Sound Source Unlimited
2985 E. Hillcrest Dr., Suite A
Westlake Village, CA 91362
800-877-4778, 805-494-9996
Fax: 805-495-0016

Wired for Sound Pro. Some packages go beyond just providing WAV sound bites. Some add pizzazz to an otherwise dull Windows. If you want total multimedia immersion, consider Aristosoft's Wired for Sound Pro. It brings sound and video elements from the sidelines and puts them smack in the middle of your daily computing routine.

You don't have to install the program's full 68M—just the media files and applications you need. Choose from 2,000 sounds, 200 video clips, 250 MIDI files, and 200 pictures, plus some so-so icons and awesome cursors.

The Wired for Sound applications (see fig. 9.10) start with a group of chatterboxes: Talking Calculator, Calendar, Clock, and System Monitor tell the facts, while Talking Minesweeper and Solitaire open their virtual mouths to help you cheat at Windows' popular games. The program lineup also includes Multimedia Jukebox, Screen Saver, Wallpaper Changer, Sound Editor, CD Browser, and Mediascape Changer. The last lets you choose an animated face and voice to front for your system; you can choose from normal-sounding folks or lame impressions of VIPs from Clinton to Schwarzenegger. Still more programs include Cursor Changer, Icon Changer, and Groupie, the last of which lets you change Program Manager group icons and nest groups within groups.

Intruder Alert, a password-protected screen saver with a realistic car-alarm sound, protects your data. Post This!, a "sticky note" utility, is also useful. And there are lots of great sounds in Wired for Sound's repertoire, organized into categories like Funny, Human, Destructive, Cartoon, Equipment, Illness, Impact, Musical, Sports, and Job Saver. Music tracks and mini-movies are similarly arranged.

Wired for Sound Pro is almost mandatory if you want to maximize your PC's multimedia capabilities.

Wired for Sound Pro ($39.95)
Aristosoft Inc.
7041 Koll Center Pkwy., Ste. 160
Pleasanton, CA 94566
800-338-2629

Fig. 9.10
Wired for Sound gives Microsoft Windows some sights and sounds.

Caring for Your Sound Card

Sound cards require little care. When handling any expansion card, you must be careful about static electricity damaging the sensitive electronic components. To drain yourself of built-up static, touch a metal object nearby, such as the inside of your computer's cover, before installing or removing the sound card. Do not touch any of the components on the sound card since any static electricity you can have can damage it. Also, do not touch the copper edge connectors. Instead, grab the card by its edges or metal bracket.

When you remove a sound card, set it aside on a clean surface, preferably on the anti-static bag the card arrived in or on a special anti-static mat.

When inserting or removing the sound card, rock the expansion card back and forth along its length. In other words, do not twist the card from side to side but rather pull up alternately on each end. Be careful where you grab the card; there may be delicate components that you may crush. Carefully grab the card by its metal bracket and edges.

When using your sound card, never connect or disconnect cables from your audio ports without the computer or other audio equipment being turned off first. You risk damaging both with the electrical energy they carry.

When using speakers rated for less than four watts, do not turn up the volume on your sound card to the maximum; your speakers may burn out from the overload.

> **Note**
>
> Your PC already has several cables connected to it. Adding audio cables makes the problem worse. To prevent these cables from getting entangled, use garbage bag twist ties to bundle related cables together. For example, you can tie all the new audio cables together. You also can buy special-purpose flex tubing that acts as a conduit for your cables.

From Here...

In this chapter, we discussed how to buy a sound card and a handful of sound card models. We reviewed budget, mainstream, portable and high-end sound cards. We also discussed accessories for your sound card, including voice recognition and screen saver software. The following chapters give you more information related to sound cards:

- Chapter 4, "Adding Sound to Your System," will give you a refresher on sound cards.

- Chapter 10, "Buyer's Guide to MIDI," discusses how a sound card can be used as a MIDI interface. By attaching to a keyboard synthesizer and other MIDI equipment, your sound card can become a musical workstation.

Chapter 10

Buyer's Guide to MIDI

This chapter offers advice about what to look for when upgrading your PC to multimedia. The chapter focuses on Musical Instrument Digital Interface equipment.

The right equipment can turn your PC into a home recording studio. With a sound card, keyboard, stereo system, and the right software, the musical hobbyist can learn about music by hearing and playing it. Musicians, on the other hand, can record, edit, arrange, print and play their compositions. This is all possible through the standard called MIDI, or Musical Instrument Digital Interface.

MIDI Buying Criteria

The Musical Instrument Digital Interface standard has been around since 1983, when manufacturers of electronic instruments developed it as a simple, low-cost technology for connecting various pieces of equipment, such as synthesizers, electronic music, keyboards, and computers.

MIDI is two-faced. It is both a digital communication language for making music and a hardware specification for using equipment for that purpose. MIDI allows multiple electronic instruments, such as keyboard synthesizers, and computers, to work with each other.

How much equipment you buy depends on your MIDI demands. At a bare minimum, creating quality, original music requires sound editing software that supports the Standard MIDI File format and a sequencer that plays back the files. Once you create a basic sequence on standard music creation software, you use sequencers to change tempos and make other changes. The sequencers also can integrate live music recorded by sound editing programs in WAV files.

If a sound card is your only synthesizer, you will have to record both synthesized and live music into a single file, but you should be careful to go back over this file with the sequencer to check balance.

You may want to invest in an external keyboard synthesizer, or a keyboard and separate sound module. If one is available, you can record live music into its own WAV file and then edit this sound and other backup tracks separately. Users may be frustrated by sequencers that commonly cannot handle multiple simultaneous WAV tracks, or WAV tracks themselves, which offer limited editing functions.

MIDI Interface

A MIDI system is like a small musical network. MIDI equipment is connected to each other and then to your PC through a MIDI interface. Each MIDI device can be independently controlled through a single MIDI line. Just as a public speaker can single out and communicate a message to one individual in the crowd, MIDI messages may be directed to a specific MIDI device.

To connect MIDI instruments to your PC, you need a sound card with a MIDI input port and a MIDI output port. Often, the joystick port on the sound card doubles as this MIDI interface. You will need a card that emulates Roland's MPU-401 MIDI interface.

With a MIDI connector box, which is often sold separately, you can connect your MIDI devices to your sound card and therefore your PC. For example, Media Vision sells the MIDI Mate for its line of MIDI-capable sound cards.

Note

You don't need to buy a MIDI connector for your sound card from your manufacturer. You can save money by buying such a connector from a local music store. The design of MIDI connectors is identical.

Adding to your MIDI network is simple. To connect MIDI devices in a network, you simply plug a cable from the MIDI out port to the MIDI in port of the new device. What MIDI devices can be connected together? A professional musician may have a drum machine for developing percussion sounds, a synthesizer for entering musical notes, and an audio mixer to blend the sounds. At home, you may be able to do everything from your own computer and perhaps an attached CD drive or stereo system. What would have cost an artist a fortune a decade ago is now within the reach of every aspiring musician.

Polyphony

When considering a synthesizer, consider how many notes it can play at the same time. This is called *polyphony*. The maximum is 64 notes, while 24 and 32 are more common.

Multitimbrality

Also, note how many separate MIDI channels you can play simultaneously. This is called *multitimbrality*. A common number is eight or 16. Since chords require, let's say, three notes, eight may be ample. The higher the number, the better, since "note stealing" won't occur as you play back music you've created.

Note stealing is basically how the keyboard determines what to play when it uses up all of its polyphony and multitimbrality. A non-intelligent way that most synthesizers use is to "steal" the first note that was played for use with notes yet to be played. Some synthesizers incorporate some intelligence when note stealing, so that the absence of the notes is not so sorely missed.

Sound Quality

Besides the number of sounds, you should consider sound quality. Sound quality varies considerably between manufacturers and models. Also, sound quality is subjective. In fact, some manufacturers tend to give their line a certain "personality." For example, Korg keyboard synthesizers are considered to sound "muddy" or "deep" while Roland products are considered "sharp" or "bright." The best advice is to audition your synthesizer.

Number of Keys

When buying a keyboard, consider how many keys it has. Some have as few as 49 keys, while others have 51, 61, 76, or 88. Ideally, 76 keys is the preferred choice of musicians, with 61 being a close second.

The number of keys needed depends on your playing ability. If you are just entering basic notes, such as during step editing, you can work with a 49-key keyboard. The style of music you play also affects how many keys you'll need. More pop-like music or music that requires one-handed chords will work with 61 keys. Anyone who uses a 76-key keyboard will rarely miss an 88-key keyboard.

Tip

A 76-key keyboard is the best all-around choice; an 88-key keyboard is often found only in professional weighted synthesizers.

Special Effects

Synthesizers include sound effects. Reverb, chorus and delay are the basic sound effects. However, some also include distortion or various types of phases. However, such effects may affect all channels, not just one specific instrument.

Multiple Audio Outputs

You should look for multiple audio outputs. If you have separate audio outputs, you can transport certain parts of a song, such as strings and bass, to a separate output. You then can run them through different parts of the mixing board, adding special effects and more.

III

Investing in Multimedia

Keyboards & Sound Modules

You can get a synthesizer in two styles:

Keyboard

Sound module

A synthesizer built into a keyboard provides you with one-stop MIDI. However, a sound module, which lacks a keyboard, allows you to invest in a better keyboard or multiple keyboards for various purposes. Many MIDI enthusiasts and musicians find a keyboard controller (without synthesizer) they like or has certain features they desire. For example, the Korg Wavestation keyboard has a joystick for vector synthesis, which lets you switch between waveforms in a sound. Other keyboards may have features such as sliders or special pitch blends.

Once a keyboard is found, buyers then seek a sound module. A sound module may come in two styles—rack-mounted or an external table-top box. Rack-mounted sound modules, the preferred choice, fit in specially-sized racks that get the module off your workstation. A rack is 19 inches wide, although half-rack units are also available. A sound module may then be a one-space, two-space, or three-space unit, where one space is 2 inches high.

> **Tip**
>
> Although a table-top sound module may be portable, a rack-mounted unit can be easily dismounted for travel.

Synthesizers can be either FM or wavetable. Wavetable synthesizers, which include sampled sounds of actual instruments, are used to achieve top-notch quality sound.

Keyboard Synthesizers

MIDI keyboards are no longer just MIDI keyboards. Through the power of electronics, a MIDI keyboard synthesizer is becoming what Korg and other manufacturers call a "music workstation."

Korg X3 Music Workstation. The Korg X3 is no beginner keyboard. It not only has 61 keys but also includes a floppy disk drive for saving and loading performances in the Standard MIDI File format (see fig. 10.1).

> **Tip**
>
> The Korg X3 can store an entire song in memory and up to 10 songs on a PC-compatible removable floppy disk.

The X3 builds on Korg's AI² Synthesis System used in the 01/W series of synthesizers. This systems enables the X3 to keep the signal entirely digital right up to the outputs on the back panel.

Its PCM (pulse-code modulation) technology is used for the X3's tone generator section, which features 6M of waveforms. A total of 340 instruments is available, including newly sampled piano, organ, and strings, along with a rich selection of guitar, bass, and ethnic instruments.

The X3 is armed with 164 drum sounds with a wide range of snare drum and bass drum variations. Two powerful stereo multi-effects systems use 47 types of effects, such as chorus, delay, overdrive, rotary speaker and more through sound-shaping control. The X3 provides 32-note polyphony for performing difficult orchestral arrangements.

Tip

A program is a certain waveform or mix of waveforms. A combination is assigning eight program sounds to certain keys or a certain velocity (the intensity of striking a key).

The X3 has two memory banks for storing up to 200 programs and 200 combinations. These sounds are synthesized from high-quality PCM data. The optional SRC-512 memory card doubles each to 400. The ROM area contains 128 General MIDI programs, one GM drum kit and seven original drum kits. In sequence mode, the X3 plays up to 16 parts by controlling as many as 16 independent programs. The sequencer can record a total of 10 songs (the capacity of the disk), and 100 patterns for a maximum of 32,000 notes (the memory limit).

Tip

32,000 is the number of notes that can be stored, but a more accurate phrase is the number of MIDI events. For example, bending the pitch of a note is a MIDI event above and beyond playing the actual note.

Note

The X3R Music Workstation is the rack-mount sound module version of the X3.

Fig. 10.1
The Korg X3 is a high-end keyboard synthesizer.

Korg X3 ($1,750)

Korg USA Inc.
89 Frost St.
Westbury, NY 11590
800-645-3188; 516-333-9100

Korg X5. The Korg X5 is an all-in-one instrument equipped with advanced synthesis to digital effects and a sequencer (see fig. 10.2). As a complete music workstation, the 61-key device uses Korg's AI Synthesis System for full digital generation and sound processing. These range from high-quality PCM sound sources to the digital effects. One hundred memory spaces store combinations, which allow you to change sound according to key velocity. The X5 also allows you to assign a maximum of eight programs to different sections of the keyboard and effectively play them as eight separate synthesizers.

Tip
With 61 keys and high-quality PCM samples, the Korg X5 is probably one of the best all-around keyboard synthesizers.

Fig. 10.2
The Korg X5 provides mid-range performance for a fair price.

Korg X5 ($1,099)

Korg USA Inc.
89 Frost St.
Westbury, NY 11590
800-645-3188; 516-333-9100

Kawai X50-D. Kawai's X50-D is a better keyboard than typically meant for MIDI consumers (see fig. 10.3). The X50-D uses four multidirectional speakers, reverb, chorus, detuning, and panning. (Kawai calls the combination Super 3-D.) These features give the high-quality pulse-code modulation (PCM) samples a chance to be heard through a keyboard.

The 61-key, velocity-sensitive MIDI controller doubles as a General MIDI sound module containing 128 16-bit PCM sampled sounds plus 47 drum/percussion sounds. It is 16-channel multitimbral and has 28 notes of polyphony. MIDI in and out ports let you connect the keyboard to a computer via either a MIDI interface or MIDI upgrade kit.

Tip

The lower-end Kawai X50-D includes background accompaniment in 100 musical styles for a price of less than $700.

The X50-D offers some highly useful performance and songwriting functions, such as an auto-accompaniment feature with 100 styles from pop funk to Hawaiian. Press the lower-register bass notes to change chords while you solo on the upper register. This is one way for potential composers to create their own songs.

If you cannot play piano, Kawai provides a one-finger ad lib function that automatically plays licks when you press and hold down one key. A built-in real-time recorder has 5 overdubbing tracks and 3,000 notes which also can be transferred over MIDI to an external sequencer/computer.

The keyboard's sounds are good and fairly diverse, ranging from Fender Rhodes electric piano sounds to funky drums. There's even a patch called fret noise to give a realistic edge to guitar sounds. Using the dual function, you can play any two sounds at the same time. This diversity is helpful when making use of the X50-D's Style Maker feature, which lets you create and solo over your own accompaniment styles. You can even create your own one-finger ad libs.

The keyboard's real breakthrough, though, is the Super 3-D sound, which creates a spacious, multidirectional, full-sounding stereo performance. In either of the two 3D modes, you can actually hear the panning in the speakers. As a combination of intuitive control and top sound quality, the X50-D will appeal to novice users and serious musicians alike.

III

Investing in Multimedia

Fig. 10.3
The Kawai X50-D is an affordable synthesizer for home musicians.

Kawai X50-D ($699)

Kawai America
2055 E. University Dr.
Compton, CA 90224
310-631-1771

Sound Modules

A sound module gets its commands from another MIDI device, such as a keyboard. A sound module provides MIDI sounds in a compact box.

Korg Wavestation SR. The Korg Wavestation SR is a rack-mounted synthesizer. It has three RAM banks and eight ROM banks for storing 550 performances, 600 with an optional card.

Designed for multitimbral use, the Wavestation SR can play a separate complex, split, and layered performance on each of 16 MIDI channels. A special set of digital effects lets you use each of the four individual outputs. The Wavestation SR provides simple front panel controls and includes 484 sampled or synthesized waveforms to use as raw sound material.

Korg Wavestation SR ($1,450)

Korg USA Inc.
89 Frost St.
Westbury, NY 11590
800-645-3188; 516-333-9100

Korg Audio Gallery for Windows 101 (AG-101). Just as Roland joined the computer industry by introducing its RAP-10 sound card, Korg is entering the computer business through multimedia's back door. The release of its Audio Gallery for Windows 101 (AG-101) provides MIDI music to Windows PCs (see fig. 10.4).

Fig. 10.4

The Audio Gallery (AG-101) bundles everything for creating a home music workstation.

The system includes Korg's AG-10 wavetable sound module, music software, and a cable to connect the AG-10 to your computer. The module has speaker and headphone connectors, and MIDI In, Out, and Thru ports as well as connectors for the AC adapter and your PC.

You don't have to shackle the AG-10 to your computer, however—you can detach the cable from the tone module and take the box on the road to use with other MIDI equipment.

> **Tip**
>
> Korg's Audio Gallery for Windows provides one-stop shopping for a sound module and sequencing software.

Setup is easy. The tone module connects to your computer via a serial port, so you don't need to open the PC's case. Plug in the AC adapter and connect some speakers, and you've finished the hardware installation. All that remains is the installation of Korg's Windows driver.

Software from Passport Designs is included, including Trax, a sequencing and scoring package; MIDI Player, a jukebox/mixer that lets you play MIDI files while mixing and matching instruments; and Quick Tunes, a collection of MIDI files.

III

Investing in Multimedia

The PGL chip set used in the AG-101 is the same found in Korg's OW/1 and Wavestation professional synthesizers, providing excellent sound quality.

Not all is perfect, however. At the present time, Korg does not yet use Microsoft's MIDI Mapper, so the software you use will have to directly support Korg's system. The only way to access the AG-10 from unsupported applications is by connecting the AG-10 to a sound card with a MIDI cable.

Audio Gallery for Windows 101 (AG-101) ($329)
Speakers 15-watt ($225/each), 5-watt ($225/pair)

Korg USA Inc.
89 Frost St.
Westbury, NY 11590
800-645-3188; 516-333-9100

Roland SC-50. The Sound Canvas SC-50 from Roland offers a high level of performance for a fair price. This compact, half-rack size sound module accommodates virtually any MIDI application for keyboard players, MIDI guitarists and percussionists, composers and computer music enthusiasts alike (see fig. 10.5).

Its digital technology provides 18-bit digital-audio conversion. It includes 226 General MIDI/GS compatible sounds. There are also eight drum kits and one sound effects kit. The SC-50 also includes built-in digital effects like reverb and chorus.

Tip

Roland's Sound Canvas SC-50 provides a good blend of polyphony and multitimbrality plus eight drum kits and one sound effects kit.

The SC-50 is 16-part multitimbral and has 28-voice polyphony. This gives you the ability to create extensive orchestrations on a sequencer like the Roland MC-50-mkII or PC-based sequencing system. The SC-50 attaches to your PC's RS-232C serial port.

Roland Sound Canvas SC-50 ($695)

Roland Corp. U.S.
7200 Dominion Circle
Los Angeles, CA 90040
213-685-5141
FAX: 213-726-8865

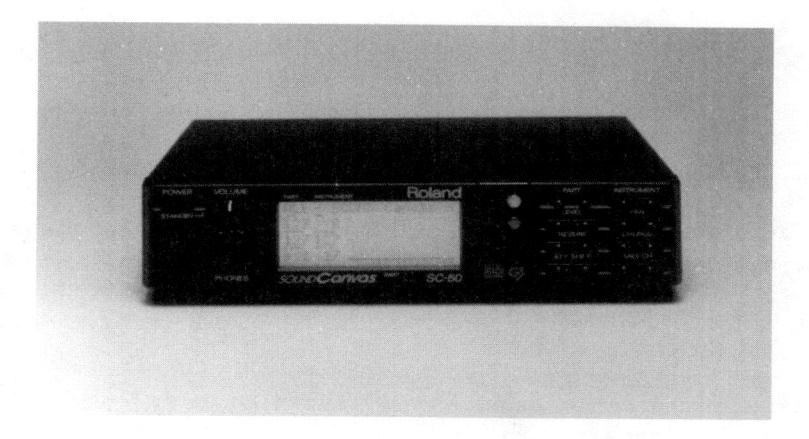

Fig. 10.5

The Roland Sound Canvas SC-50 is an affordable sound module.

Roland SC-7. The Roland SC-7 GM Sound Set contains 128 different high-quality sounds that allow you to create just about any kind of music. The SC-7 includes realistic piano, brass, strings and much more. The SC-7 has six complete drum sets including the Standard drum set that conforms to the General MIDI Percussion Map.

The SC-7 plays up to 16 different instruments at once using a maximum of 28 notes. You can "finish" your sounds using the onboard digital reverb/delay and chorus effects.

No additional MIDI interface is needed. This sound module connects directly to the RS-232C serial port of your computer. The SC-7 has two pairs of stereo audio inputs so that two external sources can be simultaneously input and mixed. For example, you can input music and voice from the computer's internal sound sources and a CD-ROM to the SC-7 and mix it with built-in sounds.

Roland SC-7 ($299)

Roland Corp. U.S.
7200 Dominion Circle
Los Angeles, CA 90040
213-685-5141
FAX: 213-726-8865

Summit. With its first entry into the high-end multimedia arena, AVM Technologies has scored big with the Summit, a General MIDI -compliant external synthesizer. The Summit, which connects to a sound card, is ideal for corporate users seeking to dazzle with music in multimedia presentations, for home users serious about MIDI, and for anyone who wants vivid music behind their DOS and Windows games.

III

Investing in Multimedia

Tip

As a portable unit, the Summit provides music to multimedia presentations for executives on the road.

Using a Wavetable Lookup synthesis chip set from Kurzweil, the Summit offers nearly 370 very convincing patches (a programmed sound such as piano or cello), as well as digital effects processing (reverb and chorus). While most professional-quality synthesizer modules and keyboards start around $900, the Summit delivers these features at a low list price of $389.

The Summit attaches easily to a sound card's joystick/MIDI port. After redirecting a MIDI application's output from your sound card's synthesis chip to the sound card's MIDI Out port, the Summit is ready for music. Its 1/8-inch stereo jack readily connects to external speakers or a home stereo.

The Summit doesn't have any front-panel controls of its own, so a MIDI sequencer application or controller is used to send MIDI Controller Codes at the beginning of a sequence. These codes specify which patch set to use on each given channel.

The Summit's 32-note polyphony capability (the number of notes you can play simultaneously) and 16-note multitimbrality (the number of patches you can play simultaneously) all but eliminate note "stealing," even during intense musical passages.

Like patch-set selection, reverb and chorus effects are also controlled using a MIDI Controller Code. Several of the reverb settings suffer from too much echo effect and as a result are of little use, but most of the reverb and chorus options greatly enhance the Summit's overall sound.

AVM's implementation of MIDI Controller Codes requires an understanding of the MIDI environment and will be confusing for the inexperienced MIDI user, but the Summit's stellar patch sets are well worth the learning curve.

Whatever the application, the Summit's low price-point makes it a great way to get into high-end wavetable lookup synthesis. Hearing is believing.

Summit ($389)

AVM Technologies Inc.
655 East 9800 South
Sandy, UT 84070
800-880-0041; 801-571-0967
FAX: 801-571-3634

Yamaha Hello!Music! Hello!Music! from Yamaha allows you to couple soundtracks to your presentations. Hello!Music! is a fully integrated portable sound system that includes a high-quality 16-bit sound module (CBX-T3), a keyboard (CBX-K3), and speakers

(CBX-S3) that let even novices record and sequence original music for use in presentations. The included software contains 35 preset instrumental songs that cover a spectrum of genres.

Tip

Hello!Music! from Yamaha includes a keyboard, speakers, 16-bit sound module, and MIDI sequencing software—all for under $500.

Hello!Music!'s sound module, the CBX-T3 Tone Generator, includes 192 16-bit instrument sounds, 10 drum kits, and digital reverb, and conforms to the General MIDI standard. The built-in MIDI interface includes a MIDI-in and -out/-thru, although you need only connect to the serial port from the To Host port to use the module.

There are 16 MIDI-channel LEDs on the CBX-T3's front panel to let you know which channels are active. Underneath, three mode buttons change from General MIDI compatibility to Yamaha Disk Orchestration Collection compatibility, or to MIDI setups for sound modules such as Roland's MT-32. Below that is an audio-in jack which can be used for live voice-overs during a presentation, and a master volume control.

The CBX-K3 keyboard has a good feel to it, and though not weighted, it is adequate for MIDI recording and even performance purposes. The CBX-K3 is a 49-key, full-sized, velocity-sensitive MIDI keyboard with modulation and pitch bend wheels.

The CBX-T3 module and the keyboard may be bought separately, but the keyboard, aside from being a good portable MIDI controller on its own, is made to work with the CBX-T3. Another controller might not be as compatible.

The software, Passport's Trax (a MIDI sequencer) and Passport's MIDI Player (a MIDI jukebox), is included. It provides preset QuikTunes, which are ready-to-play MIDI files from a variety of musical motifs ranging from rock-and-roll to new age to a category called Sports. You will actually want to take advantage of the QuikTune presets since they are well-done.

Passport's Trax software lets you sequence and compose your own music with an easy-to-use intuitive interface. Simply lay down a drum beat on one track, bass on the next, and then perhaps keyboard and strings to create an effective and professional-sounding audio background for productions. You play to the tracks through the keyboard.

Hello!Music!'s CBX-S3 speakers are great for recording and editing, as well as presentation, and have remarkably substantial volume for speakers of their size. The speakers output audio from a 70 Hz-20 KHz range.

If you're looking for a way to polish multimedia presentations, give Yamaha's Hello!Music! a listen.

III

Investing in Multimedia

Hello!Music! ($449)

CBX-K3 keyboard only ($399.95)

Yamaha Corp. of America
Consumer Products Div.
PO Box 6600
Buena Park, CA 90620
714-522-9240

Software Tools

Various software tools are available to improve your MIDI work. Waveform editors for multimedia presentations, sequencing software and sheet music notation software are just a few utilities that can help you.

Waveform Editing

Waveform editors let you modify sound files. You can stick with the Sound Recorder bundled with Windows or you can select a more sophisticated product. Following are just a few.

Sound Impression 3.5. Midisoft's Sound Impression 3.5 provides an inexpensive way for novices and professionals alike to mix and record digital audio. Its slick graphical interface mimics a set of rack-mount components, turning your desktop into an easy-to-use mixer, MIDI and CD audio player, and WAV file recorder and player. In addition to these basics, Sound Impression provides outstanding OLE support. You can transfer any supported sound data (MIDI, CD, or WAV) to an OLE client application with a few keystrokes, or even link your current Mixing Panel settings to a Windows client.

Three powerful tools augment the main program module: Wave Composer, Session Manager, and Wave Editor. Wave Composer lets you mix up to 16 separate WAV files into a composition. Special tools make it easy to precisely control the onset of any track and to change its position relative to other tracks. Session Manager lets you assign one-line descriptions to each currently opened file. The fairly powerful Wave Editor lets you clean up a sound segment with a noise filter, remove or add silence, or cut, crop, and apply other editing tools. You can add special effects such as echo, chorus, flange, fade, crossfade, and pan to parts or all of a session. Other controls let you speed up or slow down speech and music segments, and set sampling rates for recording (you can record sound in 8- or 16-bit mono or stereo at 11, 22, or 44 KHz). Insert up to 16 placemarkers into a waveform or form a stereo track by mixing two mono tracks.

Tip

With an interface that mimicks rack-mounted components, Sound Impression provides an inexpensive tool for creating and editing sound for multimedia use.

Sound Impression is an easy and cost-effective way to create and edit sound for multimedia applications. Its interface is easy to navigate, and its WAV editor and composer are ideal for generating smaller sound files.

Sound Impression 3.5 ($79.95)

Midisoft Corp.
PO Box 1000
Bellevue, WA 98009
800-776-6434; 206-881-7176

Turtle Tools 1.0. Turtle Tools for Multimedia contains just about everything a novice needs to explore the beckoning world of multimedia sound. Besides letting you create, edit, and play WAV files, Turtle Beach Systems' $89 combo includes a MIDI file editor, a full-featured MIDI sequencer, and a slick utility for attaching WAV or MIDI files to Windows events. The package also provides a KeyPlayer program that lets you create music with your PC keyboard, plus a CD-ROM containing 300 professionally recorded musical pieces and sound effects.

> **Tip**
>
> From high-end sound card manufacturer Turtle Beach Systems, Turtle Tools provides a collection of tools that lets you edit WAV files, turn your PC into a keyboard synthesizer, and more.

The WAV sound editor, Wave Tools, is easily worth the price of the entire package. This versatile and powerful utility lets you record and edit WAV files of virtually any size. You can insert place markers as navigation aids and change the sound level of selected portions of a file with the Fade In and Fade Out options. You can even use the mouse as a pencil to remove clicks, pops, and other glitches from a sound file. Wave Tools uses the same superb, easy-to-use interface as Turtle Beach's high-end editor Wave for Windows, though it lacks its big brother's support for time compression and expansion and such special effects as delay, reverb, and flanging.

Not to be outdone, Wave Tools' two MIDI utilities give you considerable control over MIDI files. The first, MIDI Tune-Up, lets you transpose instruments to different keys, adjust a song's tempo, and change such effects as reverb and panning. The utility also functions as a good general-purpose MIDI file player, letting you create lists of songs to play in sequence.

The other tool, MIDIsoft Session, provides a wide range of MIDI sequencing features. You perform most operations with the mouse, moving controls on an on-screen representation of a standard audio-tape mixer. The utility also lets you display songs as musical notation and edit the score by adding and deleting notes. Both MIDI tools support MPU-401 compatible MIDI interfaces.

III

Investing in Multimedia

In some ways, KeyPlayer is the most ambitious tool of the lot, and certainly the most fun. KeyPlayer turns your PC into a feature-packed electronic synthesizer and mixer that lets you bang out music using your keyboard. (Mouse-savvy composers can tickle the ivories of an on-screen piano keyboard.) You can compose in any of 12 musical keys and 19 musical scales, on everything from steel drums to a concert grand piano or a dulcimer.

Both good fun and a good value, The Turtle Tools for Multimedia is a talented, entertaining package for aspiring multimedia maestros.

Turtle Tools 1.0 ($89)

Turtle Beach Systems
52 Grumbacher Rd.
York, PA 17402
800-645-5640

Wave for Windows 2.0. To edit sounds like the pros, you can use Turtle Beach's Wave for Windows 2.0. This program gives Windows users many of the editing and recording capabilities of professional digital-recording systems.

You can mix up to three sound files and import and export sounds in a variety of formats, including Microsoft WAV, Creative Labs VOC, SoundStage SFI, and Microsoft ADPCM compressed files.

Tip

Wave After Wave, also from Turtle Beach, lets you professionally edit and mix sound files—thanks in part to built-in filters that clean up the sounds.

A fistful of built-in filters for cleaning up sound files and producing special effects is included. Resembling a stereo equalizer, Wave for Windows has high- and low-pass filters and a 60 Hz notch filter that screens out the annoying hum produced by poorly grounded equipment, such as a record turntable. With other filters, you can simulate an AM radio broadcast or the crackly sound of a 1930s radio news program.

For special effects, use the Auto Stutter option to manipulate voices. A reverb tool lends your music files the ambiance of a large concert hall, and your narrations the intimacy of a small room. The Speed Up/Slow Down tool lets you stretch or compress a recording while maintaining its pitch and other sound characteristics.

You can blend entire files or just previously marked portions. (You can insert up to 256 markers in a single sound file.) You can also specify delays in the files' start times and fade one file into another. Wave for Windows is a must-have package for anyone seriously interested in editing PC sound files.

Wave for Windows 2.0 ($149)

Turtle Beach Systems
52 Grumbacher Rd.
York, PA 17402
800-645-5640

MIDI Sequencing and Notation Software

Sequencing software allows you to record, edit and place any MIDI event into an output stream position that is precisely timed. For example, sequencers are useful for creating melodies and adding an ending, a beginning or a fade-out. Notation software allows you to transcribe music onto your PC.

Since MIDI was born in 1983, sequencer programs have evolved and matured. In fact, differentiating sequencers from music notation and music generation programs is a difficult task since the line between these categories has blurred. You should "audition" sequencer demonstration disks before deciding on the right product for your needs and budget.

Cakewalk Professional for Windows 3.0. Version 3.0 of Twelve Tone Systems' MIDI sequencer, Cakewalk Professional for Windows 3.0 is one of the more popular MIDI sequencers (see fig. 10.6).

Cakewalk Pro lets you record multiple performances played on a synthesizer, edit them, and play them back as individual tracks. You can create an orchestra of unlimited size and sound using external MIDI instruments or a PC sound card. The OLE-compliant Cakewalk is not only an excellent sequencer, but has hooks into Windows' Media Control Interface (MCI) that give it considerable multimedia chops.

Cakewalk is great for sophisticated MIDI recording or simple playback of prerecorded MIDI songs. It can record music straight from your synthesizer, or with a step record function that lets less accomplished keyboardists record one note at a time. It has automated punch-in and -out, and a flexible loop function that repeats a track while you play multiple takes of a performance.

Tip

Cakewalk Professional is a highly respected package that allows you to record in steps or simply play back prerecorded MIDI compositions.

Cakewalk's editing capabilities are powerful yet intuitive. The main window provides an overview of up to 256 tracks. You can click and drag to select any number of these, and then cut and paste selections. Alternatively, you can move or copy a selection by dragging and dropping it. Thus, if you're using prerecorded MIDI files, you can tailor the length of a score to fit accompanying visuals with speed, precision, and ease.

The software displays individual tracks graphically. Notes are represented by horizontal bars on a piano roll, percussion roll, or by standard musical notations or an event list. In each of these views, you can change any parameter of a note or of selected groups: pitch, duration, location in time, timbre, volume, and more. This notation view lets you display, edit, and print a score of up to 24 staves.

In its text-based event list, though, Cakewalk turns the multimedia tables. Like most MIDI sequencers, Cakewalk's event list displays notes, their qualities, and other musical data in the form of text. Cakewalk's edge is that it lets you insert any MCI command at any point in an event list. This means you can have Cakewalk not only trigger WAV digital audio, but control CD-ROM drives, audio or video tape players, and any MCI-compliant multimedia application such as Autodesk Animator or Microsoft Video for Windows.

Furthermore, Cakewalk's origins as a music program give it a rock-solid time base that's weak or absent in most visually oriented applications. If you want an animated film clip to start exactly when the fanfare does, Cakewalk is one of the few programs that can get the job done.

Fig. 10.6
Cakewalk Professional is one sequencing software program revered by many music professionals.

Cakewalk Professional for Windows 2.0 ($349)

Twelve Tone Systems Inc.
PO Box 760
Watertown, MA 02272
800-234-1171; 617-926-2480
FAX: 617-924-6657

Cakewalk Home Studio. Twelve Tone Systems also offers a lighter version of Cakewalk Professional. The arrival of Cakewalk Home Studio opens the door for amateur musicians to compose MIDI music. The Microsoft Windows-based entry-level MIDI sequencer and notation program lets you create, edit, or play back music via a sound card or external MIDI instrument. Numerous displays include a multitrack Staff view (print up to 16 staves on a single page), a Faders view (with real-time controls), and a Piano Roll view (with velocity display). With a .WAV-compatible sound card, you can embed and play back .WAV files from within a MIDI sequence.

Cakewalk Home Studio ($169)

Twelve Tone Systems Inc.
PO Box 760
Watertown, MA 02272
800-234-1171; 617-926-2480
FAX: 617-924-6657

Cubase Audio for Windows. Cubase Audio for Windows from Steinberg/Jones is a MIDI sequencing/notation and digital audio program that is revered by professional musicians. It integrates MIDI recording, score printing, and digital audio. This program requires the Yamaha CBX-D5 for audio input/output. It provides up to eight tracks of digital audio.

Tip

Cubase Audio for Windows is a highly respected program that integrates MIDI recording, printing of musical scores and digital audio.

Cubase Audio for Windows ($799)

Steinberg/Jones
17700 Raymer St., Ste. 1001
Northridge, CA 91325
818-993-4091
FAX: 818-701-7452
Tech support: 818-993-4161

Cubase LITE. Cubase also comes in a Lite version. Cubase LITE requires a PC MIDI interface with MIDI In and MIDI Out connectors that are MPU-401 compatible.

Like Cubase Audio, Cubase LITE includes an Arrange Window that is fully interactive (refer to fig. 10.7). Each track of your song can be broken down into parts. These graphic rectangles can be directly manipulated by mouse tools. The mouse-toolbox provides tools to cut and glue, move, or erase.

Cubase LITE features a real-time notation display and editor that is printable. (Cubase includes score fonts.) In Score Edit, you can step input as well, even as the sequencer is running, so you'll have immediate feedback on any changes. Score Edit includes an undo feature that can undo a whole sequence of changes, not just the last step.

Cubase LITE works with both GM and Roland GS instruments. You can adjust the volume, pan, and other features for all 16 channels. Ten MIDI songs are included along with on-line expert help. MIDI Xplained, for example, provides answers to several MIDI questions. A few clicks on the highlighted keywords lead you to the answers.

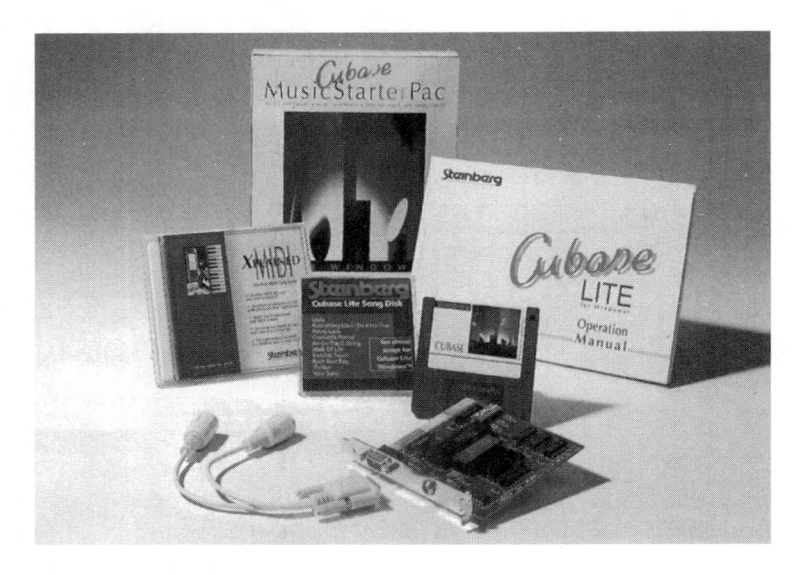

Fig. 10.7
Cubase LITE provides even more ease of use than Cubase Audio for home MIDI users.

Cubase LITE ($99)

Steinberg/Jones
17700 Raymer St., Ste. 1001
Northridge, CA 91325
818-993-4091
FAX: 818-701-7452
Tech support: 818-993-4161

Encore for Windows. Passport Designs has taken the ability to compose music on the PC to a higher level with Version 3.0 of Encore for Windows (see fig. 10.8). The user interface has new menus, tools, and palettes, plus a new array of music symbols. If you prefer Bob Dylan to Mozart, Encore 3.0 can automatically convert notes to guitar tablature, including correct fingerings, when you enter music on a MIDI keyboard. Now that Encore 3.0 supports EPS, you can export complete or partial scores to desktop publishing or word processing programs. Version 3.0 retains click-and-drag editing and real-time transcription of input from MIDI instruments.

Fig. 10.8
Encore for Windows is an excellent music notation/transcription software program.

Encore for Windows ($595)

Encore for Windows 3.0
Passport Designs Inc.
100 Stone Pine Rd.
Half Moon Bay, CA 94019
800-443-3210; 415-726-0280
FAX: 415-726-2254

MusicTime 2.0. Passport Designs' MusicTime 2.0 provides an affordable MIDI-based notation program. Instead of offering a slow, low-end, note-by-note music-entry software, Passport Designs (creator of Encore) has a software program meant for the hobbyist but powerful enough for musicians of any level.

The beauty of MusicTime is its seamless interface, which involves connecting your MIDI keyboard to a serial port via a MIDI interface and simply playing in time to a metronome. Notes appear on staves as you play, and then form into fully notated transcription beams, triplets, rests—and even your mistakes. For accurate transcription, keeping time with the metronome is essential, especially if you're quantizing to 16th or 32nd notes.

After transcription, you can play back your performance and even assign a MIDI channel to each staff. MusicTime supports most sound cards, and uses the Anastasia font, which prints clean and refined manuscripts.

Tip

MusicTime works both with and without a MIDI keyboard and is targeted at a wide range of MIDI enthusiasts. The program automatically transcribes MIDI files into ready-to-print musical scores.

If you have a sound card but no MIDI keyboard, you can enter music through the computer's keyboard. This option, although slightly clumsy, is valuable for those times when you don't have access to a keyboard, but it keeps you and MusicTime from optimum accuracy and expression. You can also edit the staves manually, adding items from a floating palette of notes, rests, articulations, and so on—perfect for fine-tuning a real-time entry, such as placing a 16th note instead of an eighth note. The software also supports and automatically transcribes MIDI files.

MusicTime handles text well, giving you the option to place lyric, chord, expression, or guitar-chord fret diagrams precisely in line with the notes. For teaching purposes, MusicTime's color capabilities let you highlight sections of a piece to work on. (Passport plans to bolster the educational front with additional learn-to-play software later this year.)

While the higher-priced Encore includes more complex notations, guitar tablatures, and playback of dynamics, articulations, and other subtleties, MusicTime works in basically the same way and is equally intuitive. However, the program is limited to eight staves per system with up to four voices per staff. If you're looking for flexible notation and more accurate dynamics, Encore can oblige, but MusicTime is perfect for charts, lead sheets, and straight playback.

MusicTime 2.0 ($149)

Passport Designs
100 Stone Pine Rd.
Half Moon Bay, CA 94019
415-726-0280

Canned Music

A good way to begin a MIDI composition is to use starter material, clip music files and programs with automated music reproduction capabilities such as Band-In-A-Box and SuperJam. For background tracks, users may only need an auto-generator.

Band-in-A-Box Pro for Windows. The amazing Band-in-a-Box, from PG Music, is a complete backup band in a software box that automatically creates a musical arrangement in a wide variety of styles, from reggae to rock to jazz. You just type in a chord progression, select a style, and jam along with the software. Band-in-a-Box is a grass-roots hit among Mac, IBM, and Atari musicians.

It plays the song you've sketched out in any of hundreds of musical styles, playing your synthesizer's bass, drum, piano, and guitar sounds in a fresh and professional way. And it comes with nearly 300 ready-to-go songs, from today's pop hits to golden oldies—and a choice of 160 musical styles, if you can believe that.

Tip

Band-in-a-Box provides backup accompaniment in a choice of 160 musical styles. You simply provide the chords.

Novices can play like pros by selecting prerecorded melodies from the program's jukebox mode, and you can save your tunes in standard MIDI files. These files can then be opened in a sequencer or notation program.

Band-in-a-Box Pro for Windows ($88)

PG Music Inc.
266 Elmwood Ave., Ste. 111
Buffalo, NY 14222
800-268-6272; 905-528-2368
FAX: 905-577-4704
Tech support: 905-528-7043

SuperJAM! 1.0. Like Band-in-a-Box, SuperJAM! allows those who have the soul of a composer, but not the talents, to compose and arrange great-sounding scores graphically. It is the perfect gift for an aspiring musician of any age.

SuperJAM! is a composition, arrangement, playback, and MIDI transcription tool that requires no previous knowledge of music or MIDI programming. It allows you to create unique musical compositions by putting the conductor's baton in your hand and several talented, attentive musicians at your command.

Tip

SuperJAM! is ideal for beginners who want to compose but may not have all of the talents for it.

SuperJAM! manages the fundamental musical structures such as key, chord, style, timbre, and tempo, while you direct the band members using a jauntily intuitive graphical interface.

The six SuperJAM! band members come prepared to play in more than 30 predefined musical styles, including everything from New Age to Waltz. Each lends a particular character to the performance, and the style may be changed on the fly, which is what makes playing along with the band so lifelike and entertaining.

Chord changes, fills, breaks, and new grooves make the SuperJAM! backup band sound great, but the best part is playing the lead after you have them jamming along. Just click the yellow trumpet on the Lead icon and use the keyboard to play your own melody over their sound.

Yet SuperJAM! is much more than just a toy. Its feature set is cleverly layered to provide sophisticated and powerful tools to MIDI aficionados, while shielding neophytes from unnecessary complexity. Nearly every aspect of SuperJAM! is configurable, from the instruments played by band members in various parts of a song, to the default chord progressions supplied by the Eas-O-Matic MusicMaker.

The six band members in the SuperJAM! House Band are the Drummer, Bass Player, Keyboard Player, Guitar Player, String Section, and Lead Player. Their names reflect their default MIDI patch assignments, but they can be assigned to play any MIDI patch. SuperJAM!'s MIDI management and configuration facilities are fully integrated with the Windows MIDI Mapper. A 16-bit sound card with wave table synthesis is recommended.

SuperJAM! 1.0 ($129)

The Blue Ribbon SoundWorks, Ltd.
Venture Center
1605 Chantilly Dr., #200
Atlanta, GA 30324
404-315-0212
FAX: 404-315-0213

Multimedia Sound Options

Buying MIDI accessories is often not an end in itself. There are other accessories that unsuspectingly raise the cost of your sound system. At the very least, you'll have to invest in a set of speakers or headphones, if you haven't already done so. You may also want to invest in a better quality microphone or joystick.

Speakers

Successful business presentations, multimedia applications, and MIDI work demand external high-fidelity stereo speakers. Although you can use standard stereo speakers, they are too big to fit on or near your desk. Smaller bookshelf speakers would be better.

> **Note**
>
> Although most computer speakers are magnetically shielded, do not leave recorded tapes, watches, personal credit cards or floppy disks in front of the speakers for long periods of time.

Quality sound depends on quality speakers. A 16-bit sound card may provide better sound to computer speakers, but even an 8-bit sound card sounds good from a quality speaker. Conversely, using an inexpensive speaker makes both 8-bit and 16-bit sound cards sound tinny.

There are dozens of models on the market, ranging from less expensive minispeakers from Sony and Koss to larger self-powered models from companies such as Bose. To evaluate speakers, you need to know the lingo. Speakers are measured by three criteria:

- *Frequency response.* Frequency response is a measurement of the range of high and low sounds a speaker can reproduce. The ideal range is from 20 Hz to 20 kHz, the range of human hearing. No speaker system reproduces this range perfectly. In fact, few people hear sounds above 18 kHz. An exceptional speaker may cover 30 Hz to 23,000 kHz. Lesser models may only cover 100 Hz to 20,000 Hz. Frequency response is the most deceptive specification, because identically rated speakers can sound completely different.

- *Total Harmonic Distortion (THD).* THD, or just distortion, is an expression of the amount of distortion or noise created by amplifying the signal. Simply put, distortion is the difference between the sound that was sent to the speaker and the sound that we hear. The amount of distortion is measured in percentages. An acceptable level of distortion is that below .1 percent (one-tenth of one percent). For some CD-quality recording equipment, a common standard is .05 percent. Some speakers have a distortion of 10 percent or more. Headphones often have a distortion of about 2 percent or less.

- *Watts.* Usually stated as watts per channel, this is the amount of amplification available to drive the speakers. Check that the company means "per channel" (or RMS) and not total power. Many sound cards have built-in amplifiers, providing up to 8 watts per channel. (Most provide 4 watts.) However, the wattage is not enough to provide rich sound. This is why many speakers have built-in amplifiers. With the flick of a switch or the press of a button, these speakers amplify the signals they receive from the sound card. If you do not want to amplify the sound, you typically leave the speaker switch to its "direct" setting. In most cases, you'll want to amplify the signal.

To power computer speakers, two or four C batteries are often used. Because these speakers require so much power, you may want to invest in an AC adapter, although more-expensive speakers include one. An AC adapter will prevent you from buying new batteries every few weeks. If yours didn't come with an AC adapter, you can pick one up from your local Radio Shack or hardware store.

You can control your speakers in various ways, depending on their complexity and cost. Typically, each speaker has a volume knob, although some share one volume control. If one speaker is further away than the other, you may want to adjust the volume accordingly. Many computer speakers include a dynamic bass boost (DBB) switch. This button provides a more powerful bass and clearer treble, regardless of the volume setting. Others have separate bass and treble boost switches or a three-band equalizer to control low, middle and high frequencies. When you rely on your sound card's power and not your speaker's built-in amplifier, the volume and dynamic bass boost controls do not have an effect. Your speakers are at the mercy of the sound card's power.

To connect to your sound card, an 1/8-inch stereo minijack is connected from the sound card output jack to one of the speakers. The signal is then split and fed from the first speaker to the remaining one through a separate cable.

Before purchasing a set of speakers, check that the cables between the speakers are long enough for your computer setup. For example, a tower case sitting alongside one's desk may require longer speaker wires than a desktop computer.

Beware of speakers that have a tardy built-in "sleep" feature. When such speakers are not in use, they turn themselves off to save electricity. However, they may have an annoying habit of clipping the first part of a sound after a period of inactivity.

Note

Headphones are an option when you can't afford a premium set of speakers. Headphones provide privacy while allowing you to play your sound card as loud as you'd like.

Powered Partners AV22. At the bottom of the price range, consider the Advent 22 speakers from the Advent division of International Jensen Inc. You'll pay about $109 a pair for them, and if you're used to the tinny sound of bundled speakers, you'll be astonished. The AR 22s are compact, fitting easily onto the typically crowded PC desktop. The speakers don't provide much bass below 100 Hz, but that's expected, considering their small size and price.

Powered Partners AV22 ($109/pair)

Advent (division of International Jensen Inc.)
25 Tri-State, International Office Center, Ste. 400
Lincolnshire, IL 60069
800-323-0707; 708-317-3700
FAX: 708-317-3836

Yamaha YST-M10. With a street price of about $99, Yamaha's YST-M10s are the next step up. About half as large as the Advent 22s, the M10s sound great with more bass. They have a frequency response of 80 Hz to 20 kHz.

YST-M10 ($149.95/pair)

Yamaha Corp. of America (Consumer Products Division)
PO Box 6600, 6600 Orangethorpe Ave.
Buena Park, CA 90622-6600
714-522-9937
FAX: 714-228-3913

Sony SRS-58PC. Close competitors to the Yamahas are Sony's SRS-58PCs, also with a street price of about $90. You may find the Yamaha speakers better for music. These two satellite speakers have a frequency response of 100 Hz to 20 kHz. They can be AC or battery powered. Battery life is about 120 hours.

SRS-58PC ($129.95/pair)

SONY Electronics, Inc. (Computer Peripheral Products Co.)
3300 Zanker Rd.
San Jose, CA 95134
800-352-7669; 408-432-0190
FAX: 408-943-0740
Tech support: 408-894-0555
Tech support BBS: 408-955-5107

ACS-301. For better sound (and perhaps more volume), you need to move into what amounts to serious speakers. If you want the very best in computer speakers and can afford them, consider the three-part ACS301 from Altec Lansing Consumer Products.

The $350 ACS301 features two clamshell satellite speakers that provide the midrange and treble part of the sound. A lunch-box size subwoofer delivers the bass. By adjusting the open angle of the clamshells, you can position the speakers precisely, so that none of the sound is muffled on the desktop. You close the clamshells when you're done using them.

The small size of the satellite speakers ($3^1/_2 \times 5 \times 7$ inches) allows them to be mounted on a wall or placed beside your monitor or on your desk. Each satellite has a 4-inch woofer

III

Investing in Multimedia

and a half-inch dome tweeter. The accompanying subwoofer picks up where the satellites leave off, reproducing bass notes below 120 Hz. The subwoofer, although not magnetically shielded, can be hidden under a desk.

Altec includes a variety of controls, including controls for volume, treble, bass, balance and digital signal processing (DSP) enhancement. Controls are also provided for mixing and balance; the AB mixing control allows you to preview and set the two sound sources for the best possible combination.

The ACS301 has a 36-watt-per-channel amplifier and a rated frequency response of 35 Hz to 20 KHz (+ or - 3 decibels), with total harmonic distortion (THD) less than 0.8 percent.

ACS301 ($350/pair)

Altec Lansing Multimedia (Consumer Products Division)
PO Box 277
Milford, PA 18337-0277
800-648-6663; 717-296-2818
FAX: 717-296-1222
Tech support: 800-258-3288

Bose Roommate Computer Monitor. The Bose name has always connoted sound quality. Bose Corp.'s Bose Roommate Computer Monitors have been out awhile, but still are excellent speakers. Housed in tough $6 \times 9 \times 6$-inch (HWD) molded styrene cabinets, this pair of speakers combines woofer, midrange, and tweeter into the same 4 1/2 inch driver. However, the size makes the speakers a bit clumsy for your desktop. The rugged design makes them ideal for the traveling presenter.

Controls are simple on the Bose Roommate. One volume knob adjusts the level of both speakers; most other adjustments are made automatically, including dynamic equalization to ensure the proper proportion of high and low frequencies at loud and quiet volumes.

Bose Roommate Computer Monitor ($329/pair)

Bose Corp.
The Mountain
Framingham, MA 01701-9168
800-444-2673; 508-879-7330
FAX: 508-229-3795

Roland MA-12C Micro Monitor. If you are a serious MIDI user and musician, consider buying the Roland MA-12C Micro Monitors. These speakers are very rugged and adaptable speakers. Each speaker has three 1/4 inch jack inputs located on the back: a line input (to be used for a CD player or an audio card), a microphone input, and an instrument hookup—perfect for MIDI users.

These speakers lack a headphone jack, but Roland is one of the few companies to offer an on/off power button on each speaker.

At 8 $^1/_2$ × 5 × 6$^1/_4$ inches (HWD), the Roland speakers may be a little large for typical desktops, but the thick plastic speaker cabinets and heavy-duty power cords make them ready for the road. Each speaker has a single driver and an independent 10-watt power amplifier with individual controls for volume, bass, and treble.

Like Bose Corp., Roland doesn't provide ratings for the speakers' frequency response or total harmonic distortion.

Roland MA-12C Micro Monitor ($290/pair or $124.50/each)

Roland Corp. U.S.
7200 Dominion Circle
Los Angeles, CA 90040
213-685-5141
FAX: 213-726-8865

Powered Partners AV570. The best high-end PC sound I've heard comes from the AR 570 speakers, also from Advent. Their relatively large wedge shape (about 10 inches high with a 6 × 7-inch footprint) may be hard to accommodate on your desk. Of course, you can put them under your desk if that doesn't spoil the stereo effect for you. At about $300 per pair, the AR 570s aren't cheap, but they're very, very good. In fact, they're better speakers than many of us have in our stereo systems.

Powered Partners AV570 ($399/pair)

Advent (division of International Jensen Inc.)
25 Tri-State, International Office Center, Ste. 400
Lincolnshire, IL 60069
800-323-0707; 708-317-3700
FAX: 708-317-3836

Note

You can bypass a set of speakers and simply connect your PC sound card to your stereo. The output of sound cards is compatible with the Aux, CD, Video, Tape In, and Line In inputs of almost any stereo, and even the smallest mini-stereo speakers will sound better than the cheap speakers bundled with sound cards and multimedia PCs. If your PC and stereo are in the same room, give it a try.

Microphone

Most sound cards do not include a microphone. You'll need one to record your voice to a WAV file. Selecting a microphone is quite simple. You need one that has a 1/8-inch minijack for plugging into your sound card's microphone, or audio in, jack. Most have an on/off switch.

III

Investing in Multimedia

Like speakers, a microphone is measured by its frequency range. However, this buying factor is not important since the human voice has a limited range. If you are recording only voices, consider an inexpensive microphone that covers a lesser range of frequencies. An expensive microphone extends its recording capabilities to frequencies outside the voice's range. Why pay for something you won't be needing?

If you are recording music, invest in an expensive microphone, although an 8-bit sound card can record music as well with an inexpensive microphone as an expensive one.

Your biggest decision is selecting a microphone that suits your recording style. If working in a noisy office, you may want an unidirectional microphone that will prevent extraneous noises from being recorded. An omnidirectional mike would be best for recording a group conversation. If you want to leave your hands free, you may want to shun the traditional handheld microphone for a lapel model.

Some sound cards include a microphone. For example, the Media Vision Pro AudioStudio 16 includes a small lapel microphone and a holster in which to place it. The Sound Blaster 16 ASP includes a handheld microphone.

Joysticks

Many sound cards include a joystick, or game, port. (This joystick port often doubles as a connection to a MIDI device.) A joystick is ideal for gameplaying, such as simulating a Cessna aircraft flight. Like a speaker, a joystick is best chosen through hands-on experience.

A joystick includes a fire button on top of a center wand you move in any of eight directions. A second button or pair of buttons are located on the base of the joystick.

Good joysticks have resistance that increases the further you move the center wand from dead center. Some joysticks include suction cups that mount the unit to your desk. If short on desk space, you may prefer a smaller joystick that fits in your hand. If you are left-handed, look for an ambidextrous joystick, not one that is contoured for right-handers.

Some joysticks are especially meant for flight simulation games. The Flightstick Pro from CH Products provides additional buttons for firing and selecting missiles, and looking in different directions.

Flightstick Pro ($99.95)

CH Products
970 Park Center Dr.
Vista, CA 92083
800-624-5804; 619-598-2518
FAX: 619-598-2524
Tech support: Use main no.
Tech support BBS: 619-598-3224

From Here...

This chapter discussed some key criteria for buying MIDI equipment. You learned about polyphony and multitimbrality and their importance in reducing note stealing. You learned about the configurations of synthesizers, either built into a keyboard controller or as a separate table-top or rack-mounted module. Lastly, you learned about some of the more predominant keyboard and sound module synthesizers and accessories.

■ Chapter 5, "MIDI: Music to Your Ears," discusses MIDI in more detail.

■ Chapter 11, "Buyer's Guide to Video," discusses video cards, including video capture boards.

III

Investing in Multimedia

Chapter 11

Buyer's Guide to Video

If the eyes are the windows to the soul, then your monitor is the window to multimedia. Your monitor provides the vital link between you and your computer. While you can get rid of your printer, disk drives, and expansion cards, you can't sacrifice your monitor. Without it, you operate blind.

The first microcomputers were small boxes that lacked displays. Instead of reading output as it ran across a monitor, you had to wait for the final, entire output to be printed by a printer. When the monitor was added, the computer became accessible to a wider audience. This trend continues today with graphical user interfaces such as *Microsoft Windows*.

In this chapter, you will learn about the combination of video cards and monitors and the criteria for buying each. We also review some multimedia-capable monitors and video cards. How video capture cards enable you to capture images from a TV screen or display computer images onto a TV or video cassette also is covered.

The video portion of an MPC consists of two main components:

> Monitor (or video display)

> Video adapter (also called the video card, video adapter, or graphics card)

You also can get accessories, such as a video capture board for capturing TV screens to your computer or displaying computer images to a TV screen or VCR. This chapter explores the range of MPC-compatible video adapters and the displays that work with them.

Video Cards

The monitor is, of course, the display found on top of, near, or built inside your computer. Like any computer device, a monitor requires a source of input. That input comes from the video card (also called a video board, video adapter, or graphics card).

In the good old days, buying a video card was simple: If you had an EGA monitor, you bought an EGA card; if you had a VGA display, you opted for VGA. Maybe you gave a moment's thought to how much memory you wanted onboard (256K, or a hefty 512K for VGA power users), but otherwise, you shopped for the best price and were done with it. Those days are gone, thanks to Windows, desktop publishing, and multimedia. Today, even the phrase "video card" is being stolen by a different class of boards, those that capture full-motion video. Cards for the more basic purpose of putting data on your PC's display are now referred to as "graphics cards" or "graphics adapters."

Video Card Buying Criteria

Most video cards follow one of several industry standards:

MDA	Monochrome Display Adapter
CGA	Color Graphics Adapter
EGA	Enhanced Graphics Adapter
VGA	Video Graphics Adapter
SVGA	Super VGA
XGA	eXtended Graphics Array

Tip

Standards such as MDA, CGA, and EGA have fallen by the wayside, while XGA was mostly promoted by IBM, it's creator. Today's hottest video standards are VGA and SVGA.

There have been many efforts recently to improve the speed of video adapters. This is due to the complexity and sheer data of the high-resolution displays needed to use much of today's software. Video card improvements were made in the following areas:

- Resolution (VGA, SVGA, etc.)

- Video memory and design (VRAM and DRAM)

- Chip and circuitry design (Windows accelerators, S3 coprocessors, etc.)

- Bus design (PCI or VL-Bus)

Each of these will be discussed in the next few sections.

VGA: The Minimum. The MPC Level 2 specifications call for VGA resolution, which is 640×480 picture elements, referred to as pixels. The specifications also call for the display of 65,536 colors, which provide near photographic quality output. You can easily step up to super-VGA (SVGA) video cards for even higher resolutions. Most people do.

Super-VGA does not refer to a card that meets a particular specification, but to a group of cards with different, heightened capabilities. For example, one card may offer two resolutions (800×600 and 1024×768) which are greater than those achieved with a regular VGA, while another vendor may offer a card that provides those resolutions but also provides more color choices at each one. While these cards have different capabilities, they are nonetheless both classified as super-VGA. To help standardize SVGA cards, the Video Electronics Standards Association (VESA) proposed a programmer's interface for SVGA cards.

> **Note**
>
> VESA includes video card manufacturers ATI Technologies, Genoa Systems, Orchid Technology, Renaissance GRX, STB Systems, Techmar, Headland Technology (formerly Video Seven), Western Digital Imaging/Paradise Systems, and NEC.

Video Memory. A video card relies on memory for holding the contents of your screen for your monitor to "paint." Often, you can select how much memory you want on your video card, such as 256K, 512K, 1MB, 2M, or even 4M. Finding only 256K on a VGA card is rare; most cards come with at least 1M, if not 2M. The 1M or 2M of memory is not intended to speed up your video card, rather, it allows your monitor to display more colors and/or higher resolutions. For 256 colors drawn from a palette of 256,000, you need at least 512K of video memory. At 1024×768 pixels, you need at least 1M. If you want 24-bit (true-color) resolution for viewing images at photographic quality, you need 2M.

How do you know how much you need? A simple formula is to multiply the horizontal and vertical resolution and multiply it by the bits required for the number of colors you want to view. Then, divide by eight (8 bits in a byte). This is how much memory you need.

For example, if you wanted to view 800×600 pixels at 8-bit color ($2^8 = 256$ colors):

$(800 \times 600 \times 8) / 8 = 480,000 = 468K$

If you wanted to view 800×600 pixels at 24-bit (photographic) color ($2^{24} = 16,777,216$ colors):

$(800 \times 600 \times 24) / 8 = 1,440,000 = 1,406K = 1.4M$

Most video cards use regular dynamic RAM (DRAM) to store video images. Although it is inexpensive, DRAM is rather slow as well. However, using an odd/even interleaved design, DRAM video cards perk up. Newer video cards, however, use specialized video RAM (VRAM).

III

Investing in Multimedia

> **Tip**
>
> If you are buying a video card, consider models that use DRAM, not VRAM. DRAM memory is half the price of VRAM. Advances in DRAM interleaving make DRAM video cards almost as fast as the costlier VRAM models.

A 24-bit (or true-color) video card can display photographic images by using 16.7 million colors. If you spend a lot of time working with graphics, you may want to invest in a 24-bit video card. Two years ago true-color cards cost as much as a decent PC. Today, you can buy one for well under $500.

Accelerators and Coprocessors. There are three types of processors, or chip sets, that can be used in designing a video card. The oldest is frame buffer technology, where individual frames of an image are held in memory. This places a heavy burden on your computer, which could be busy completing other multimedia tasks.

Accelerator chips take a different approach by relieving your computer's CPU from certain video processing duties. Coprocessors go a step further. A software driver controls how the video board performs calculations—which allows drivers to be tuned for specific applications. A coprocessor assumes a large portion of the video duties.

Bus. Video cards are designed for various buses. The bus system you use in your computer (ISA, EISA, VL-Bus, PCI, or MCA) affects the speed at which your system can process video information. For example, the VGA video card originally was designed to be used with the PS/2's MCA bus.

The introduction of the VESA local bus (VLB or VL-Bus) standard has sped up video cards immensely. The VLB allows you to have high-speed video cards that can pass video information in 32-bit chunks at 40 MHz. A newer alternative bus is Intel's 32-bit Peripheral Component Interconnect (PCI). PCI video cards, like VL-Bus video cards, can increase video performance dramatically. PCI video cards, by their design, are meant to be "plug and play," requiring little configuration.

Drivers

If you are shopping for a video card to provide super-VGA or sharper resolutions, you require special software drivers for each of your software programs to take advantage of this resolution. Otherwise, your video card acts as a typical VGA card. For example, if you use Microsoft Windows (who doesn't?), you need a software driver for your SVGA video card to display more of the page on the screen. (Windows does include a generic SVGA driver.)

When shopping for a higher-resolution video card, ensure it has drivers that support the software packages you own. Otherwise, your software will operate in the typical

VGA mode. Don't expect many drivers to be available. Drivers are usually only provided for a handful of the following programs: AutoCAD, Autoshade, CADKEY, Framework, GEM Desktop, Lotus 1-2-3, Microsoft Windows, Microsoft Word, P-CAD, Symphony, Ventura Publisher, VersaCAD, WordPerfect, WordStar, OS/2 Presentation Manager, and Quattro Pro.

Video drivers not only provide sharper resolutions but also optimize your specific video card for the work it does. For example, a Windows accelerator card is put into high gear when it is used with its appropriate driver. With a generic driver, it slows down to a snail's pace.

Some software programs have built-in support for a higher-resolution video card. For example, Microsoft Windows has drivers for most video cards, although your video card may include a newer, more-powerful version. After the software driver is installed for its intended program, your video card will perform to its fullest. For example, you may be able to see more on your screen. Characters on the screen will be easier to read because more pixels are being used to form the letters, and graphical images will be smoother and more representative of how they will look when printed. If you use Windows, you'll need to run the Windows Setup program from DOS to install your new video card's drivers. Other video cards add an icon to the Windows Control Panel from which you can change resolutions and number of colors.

Because video card drivers directly control your video card, they are often the first suspect when Windows becomes troublesome. Often, the most current version of a video card software driver solves these problems.

Tip

Newer drivers can be received directly from your video card's manufacturer or downloaded from an on-line service, such as CompuServe or America Online.

Selected Video Cards

Selecting a video card is a choice between blazing 64-bit speed and more affordable 32-bit video cards. For multimedia work, you need a VLB- or PCI-capable card so that video data can be moved quickly around your system. To save money, consider the "older" 32-bit video cards, which are not far behind the newer 64-bit models.

Next is a review of some of the top video cards for multimedia work. Table 11.1 summarizes video card specs, which are described in more detail throughout the rest of this section.

III

Investing in Multimedia

Table 11.1 Multimedia Video Cards

Model	Maker	Design	Maximum resolution
MGA Ultima Plus VL	Matrox	64-bit	1600x1280
MGA Ultima Plus PCI	Matrox	64-bit	1600x1280
Number Nine GXE64 Pro PCI	Number Nine	64-bit	1600x1280
Number Nine GXE64 Pro VL	Number Nine	64-bit	1600x1280
Stealth 64 VLB	Diamond Computer Systems	64-bit	1280x1024
Stealth 64 PCI	Diamond Computer Systems	64-bit	1280x1024
Graphics Pro Turbo VLB	ATI Technologies	64-bit	1280x1024
Graphics Pro Turbo PCI	ATI Technologies	64-bit	1280x1024
Diamond Viper Pro PCI	Diamond Computer Systems	32-bit	1280x1024
Diamond Viper Pro VLB	Diamond Computer Systems	32-bit	1280x1024
Pro Graphics 1024 VLB	Media Vision	32-bit	1024x768

Matrox MGA Ultima Plus. If you want the fastest Windows video card you can buy, consider Matrox's MGA Ultima Plus. Offered in both PCI and VLB version, the Ultima Plus has an innovative 64-bit chip design that pushes Windows to its limits. The Ultima Plus includes a Consistent Color color-correction utility and WinSqueeze, a JPEG compression program. The Ultima Plus also has the most detailed monitor-configuration controls.

The Ultima Plus has impressive Windows performance and delivers the best 24-bit color performance in Windows by far. It is among a few video cards that supports 1600×1200 resolution. It supports 1600×1200 resolution in 256-color mode and up to 65,536 colors in 1280×1024 mode—all at refresh rates above 60 Hz. Unfortunately, the Ultima Plus has its drawbacks, including that it's slow when you're running DOS applications. Drivers for 3D Studio, AutoShade, and MicroStation are included.

MGA Ultima Plus PCI (Ult/2+/P) ($499)

MGA Ultima Plus VLB (Ult/2+/V) ($549)

Matrox Electronic Systems, Ltd.
1055 St. Regis Blvd.
Dorval, QB, CD H9P 2T4
800-361-4903; 514-685-2630
Direct sales: 800-361-4903
FAX: 514-685-2853
Tech support: 800-810-2338
Tech support BBS: 514-685-6008

Maximum # of colors	Standard RAM	Graphics Coprocessor	Bus Type	Price
16.7M	2M	MGA 64	VLB	$549
16.7M	2M	MGA 64	PCI	$499
16.7M	2M	S3 Vision964	PCI	$499
16.7M	2M	S3 Vision964	VLB	$499
16.7M	2M	S3 Vision964	VLB	$399
16.7M	2M	S3 Vision964	PCI	$399
16.7M	2M	ATI Mach64	VLB	$449
16.7M	2M	ATI Mach64	PCI	$449
16.7M	2M	P9100	PCI	$479
16.7M	2M	P9100	VLB	$479
16.7M	1M	na	VLB	$449

Number Nine GXE64 Pro. The GXE64 Pro from Number Nine Computer Corp., as shown in figure 11.1, provides above-average speeds for DOS programs and good overall Windows performance. Although not the fastest card, it provides easy-to-use utilities and high refresh rates that provide relief for your eyes.

The GXE64 Pro is based on the S3 Vision964 accelerator chip. The GXE64 Pro is the only board I know of that has the new 32-bit VESA Advanced Feature Connector (VAFC) in addition to the standard 8-bit connector for faster transfer of motion video and additional data from other cards.

The GXE64 Pro has no jumpers, making installation easy. Instead, settings are preserved on the board in non-volatile memory. A Monitor Adjustment applet makes tuning the card simple. Drivers for 3D Studio, AutoShade, and MicroStation are included.

Number Nine GXE64 Pro VL (2 meg: $499; 4 meg: $749)

Number Nine GXE64 Pro PCI (2 meg: $499; 4 meg $749)

Number Nine Computer Corp.
18 Hartwell Ave.
Lexington, MA 02173
800-GET-NINE; 617-674-0009
FAX: 617-674-2919
Tech support: Use main number
Tech support BBS: 617-862-7502

Fig. 11.1
The GXE64 Pro from Number Nine has no jumpers, easing installation.

Diamond Stealth 64. Diamond Computer Systems provides an affordable 64-bit card with its Stealth 64 PCI and VL-Bus cards. These cards, like the Number Nine XGE64 Pro, use the S3 Vision964 graphics chip. The Stealth 64 is one of the faster DOS cards, and game-lovers should take note of the Stealth 64 for this reason (see fig. 11.2).

Under Windows, the Stealth 64 is fast. The VL-Bus model has a jumper, while the PCI version dumps jumpers or addresses—a true plug-and-play board.

Diamond uses the same InControl Tools utility in Windows across multiple models. InControl's Display and Desktop selections define your monitor and its refresh information, allowing you to set screen resolution, the number of colors, font, cursor size and color, and even dots per inch. Like other cards, Diamond supports power management. In fact, you can have a Windows screen saver kick in for a specified duration before the monitor is suspended and then powered off.

Stealth 64 PCI (2 meg: $399; 4 meg: $599)

Stealth 64 VLB (2 meg: $399; 4 meg: $599)

Diamond Computer Systems, Inc.
1130 E. Arques Ave.
Sunnyvale, CA 94086
408-736-2000
FAX: 408-730-5750
Tech support BBS: 408-524-9301

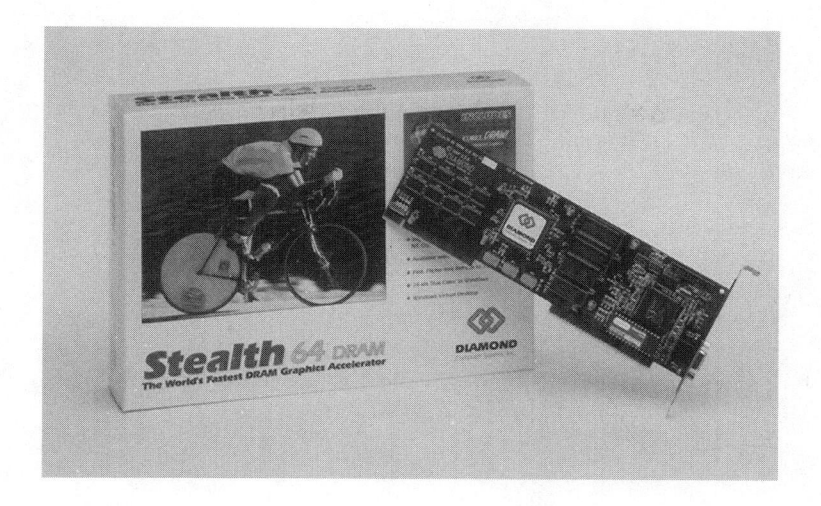

Fig. 11.2

The Stealth 64 provides both great Windows and DOS performance.

ATI Graphics Pro Turbo. The ATI Graphics Pro Turbo uses the Mach64 graphics accelerator chip. With 4MB of VRAM, (2MB onboard and 2MB on a proprietary daughtercard), the Graphics Pro Turbo provides an above-average mix of features and performance.

Installing the Graphics Pro Turbo is virtually plug-and-play for both buses. VL-Bus owners can turn the memory aperture on or off if they run into problems. (The memory aperture is a technique for speeding up getting video information into the card's frame buffer.) The only flaw is that both versions eat up COM4 by using port address 2E8h. Whatever uses that fourth serial port will have to be reconfigured.

The Graphics Pro Turbo is the only card that provides built-in motion-video enhancement through a set of included drivers (see fig. 11.3). The card provides crisp color with refresh rates as high as 100 Hz up to 1280 × 1024 resolution. Windows performance is top of the line, especially in 24-bit color. The Graphics Pro Turbo is the only card I know that provides 24-bit color at 1280 × 1024 resolution.

Graphics Ultra Pro PCI ($399)

Graphics Ultra Pro VLB ($399)

ATI Technologies, Inc.
33 Commerce Valley Dr., E
Thornhill, ON, CD L3T 7N6
905-882-2600
FAX: 905-882-2620
Tech support: 905-882-2626
Tech support BBS: 905-764-9404

III

Investing in Multimedia

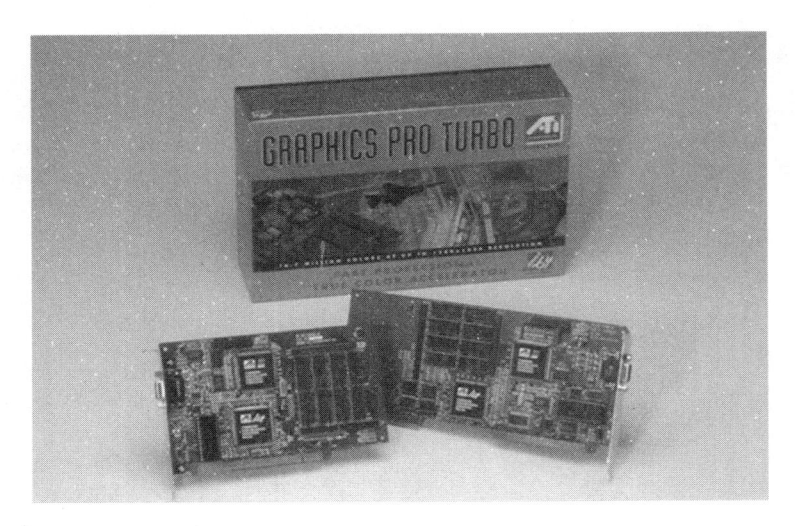

Fig. 11.3
The Graphics Pro Turbo from ATI Technologies includes motion-video enhancement.

Diamond Viper Pro PCI/VLB. If you're looking for a fast, affordable graphics accelerator, consider the Diamond Viper Pro, which is available in both VL-Bus and PCI models (see fig. 11.4). The 32-bit Viper Pro uses Weitek's P9100 graphics accelerator chip. The Viper Pro provides 1280 × 1024 resolution at 24-bit color in only 4M of VRAM at a refresh rate of 75 Hz.

Unfortunately, Diamond doesn't complement this card's high-performance hardware with full software functionality, such as a virtual desktop or color calibration. Superior software, such as that offered by ATI and Matrox, also offer gamma correction, as well as on-the-fly mode switching and color dithering, which are essential for intensive graphics use.

Diamond Viper Pro PCI (2 meg: $479; 4 meg: $699)

Diamond Viper Pro VLB (2 meg: $479; 4 meg: $699)

Diamond Computer Systems, Inc.
1130 E. Arques Ave.
Sunnyvale, CA 94086
408-736-2000
FAX: 408-730-5750
Tech support BBS: 408-524-9301

Fig. 11.4
A 32-bit card, such as the affordable Diamond Viper Pro, may be suitable for all but the most demanding multimedia needs.

Media Vision Pro Graphics 1024 VLB. High resolution and 24-bit color have, until recently, been a cost-prohibitive combination. However, the Media Vision Pro Graphics 1024 provides high-resolution true color that is affordably priced for all of us.

With the basic Pro Graphics card, which offers 768K of VRAM at a retail price of only $449, you get true color at lower resolutions or 256 colors at 1024 × 768 resolution. A $200 upgrade increases the onboard VRAM to 2.25M and allows true color at 1024 × 768.

To provide true color with such little memory, Media Vision employed a patented process called three-way interleaving. The process also allows the video card to operate at very high speeds.

Media Vision ProGraphics 1024 VLB ($449)

Media Vision, Inc.
47300 Bayside Pkwy.
Fremont, CA 94538
800-348-7116; 510-770-8600
Direct sales: 800-845-5870
FAX: 510-770-9592
Tech support: 800-638-2807
Tech support BBS: 510-770-0527

III

Investing in Multimedia

Monitor Required

We often take our computer monitor for granted. We look at it constantly when using our PC, and yet never consider how important it really is. For multimedia, your monitor is the key to enjoying the best presentations and games.

The trick is to pick a monitor that works with your selected video card. You can save money by purchasing a single-standard (fixed-frequency) monitor and a matching video card. For example, you can order a VGA monitor and a VGA video card. For greater flexibility, get a multiscanning (multisync) monitor that accommodates a range of standards.

Monitor Buying Criteria

A monitor may account for as much as 50 percent of a computer system's price. What should you look for when shopping for a monitor? You can compare monitors based on these characteristics:

- Size
- Resolution
- Dot pitch
- Tube design
- Controls
- Interlacing

Size: More Real Estate. When working in Windows, having a larger monitor provides a definite boost in productivity. For example, moving up from a 14-inch monitor to a 17-inch monitor enables you to comfortably bump the pixel resolution from 640×480 to 800×600 or even 1024×768. That's nearly 60 percent more on-screen real estate. Yet because you are using a larger monitor, you won't suffer eyestrain from the tightly packed pixels.

Monitors come in sizes ranging from a 12-inch monochrome monitor to a 42-inch color monitor. The larger the monitor, of course, the higher the price tag. The most common sizes are the 15-, 17-, and 21-inch models. Unfortunately, these diagonal measurements are not for the actual screen that will be displayed, but for the size of the tube. So comparing one company's 15-inch monitor to another's may be unfair unless you actually measure the active screen area. For example, one company's 15-inch monitor may display a 13.8-inch image. Another company's 14-inch monitor may present a 13.5-inch image. Don't be misled, and bring your ruler.

Tip
Some computer magazine reviews of monitors often provide the actual "live" screen measurements.

Larger monitors are mandatory for multimedia, where the smallest details must be clearly seen. Consider at least a high-quality 15-inch monitor, although we recommend 17-inch models and larger.

Tip

Consider the size of your desk before you think about monitors 15 inches or larger. A 15-inch monitor is typically at least a foot-and-a-half deep.

High Resolution. *Resolution* is the amount of detail a monitor can render, expressed in pixels. Although the MPC Level 2 specifications require a VGA resolution (640×480), you will probably want to use a higher resolution. To use, let's say, 1024×768, you would probably want to use a 17-inch monitor so that the images are not so small your eyesight suffers.

Dot Pitch. Another buying concern is the *dot pitch*, the distance, measured in millimeters, between the phosphor triads that make up your monitor. (The phosphor triad is the red, green and blue elements that make up a pixel.) Screens with a smaller dot pitch that contain less distance between the phosphor triads produce a sharper picture.

Tip

Although the resolution of a monitor may be high, its dot pitch may be very large, creating a fuzzy-looking picture. Often, stores may be open about the resolution but fail to advertise its dot pitch.

Most monitors have a dot pitch between .25 and .52 mm. To avoid grainy images, look for a dot pitch of .28 mm or smaller for 14- and 15-inch monitors, or .31 mm or smaller for 16-inch and larger monitors. The state-of-the-art displays marketed today have a dot pitch of .28 mm or less.

You can save money by either picking a smaller monitor or one with a higher dot pitch. The tradeoff, of course, is clarity. Don't be too discerning; selecting a monitor with a .31 mm dot pitch over one with a .28 mm dot pitch may save you dollars. Never buy a monitor with a dot pitch greater than .31 mm. If you spend long hours at a PC monitor, insist on .28 mm or sharper.

Tube Design. Many inexpensive monitors are curved because it's easier to send an electron beam across them. Flat-screen monitors, which are a bit more expensive, look better to most people. As a general rule, the less curvature a monitor has, the less glare it will reflect.

Trinitron tubes are a compromise between the two. They are flat in the vertical and curved on the horizontal. A Trinitron tube provides an affordable design with less glare than traditional spherical-shaped monitors. True flat tubes are flat on all sides, while the newer flat-square tubes have only minor curves. Flat-square screen technology has gained increasing popularity in the 17-inch monitor market, and most monitors use it.

> **Tip**
>
> If a it's a toss-up between a Trinitron tube and a flat-screen monitor, choose the flat-screen model.

Controls. Sophisticated controls to adjust image size, position, color, and other settings are essential. Get a monitor with horizontal and vertical positioning and image controls that can be easily reached. Look for more than basic contrast and brightness controls; some monitors let you adjust the width and height of your screen images so that you can maximize the image to the full width and height of your screen and adjust for any distortions.

Better monitors allow you to save custom image settings, including color. Every video resolution has a different set of ideal image parameters. In high-end monitors with digital controls, a microprocessor chip allows you to select the best image settings for a particular resolution, then automatically save those settings in memory. When your PC changes resolutions, the monitor receives horizontal and vertical video frequencies, which are routed to a microprocessor chip in the monitor. This processor checks its electrically erasable programmable ROM (EEPROM) for the best size, position, and other settings for those frequencies, then automatically adjusts the displayed image.

Color matching is provided on some monitors. This feature was developed in response to the rising popularity of color printing and the subsequent complaints by users that colors being displayed on their monitors were not the same as the colors being printed. Color matching lets you adjust (via digital controls) the strength of the red, green, and blue electron beams so screen colors more closely match printed colors, regardless of the color-printing scheme (CMYK, Pantone, and so on) being used. Beware: color-matching technology is improving but still lacks precision.

Some monitors, such as the NEC MultiSync 4FGe, provide a degauss button that clears built-up magnetic fields that can distort the picture. Others, following the lead of VCRs, provide on-screen display. ETC Computer Inc.'s ViewMagic CA-1565LSP color monitor, for example, provides this feature. With on-screen display, you can adjust bar graphs of various monitor settings, such as brightness and contrast.

> **Tip**
>
> Your monitor should include a tilt-swivel stand, allowing you to move the monitor to the angle that best suits you.

Interlaced Versus Noninterlaced. To keep the horizontal frequency low, some video cards use interlacing signals, alternately displaying half of the lines of the total image. With some monitors, interlacing can produce a pronounced flicker. For this reason, your monitor should synchronize to twice the vertical frequency of the video card in order to counteract it. For example, the IBM XGA video standard uses a frame rate of 43.5 Hz. To match those signals, a monitor must accept a vertical frequency of 87 Hz and a horizontal frequency of 35.5 kHz.

When shopping for a VGA monitor, make sure the monitor supports a horizontal frequency of at least 31.5 KHz, the minimum a VGA card needs in order to display a 640 × 480 screen. The VESA super-VGA (800 × 600) standard requires a 72 Hz vertical frequency and a horizontal frequency of at least 48 kHz. The sharper 1024 × 768 image requires a vertical frequency of 60 Hz and a horizontal frequency of 58 kHz. If the vertical frequency is upped to 72 Hz, the horizontal frequency must be 58 kHz. If flicker-prone interlacing is used, a 1024 × 768 video card needs a monitor with a 43.5 Hz vertical frequency and a 35.5 kHz horizontal frequency.

Energy and Safety. An energy-saving monitor is a good buy. Many monitor manufacturers are trying to meet the Environmental Protection Agency's Energy Star requirements. Any PC and monitor combination that consumes less than 70 watts (35 watts apiece) can use the Energy Star logo in their advertisements. Some figures show that each "green" PC can cut electricity bills by about $70 per year.

Because monitors are one of the most power-hungry computer components, an energy-efficient monitor can contribute to those savings. Perhaps the best-known energy-saving standard for monitors is VESA's Display Power-Management Signaling (DPMS) spec, which defines the signals that a computer sends to a monitor to indicate idle times. When the video card isn't being used, the monitor shuts down, saving electricity.

Another trend in green monitor design is to minimize the user's exposure to potentially harmful electromagnetic fields. The concern is that VLF (very low-frequency) and ELF (extremely low-frequency) emissions may cause miscarriages, birth defects and cancer.

These two frequencies are covered by the new Swedish monitor-emission standard called SWEDAC, named after the Swedish regulatory agency. In many European countries, government agencies and businesses buy only low-emission monitors. The MPR II standard, established in 1990, is the level of protection you're most likely to find in low-emission monitors today. A more stringent 1992 standard, called TCO, further tightens the MPR II requirements.

Tip
If using a monitor for hours at a time, insist on one that meets at least the MPR II requirements.

III

Investing in Multimedia

A low-emission monitor costs about $20 to $100 more than similar, regular-emission monitors. When shopping for a low-emission monitor, don't just ask for a low-emission monitor. Find out if a monitor limits specific types of emission. Use the three electro-magnetic emission standards just discussed as a guideline.

> **Note**
>
> If you decide to not buy a low-emission monitor, you can take other steps to protect yourself. The most important is to stay at arm's length (around 28 inches) from the front of your monitor. After a couple of feet, ELF magnetic emission levels usually drop down to those of a typical office with fluorescent lights. Also, monitor emissions are weakest from the front of a monitor, so keep at least three feet from the sides and backs of nearby monitors and five feet from any copier—a very strong source of ELF. Also, some add-on anti-glare screens reduce these emissions.

Selected Monitors

Selecting a monitor depends on your budget and need. For multimedia work, you want to buy at least a 17-inch monitor. However, if the cash is tight and your demands are reasonable, a quality 15-inch monitor will do.

State-of-the-art 20- and 21-inch displays can give you a whole new outlook on the video, animation, and graphics that make multimedia so seductive. And to display multiple windows and applications in Windows simultaneously, big screens offer the ideal combination of high resolutions (1280×1024 pixels and higher) and generous screen real estate. Such large monitors should support the EPA Energy Star standard, or some other type of power management, because displays this large account for as much as 80 percent of the total energy consumed by your computer.

Table 11.2   Monitors (15 Inches or Larger)

Model	Maker	Display size	Dot pitch	Max. Supported Resolution (Non-interlaced)
MultiSync 4FGe	NEC Technologies	15"	.28 mm	1024x768
Brilliance 15	Philips	15"	.28 mm	1024x768
Multigraph 449E	Nokia	15"	.28 mm	1024x768
MultiSync 5FGe	NEC Technologies	17"	.28 mm	1024x768
Nanao 550i-W	Nanao USA	17"	.28 mm	1024x768
Nanao 560i-W	Nanao USA	17"	.26 mm	1280x1024
Multigraph 447X	Nokia	17"	.26 mm	1600x1280
MultiSync 6FGp	NEC Technologies	21"	.28 mm	1280x1024
MultiSync 4PG	NEC Technologies	27"	.28 mm	800x600

Most likely, a 17-inch monitor provides a middle-of-the-road monitor for multimedia work. For example, 17-inch monitors are considerably lighter and less bulky than the 19- to 21-inch models.

Table 11.2 reviews some of the top monitors for multimedia work and describes some key data on each monitor discussed.

NEC MultiSync 4FGe. The MultiSync 4FGe from NEC Technologies has a 15-inch flat-square tube. It is rated as MPR II-compliant and includes Intelligent Power Manager (IPM), which works with your computer's video card to save power. The NEC 4FGe has a superior manual and a three-year warranty covering parts and labor.

The monitor is designed to run at higher resolutions than most of the others in its class. It can handle resolutions up to 1024×768 at a 76-Hz refresh rate that will banish flickering.

One minor drawback is that the NEC 4FGe has a tendency to cause glare; most users will want to get NEC's light gray glass glare filter (about $70).

The monitor comes with digital controls for altering position and size. The same controls do double-duty for color balancing and pincushioning. (Pincushioning is a screen distortion in which the sides bow in.) There are three color settings—one factory-preset and two user-definable. There are also a degaussing button (which is also used to change modes for the digital controls) and analog brightness and contrast controls. The monitor comes with an excellent manual as well, which includes useful information on color theory.

Max. Supported Resolution (Interlaced)	Max. Horizonta Scanl	Vertical Scan	MPR II -compliant	Flat screen	Price
1024x768	31-62 kHz	55-90 Hz	Yes	Yes	$655
na	30-58 kHz	50-100 Hz	Yes	Yes	$499
1024x768	30-62 kHz	48-100 Hz	Yes	Yes	$630
1024x768	31-62 kHz	55-90 Hz	Yes	Yes	$1,045
1024x768	27-65 kHz	55-90 Hz	Yes	Yes	$1,199
1024x768	30-82 kHz	55-90 Hz	Yes	Yes	$1,499
1024x768	30-82 kHz	50-110 Hz	Yes	Yes	$1,250
1024x768	27-79 kHz	55-90 Hz	Yes	Yes	$2,125
800x600	15.5-50 kHz	40-100 Hz	na	Yes	$3,695

III

Investing in Multimedia

> **Note**
>
> NEC Technologies divided its multiscan monitors into three product lines: the V series, for budget-conscious, entry-level buyers; the E series, which complies with the government's new Energy Star power-management specification; and the high-end P series, which replaces the current FG line and adds both power management and antiglare coatings. The more features, the higher the price.

NEC 4FGe ($655)

NEC Technologies Inc. (subsidiary of NEC Corp.)
1414 Massachusetts Ave.
Boxborough, MA 01719-2298
800-632-4636; 508-264-8000
Direct sales: 800-374-8000 (NEC Select)
FAX: 508-264-8245
Tech support: 800-388-8888
Tech support BBS: 508-635-4706

Philips Brilliance 15. The Philips Brilliance 15 ($499) is an attractive monitor that couples sound capabilities with video. The Brilliance 15 is based on a 15-inch .28-mm-dot-pitch flat-square tube. It is capable of up to 1024 × 768 resolution with a 72-Hz vertical refresh rate. The Brilliance 15 complies with the MPR II low-emissions standard, though it doesn't meet Energy Star power-conservation requirements.

Two stereo speakers are concealed within the Brilliance 15's attractive chassis, and a front-panel mini-jack with volume control accommodates headphones for private listening. In back, there are two stereo RCA-style audio input jacks for connecting the monitor to a PC's sound board. In giving this monitor audio capabilities, Philips has made a few sacrifices. The monitor does not have any power-saving features, and it uses standard analog display controls. All the image-adjustment dials are lined up on the front panel, but there is no microprocessor to store settings; further, the monitor has neither a pincushioning nor a trapezoidal distortion control. (Trapezoidal distortion is also called barrel distortion, in which the sides of the image bow out.)

The Brilliance 15's audio capabilities make this monitor sufficient for common business audio uses but not for professional multimedia presentations or for playing back high-fidelity sound. The internal speakers lack the bass response for such tasks, and although they provide enough volume to fill a cubicle, when the volume is pushed higher there is some noticeable distortion. Still, the arrangement is fine for multimedia novices.

Philips Brilliance 15 (Model 1520AS) ($499)

Philips Consumer Electronics Co. (division of North American Philips Corp.)
One Philips Dr., P.O. Box 14810
Knoxville, TN 37914-1810
800-835-3506; 615-521-4316

Direct sales: 615-475-8869
FAX: 615-521-4406
Tech support: 800-835-3506

Nokia Multigraph 449E. Nokia Corp.'s Multigraph 449E is a 15-inch monitor that provides a high-quality picture, while cutting down the level of electromagnetic emissions. (This model meets general Swedish emission standards.) The Multigraph's Invar mask, 80 MHz of bandwidth and .28mm-dot-pitch screen produce crisp displays with 1024×768 resolution without any flickering.

A variety of digital controls allow users to manipulate picture position and size, control brightness and contrast, and select different screen options. The compact monitor includes other impressive features, such as a non-glare, anti-static coating and Energy Star-winning power-saving features.

Multigraph 449E ($630)

Nokia Display Products, Inc. (division of Nokia Consumer Electronics)
3000 Bridgeway Blvd.
Sausalito, CA 94965
800-BY-NOKIA; 415-331-0322
FAX: 415-331-0424
Tech support: Use toll-free number
Tech support BBS: 800-483-7952

NEC MultiSync 5FGe. The NEC MultiSync 5FGe is an excellent 17-inch monitor. It is equipped with digital controls, including side pincushion, a large flat-square screen, and tight dot pitch.

Digital controls for horizontal and vertical position and size occupy most of the control panel compartment. Other controls in the compartment include a degauss button, which also serves as a means to switch to the pincushion correction modes; a sync switch to toggle-set for normal sync, or composite and sync on green input signals. Brightness and contrast controls are actuated by thumbwheels that have no way to accurately return to factory preset conditions. The power button is conveniently flush-mounted on the front-right corner and has a noticeable but inconspicuous narrow horizontal LED.

The MultiSync 5FGe is a midrange monitor possessing 1024×768 maximum resolution and 80-MHz bandwidth. However, most Windows users operate in this mode or in lesser resolutions, and the 5FGe's performance is generally excellent for the purposes for which it was intended. Moreover, NEC's pricing of the 5FGe should make it attractive to all looking for a quality 17-incher. The dot pitch is a good .28 mm and display clarity is excellent. The available screen filter turns the large screen into a nearly ideal display, retaining its bright and clear characteristics while alleviating most of the reflection. This is definitely an option worth considering.

NEC MultiSync 5FGe ($1,045)

NEC Technologies Inc. (subsidiary of NEC Corp.)
1414 Massachusetts Ave.
Boxborough, MA 01719-2298
800-632-4636; 508-264-8000
Direct sales: 800-374-8000 (NEC Select)
FAX: 508-264-8245
Tech support: 800-388-8888
Tech support BBS: 508-635-4706

Nanao FlexScan F550i-W and F560i-W. The FlexScan F550i-W and F560i-W monitors share identical physical characteristics and controls but differ in specifications and capabilities. As shown in figure 11.5, these monitors offer a power-saving mode and combine this feature with color controls, full digital distortion controls, and MPR-II compliance.

The F550i-W's frequency-synchronization range is quite comfortable for today's video adapters, while the F560i-W boasts extended frequency-synchronization ranges to better prepare it for future video modes.

The F560i-W's display is more impressive, as its extended frequency-synchronization range and tighter dot pitch produce an even clearer and more precise display. All super-VGA modes look excellent, and the 1024×768 mode is particularly well-suited to the F550i-W. The F560i-W, with its maximum 1280×1024 noninterlaced resolution, is better able to display higher resolutions and is clearer and more comfortable at these resolutions than its lesser sibling.

While the F550i-W is more suited to general Windows applications, the senior Nanao, with its impressive specifications and marvelously tight .26-mm dot pitch, approaches perfection for all applications.

FlexScan F550i-W ($1,099)

FlexScan F560i-W ($1,299)

NANAO USA Corp.
23535 Telo Ave.
Torrance, CA 90505
800-800-5202; 310-325-5202
Tech support: 800-800-5202, ext. 114
FAX: 310-530-1679

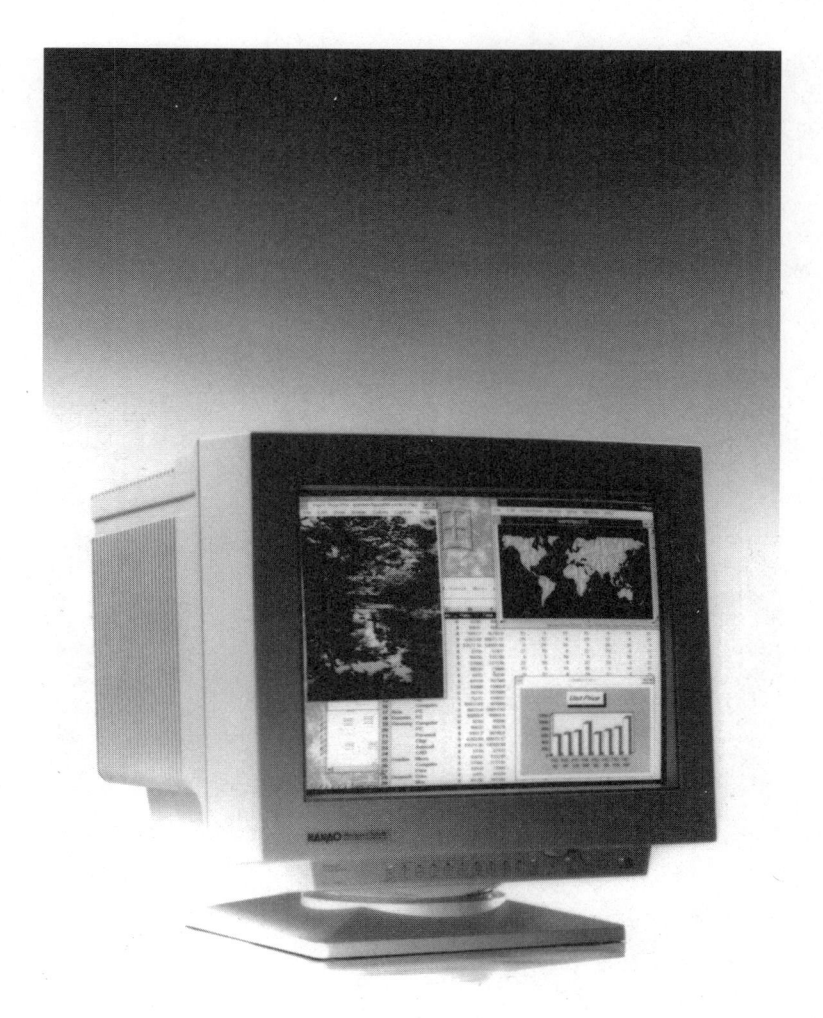

Fig. 11.5
The FlexScan F560i-W provides the best image at higher resolutions.

Nokia Multigraph 447X. The Nokia Multigraph 447X features a sharp picture and clever on-screen menu controls (see fig. 11.6). The 17-inch 447X gets its sharp picture from the smaller .26-mm Trinitron tube. The monitor also uses Sony's silicon coating to effectively reduce screen glare.

The 447X runs without flicker at 1280 × 1024 noninterlaced resolution with a 75-Hz refresh rate, although the 1024 × 768 mode at 95 Hz is best for most uses.

The 447X has sophisticated image adjustments, including trapezoidal, orthogonal, color-temperature, and tilt controls. All of these controls are accessed through on-screen menus that resemble those that you find on TVs and VCRs—a rare and accommodating control scheme for a monitor.

The 447X complies with the EPA Energy Star standards. The 447X also meets MPR II's guidelines for electromagnetic emissions. Nokia optionally plans to offer compliance with the Swedish union TCO's stricter standard.

Fig. 11.6
Monitor newcomer Nokia provides excellent controls with its Multigraph 447X monitor.

Multigraph 447X ($1,250)

Nokia Display Products, Inc. (division of Nokia Consumer Electronics)
3000 Bridgeway Blvd.
Sausalito, CA 94965
800-BY-NOKIA; 415-331-0322
FAX: 415-331-0424
Tech support: Use toll-free number
Tech support BBS: 800-483-7952

NEC MultiSync 6FGp. The 21-inch NEC MultiSync 6FGp provides a variety of resolutions up to 1280 × 1024 pixels at a 74 Hz screen-refresh rate. The 6FGp is the replacement model for the earlier 6FG. The new model offers an anti-reflective surface that reduces glare and improves contrast. Also, the NEC 6FGp uses NEC's power-management system, which reduces power consumption of idle monitors to about 70 percent.

The 6FGp features a .28 mm dot pitch and front-panel digital controls for brightness, contrast, horizontal size and position, and pincushioning.

NEC MultiSync 6FGp ($2,125)

NEC Technologies Inc. (subsidiary of NEC Corp.)
1414 Massachusetts Ave.
Boxborough, MA 01719-2298
800-632-4636; 508-264-8000
Direct sales: 800-374-8000 (NEC Select)
FAX: 508-264-8245
Tech support: 800-388-8888
Tech support BBS: 508-635-4706

NEC MultiSync 4PG Multimedia Monitor. The 27-inch NEC MultiSync 4PG Multimedia Monitor is two monitors in one. This video and RGB monitor can be either a multipurpose presentation monitor for your boardroom or a sturdy monitor to show training tapes or to demonstrate software programs. Its $3,499 estimated selling price keeps the 4PG out of the reach of typical PC users, but it is no typical monitor.

With two RGB inputs and two inputs for video signals, the 4PG can be hooked simultaneously to a television input, a VCR or video camera, and two computers (PC and Macintosh video signals are both supported). Both video inputs and one of the RGB inputs include stereo audio inputs for quality sound that can be played through internal stereo speakers or output to an external amplifier or speakers. Every video and audio input has a corresponding set of output plugs so you can rig up to 50 monitors in a series for spectacular large-room presentations.

The 4PG comes with a wireless remote control (which can also operate with an included 12-foot wire) to select the display device; adjust image size, position, pincushioning, contrast, brightness, color, and tint; and control sharpness. The remote control also has a monitor degauss button, and volume and mute controls.

With its flat-square shadow mask tube, the 110-pound 4PG is a multisync monitor with a horizontal scanning range of 15.5 to 50 kHz and vertical range of 40 to 120 Hz. Maximum rated resolution is 1024×768 at 60 Hz. Video support includes VGA, XGA2, NTSC, M-NTSC, PAL (European), and S-Video signals.

The 4PG is best used as an all-purpose presentation monitor. Whether your presentations are straight from software such as Lotus Freelance Graphics or Microsoft PowerPoint (saving the expense and time of printing hard copies in color), live computer demonstrations, broadcast television, camera, or videotape, the 4PG displays a big, bright image and lets you easily switch between input sources.

NEC MultiSync 4PG Multimedia Monitor ($3,499)

NEC Technologies Inc. (subsidiary of NEC Corp.)
1414 Massachusetts Ave.
Boxborough, MA 01719-2298
800-632-4636; 508-264-8000

III

Investing in Multimedia

Direct sales: 800-374-8000 (NEC Select)
FAX: 508-264-8245
Tech support: 800-388-8888
Tech support BBS: 508-635-4706

Tire Kicking a Monitor

A monitor is such an important part of your computer that knowing its technical specifications doesn't go far enough. Knowing the monitor has a .28 mm dot pitch doesn't necessarily tell you that it is ideal for you.

It's best to "kick the tires" of your new monitor at a showroom, or with a liberal return policy that lets you learn in the privacy of your office. To test your monitor:

- Draw a circle with the graphics program. If the result is an oval, not a circle, this monitor won't serve you well with graphics or design software.

- Type some words in 8- or 10-point type (one point=1/72 inches). If they are fuzzy or if the black characters are fringed with color, select another monitor.

- Turn the brightness up and down while examining the corner of the screen's image. If the image blooms or swells, it's likely to lose focus at high brightness levels.

- Load Microsoft Windows to check for uniform focus. Are the corner icons as sharp as the rest of the screen? Are the lines in the title bar curved or wavy? Monitors are usually sharply focused at the center, but seriously blurred corners indicate a poor design. Bowed lines may be the result of a poor graphics card, so don't dismiss a monitor that shows them without double-checking with another card.

Video Capture Cards

Putting short video clips into multimedia presentations, adding them to corporate newsletters on a network, or capturing video clips for training applications can be done for a reasonable price and, in most cases, with much less fuss than ever before. Video-capture boards have street prices that range from just over $200 to $600, accept standard video sources such as VHS VCRs or Hi-8 camcorders, and can capture and compress acceptable motion video in a 320 × 240-pixel window.

Video Capture Criteria

Many video-capture boards improve the capture rate and obtain better motion video by reducing the number of colors captured. In 8-bit palletized mode, for example, most cards capture 10 to 30 percent more frames. Unfortunately, the resulting clips look like a bad MTV video. On the other hand, using a compression codec such as Indeo or Cinepak still means you lose either color or image detail, or a little of both.

For accurate captures, look for a video-capture board that does a good job of capturing uncompressed video in 24-bit RGB mode. This gives the best frame-by-frame source material and turns out higher-quality compressed files after you've finished editing. It does, however, mean sacrificing motion and dropping more frames unless you stick to a smaller 160 × 120 window.

For near-full-motion in a larger window, select a capture board that records clips in the YUV digital format. The format provides images that are sharper than compressed video images, captures more frames than straight RGB, and results in minimal color loss. YUV separately samples the brightness, or luminance, portion of the video signal (represented by the "Y") and the two color coordinates (represented by the "U" and "V") of a given signal. A YUV 4:1:1 ratio uses 4 bits to sample the luminance and 1 bit each to sample the color portions of the signal. Hence, YUV 4:2:2 will render even better color accuracy.

Media Vision Pro MovieStudio. Media Vision's $449 Pro MovieStudio offers several attractive features, including hardware-based compression, superior ease of use, and convenient software controls. A lack of 24-bit color support and its reliance on Microsoft Video 1 compression readies this capture board more for business applications than for multimedia.

The Video 1 compression support was first developed by Media Vision for Microsoft. The Video 1 codec supports 16-bit color, which is sufficient for most Desktop applications. The board captures a 10-second video clip in a 320 × 240-pixel window at 30 frames per second (fps) without dropping frames. You get better results in terms of image clarity by using Pro MovieStudio's RGB capture mode, but only by sacrificing frames. In RGB capture mode using a 320 × 240 window, the Pro MovieStudio lost about 87 percent of the frames at the 30-fps setting and about 50 percent of frames in 15-fps mode.

The Pro MovieStudio is easy to use. Pro MovieStudio is simple to install, without any of the jumper headaches encountered with other boards. All address and IRQ settings are selected through the setup software.

Also, Media Vision's software allows you to scale the capture window from 44 × 32 up to 320 × 240 pixels, or to a full-screen 640 × 480 size. You can also modify images by adjusting the color gain, hue, horizontal and vertical centering, and by selecting various filters.

Pro MovieStudio ($449)

Media Vision, Inc.
47300 Bayside Pkwy.
Fremont, CA 94538
800-348-7116; 510-770-8600
Direct sales: 800-845-5870
FAX: 510-770-9592
Tech support: 800-638-2807
Tech support BBS: 510-770-0527

Studio Magic Controls. You can make any video have the look of an MTV hit with Studio Magic Corp.'s Studio Magic Controls Desktop video-editing system. The 16-bit expansion board works with regular home-video cameras but uses advanced tape transport protocols (either infrared, Control L, or Control M) to control up to two devices simultaneously. A $200 price tag makes the card affordable for the novice, yet the software tools are designed to give you total control of video editing and organization.

The Studio Magic bundle has help-sensitive icons that explain their functions when your cursor passes over them. Your tapes and clips appear grouped by project in lists so you can plan edits and then move the files into correct sequence by dragging filenames. The software then makes your changes automatically to the actual images. The search feature lets you display files in your choice of views, and search clips and tapes by name, date, or description.

Studio Magic Controls ($199.95)

Studio Magic Corp.
1690 Dell Ave.
Campbell, CA 95008
408-378-3838
FAX: 408-378-3577

Personal Video Studio. Studio Magic Corp., besides the low-priced Studio Magic Director, also offers a higher-end Personal Video Studio. This hardware/software video-editing system consists of a controller card and software. It is not a digital video product; movies created with it play on a standard VCR. The controller card provides connections for cameras, VCRs, CD-ROMs, and other signal sources.

Launching the software program brings up a screen with six windows across the top; one displays selected overlays, two display graphics, two live video, and the last background colors. Users can control sound effects or mix audio from CDs via a menu bar option.

Personal Video Studio allows the creation of powerful macros for assembling parts of a video production quickly. It is an excellent tool for converting previously recorded video input into professional-looking tapes with sound, video, special effects, and animation.

Personal Video Studio ($499.95)

Studio Magic Corp.
1690 Dell Ave.
Campbell, CA 95008
408-378-3838
FAX: 408-378-3577

VideoBlender, WaveWatcher-TV, and VideoSurge. AITech's VideoBlender allows users to capture Video for Windows video at 320 × 240 pixels at 30 frames per second using Intel Corp.'s Indeo. On a 33-MHz 486DX, the card captures at 15 fps at a resolution of 160 × 120. You can also capture at 30 fps in a window measuring 80 × 60 pixels.

The $449 WaveWatcher-TV provides 2 million colors at 640 × 480 resolution. The $695 VideoSurge is a high-end, 24-bit video capture board capable of 16.7M colors.

VideoBlender ($299)

WaveWatcher-TV ($449)

VideoSurge ($695)

AITech International
47971 Fremont Blvd.
Fremont, CA 94538
800-882-8184; 510-226-8960
FAX: 510-226-8996
Tech support: 510-226-8267

MegaMotion. The $995 MegaMotion multimedia video board, from Alpha Systems Lab, allows you to fill your Windows screen with not one, not two, but four video images (two with full motion). It also provides capturing and compressing of NTSC, PAL composite, and S-video sources to disk, or sending them from your hard disk to a video monitor or videotape.

MegaMotion can rotate images 90 degrees, create scrolling titles, freeze frames, and do gamma correction. With the appropriate software, you can cut, wipe, or dissolve from one image to the next. MegaMotion is not a professional product; it is just shy of a full 640 × 480 resolution at 30 fps. Its chips and interfaces constrain the board to 15 fps at full resolution or 320 × 240 resolution at full speed.

As a workaround, you can fill your 1024 × 768 monitor by interpolating images, or tile it with up to eight images in MegaMotion's four overlays.

Adobe Premiere 1.0, software for creating and editing video movies under Windows, is included with MegaMotion.

MegaMotion (Non VTA version: $995; Full version: $1095)

Alpha Systems Labs Inc.
2361 McGaw Ave.
Irvine, CA 92714
800-576-4275; 714-252-0117
FAX: 714-252-0887

ProPC/TV Plus and gamePlayerTV. Unlike the previous products examined, the ProPC/TV Plus and gamePlayerTV do not capture images. Instead, they allow you to output your computer's monitor image to a TV screen or VCR. For example, you could demonstrate software live on a big TV screen and pause to answer questions. You can also place multimedia presentations on VHS tape to send to potential customers.

The AITech's Pro PC/TV Plus is a six-ounce box that changes your computer's digital output to an NTSC or PAL signal for live simultaneous viewing on a PC monitor and television screen. The gamePlayerTV essentially is an internal version of the same product.

The Pro PC/TV encoder box comes with an RCA phono cord to plug into the TV or VCR's video-in connector; an S-VHS 4-pin DIN cord in case you have a TV or VCR equipped for the higher-quality signal; a 15-pin male-to-male cord that hooks up to the VGA port on the back of your video card; a 15-pin male-to-female cord that attaches to the monitor cord; and an AC power cord. Everything is external—there's no reason to open your PC. Users supply the standard co-ax connection between VCR and TV, as well as the audio source and cable if sound is desired.

Routing through a VCR, you can tape your presentation by pushing Record and Play, just as though you were recording Monday Night Football. You can even use Pro PC/TV Plus to play games on a bigger screen.

PC/TV's software includes software drivers, demo animation, and graphics. After the cords are plugged in and the software is copied, use your VCR's switch or on-screen menu to set input to AV, rather than tuner. Then type a single command to the PC and everything appears on both screens, whether you're in DOS or Windows. Hot keys are available in case you need to change text fonts, adjust picture position, remove the driver from memory, or reduce flicker.

PC/TV Plus' 6-ounce base unit measures 5.5 × 4 × 1 inches and tucks painlessly into a laptop carrying case. Unfortunately, the documentation is small and light as well, but it includes a diagram of what to plug in and where to plug it.

With minimal documentation as its only drawback, PC/TV Plus is an asset to anyone who wants to demonstrate software navigation in real time, tape a PC session, or demo for audiences anywhere in the world.

ProPC/TV Plus ($249)

gamePlayerTV ($269)

AITech International
47971 Fremont Blvd.
Fremont, CA 94538
800-882-8184; 510-226-8960
FAX: 510-226-8996
Tech support: 510-226-8267

MultiPro CTV. AITech International also offers the MultiPro CTV. MultiPro CTV is a more sophisticated version of the ProPC/TV Plus. More importantly, the product works with both IBM PCs and Apple Macintosh computers, allowing you to display or record the screens of either platform.

MultiPro CTV ($399)

AITech International
47971 Fremont Blvd.
Fremont, CA 94538
800-882-8184; 510-226-8960

FAX: 510-226-8996
Tech support: 510-226-8267

Video Tools

There is a myriad of software products you can buy to improve and protect your monitor. These range from entertaining screen savers to wrist-saving ergonomic utilities.

Screen Savers with Sound

As you probably know, a screen saver is a software program that either blanks your screen or replaces it with moving images after a preset amount of time. This prevents the current image from being "burned" into the monitor's phosphor surface. Screen savers often include passwords to protect your work from being seen by prying eyes. For example, Microsoft Windows 3.1 has a built-in screen saver with password protection.

While your Microsoft Windows screen saver may blank your screen, other screen savers can fill your ears. Screen savers, such as Berkeley Systems' After Dark for Windows include sounds. In After Dark, the nocturnal module howls and chirps, the aquatic scene bubbles, and the space toasters flap their wings.

Jurassic Park: The Screen Saver. Enjoyed the movie? Relive it with Jurassic Park: The Screen Saver. This screen saver is available on both floppy disks and CD-ROM. The newer CD-ROM version includes a variety of new wallpaper scenes and sound effects.

Jurassic Park: The Screen Saver includes over 35 screen savers, with more than half of those new since the release of the floppy disk version. Titles include Run Through The Jungle, Nedry's Adventure, What's for Dinner, and Feeding Time. You also get a Dinosaur Encyclopedia, which contains facts and statistics on the dinosaurs of Jurassic Park.

Jurassic Park: The Screen Saver ($19.95, $34.95 CD-ROM)

Asymetrix Corp.
110 110th Ave., NE, Suite 700
Bellevue, WA 98004-5840
800-448-6543; 206-462-0501
Direct sales: 800-448-6543
FAX: 206-637-1504
Tech support: Use main number
Tech support BBS: 206-451-1173

Star Trek. Berkeley Systems offers Star Trek: The Screen Saver 2.0 for $49.99. This software program is a collection of 14 screen-saver modules that are funny and reminiscent of the popular television show Star Trek. One module features the character Spock pacing across the screen taking readings and muttering 'fascinating,' another plays the theme from the show, and another makes the screen resemble a computer on the starship Enterprise.

Star Trek Screen Saver for Windows ($49.99)

Berkeley Systems, Inc.
2095 Rose Street
Berkeley, CA 94709-4303
800-877-5535; 510-540-5535
Direct sales: 800-344-5541
FAX: 510-540-5630

T-2: The Screen Saver. Besides audio snippets, Sound Source Unlimited also offers T2: The Screen Saver. This Windows screen saver lets you set up passwords to protect your work while you're away, or silence the screens, but the real point of the software is to crank up the volume and enjoy.

With T-2, you can have the evil T-1000 stretch through your desktop the way it stretched through the floor at the asylum, then took shape as a metal man. Gunshot Morphs put liquid metal behind your screen and start shooting holes through it.

For more action, try Desktop Terminators. There's Arnold Schwarzeneggar in a full leather jacket, twirl-cocking his shotgun between comments and blasts. Then the T-1000 smashes his metal arms through your Windows as he hoists himself from the bottom of your screen to the top. Finally, the original Terminator, stripped to a skeleton, advances across your spreadsheet with his spurred feet and glowing eyes.

For an unnerving glimpse of the future, visit Terminator Factory. Or spy on Skynet through the Skynet World Clock. The clock also shows your local time and that of seven locations worldwide.

T-2: The Screen Saver ($19.95)

Sound Source Unlimited
2985 E. Hillcrest Dr., Suite A
Westlake Village, CA 91362
800-877-4778, 805-494-9996
Fax: 805-495-0016

Video Tools

Several video utilities are available, such as editors and sound track utilities. I've listed just a few of the more notable ones.

Adobe Premiere 1.1. Premiere 1.1 lets you capture video from within the application and supports machine control on compatible decks. It can also import a wide variety of graphics, animation, and audio clips, as well as AVI or QuickTime digital-video files.

Premiere allows you to organize your media files into libraries, which can be accessed from any editing project. Each clip appears as a thumbnail image with information about file type and duration. There's also space to enter notes about each clip, a feature that significantly improves the capture and logging process.

Premiere supports two video tracks—a graphics track and an overlay track, which can contain either video or graphics. There are also three audio tracks, which can fade up or down by adjusting them in the Construction Window.

The editing tools and time line are sensible and easy to access, demonstrating a good understanding of the editing process. You can have several Clip Windows open simultaneously, a welcome departure from the two-screen viewing setup found in traditional editing packages. Another useful feature is the ability to place markers in your video or audio clips, as well as in your project time line. This speeds the editing process by allowing fast and easy synchronization of clips to precisely marked points.

Adobe Premiere 1.1 ($295)

Adobe Systems Inc.
P.O. Box 7900, 1585 Charleston Rd.
Mountain View, CA 94039-7900
800-833-6687; 415-961-4400
Direct sales: 800-642-3623
FAX: 408-655-6096
Tech support: 415-961-4992
Tech support BBS: 408-562-6839

Digital Video Producer 2.5. Asymetrix's Digital Video Producer 2.5 packs a solid set of video-editing tools into a simple Windows interface. It offers many of the same features and capabilities as Premiere, but it has a distinctly different feel. The Digital Video Producer is not a stand alone product, however; you must buy it as a part of a bundle.

Digital Video Producer provides two players for screening clips or scenes that have been assembled on its time line. Digital Video Producer's time line contains two video tracks and two audio tracks.

Like Premiere, Digital Video Producer contains a capture module and supports machine control on compatible decks. Although Digital Video Producer doesn't have a clip library, its Clip Window is equivalent to Premiere's Project Window, with information about each clip's name, file type, duration, and screen size. To take full advantage of this powerful tool, you'll want to plan your effects out in detail.

This advice applies to Digital Video Producer as a whole—it's aimed more at video-editing purists than dabblers moving up from presentation packages, so forethought is essential, but that doesn't detract from its performance.

Digital Video Producer 2.5 (Part of a bundle)

Asymetrix Corp.
110 110th Ave., NE, Suite 700
Bellevue, WA 98004-5840
800-448-6543; 206-462-0501
Direct sales: 800-448-6543

III

Investing in Multimedia

FAX: 206-637-1504
Tech support: Use main number
Tech support BBS: 206-451-1173

SoundTrack. SoundTrack is an inexpensive utility that gives you control over the audio portions of your Video for Windows (AVI) video clips. The $89.95 CD-ROM version includes a library of AVI and WAV audio clips, while the floppy disk version, with fewer samples, costs $79.95.

SoundTrack can take an AVI file and separate the video from the audio, creating a new WAV file for the latter. With video and sound separated, the possibilities for both are expanded.

The first audio track—the one that's part of the original AVI file—remains unchanged. After the loading and separation process, a second audio track appears as a blank screen; you can record this new track with a microphone, or by connecting another audio source to an MCI-compatible audio card. You can replace the first track with the second to create a completely new AVI movie, or cut and paste sounds onto either track to add special effects or customize a presentation. A mixer can even combine the sound on the two tracks.

Sound and video can be synchronized or played individually. SoundTrack's video player complements the editing process, letting you advance frame by frame. You can even snip sound from an audio track to create new sound files—for example, capturing a sound effect that can be used as a system prompt.

SoundTrack is at its best when working with small files. When loading a large video clip, you may have to wait a number of minutes as the program digitizes the AVI's audio. Worse, SoundTrack creates large WAV files that take up lots of hard disk space. If you're running tight on system resources, SoundTrack may not be able to handle larger files.

Still, SoundTrack makes it fairly easy to create a custom sound track or get more use out of your video clips. Marketed as a fun utility, it lacks the sort of documentation or tutorial that novices look for. But its potential as more than an entertainment item—for business presentations and other tasks that use AVI videos—shouldn't be overlooked.

SoundTrack ($89.95 CD-ROM, $79.95 floppy)

Access Softek
2550 9th St., Suite 206
Berkeley, CA 94710
510-848-0606
Fax: 510-848-0608
Tech support: Use main number

DisplayMate. This last utility actually has nothing to do with video capture or editing. But, it still may be valuable. As computer users, we spend a large part of the day staring into the glass eye of our monitors, yet few of us take the time to adjust the image for optimal results. Aside from playing with the brightness and contrast dials a little, many of us take a fatalistic attitude about our monitor image and simply accept what we see.

But if you want to make sure you're getting the most from your monitor, the tests and utilities in DisplayMate for Windows can help you set up and adjust your display system for best results.

The program can be run directly from a floppy disk without any installation, making it easy to run on different computers. In addition to details about what to look for in the test images it displays, the program also gives instructions on how to use your monitor's controls to get improved results.

DisplayMate for Windows does not draw the line at your monitor's controls, either. The information screens also include suggestions about other hardware factors, including cabling and your graphics adapter. By using the monitor controls in conjunction with graphics adapter adjustments, you can often achieve noticeable improvements in image quality.

The package relies on the Windows display driver, so you don't need to hassle with configuring the software to match your hardware. The program supports color depths up to 24-bit, and it runs in any Windows-supported resolution.

You can configure the program to make it as complex or simple as you want. By default, it displays brief explanations and uses a subset of the test suite, but you can choose the full explanations and use all the tests if you prefer.

DisplayMate for Windows ($79)

Sonera Technologies, P.O. Box 565
Rumson, NJ 07760
800-932-6323; 908-747-6886
FAX: 908-747-4523

From Here...

In this chapter, you learned about key criteria for buying video cards and monitors. For video cards, you learned about video card standards, high-speed design, using VRAM vs. DRAM, various local-bus designs, and graphics coprocessors. Monitor buying criteria were covered, including resolution, interlacing vs. non-interlacing, and dot pitch, Lastly, video-capture boards were discussed that either capture TV images to one's computer or play computer images onto a TV screen or VCR.

For more information about video equipment see:

- Chapter 6, "Upgrading Your Video," describes in detail information about multi-media video.

III

Investing in Multimedia

Part IV

Appendixes

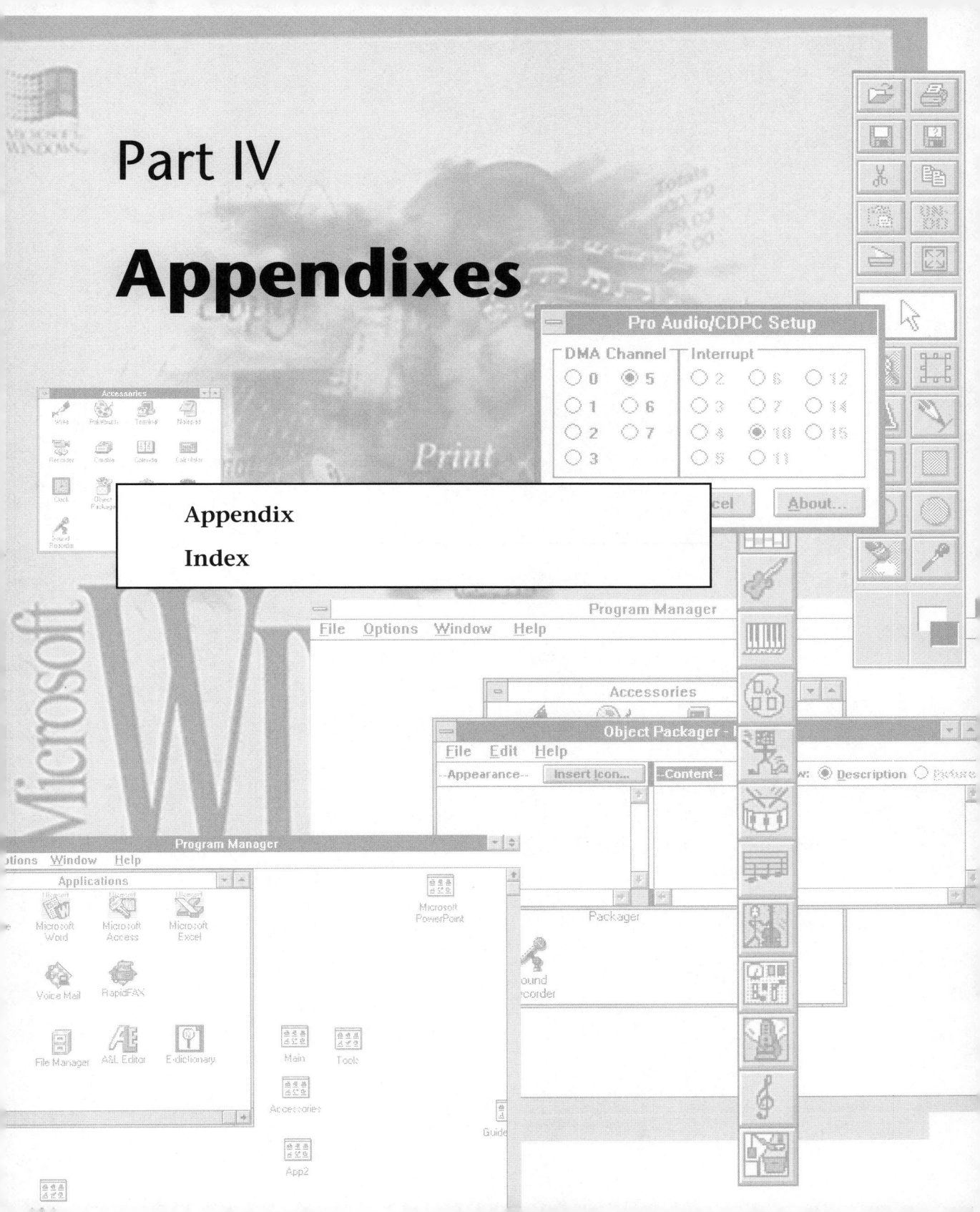

Appendix

Index

Appendix A

Resources

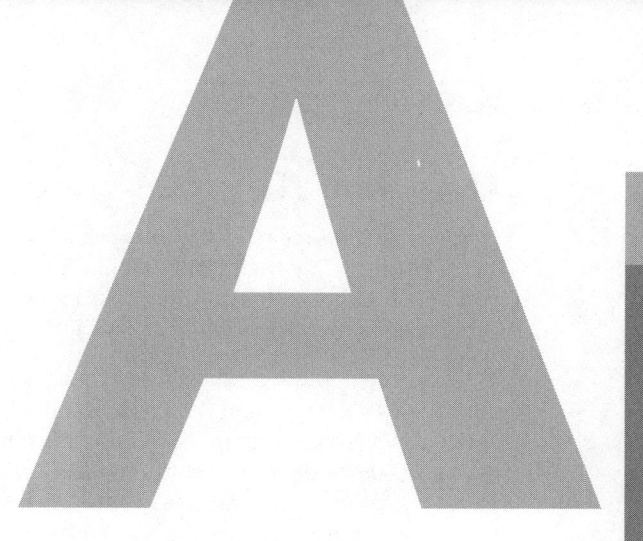

There are many resources available to assist you with upgrading and learning about multimedia. Some of these resources include groups, organizations, peers, on-line services, training institutions, books, magazines, and user groups. Many of these resources complement each other; for example, you can use on-line services to locate user groups or to locate books or magazines. Recognizing these resources, and learning how to use them to your benefit, will help you achieve a greater measure of success.

Groups, Organizations, Peers

The following is a list of some of the many institutions and standardization committees associated directly or indirectly with multimedia (each organization maintains a wealth of information):

- Multimedia PC Council (MPC)
- Association of PC User Groups (APCUG)
- International Standards Organization (ISO)
- American National Standards Institute (ANSI)
- Joint Photographic Experts Group (JPEG)
- Motion Picture Experts Group (MPEG)
- National Television Standards Committee (NTSC)
- Video Electronics Standards Association (VESA)

Peers also are a good resource. Often, individuals begin seeking information by going outside their immediate circle of friends. Checking with peers (co-workers, schoolmates, friends, and so on) may offer much quicker, more credible results. If there are no resources available in your immediate circle of contacts, then you can seek advice from organizations. You can, for example, go to a library and look at reference material to locate organizations and associations that deal with your area of interest (ask the librarian for assistance.) On-line services also are a good place to start your search.

On-Line Advice

If you're not *on-line* then you're *off-line*. This means that you are missing out on all the benefits offered by the highly publicized information superhighway. This resource is so valuable because of the copious amounts of up-to-date information available. You can access this information without ever leaving your home.

To access an on-line service you need a *modem*, a hardware device that connects your computer to a telephone. You also will need communications software to operate the modem. Software programs like Procomm or Crosstalk are available at most computer stores. Modems operate at different speeds. The slower the modem (1200, 2400, 4800 baud) the more time it takes to communicate over the telephone lines. The more time it takes, the more expensive the telephone call. Therefore, make sure you have a fast modem (9600 baud or 1.44 baud) to keep the phone charges down. A 9600 baud (baud is a term used to indicate *bits-per-second*) modem is common, although you should try to obtain a 1.44 baud modem. At 1.44K baud you can send and receive faxes (provided you have the proper software).

There are several on-line services available, including CompuServe, America On-Line, Prodigy, Delphi, and GEnie. Also, there are many service providers that offer access to the Internet, the backbone of the information superhighway. Some of the commercial services allow access (some limited, others complete) to the Internet. Table A.1 identifies the common commercial services.

Table A.1 Commercial On-Line Services		
On-Line Service	**Fee[1]**	**Contact Info**
CompuServe	$8.95/mo	800-848-8199
America Online	$9.95/mo(5 hrs) $3.50/additional hr	800-827-6364
Delphi	$10/4 hrs. $4/additional hr	800-544-4005
GEnie	$8.95/mo(4 hrs.) $3/additional hr	800-638-9636
Prodigy	$7.95/mo	800-822-6922

[1] *Fees vary based upon alternate plans. Basic plans are listed in this table. Contact the appropriate on-line service for a current price quote.*

If you prefer to use Internet as your primary on-line resource (many people use Internet in addition to a commercial service like CompuServe) then you need access via an Internet provider. Some businesses and institutions (colleges, universities, and so on) provide free access to their members. If you don't have an Internet provider then you can choose from several commercial services. Some Internet providers advertise in magazines and books. Some providers are listed in Table A.2.

Table A.2   Internet Service Providers

Service Provider	Fee	Contact
a2i Communications	$15	408-293-9020*
Anomaly	$13	401-273-4669
APK	$35	216-481-9428
The Black Box	$22	713-480-2684
CAPCON Library Network	$13	202-331-5771
Colorado SuperNet	$15	303-273-3471
Communications Accessibles	$25	514-931-0749
Community News Service	$10	719-520-1700*
CRL	$20	415-381-2800
CTS Network Services	$18	619-637-3640
The Cyberspace Station	$20	619-944-9498
Delphi[1]	$13	800-695-4005
Dial n' Cerf	$20	800-876-2373
DSC BBS	$15	215-674-9290
Eskimo North	$13	206-367-3837*
Express Access	$15	301-220-0258
HoloNet	$6	510-704-0160
The IDS World Network	$15	401-884-7856
Maestro	$15	212-240-9600
MCSSNet	$25	312-248-8649
The Meta Network	$20	703-243-6622
MindVox	$18	212-989-2418
MsenLink	$20	313-998-4562
NeoSoft	$30	713-684-5969
Netcom On-line Communications	$20	800-488-2558
Net Guide Online[2]	$15	800-NET-1133
North Shore Access	$9	617-593-3110
Northwest Nexus/Halcyon	$20	617-593-3110
NovaLink	$13	800-274-2814
Old Colorado City Com. Srv.	$30	719-632-4848
Panix	$19	212-787-6160
The Portal System	$20	408-973-9111
PUCnet	$hrly	403-448-1901
Telerama	$20	412-481-3505
Texas Metronet	$10	214-401-2800
Vnet Internet Access, Inc.	$25	704-347-0779
The WELL	$15	415-332-4335
The World	$5	617-739-0202
Wyvern Technologies Inc.	$20	804-622-4289

* Modem number provided.
[1] *Includes access to both Delphi and Internet.*
[2] *Netguide book lists all details associated with each of the service providers listed above.*

Appendix

Bulletin Board Systems (BBS) are another resource worth pursuing. A BBS is usually an independently operated on-line service, although companies and other organizations may also offer BBS services. The content of each BBS varies. You need to find a BBS that satisfies your area of interest. There are several ways to locate BBS's. In fact, on some BBS's you can *download* (copy from the BBS onto your PC) directories of other BBS's throughout the country. To do this, you need to access the BBS first, and then you can download the file.

Local newspapers and other publications (such as Recycler or ComputerEdge Magazine) often list BBS numbers. A common BBS listing will include the phone number and communication protocol. An example of a common protocol would be 9600,N,8,1. This refers to the baud rate, parity, data bits, and stop bits, respectively (9600 baud, no parity, 8 data bits, and 1 stop bit). Another common protocol is 2400,7,E,1 (2400 baud, 7 data bits, even parity, and 1 stop bit). The individual parameters of the protocol vary. You may find that 2400 baud is more common than 9600. However, 9600 is faster and is preferred. If you locate a BBS listing that you want to access, you first need to make the protocol settings in your own communication software, then dial the BBS number. After the connection is established, you can sign-on to the BBS (you usually need to press Enter several times).

Additional Training

Multimedia training is becoming more available. Community colleges offer courses and extension programs are available at major universities. Also, businesses that specialize in training offer various multimedia training programs.

Table A.3 CompuServe's Computer Books (GO CBK)		
Description	**Author(s)**	**Price ($)**
General Graphics		
Computational Geometry in C	O'Rourke	24.95
Computer Graphics Principles & Practice, 2/E	Foley	58.61
JPEG Still Image Data Compression Standard	Pennebaker, Mitchell	59.95
Computerized Document Imaging Systems	Muller	67.15
Symmetry in Chaos: A Search for Pattern in Mathematics	Field, Golubitsky	29.75

Books

In addition to traditional methods of acquiring books (retail bookstore, library), there also are modern methods. The benefit of modern methods is that searches are automated and can be performed in the convenience of your own home. Most on-line services provide forums for book acquisition or reviews (see table A.3).

In table A.3, the Level column refers to the levels of audience for which the book is written. The levels are 1-Beginner; 2-Intermediate; 4-Advanced. Levels can be added together to form combinations (6=Int(2)+Adv(4)).

The Price ($) column represents the CompuBooks (CBK) price.

The Number (#) is the book number used when ordering.

The Type can be any of the following: UG-User Guide; RM-Reference Manual; OT-Other; PM-Programming Manual; QR-Quick Reference.

Note

You can order any of the books shown in table A.3 directly from CBK (type **GO CBK** from the CompuServe prompt). There are several other ways to order:

> CompuServe e-mail: 70007,1333
> Phone: 800-880-6816
> Fax: 512-321-4525
> Mail: RR 1 Box 271D
> Cedar Creek, TX 78612-9733

An electronic catalog of current CompuBooks (CBK) can be requested from the Download our Catalog on the main menu (**GO CBK**).

Number (#)	Type	Level
5764	PM	6
843	RM	7
2824	OT	6
3333	OT	4
4613	OT	4

(continues)

Table A.3 Continued

Description	Author(s)	Price ($)
General Graphics		
Mastering 3D Studio:Vol 1-Adv Modeling & Rendering	Payne, Drust	54.95
Fractals Everywhere,2/E	Barnsley	49.95
Evolutionary Art & Computers	Todd, Lathan	39.95
Virtual Community	Rheingold	19.51
Computer Illusion in Film & TV	Baker	17
Frontiers of Scientific Visualization	Pickover, Tewksbury	29.71
General Computer Books on Software		
Video Demystified: Handbook for the Digital Engineer	Jack	25.46
CD-ROM Buyer's Guide & Handbook, 3/E (1993)	Nicholls	38.21
CD-ROM Directory W/Multimedia CD'S-1994 (Int'l 11/E)		123.25
CD-Recordable Bible	Pahwa	21.21
General Computer Books		
Radiosity & Realistic Image Synthesis	Cohen, Wallace	42.46
Computer Adventure Games Secrets-The Condor	Barba	16.96
Best of BYTE: Two Decades on the Leading Edge	Ranade, Nash	21.21
Technology in Education Reform	Means	24.61
Journals on CD-ROM		
Hobbes OS/2 CD-ROM (Largest Internet FTP Archive)	Walnut Creek	29.95
C User Group Library CD-ROM Dec 1993 (user sup C source code)	Walnut Creek	49.95
Jamsa's C++ Multimedia Trilogy (CD-ROM)	Jamsa	42.46
Internet Tools CD-ROM Jan 1994: TCP/IP Tools & Util	Infomagic	36
USENET CD-ROM-Jan 1994: Archive of USENET news groups	InfoMagic	20
CICA Archive for MS Windows 2 CD-ROM Set-April 1994	InfoMagic	21.21
Standards CD-ROM (incl RFC's) Domestic/Int'l Stds & Doc-Jan 1994	InfoMagic	36

Number (#)	Type	Level
4891	UG	6
5263	OT	6
5569	OT	6
5706	OT	7
6376	OT	7
6700	OT	4
6113	UG	6
5445	UG	6
5967	UG	7
5968	UG	7
5187	UG	6
5965	UG	7
6553	OT	7
6888	OT	6
6145	OT	6
6146	OT	6
6487	PM	7
3469	OT	7
3471	OT	6
3473	OT	6
3924	OT	6

(continues)

Table A.3 Continued		
Description	**Author(s)**	**Price ($)**
Journals on CD-ROM		
Source Code CD-ROM-Jan 1994 (incl BSD Net/2 Distribution)	InfoMagic	40
SIMTEL20 Archive for MS-DOS 2 CD-ROM Set-March 1994	InfoMagic	21.21
Windows Bible CD-ROM	Davis	29.71
CD-ROMs in Print (1994 1st Rel Dos/Win)	Meckler	42.46
Proceedings		
Graphics Interface 1993 Proceedings		34
Multiple Platform Books on Data Communications		
Internet System Handbook	Lynch, Rose	50.36
How to Get the Most Out of CompuServe,5/E	Bowen, Peyton	21.25
Exploring the Internet:A Technical Travelogue	Malamud	22.91
Internet Guide for New Users	Dern	23.76
Whole Earth On-Line Almanac: Info From A-Z	Rittner	28.01
Exploring the World of Online Services	Resnick	15.26
Connecting to the Internet	Estrada	13.56
Internet: Getting Started, 1993 Updated Ed	SRI	23.8
Internet: Mailing Lists, 1993 Updated Ed	SRI	24.65
Welcome to Internet:From Mystery to Mastery	Badgett, Sandler	16.96
Internet Navigator	Gilster	21.21
Internet for Dummies	Levine	16.96
Internet: The Complete Reference	Hahn	25.46
Internet Companion Plus	LaQuey, Ryer	16.96
Using the Internet,Special Ed.	Tolhurst, Pike	33.96
Complete Idiot's Guide to the Internet	Kent	16.96
Internet Resource Quick Reference	Tolhurst, Pike	15.29
How to Connect: Driver's Ed for the Info Highway	Shipley	21.21
Internet Directory	Braun	25
Internet Yellow Pages	Hahn	23.76

Number (#)	Type	Level
3980	OT	7
5006	OT	6
5847	OT	6
7328	RM	7
4374	OT	4
2458	RM	6
2851	UG	7
3164	UG	7
3689	UG	1
3763	RM	6
4315	OT	6
4339	UG	6
4816	UG	7
4817	UG	7
4854	UG	3
4867	UG	7
5020	UG	7
5028	RM	6
5474	UG	7
5499	RM	7
5514	UG	3
5863	QR	7
5866	UG	7
5953	RM	7
6078	UG	7

(continues)

Table A.3   Continued

Description	Author(s)	Price ($)
Multiple Platform Books on Data Communications		
Navigating the Internet,Dx Ed w/Windows Internet Software	Smith, Gibbs	25.46
Internet Unleashed (PC or Mac software & Internet Tools)	Sams	38.21
Success with Internet w/disk	Wyatt	25.46
On Internet 1994:An International Guide	Meckler	38.25
Internet Basics: Your On-line Access to the Global Elec Super Hwy	Lambert, Howe	22.95
Traveler's Guide to the Information Highway	Tweney	21.21
Hitchhiker's Guide To The Electronic Highway	Glossbrenner Kane	18.66
How to Use the Internet	Butler	15.26
Multiple Platform Books on Graphics		
FractalVision: Put Fractals to Work For You	Oliver	33.96
Multiprocessor Methods for Computer Graphics Rendering	Whitman	33.96
Inside I/RAS B: Complete Guide to Intergraph's Binary Raster Edit Sftw	Marshall	42.46
MicroStation Bible (vers 4.X/5.X)	Cowden, Hayward	42.46
Inside Microstation 5	NRP	33.96
Real World Scanning & Half Tones	Blatner, Roth	21.21
Multimedia Production Handbook for the PC,Mac, & Amiga	Yager	30.56
Multiple Platform Books on Other (Misc) Topics		
Musician's Guide to MIDI (incl MIDI Std)	Braut	33.99
MULTIPLE PRG Introduction to Computer Graphics (in C)	Foley, van Dam	42.08
Multimedia Apps Development,2/E: Using Indeo Video & DVI Tech	Bunzel, Morris	38.25
Intelligent Multimedia Interfaces	Maybury	33.96
Multiple Platform Books on Desktop Publishing		
Publish Yourself on CD-ROM (with CD-ROM)	Caffarelli, Straughan	42.5
Advertising from the Desktop	Floyd, Wilson	21.21

Number (#)	Type	Level
6217	UG	3
6219	UG	7
6258	UG	7
6273	UG	6
6555	UG	7
6883	UG	6
7077	UG	3
7089	UG	3
4331	UG	3
4590	UG	4
4784	UG	7
5076	RM	7
5173	UG	7
5246	UG	7
6007	UG	7
5723	UG	6
3936	OT	7
5498	PM	6
5653	PM	6
3492	UG	6
5230	UG	3

(continues)

Table A.3 Continued		
Description	**Author(s)**	**Price ($)**
PC Books on Data Communication		
CompuServe InformationManager/Windows (incl membership kit)	Davis	25.46
Using CompuServe	Que	16.96
CompuServe From A to Z: The Ultimate CompuServe Ref,2/E	Bowen	24.65
PC Internet Tour Guide: Cruising the Internet the Easy Way	Frease	21.21
Internet Starter Kit For Windows 3.1	Engst, Low	25.46
Windows Internet Tour Guide	Fraase	21.21
DOS User's Guide to the Internet	Gardner	29.71
Cruising Online: Larry Magid's Gde to the New Dig Hwy	Magid	21.25
Internet White Pages (1994)	Godin	25.46
Welcome To...CompuServe w/disk	Banks	21.21
PC Books on Graphics		
Photorealism & Ray Tracing in C	Watkins, Coy	38.21
Fractal Image Compression	Barnsley, Hurd	42.46
Object-Oriented Graphics Programming in C++	Stevens	33.96
Using Freelance Graphics 2.0 for Windows	Sagman	23.76
Imaging & Animation for Windows	Barkakati	29.71
AutoCAD for Windows Book (Rel 12)	Grabowski	29.71
Graphics File Formats	Kay, Levine	21.21
Inside AutoCAD Rel 12	New Riders	32.26
Maximizing AutoLISP (Rel 12)	Gesner, Smith	33.96
Tricks of the Graphics Gurus	Oliver	42.46
AutoCAD Release 12: The Professional Reference	New Riders	36.51
Practical Ray Tracing in C	Lindley	42.46
Inside CorelDRAW! Ver 4.0,Spec Ed	Gray	29.71
AutoCAD Professional's API Toolkit	New Riders	42.50
Inside 3D Studio w/CD-ROM	Elliott, Miller	42.46
Morphing Magic	Anderson	25.46
Adventures in Ray Tracing	Hermida	23.76
Inside Adobe Photoshop 2.5 for Windows(w/CD ROM)	Bouton	35.70
Inside AutoCAD Rel 12 for Windows	New Riders	32.26

Number (#)	Type	Level
5587	UG	7
6201	UG	3
6226	RM	7
6251	UG	6
6308	UG	7
6510	UG	3
6528	UG	7
6652	UG	3
7033	UG	7
7079	UG	3
3237	PM	2
3370	PM	4
6300	PM	6
3762	UG	3
4358	UG	6
4783	UG	6
1702	UG	3
1849	RM	3
3174	UG	6
3248	UG	6
3343	RM	7
3379	PM	6
3575	UG	7
3648	UG	4
3682	UG	6
3907	UG	3
4140	UG	7
4149	RM	7
4218	UG	7

(continues)

Table A.3 Continued

Description	Author(s)	Price ($)
PC Books on Graphics		
3D Studio Applied(Version 3.0)- with CD ROM	Fulton	39.95
Virtual Reality Madness! w/CD-ROM	Wodaski	33.96
Adobe Photoshop Now!w/CD-ROM (ver 2.5/windows)	Bouton	29.75
Teach Yourself CorelDRAW! 4.0 for the PC	Erdos	18.66
CorelDraw! 4.0 Unleashed W/CD ROM	Coburn	33.96
Adobe Photoshop for Windows: Classroom in a Book w/CD-ROM	Adobe Systems	38.21
CorelDRAW 4.0 Now!	New Riders Staff	18.66
Learn CAD With Autosketch for Windows	New Riders Editors	29.71
Killer AutoCAD Utilities (Rel 11/12)	New Riders	38.25
Customizing AutoCAD Release 12	Tickoo	28.01
Using AutoCAD, Rel 12	Que	29.71
CorelDraw! Special Effects (Ver 3&4)	Gray	33.96
Adventures in 3-D	Wolfgram	21.21
Modern Image Processing: Warping,Morphing, & Classical Tech	Watkins, Sadun	42.46
Using Harvard Graphics ver 2.0 for Windows	Que	23.76
Multimedia Madness! w/2 CD-ROMs, Deluxe Edition	Wodaski	46.75
AutoCAD Release 12 Certification Exam Prep Manual	Kalameja	28.01
Image Processing in C w/disk	Phillips	34
Fractal Creations,2/E (w/CD ROM)	Wegner, Tyler	29.71
AutoCAD for Architecture	Jefferis, Jones	28.01
Framemaker 4 for Windows	Tolman	16.11
Real-World Fractals (DOS/Borland C++ 3.1)	Finlay, Blanton	33.96
Freelance Graphics for Windows Quick Start	Que	18.66
Super Scanning Techniques: H-P Guide to B&W Imaging	Day	20.40
CorelDraw 4 Revealed	Harrel	21.21
High Resolution Video Graphics	Sanchez, Canton	36.51
Harnessing MicroStation ver 5	Krishnan, Rhea	33.96

Number (#)	Type	Level
4276	OT	6
4280	OT	6
4333	UG	6
4378	UG	3
4682	UG	6
4701	UG	7
4706	UG	6
4707	UG	6
4733	UG	6
4787	UG	6
4913	UG	7
5104	UG	7
5132	UG	7
5186	UG	6
5251	UG	7
5280	UG	6
5343	UG	6
5404	PM	6
5439	PM	7
5510	UG	7
5527	UG	7
5530	PM	2
5547	UG	6
5584	UG	7
5702	UG	3
5707	UG	6
5770	UG	7

(continues)

Table A.3 Continued

Description	Author(s)	Price ($)
PC Books on Graphics		
Authoring Interactive Multimedia (w/CD-ROM)	Luther	42.46
Scanning & Image Processing for the PC	Baeseler	23.76
Multimedia Programming for Windows w/CD-ROM	Rimmer	33.96
Walkthroughs & Flybys (w/CDROM)	Shatz	28.01
Multimedia Authoring:Building & Dev Documents	Fisher	29.71
MS PowerPoint 4 for Windows Step by Step	Perspection	25.46
Hands-On AutoCAD Rel 12:College Student's Guide	Boyce	21.21
Inside Adobe Illustrator Ver 4 for Windows	Plumley	33.96
Graphics Gems IV(IBM Version)	Heckbert	42.46
Discovering Generic Cadd 6.0/6.1	White	25.46
Inside AutoCAD LT for Windows	Gersner	25.46
PCLL Teaches CorelDRAW! 4.0	PCLL	19.51
PCLL Teaches PowerPoint 4.0 for Windows	PCLL	19.51
PowerPoint 4 for Windows QuickStart DiskPack	Que	25.48
Using PowerPoint for Windows	Que	25.49
PowerPoint 4/Windows Visual Learning Guide	Beatty, Gardner	16.96
Virtual Reality Excursions w/Progs in C	Watkins, Marenka	33.96
MS Multimedia Viewer How-To	Pruitt	33.96
Multimedia Developer's Guide(w/CD ROM)	Perry	42.46
Creating Multimedia Presentations w/CD ROM	Que	33.99
3-D Modeling Lab	Shaddock	29.71
Making Movies with Your PC	Hone, Kuntz	21.21
Build Cell v1.0 (DOS Utility Program/Microstation)	Steinbock	33.96
Using Windows Sound System 2	Moore	21.24
Running MS PowerPoint 4 for Windows	Sagman	21.21
How to Digitize Video w/CD-ROM for Win/Mac	Johnson	33.96

Number (#)	Type	Level
5853	UG	6
5963	UG	6
5982	PM	6
5986	OT	6
6083	UG	7
6111	UG	3
6121	UG	3
6122	UG	6
6128	UG	6
6152	UG	7
6158	UG	6
6180	UG	3
6182	UG	3
6202	UG	3
6225	UG	3
6259	UG	3
6268	PM	6
6296	UG	6
6335	RM	6
6350	UG	3
6460	UG	7
6461	UG	7
6490	PM	4
6630	UG	7
6689	UG	6
6692	UG	

(continues)

Table A.3   Continued

Description	Author(s)	Price ($)
PC Books on Graphics		
Power Graphics Using Turbo C++	Heiny	23.76
How to Use CorelDRAW! 4.0 (DOS/Windows)	Craig	15.26
Mastering CorelDraw 4	Dickman	29.71
Adobe Illustrator 5.0,4/E	Bove	22.95
PC Books on Hardware		
PC Video Madness! (w/CD ROM)	Wodaski	33.96
PCI System Architecture,2/E	Shanley	25.46
Sound Blaster:The Official Book,2/E	Ridge, Golden	29.71
PC Books on Other Topics		
Audible PC	Rubin, Tully	29.71
ISO 9000 Doc Toolkit w/ Word Process Templates (Word 6/WP 6)	Novack	67.96
PC Books on Programming		
Bitmapped Graphics Programming in C++	Luse	32.26
Power Graphics Using Turbo Pascal 6 Bk/Disk Combo	Weiskamp, Heiny	35.66
Advanced Graphics Prog Using C/C++ Bk/Disk Combo	Heiny	40.76
Object-Oriented Ray Tracing in C++ (book only)	Wilt	31.41
Programming for Graphic Files in C & C++ (book/disk combo)	Levine	42.46
Flights of Fantasy: Program 3-D Video Games in Borland C++	Lampton	29.71
Portable GUI Development With C++	Watson	25.46
PC Books on Windows, GUIs, and Multitasking Env.		
Bytes Windows Programmer's Cookbook (w/CD-ROM)	Ribar	29.71
GUI Guide (Euro Ed.) International Terminology to Windows Interface	Microsoft	25.46
CD-MOM:The Mother of All Windows Packages w/CD-ROM	Leonhard, Simon	42.46

Number (#)	Type	Level
6701	PM	4
6886	UG	1
7037	UG	7
7092	UG	7
3755	OT	3
4808	OT	6
6126	UG	7
6067	OT	6
6704	UG	6
3424	PM	6
5216	UG	6
5218	PM	4
5835	PM	6
5991	PM	6
2846	PM	7
3161	PM	
6552	PM	6
3034	PM	6
5484	UG	7

(continues)

Table A.3 Continued		
Description	**Author(s)**	**Price ($)**
PC Books on Desktop Publishing		
Adobe Photoshop Handbook,2/E (Ver 2.5)	Biedney, Monroy	24.65
Adobe Illustrator for Windows: Classroom in a Book	Adobe Systems	38.21
Photoshop in Black & White	Rich, Bozek	15.3
Photoshop Wow! Book (ver 2.5/windows)	Dayton, Davis	29.71
How Desktop Publishing Works	Pfiffner, Fraser	21.21

Magazines

There are several magazines that discuss multimedia. Some magazines address different genres (MIDI, animation, sound, video, graphics) more than others. To identify the different magazines, and the topics they discuss, a research project was conducted using Melvyl, an on-line database that contains all the periodicals available to students at California Universities. Table A.4 shows the research results. All the magazines listed have articles based upon one or more genres of multimedia, or on *multimedia*. The search was focused on magazines published since 1988.

Table A.4 Magazines with Multimedia Stories			
Title/Description	**Yr[1]**	**MM[2]**	**MI**
Multimedia World[3]	1994	15	3
Multimedia Business Report	1992	149	1
Multimedia Computing & Presentations	1991	167	0
Windows Magazine	1993	18	3
Computer Shopper[4]	1993	250	14
PC Week	1988	637	10
THE Journal (Tech. Horizons in Education)	1988	201	5
Electronic Design	1988	25	1
Digital Media	1991	150	2
PC World	1988	137	10
Electronic Engineering Times	1988	180	2
Window Sources	1993	57	3
Byte	1988	70	18
IEEE Computer Graphics & Applications[5]	1988	21	1
EDGE: Workgroup Computing Report	1990	269	1

3738	UG	7
4700	UG	7
5850	UG	6
5976	UG	7
6501	UG	3

The list of magazines in table A.4 is not all inclusive. There are other magazines that are highly recommended. Also, new magazines arrive on the newsstand every day. Two magazines, specifically recommended by multimedia developers, are:

- *Morph's Outpost on the Digital Frontier:* By developers, for developers. Hands-on, how-to. The subscription rate is $39.95 U.S. (1 year, 12 issues), by Morph's Outpost, Inc., Orinda, CA.

- *New Media:* Industry news, product and title reviews.

AN	SO	VI	GR
1	3	4	8
4	3	71	0
11	7	86	33
2	18	9	57
11	115	162	352
56	126	816	2285
40	31	158	347
0	4	56	94
6	4	145	28
7	43	90	347
2	38	300	385
4	66	83	234
10	39	124	307
27	1	14	405
7	58	193	265

(continues)

Table A.4 Continued			
Title/Description	**Yr[1]**	**MM[2]**	**MI**
InfoWorld	1988	378	4
DR. Dobbs Journal	1988	16	1
Computer Graphics World	1988	56	2
C Users Journal	1991	6	2
PC Sources	1990	45	7
Technology & Learning	1990	71	2
LAN Magazine	1989	16	1
Electronic Learning	1988	30	2
EXE	1989	6	1
A+	1988	0	9
PC-Computing	1988	93	13
Rainbow	1988	0	2
EDN	1988	22	2
Computer Reseller News	1988	247	7
Classroom Computer Learning	1988	8	1
M.D. Computing	1988	2	1
IEEE Spectrum	1988	15	0
IEEE Software	1988	10	0
Computing Canada	1988	124	0
Government Computer News	1988	82	0
Publish	1988	56	0
Desktop Communications	1993	10	0
Home Office Computing	1990	11	0
Industrial Engineering	1988	0	0
Computerworld	1988	120	0
Computers & Operations Research	1989	0	0
Business Week	1989	62	0
Digital Review	1988	55	0
CAD-CAM International	1988	0	0

[1] *Year of oldest article in database back to 1988.*
[2] *MM=Multimedia; MI=MIDI; AN=Animation; SO=Sound; VI=Video; and, GR=Graphics. These are the topics searched on.*
[3] *Newer publications won't have as many articles because of smaller time span.*
[4] *Computer Shopper is an excellent resource for sources of products and services; articles are also very informative.*
[5] *Some magazines are received by being a member of an association.*

There also are magazines dedicated to a specific aspect of multimedia. MIDI, for example, is a topic of several magazines. These include the following:

AN	SO	VI	GR
42	87	393	1093
17	76	11	86
143	4	98	657
2	3	2	47
7	23	87	361
3	2	22	8
0	1	10	17
0	0	38	17
2	3	14	76
6	3	3	44
7	57	167	386
2	3	1	26
0	16	71	108
11	21	199	428
1	2	4	8
0	0	3	3
1	0	13	32
2	0	2	19
3	13	113	294
4	13	81	361
17	2	46	299
3	0	7	27
1	3	28	55
2	0	2	11
6	8	100	219
1	0	0	3
4	9	55	26
13	9	46	586
4	0	5	63

- *midi: written for the mind of the musician*: published bi-monthly, GW Publishing Company, Wellesley, MA. Special issues are published in July and December. The subscription rate is $19.95 U.S. (1 year, 8 issues)

- *Electronic Musician*: published monthly, Cardinal Business Media, Inc., Horsham, PA. The subscription rate is $24 U.S. (1 year, 12 issues)

There are many other magazines. Some are more general, occasionally covering multimedia topics and reviews on hardware and software. Others are very focused, specializing on one aspect of multimedia.

Multimedia magazines are also surfacing. Literally, different mediums are being used to distribute magazines. The *NautilusCD* magazine is distributed on a CD (call 800-637-3472 for further information). Ziff-Davis Publishing Company published *The Computer Life Guide to Mastering New Media.* This electronic magazine is distributed on a disk.

Your interests may vary over time. A magazine that is beneficial to you today may not serve your needs tomorrow. It's possible that a magazine is useful to you occasionally, but is not worthy of the subscription rate. These factors must be balanced out.

If you are looking for articles on a specific subject then you have a variety of resources available. On-line services provide up-to-date information on the latest articles (refer to preceding section, *On-Line Advice*). Some services offer full-text of the article for a nominal fee, usually much less than the magazine cost itself; however, pictures and illustrations are not usually included. CompuServe, for example, offers several services related to searching and retrieving magazine articles, journals, newsletters, and other publications:

- *GO BUSDB: (Business Database Plus).* Provides full-text articles from more than 500 regional, national, and international business publications. Articles from more than 550 specialized business newsletters that often focus on specific industries or geographic locations can also be found.

- *GO BUSDATE: (Business Dateline).* Provides full-text articles from over 115 business publications.

- *GO COMPDB: (Computer Database Plus).* A comprehensive collection of computer-related abstracts and/or full-text from leading computer industry publications covering hardware, software, electronics, engineering, communications, and technology applications. Includes over 230 magazine, newspaper, and journal titles. Over 370,000 articles are included in the database.

- *GO CONSUMER: (Consumer Reports).* Provides reports on the features, brand ratings, and recommendations from *Consumers Union,* on a variety of consumer products.

- *GO DPNEWS: (Data-Processing Newsletters).* Provides articles from several leading newsletters covering the computer, electronics, and telecommunications industries. It gives facts, figures, analysis, current company conditions, company activities, new products and technologies, government policies and trade agreements.

- *GO DISSERTATION: (Dissertation Abstracts).* Provides information on dissertations for academic doctoral degrees at accredited U.S. institutions since 1861, selected masters theses, and dissertations accepted at Canadian and many other non-U.S. institutions.

- *GO EBF: (Entrepreneur's Business Franchise and Opportunities Database).* Provides information about franchising and business opportunities in *Entrepreneur* magazine's Business Franchise and Opportunities Database. Based on the magazine's annual *Guide to Franchise and Business Opportunities,* the database provides a description of franchising and business opportunities throughout the United States.

■ *GO ERIC: (Education Research).* Contains abstracts of articles covering all aspects of education, including vocational education, counseling, teacher education, and testing. Information extends back to 1966 and is updated monthly. There are two subfiles within ERIC: the *Resources In Education (RIE)* file and the *Current Index to Journals in Education (CIJE)* file. The RIE subfile contains research/technical reports, conference papers and proceedings, program descriptions, opinion papers, bibliographies, reviews, dissertations, teaching and curriculum materials, and lesson plans and guides. The CIJE subfile contains abstracts of articles from 750 education related professional journals.

■ *GO GOVERNMENT: (Government Information).* Provides a menu of information on government services and publications.

■ *GO GPO: (Government Publications).* There are two basic parts to this program. The first is a catalog of government publications, books, and subscription services. The second part has on-line consumer information articles for government publications.

■ *GO IQUEST: (IQUEST).* Provides access to more than 850 databases from companies such as Dialog Information Services Inc., BRS Information Technologies, NewsNet Inc., Data-Star, ORBIT Search Service, H.W. Wilson Company, FT Information On-line, Ltd., G. Cam-L'Europeenne De Donnees, Questel Inc., and VU/TEXT Information Services Inc. All types of information are included—from scholarly to popular press, business-related to the obscure. Both bibliographic and full-text documents are provided. Source materials include magazines, newspapers, indexes, conference proceedings, directories, books, newsletters, government documents, dissertations, encyclopedias, patent records, and reference guides.

■ *GO KI: (Knowledge Index).* Provides access to over 500,000 journals through more than 100 full-text and bibliographic databases available through Dialog.

■ *GO MAGDB: (Magazine Database Plus).* Provides access to more than 130 publications.

■ *GO MGMTRC: (Marketing/Management Research Center).* Provides full-text articles of major U.S. and international business, management, and technical magazines. Also provides indices to market and industry research reports, market studies, and statistical reports. Finally, provides U.S. and international company news releases.

■ *GO NTIS: (NTIS-Government Sponsored Research).* National Technical Information Service offers a database of references to articles from government-sponsored research, development, and engineering reports.

■ *GO PATENT: (Patent Research Center).* Provides access to databases containing summaries of U.S. patents granted and patents granted internationally.

■ *GO UKMARKETING: (UK Marketing Library).* Provides market research reports compiled by top marketing analysts. The information is gathered from a variety of sources and includes reports from the ICC Key Note series, Marketing Surveys

Indexes, Mintel Research Reports, and Mintel Special Reports, and MSI Market Research Reports.

A more traditional approach to finding periodicals is to use your local library. There you can find reference resources of periodicals. One example is *Readers Guide to Periodical Literature,* by the H.W. Wilson Company. The current version of this guide references several categories related to multimedia (see table A.5).

Table A.5 Readers Guide to Periodical Lit. Categories	
Category	**Subcategory**
Multimedia	Business Use
	Educational Use
	Exhibitions
	Journalistic Use
	Testing
Multimedia Databases	
Video Display Terminals	
Videodisc	
Graphical User Interface	
Graphics	
Animated*	
Computers	Musical Use
Interactive*	
Sound*	

* Implies several subcategories also listed.

Other subtopics included in this appendix provide additional resources. Refer to the topics preceding and succeeding this section.

User Groups

There are more to user group meetings than eating donuts and drinking coffee. A user group can be an excellent resource for keeping abreast of technology. You also can meet individuals who share, among other things, the same interests, geographic location, and possibly the same job functions as do you. Entrepreneurs, scholars, and other career-oriented individuals are typical members.

One of the more valuable deliverables of a user group is a newsletter. Some are very professional and provide a wealth of knowledge. Bulletin Board Systems (BBSs) are used by some user groups. A side benefit of all the contacts that you establish is the ability to call up individuals on a personal basis for technical support. Keep in mind that they will probably do the same, especially if you are knowledgable on the subject in question.

If you have available time, you can be very supportive to a user group. You should locate the user groups in your area and become a member of the one that: a) provides direct benefits to you; b) has a good reputation; and c) you can actively support, if only in a small role. You want to approach a user group with a mutually beneficial attitude, you are an asset to the group, and the group is a resource for you.

There are several ways to locate user groups in your area. Here are some possible sources:

- *Newspapers.* Classified sections of newspapers sometimes mention user groups.

- *Bulletin Board Systems (BBSs).* It's usually easier to locate a local BBS number than it is a user group. However, BBS systems often have files that you can download which refer you to user groups. To access a BBS you need a modem and communications software like Procomm (any retail computer store can assist you). With the proper hardware and software you are ready to dial the BBS number and connect your computer. (Refer to the section *On-line Advice* earlier in this chapter.)

- *On-line services.* Services like CompuServe, Internet, America On-line, and Protegy can be used to locate a user group in your area (refer to *On-line Advice* in this chapter).

- *Magazines and Periodicals.* Larger user groups may be advertised in more well-known magazines. The smaller groups may not be able to afford the advertising costs, although publications sometimes allow user groups to advertise free of charge. *The Computer Shopper* has a section listing user groups. If you have access to a free, local computer periodical like *Computer Edge* you will also find groups listed there. Even the well known *Recycler* is fairly thorough in user group listings.

- *ASPCUG.* You always have access to the Association of PC User Groups. This is a user group for *user groups.*

The Association of PC User Groups is helpful for finding out information regarding other user groups. A user group locator service is provided by dialing 914-876-6678. This is an automated telephone system that allows you to locate user groups in any area of the U.S., and even locations outside of North America. You can search for user groups by area code, state, or zip code. Additional information is also provided on the APCUG by selecting option 5, after the recorded voice prompts you.

The blessing and the curse of the computer industry is that there is a lot of *free advice* available. Everyone is willing to give you their opinion, whether it is *right* or *wrong*. The challenge you have is to identify the good advice and ignore the bad advice. If you can develop the ability to recognize good advice, then your multimedia upgrade will be more enjoyable and will result in a better overall investment.

Index

B